Methodological Advances in Educational Effectiveness Research

Methodological Advances in Educational Effectiveness Research is an important new work by some of the leading researchers in the field of Educational Effectiveness Research (EER). This book provides a state-of-the-art snapshot of the methodology of EER now and clearly demonstrates the way it is applied in both research and evaluation. It shows how developments in the research methodology area, such as the use of multilevel modelling approaches to analyse nested data, have promoted the knowledge base of educational effectiveness. But at the same time, as the authors show, the knowledge base of educational effectiveness and the attempt to establish theoretical models do paradoxically challenge the development of methodologically appropriate studies, including ways of analysing data.

This book guides readers though the effective and appropriate use in educational effectiveness of:

- longitudinal studies
- experimental studies
- mixed research methods
- meta-analyses of effectiveness studies
- using Item Response Theory to measure outcomes and factors
- using Generalizability Theory to test the quality of data
- multilevel modelling
- Structural Equation Modelling techniques.

The authors draw in the expertise of scholars from around the world to show the mathematical background of each technique, current and future applications and specific examples of applying each orientation to help the readers design their own effectiveness studies using specific methodological tools.

Bert P.M. Creemers is Professor and Director of the Centre for Learning and Teaching, University of Groningen.

Leonidas Kyriakides is Associate Professor of Educational Research and Evaluation, Department of Education, University of Cyprus.

Pam Sammons is Professor of Education, Department of Education, University of Oxford.

Quantitative Methodology series
Series Editor: George A. Marcoulides

This series presents methodological techniques to investigators and students. The goal is to provide an understanding and working knowledge of each method with a minimum of mathematical derivations, while retaining the clarity and rigor of quantitative research. Each volume focuses on a specific method – for example factor analysis, multilevel analysis, structural equation modelling, providing an up-to-date snapshot of current methodological practice in qualitative studies.

The authors and contributors draw upon the expertise of scholars from around the world to show the diversity and demands of quantitative research, providing current and future applications, as well as specific examples to help readers design their own studies using methodological tools.

Previous titles in the series include:

Modern Methods for Business Research
George A. Marcoulides

Latent Variable and Latent Structure Models
George A. Marcoulides and Irini Moustaki

Multilevel Analysis: techniques and applications
Joop Hox

Studying Educational and Social Policy: theoretical concepts and research methods
Ronald Heck

New Developments in Categorical Data Analysis for the Social and Behavioral Sciences
L. Andries Van der Ark, Marcel Croon and Klaas Sijtsma

An Introduction to Latent Variable Growth Curve Modeling: concepts, issues, and applications (second edition)
Susan Duncan and Lisa Strycker

An Introduction to Multilevel Modeling Techniques (second edition)
Ronald Heck and Scott Thomas

Applying Generalizability Theory Using EduG
Jean Cardinet, Sandra Johnson and Gianreto Pini

Multilevel and Longitudinal Modeling with PASW/SPSS
Ronald Heck, Scott Thomas and Lynn Tabata

Multilevel Analysis: techniques and applications (second edition)
Joop Hox

Methodological Advances in Educational Effectiveness Research

Bert P.M. Creemers,
Leonidas Kyriakides and
Pam Sammons

Routledge
Taylor & Francis Group

LONDON AND NEW YORK

First published 2010
by Routledge
2 Park Square, Milton Park, Abingdon, Oxon OX14 4RN

Simultaneously published in the USA and Canada
by Routledge
270 Madison Avenue, New York, NY 10016

Routledge is an imprint of the Taylor & Francis Group, an informa business

© 2010 Bert P.M. Creemers, Leonidas Kyriakides and Pam Sammons
for selection and editorial material. Individual contributions, the
contributors.

Typeset in Galliard by
Florence Production Ltd, Stoodleigh, Devon
Printed and bound in Great Britain by
CPI Antony Rowe, Chippenham, Wiltshire

British Library Cataloguing in Publication Data
A catalogue record for this book is available from the British Library

Library of Congress Cataloging-in-Publication Data
Creemers, Bert P.M.
Methodological advances in educational effectiveness research/Bert
P.M. Creemers, Leonidas Kyriakides, and Pam Sammons. – 1st ed.
p. cm.
Includes bibliographical references and index.
1. Education – Research – Methodology. I. Kyriakides, Leonidas.
II. Sammons, Pam. III. Title.
LB1028.C736 2010
370.7'2–dc22   2009048160

ISBN10: 0–415–48175–9 (hbk)
ISBN10: 0–415–48176–7 (pbk)
ISBN10: 0–203–85100–5 (ebk)

ISBN13: 978–0–415–48175–5 (hbk)
ISBN13: 978–0–415–48176–2 (pbk)
ISBN13: 978–0–203–85100–5 (ebk)

Contents

PART C
Methodological advances and EER: retrospect and prospect

Contributors

Authors of the book

Bert P.M. Creemers, Centre for Learning and Teaching, University of Groningen. b.p.m.creemers@rug.nl

Leonidas Kyriakides, Department of Education, University of Cyprus. kyriakid@ucy.ac.cy

Pam Sammons, Department of Education, University of Oxford. pamela.sammons@education.ox.ac.uk

Authors of/contributors to Part B of the book

Jan-Eric Gustafsson, University of Gothenburg, Sweden. jan-eric.gustafsson@ped.gu.se

Hans Luyten, University of Twente, Department of Educational Organisation and Management. j.w.luyten@gw.utwente.nl

George A. Marcoulides, Graduate School of Education, University of California, Riverside. georgem@ucr.edu

Robert E. Slavin, Johns Hopkins University and University of York. rslavin@successforall.org

Charles Teddlie, Department of Educational Theory, Policy and Practice, Louisiana State University. edtedd@lsu.edu

Norman Verhelst, CITO, the Netherlands. norman.verhelst@cito.nl

Figures

Tables

Preface

Compared to other areas of research in the social sciences and even in education, Educational Effectiveness Research (EER) has had a relatively short history of about 40 years. This short history is, however, already fairly well documented and in most cases the authors have given recommendations for the development of EER in the future. However, although there have been many reviews and several handbooks focusing on EER, there has been little systematic attention paid to documenting and analysing methodological advances. In this book, therefore, we seek to provide an overview of the methodological development of EER and make a plea for a more theoretical orientation in educational effectiveness, for more experimental and longitudinal research and for further rigorous evaluation of improvement projects in schools and classrooms.

We were already convinced – and after reading the contributions to this publication our conviction has been strengthened – that EER makes progress through the advancements in the research methodology of, and the statistical techniques used in, the analysis of relevant hierarchically structured data sets. However, in our view it is not only the quality of the research design, the instruments and the statistical analysis that promote the knowledge base of educational effectiveness but also the development of better theories about the complex nature of educational effectiveness. In our opinion, the theoretical development of educational effectiveness both asked for and also promoted methodological advances, and the further development of educational effectiveness theory is thus facilitated by various methodological and technical advances that have been made over the last two decades or so. These advances have enabled researchers to test the various components of theories of educational effectiveness and to evaluate improvement practices, which in turn have pushed our thinking and theory development further.

In this publication we concentrate on describing and explaining the main methodological advances that we believe will help readers to improve the quality of future EER studies. Thus, we do not restrict ourselves to a simple overview of different research tools, but instead we choose to present them from the perspective of the development and testing of a theoretical body of knowledge about effectiveness. For this reason we provide the readers in the first part of the book with an analysis of the background to EER, an account of the advances in research and theory made in the past and an analysis of the mutual relationship between methodological advances and progress in theory development. Special attention is given to two issues related to our theoretical orientation in educational effectiveness: first, the difficulties in demonstrating causal relations between the various context, input, output and process factors of interest in EER and the most fruitful avenues for identifying causality, and second, an analysis of the implications of this orientation for research design. The second issue is concerned with the purpose of EER, to have an impact on educational practice in classes, schools and on policy and ways to promote this impact and evaluate it.

In the second part of the book – the main core of the publication – we provide readers with a state-of-the-art overview of advances in the EER methodology with respect to design measurement theories and data analysis. Experts in each of the areas (in most cases in collaboration with the editors) provide the background to each of the specific approaches of particular interest, present a comprehensive overview and give examples of the use of the approach and/or technique in specific EER studies to illustrate their application. After this presentation of advances made in research design, measurement and data analysis, we return in the third part of the book to a discussion of the main implications for EER. We draw conclusions about the implications of such methodological advancements for the future of EER, especially with respect to the prospect for improved development and testing of theories about educational effectiveness, which can have an impact on practice and policy. In order to promote excellence in research we provide readers with an instrument (which we regard as analogous to a conceptual road map or guide) that will support them in making decisions in the development of their own research plans and in the implementation of those plans.

In writing this book we received support from many colleagues, policymakers, practitioners and our families. We would like to mention some of them, especially the following. Our colleague Dr James Hall provided us with constructive feedback of the early draft of the book and challenged us to sharpen our arguments. Our friend Ioannis Yiannakis, who is currently an inspector and used to be a teacher for many years, gave us comments that helped us identify the extent to which our work could contribute in the improvement of policy and practice. We also thank him for helping us to draft figures of the proposed conceptual map for conducting methodologically appropriate effectiveness studies. The research assistants on our team and especially our PhD students gave us comments from the perspective of young researchers in the field of EER. Evi Charalambous helped us in the production of the manuscript and supported us in the process of linguistic editing. Finally, our universities were supportive in facilitating our academic efforts to write the book.

As we have already mentioned, in producing this volume our main purpose is to promote future high-quality research in educational effectiveness. We see the current advancements in methodology and statistical techniques as great opportunities to improve the quality of EER. Moreover, the relationship can be seen as reciprocal because, as we show, some of the key advancements have been promoted and fostered by research in the educational effectiveness field. We welcome comments, criticism and contributions to its further development and anticipate that new knowledge will be produced by readers with different perspectives in education and research. We hope that readers, and especially students, will be challenged to conduct high-quality research in this area in order to contribute to the growing EER evidence base and to enhance current understanding and the use of EER in the improvement of educational practice.

Part A

The state of the art of Educational Effectiveness Research

Challenges for research methodology

Chapter 1

Background to Educational Effectiveness Research

Introduction

The essential difference between this book and other books on research methodology is a focus on methodological advances in a specific area within research on education, namely Educational Effectiveness Research (EER). Thus, this introductory chapter offers a background to EER and helps readers recognize the importance of the progress that has been made in research methodology for this field. This chapter also seeks to enable EER researchers to identify ways of making use of advanced research methods that will further promote the development of this field. At the same time, this chapter also provides readers who are more generally interested in research methodology with a brief account of the background to EER in order to help them understand the specific context in which advanced research methods can be applied and so contribute to the ongoing development of this field.

In this introductory chapter we give a short outline of the history of EER, identify its essential characteristics and illustrate the strengths and weaknesses of this field. The progress made in modelling educational effectiveness is presented and major research questions are identified that have implications for the choice of most appropriate research methodology. It is shown that developments in research methodology, such as in multilevel modelling to analyse nested data, have promoted the knowledge base of educational effectiveness. Further, this chapter outlines attempts by researchers to establish theoretical models and describes how the complexity of educational effectiveness has provided challenges to the development of methodologically appropriate studies, including ways of analysing data. Finally, the aims of this book and its structure are then outlined.

Educational Effectiveness Research can be seen as an overarching theme that links together a conglomerate of research in different areas, including research on teacher behaviour and its impacts; curriculum; student grouping procedures; school organization; and educational policy. The main research question underlying EER is the identification and investigation of which factors in the teaching, curriculum and learning environments (operating at different levels, such as the classroom, the school, and levels above the school) can directly or indirectly explain measured differences (variations) in the outcomes of students.

Further, such research frequently takes into account the influence of other important background characteristics, such as student ability, socio-economic status (SES) and prior attainment. Thus, EER attempts to establish and test theories that explain why and how some schools and teachers are more effective than others in promoting better outcomes for students. However, it is also important to note that the three terms – school effectiveness, teacher effectiveness and educational effectiveness – are used inconsistently in the literature and that these are themselves interrelated. In this book, 'school effectiveness' is taken to mean the impact that school-wide factors, such as a school policy for teaching, school climate and the 'mission' of a school, have on students' cognitive and affective performance. On the other hand, 'teacher effectiveness' is taken to mean the impact that classroom factors have on student performance, and includes teacher behaviour, teacher expectations, classroom organization and use of classroom resources.

Teddlie (1994) argued that most teacher effectiveness studies have been concerned only with the processes that occur within classrooms, to the exclusion of school-wide factors, whereas most school effectiveness studies have involved phenomena that occur throughout the school with little emphasis on particular teaching behaviours within individual classrooms. Only a few EER studies have attempted to examine both school and classroom effectiveness simultaneously (Mortimore et al. 1988; Teddlie and Stringfield 1993), although this weakness has begun to be addressed in recent studies (de Jong et al. 2004; Kyriakides 2005; Reynolds et al. 2002; Opdenakker and Van Damme 2000). The attempts to deal with both teacher and school influences can be seen as a significant development in EER, since joint studies on school and teacher effectiveness reveal that neither level can be adequately studied without considering the other (Reynolds et al. 2002). In this context, we are using the term educational effectiveness rather than teacher and/or school effectiveness to emphasize the importance of conducting joint school and teacher effectiveness research, which can help us identify interactions between the school, classroom and student levels and their contributions in explaining variation in student outcomes, both cognitive and non-cognitive. Finally, it is important to note that EER also refers to the functioning of the educational system as a whole, and this research can, therefore, also be used to support the development and testing of different models of effectiveness (Creemers 1994; Creemers and Kyriakides 2008; Scheerens 1992; Stringfield and Slavin 1992). In turn, these models of effectiveness ultimately attempt to explain why educational systems and their subcomponents perform differently, with the aim of providing relevant evidence for policymakers.

History of Educational Effectiveness Research

The origins of EER largely stem from reactions to seminal works on equality of opportunity in education that were conducted in the United States and undertaken by Coleman et al. (1966) and Jencks et al. (1972). These two innovative studies from two different disciplinary backgrounds – sociology and psychology, respectively – drew very similar conclusions in relation to the amount of variance in student outcomes that can be explained by educational factors. Although the studies did not suggest schooling was unimportant, the differences in student outcomes that were attributable to attending one school rather than another were modest. However, these studies were also criticized for failing to measure the educational variables that were of the most relevance (Madaus *et al.* 1979). Nevertheless, it is important to note that these two studies both claimed that, after taking into consideration the influence of student background characteristics such as ability and family background (for example, race and SES), only a small proportion of the variation in student achievement could be attributed to the school or educational factors. This pessimistic sense of not knowing what, if anything, education could contribute to reducing inequality in educational outcomes and in society as a whole was also fed by the apparent failure of large-scale educational compensatory programmes, such as 'Headstart' and 'Follow Through' conducted in the United States, which were based on the idea that education in pre-school/schools would help compensate for initial differences between students. Similarly disappointing results have since also been reported for the effects of compensatory programmes that have been conducted in other countries (Driessen and Mulder 1999; MacDonald 1991; Schon 1971; Taggart and Sammons 1999; Sammons *et al.* 2003).

The first two school effectiveness studies that were independently undertaken by Edmonds (1979) in the United States and Rutter *et al.* (1979) in England during the 1970s were concerned with examining evidence and making an argument about the potential power of schooling to make a difference in the life chances of students. This was an optimistic point of view, because many studies published in that period had shown that teachers, schools and maybe even education in general had failed to make much of a difference. The early appearance of these two independent research projects in different countries that asked similar questions and drew, to a certain extent, on similar quantitative methodologies demonstrated the potential for establishing a scientific domain dealing with effectiveness in education (Kyriakides 2006). Thus, the publications by Brookover *et al.* (1979) and Rutter *et al.* (1979) were followed by numerous studies in different countries on educational effectiveness and the development of international interest and collaboration through the creation of the International Congress for School Effectiveness and Improvement (ICSEI) in 1990 (Teddlie and Reynolds 2000). Looking at the history of EER, we see four sequential phases in the field, which address different types of research questions and promote the theoretical development of EER.

- **First phase: a focus on the size of school effects. Establishing the field by showing that 'school matters'.**
  During the early 1980s, the studies that were conducted attempted to show that there were differences in the impact that particular teachers and schools

have on student outcomes. This research showed how important it is for students to have effective teachers and schools, and that school and teacher effects tend to be larger for disadvantaged groups (Scheerens and Bosker 1997).

- **Second phase: a focus on the characteristics/correlates of effectiveness. Searching for factors associated with better student outcomes.**
  In the late 1980s and early 1990s, researchers in the area of EER were mainly concerned with identifying factors that were associated with student outcomes. These studies resulted in a list of factors that were treated as characteristics of effective teachers and schools (Levine and Lezotte 1990; Sammons *et al.* 1995; Scheerens and Bosker 1997).

- **Third phase: modelling educational effectiveness. The development of theoretical models that show why specific factors are important in explaining variation in student outcomes.**
  By the late 1990s and early 2000s several integrated models of educational effectiveness (Creemers 1994; Scheerens 1992; Stringfield and Slavin 1992) had been developed. These models sought to explain why factors that operate at different levels are associated with student outcomes, and these models guided not only the theoretical development of EER but also the design of empirical studies within this field (Kyriakides *et al.* 2000; de Jong *et al.* 2004).

- **Fourth phase: focus on complexity. A more detailed analysis of the complex nature of educational effectiveness that developed further links with the study of school improvement.**
  A gradual movement from the third to fourth phase was observed particularly after 2000. This featured a focus on change over time and addressed issues such as consistency, stability, differential effectiveness and departmental effects. Researchers increasingly gave attention to the study of complexity in education and pointed to the fact that the theoretical models of the third phase had not emphasized the *dynamic* perspective of education nor had they paid sufficient attention to the differential character of some factors (Creemers and Kyriakides 2006). Moreover, this gradual movement also saw an interest develop in investigating the question of changes in the effectiveness of schools, rather than exploring the extent of stability in effectiveness (Kyriakides and Creemers 2009). The move away from seeing effectiveness as an essentially stable characteristic of different schools or teachers to one that varies across years, and may differ for different student outcomes or in relation to different student groups, places change at the heart of EER. As such, the field became increasingly linked with the growth of larger scale, systematic investigations of the long-term effect of teachers and schools (Kyriakides *et al.* 2009; Pustjens *et al.* 2004). As a consequence, EER is seeing a growth in interest concerning the processes of school improvement, which is leading to the use of new theories such as the dynamic model (Creemers and Kyriakides 2008). Such developments

also point to the value of building links with other research areas such as organizational change in educational administration.

Although these four phases are analysed in more detail below, it is argued that EER has gradually evolved from focusing on a single issue (that is, schools and education 'matter') into a more intellectually sophisticated and mature area within the educational sciences. This has come about through EER trying to explain the complex and essentially dynamic nature of educational effectiveness and educational change. In this book, it is stressed that the above theoretical developments in the field were greatly facilitated by developments in research methodology that were increasingly adopted by EER in order to understand the complexity of the links between educational processes and outcomes. As a result, during these four phases one can also observe further parallel development in the methods used within EER. For example, there has been a movement from outlier studies (during phase one) to cohort studies (phases two and three) and most recently to longitudinal and experimental studies (phases three and four). Advanced techniques in analysing the data of effectiveness studies can be especially identified after the mid-1980s when multilevel modelling techniques (Goldstein 1995) were systematically employed. Therefore, it can be assumed that further developments in the field will continue to involve close links between theoretical and methodological advances.

First phase: establishing the field by showing that school matters

The studies from the first phase of EER were mainly concerned with revealing that teachers and schools differ among themselves in their impact on student performance and thereby that student progress in part depends on who is their teacher and which school they attend. The extent to which schools differ was the next question raised by researchers in the field, with a more precise version of this question being how much schools differ in terms of student outcomes when they are more or less equal in terms of the innate abilities and socio-economic background of their students (using statistical controls for variations in student intake characteristics). EER aimed to make fair comparisons between teachers and schools in order to assess the impact of schooling on student achievement that could be uniquely attributed to, for example, teacher A or school X, rather teacher B or school Y. Such research was enabled through the use of multilevel models that allowed for clustering of the data at the teacher (class) level and at the school level, which enabled more precise estimates of variation between schools and the identification of individual school effects (through residual estimates and their associated confidence limits). By the end of this phase, a clear message about the important role of teachers and schools had emerged from a large number of studies conducted in various countries and these provided a strong argument against critics who had argued that teachers and schools did not matter for student outcomes (Scheerens and Bosker 1997; Teddlie and Reynolds 2000). However, the issue of educational effectiveness did not end by assessing the differences between schools and teachers in terms of their effectiveness. Rather, this was merely a prelude to exploring what matters in schools.

Second phase: searching for factors associated with student outcomes

The main research question of the second phase of EER attempted to identify those factors that help to explain differences in the effectiveness of schools. The results of studies conducted during this phase produced lists of correlates that were associated with better student achievement and which were treated as key effectiveness factors. One of the first of these was concerned with the so-called 'five-factor model' (Edmonds 1979). These five correlates of educational achievements were:

- strong educational leadership;
- high expectations of student achievement;
- an emphasis on basic skills;
- a safe and orderly climate;
- frequent evaluation of student progress.

This initial model has since been criticized on methodological (Ralph and Fennessey 1983) and also conceptual grounds (Scheerens and Creemers 1989). However, more refined models of educational effectiveness were also developed from this (Clauset and Gaynor 1982; Duckworth 1983; Ellett and Walberg 1979; Glasman and Biniaminov 1981; Murphy *et al.* 1982; Schmuck 1980; Stringfield and Slavin 1992; Squires *et al.* 1983). These later models elaborated on the framework for a causal model of educational effectiveness as developed by Scheerens and Creemers (1989). This framework stressed the fact that various levels in education can be seen to contribute to variations in student performance. The characteristics for educational effectiveness that are found in this phase of research can also be placed (that is, be seen to operate) at different levels. However, this framework does not answer why certain characteristics correlate positively with achievement. Finally, it is also important to note that reviews of the results of the studies conducted during this phase (Levine and Lezzotte 1990; Sammons *et al.* 1995) resulted in numerous correlates for effective classrooms, schools and above-school levels (districts, states, country). Together, these studies emphasized once more the importance of further developing the relatively limited theoretical foundation of EER by including the combination of correlates into categories.

Third Phase: development of theoretical models

The third phase of EER saw researchers use several theoretical orientations to help explain why certain characteristics might contribute to educational effectiveness (Scheerens and Bosker 1997). Generally speaking, there are three perspectives within EER in this phase, which attempted to explain why and how certain characteristics contribute to educational effectiveness, and three relevant theoretical models that emerged from these approaches.

First, in order to explain variation in the effectiveness of teachers and schools, economists have focused on variables concerned with resource inputs, such as per-student expenditure. Specifically, this economic approach is focused on producing a mathematical function that reveals the relationship between the 'supply of selected purchased schooling inputs and educational outcomes controlling for the influence of various background features' (Monk 1992: 308). This function may be viewed as either linear, consisting of main effects and interaction effects, or nonlinear (Brown and Saks 1986). Thus, the associated emergence of 'education production' models (Brown and Saks 1986; Elberts and Stone 1988) were based on the assumption that increased inputs will lead to increments in outcomes. These models are mainly concerned with: (a) the selection of relevant resource inputs as the major type of selection of antecedent condition, (b) the measurement of direct effects, and (c) the use of data at only one level of aggregation (that is, either at micro [for example, student] level or aggregated [for example, school] level).

The second model to emerge from this phase of EER featured a sociological perspective and focused on factors that define the educational and family background of students, such as SES, ethnic group, gender, social-capital and peer group. This perspective examined not only student outcomes but also the extent to which schools manage to ameliorate or increase the variation in student outcomes when compared to prior achievement. Two dimensions of measuring school effectiveness emerged from this perspective and concerned the quality of schools (students reaching high outcomes) and enhancing the equity in schools (reducing the achievement gaps between advantaged and disadvantaged groups). Moreover, the sociological perspective also brought attention to school processes that emerged from organizational theories (including climate, culture and structure) and to contexts such as the concentration of disadvantaged students and the impacts of this on student outcomes and school and classroom processes.

Finally, educational psychologists in this period focused on student background factors such as 'learning aptitude' and 'motivation', and on variables measuring the learning processes that take place in classrooms. Further, an interest in identifying and understanding the features of effective instruction practice was also observed and led to a list of teacher behaviours that were positively and consistently correlated with student achievement over time. For example, Rosenshine (1983) identified general teacher factors associated with achievement, which he labelled the 'direct instruction model' of teaching, sometimes called a 'structured approach'. From this, a slightly different model called 'active teaching', with more emphasis put on the involvement of students in the learning and teaching process, was then also developed.

However, more recent research on teaching has featured a gradual trend toward less interest in teacher behaviour and the effects of teacher and instructional behaviour, and more interest in teacher cognition and teacher thinking about their professional practice (Creemers 2008). Within EER at this time, attention was initially directed to the effects of schools; however, after the introduction of multilevel analysis and a more theoretical orientation of EER, more emphasis was put on the learning and instructional level (Teddlie and Reynolds 2000). Theoretically, it was expected that student outcomes were related to learning activities that take place mostly at the learning/instructional level. This resulted in a re-orientation, empirically and theoretically, of effectiveness research toward a more explicit focus on the processes taking place at the teaching/learning level. Factors at the classroom level or the teaching and learning level are therefore seen as the primary effectiveness factors (Creemers and Kyriakides 2008). When a better foundation for EER was sought, this was therefore also concerned with an orientation towards developing theories and models about learning in schools. These theories and models were seen as a possible bridge between learning outcomes, which are used as criteria for effectiveness, and processes at the classroom and school level.

Fourth phase: analysing in more detail the complex nature of educational effectiveness

During the fourth phase, researchers attempted to respond to a major criticism of earlier EER that was concerned with the failure of the field to contribute significantly to the establishment of strong links between research on effective factors and developmental work intended to improve the quality of education. However, a dynamic perspective on education is now being taken into account more explicitly in theoretical and empirical EER studies (Creemers and Kyriakides 2006). Thus, in this phase, teaching and learning are seen as dynamic processes that are constantly adapting to changing needs and opportunities. This thereby has seen studies investigating the process of change in schools gradually emerge (Opdenakker and Van Damme 2006), which has had implications for modelling educational effectiveness in a way that takes into account the complex nature of education (Creemers and Kyriakides 2008). Moreover, such studies have helped us look at the functioning of each effectiveness factor using a dynamic rather than an instrumental perspective. This also implies that specific developments in the methodology of EER are needed since this research does not support the traditional approach of modelling effectiveness as a static feature or attribute of schools or teachers. Modelling effectiveness or change should not be restricted to fitting conditional models in which measures of student learning outcomes (adjusted for background characteristics such as SES, gender and prior knowledge) are regressed on a set of explanatory variables. Further, measures of change based on only one or two time points are also unreliable (Bryk and Raudenbush 1987; Goldstein 1997; Willet 1988) and so provide an inadequate basis for studying change (Bryk and Weisberg 1977; Rogosa et al. 1982).

Therefore, the approach promoted in the current phase of EER does not place undue emphasis on measuring the short-term outcomes of the immediate effect of schools and teachers on student achievement gains during a single school year. In contrast, this approach instead reveals a need for longitudinal research to study results of schools and classrooms and their functioning over a longer period, modelling the growth in student outcomes over at least three time points. The progress made in the way educational effectiveness is conceptualized by EER also reveals that theoretical developments in the field have been facilitated by several methodological developments, as is shown in the next section.

Methodological developments promoting theory and research on effectiveness

This section attempts to show that much of the progress in EER is due to advances in methodology made during the last 30 years. During the first phase of EER, major emphasis was given to conducting outlier studies and comparing the characteristics of more effective schools with those of less effective schools (for example, the Louisiana Study). However, the emphasis on identifying outliers was criticized both for conceptual and methodological reasons (Goldstein 1997). During the 1980s, researchers moved to the use of mainly cohort and longitudinal designs involving larger numbers of schools and students, and such studies multiplied in the 1990s. In addition, the development of hierarchical regression approaches involving multilevel modelling techniques enabled researchers in the area to take the multilevel structure of educational systems into consideration and thereby deal with the methodological weaknesses of earlier studies that used only uni-level regression analysis (for example, the *Fifteen thousand hours* study by Rutter et al. 1979). Early examples of studies that made use of hierarchical regression approaches include the *School matters* study (Mortimore et al. 1988) and the *Young children at school in the inner city* research (Tizard et al. 1988) in England. Gradually, the way of measuring the links between inputs, outcomes and processes became more sophisticated, particularly through the development of contextual value-added models that controlled for student level, prior attainment and background as well as contextual measures of school or class composition (Sammons et al. 1997). Moreover, progress in the area of developing tests and other assessments helped researchers establish better measures of achievement not only in the area of basic skills such as reading, writing and mathematics but also in higher-level cognitive outcomes, and even in the affective and social domains.

During the second and third phase of EER, a large number of reviews were conducted and their main purpose was to provide the research community and policymakers with the latest developments from the field (Creemers and Reezigt

1996; Levine and Lezotte 1990; Sammons *et al.* 1995). However, although these reviews were usually based on a collection of studies that were seen by the authors as providing good examples of research (Creemers and Reezigt 1996, Sammons *et al.* 1995), their judgements of the methodological deficiency of studies that were excluded were not necessarily systematic and were often based on implicit rather than explicit criteria. On the other hand, the reviews that were not selective resulted in a huge number of factors for which not much information about their empirical support was provided (Levine and Lezotte 1990). As a consequence, the results of these early reviews can be questioned. In this context, carrying out meta-analyses using advanced quantitative approaches can be seen as a major methodological development that promotes theoretical development in the field and enables researchers to identify generic and more specific factors the impact of which is dependent on the educational setting in which they are operating (Scheerens and Bosker 1997).

During the third and the fourth phases of EER, emphasis was given not only to searching for predictors with direct effects on student outcomes but also those with indirect effects (for example in studies of school leadership and the links with student outcomes (Silins and Mulford 2002). Moreover, the theoretical models that have been developed during this phase refer to relations among factors situated at different levels (Creemers and Kyriakides 2008; Scheerens and Bosker 1997). In this context, the development of multilevel Structural Equation Modelling (SEM) approaches (Heck and Thomas 2000; Hox 2002; Muthén 1997) enables researchers to search for indirect effects and/or test the validity of the current models of EER in relation to this assumption (de Fraine *et al.* 2007; de Maeyer *et al.* 2007).

During the fourth phase of EER, emphasis has been given to modelling the dynamic nature of effectiveness. This implies, among other things, that longitudinal studies that last for at least three years should be conducted in order not only to measure the long-term effect of schools and teachers but also to find out how changes in the functioning of factors are associated with changes in educational effectiveness (Kyriakides and Creemers 2009). For this reason, developments in advanced quantitative research methods such as the use of growth modelling techniques are to be welcomed because they can help us answer such research questions. Moreover, conducting longitudinal studies enables researchers to search for reciprocal relations that, according to current theoretical developments in the field of EER, are expected to exist. Such relations are often included in relevant statistical models and refer to the relation of student factors that are likely to change with achievement (Creemers and Kyriakides 2008). For example, advanced SEM techniques can be used to search for reciprocal relations between motivation or academic self-concept and student achievement by making use of data collected at different points of time (Marsh *et al.* 2006).

At this point, we would like to claim that a challenge for EER is to make better use of current developments and progress in research methodology and to provide empirical support for new ways of conceptualizing the dynamic nature of educational effectiveness. At the same time, it is acknowledged that the knowledge base of educational effectiveness and its attempt to establish theoretical models challenge the development of methodologically appropriate studies and ways of analysing data. An example is the development of SEM and multilevel techniques, which help EER to search not only for linear but also for non-linear relations between effectiveness factors and student achievement. Furthermore, a challenge for EER research methodology is to establish and use advanced quantitative techniques that will identify meaningful groupings of factors (Kyriakides *et al.* 2009). Such a development would contribute to the establishment of stronger links between EER and those who are involved in school/teacher development or improvement projects that seek to promote better practice (defined as that which promotes better outcomes for students) and offers the hope that more comprehensive strategies for school improvement will eventually emerge.

Aims and outline of the book

The aims of the book

The main aim of this book is to provide an authoritative account of the history and current developments in the methodology of EER and the way EER has evolved and is being applied in research and evaluation. By doing so, we hope to promote the further development of theory and research in educational effectiveness, which in turn depends on the further development of research methodology. At the same time, this book shows that the knowledge base of educational effectiveness and its attempt to establish theoretical models offer a challenge to the development of methodologically appropriate studies, including better ways of analysing clustered data. Next to this more theoretical perspective of the book, there is also a very practical argument for the promotion of the appropriate use of advanced research techniques by researchers in the area of EER. We try to do so by giving a sufficient background for each method and cite examples of using each within the context of EER.

The nature and structure of the book

This book is organized in three parts, which feature a summary of the main points therein. In the last chapter, the main conclusions emerging from the book are then outlined and their implications for further methodological development are considered.

Part A presents an overview of the state of the art of educational effectiveness studies and pinpoints challenges for the development of EER and research methodology. Chapter 2 provides an overview of major methodological issues in EER. More specifically, this chapter refers to the main research questions prevalent in EER and how these are related to methodological issues that are connected to both designing studies and using advanced techniques to analyse quantitative and qualitative data, including their integration in mixed-methods designs. Moreover, issues concerned with the development of appropriate instruments and the process of investigating their psychometric properties are also discussed. In Chapter 3 by contrast, we argue that searching for causality is an important issue within EER since it promotes the theoretical and method-ological development of the field. We also discuss causality's meaning and how it can be addressed by looking at different orientations within the research methodology. In the last chapter of this part of the book, we discuss the impact of EER on the design and evaluation of reform policies and the establishment of strategies to improve practice. It is argued that EER can contribute to the development of theory-driven evaluation studies that will serve both policymakers and educational practice, as well as promoting further theoretical development of the field. Thus, in this chapter, we provide guidelines to readers on how to design theory-driven evaluation studies that will contribute to the establishment of an evidence-based approach in policymaking and a theory-driven approach to improving education.

In Part B, each chapter is designed to help the readers understand why each methodological orientation is important for EER, and the mathematical background of each technique is summarized to help readers understand its current and future applications. Specific examples of applying each orientation are offered to help readers design their own effectiveness studies using the method-ological tools presented here. The sequence used to present the methodological tools of EER follows the main decisions that have to be taken in designing original studies. Initially, different types of original studies are presented before we then refer to the two main measurement theories that can be used to develop research instruments and test their validity. Next, advanced statistical tech-niques that can be used to analyse nested and longitudinal data are presented before, finally, we then promote the use of meta-analyses and secondary analyses of international studies and explain how to conduct them. Specifically, in Chapters 5, 6 and 7, we illustrate the importance of using different types of research design in EER (that is, longitudinal studies, experimental studies and mixed research methods, respectively). It is shown that each research method can address specific research questions in an appropriate way. Chapters 8, 9 and 10 refer to two different measurement theories and show how Item Response Theory and Generalizability Theory can be used for developing and testing the validity of psychometrically appropriate research instruments. The next two chapters (11 and 12) refer to advanced techniques in analysing data. Chapter 11 examines the use of multilevel modelling techniques and their application, whereas Structural Equation Modelling techniques are discussed in Chapter 12. Finally, Chapter 13 examines the importance of conducting quantitative syntheses of original studies. The importance of testing and developing theoretical models of educational effectiveness by conducting meta-analyses is also stressed. Beyond illustrating how meta-analyses can be conducted to search for generic and differential factors of effectiveness, we also refer to the importance of conducting secondary analyses of comparative international studies such as the Programme for International Student Assessment (PISA) and the Third International Mathematics and Science Study (TIMSS). Advantages and limitations of these approaches are also discussed.

In the very last part of the book, we relate the further development of theory and research in educational effectiveness to current trends and advances in the methodology used within the social sciences. Topics for further development concerning both EER and research methodology that are adopted in such studies are identified and a conceptual map for further methodological advancements in EER is provided.

References

Brookover, W.B., Beady, C., Flood, P., Schweitzer, J. and Wisenbaker, J. (1979) *School systems and student achievement: schools make a difference*, New York: Praeger.

Brown, B.W. and Saks, D.H. (1986) 'Measuring the effects of instructional time on student learning: evidence from the beginning teacher evaluation study', *American Journal of Education*, 94: 480–500.

Bryk, A.S. and Raudenbush, S.W. (1987) 'Application of hierarchical linear models to assessing change', *Psychological Bulletin*, 101(1): 147–58.

Bryk, A.S. and Weisberg, H.I. (1977) 'Use of the nonequivalent control group design when subjects are growing', *Psychological Bulletin*, 84: 950–62.

Clauset, K.H. and Gaynor, A.K. (1982) 'A systems perspective on effective schools', *Educational Leadership*, 40(3): 54–9.

Coleman, J.S., Campbell, E.Q., Hobson, C.F., McPartland, J., Mood, A.M., Weinfeld, F.D. and York, R.L. (1966) *Equality of educational opportunity*, Washington, DC: US Government Printing Office.

Creemers, B.P.M. (1994) *The effective classroom*, London: Cassell.

Creemers, B.P.M. (2008) 'The AERA handbooks of research on teaching: Implications for educational effectiveness research', *School Effectiveness and School Improvement*, 19(4): 473–7.

Creemers, B.P.M. and Kyriakides, L. (2006) 'A critical analysis of the current approaches to modelling educational effectiveness: the importance of establishing a dynamic model', *School Effectiveness and School Improvement*, 17(3): 347–66.

Creemers, B.P.M. and Kyriakides, L. (2008) *The dynamics of educational effectiveness: A contribution to policy, practice and theory in contemporary schools*, London: Routledge.

Creemers, B.P.M. and Reezigt, G.J. (1996) 'School level conditions affecting the effectiveness of instruction', *School Effectiveness and School Improvement*, 7(3): 197–228.

de Fraine, B., Van Damme, J. and Onghena, P. (2007) 'A longitudinal analysis of gender differences in academic self-concept and language achievement: A multivariate multilevel latent growth approach', *Contemporary Educational Psychology*, 32(1): 132–50.

De Jong, R., Westerhof, K.J. and Kruiter, J.H. (2004) 'Empirical evidence of a comprehensive model of school effectiveness: A multilevel study in mathematics in the 1st year of junior general education in the Netherlands', *School Effectiveness and School Improvement*, 15(1): 3–31.

De Maeyer, S., Rymenans, R., Van Petegem, P., van den Bergh, H. and Rijlaarsdam, G. (2007) 'Educational leadership and pupil achievement: The choice of a valid conceptual model to test effects in school effectiveness research', *School Effectiveness and School Improvement*, 18(2): 125–45.

Driessen, G.W.J.M. and Mulder, L.W.J. (1999) 'The enhancement of the educational opportunities of disadvantaged children', in R.J. Bosker, B.P.M. Creemers and S. Stringfield (eds) *Enhancing excellence, equity and efficiency: Evidence from evaluations of systems and schools in change*, Dordrecht: Kluwer Academic Publishers, pp. 37–64.

Duckworth, K. (1983) *Specifying determinants of teacher and principal work*, Eugene, OR: Centre for Educational Policy and Management, University of Oregon.

Edmonds, R.R. (1979) 'Effective schools for the urban poor', *Educational Leadership*, 37(1): 15–27.

Elberts, R.W. and Stone, J.A. (1988) 'Student achievement in public schools: Do principles make a difference?', *Economics Education Review*, 7: 291–9.

Ellett, C.D. and Walberg, H.J. (1979) 'Principal competency, environment and outcomes', in H.J. Walberg (ed.) *Educational environment and effects* 140–67, Berkeley, CA: McCutchan.

Glasman, N.S. and Biniaminov, I. (1981) 'Input–output analyses of schools', *Review of Educational Research*, 51: 509–39.

Goldstein, H. (1995) *Multilevel statistical models*, London: Edward Arnold.

Goldstein, H. (1997) 'The methodology of school effectiveness research', *School Effectiveness and School Improvement*, 8(4): 369–95.

Heck, R.H. and Thomas, S.L. (2000) *An introduction to multilevel modelling techniques*, Mahwah, NJ: Lawrence Erlbaum Associates.

Hox, J. (2002) *Multilevel analysis. Techniques and applications*, Mahwah, NJ/London: Lawrence Earlbaum Associates.

Jencks, C., Smith, M., Acland, H., Bane, M.J., Cohen, D., Gintis, H., Heyns, B. and Michelson, S. (1972) *Inequality: A reassessment of the effects of family and schooling in America*, New York: Basic Books.

Kyriakides, L. (2005) 'Extending the comprehensive model of educational effectiveness by an empirical investigation', *School Effectiveness and School Improvement*, 16(2): 103–52.

Kyriakides, L. (2006) 'Using international comparative studies to develop the theoretical framework of educational effectiveness research: A secondary analysis of TIMSS 1999 data', *Educational Research and Evaluation*, 12(6): 513–34.

Kyriakides, L., Antoniou, P. and Maltezou E. (2009) 'Investigating the short- and long-term effects of secondary schools upon academic success and development', paper presented at the 90th Annual Meeting of the American Educational Research Association, San Diego, USA.

Kyriakides, L., Campbell, R.J. and Gagatsis, A. (2000) 'The significance of the classroom effect in primary schools: An application of Creemers' comprehensive model of educational effectiveness', *School Effectiveness and School Improvement*, 11(4): 501–29.

Kyriakides, L. and Creemers, B.P.M. (2009) 'Explaining stability and changes in schools: A follow-up study testing the validity of the dynamic model', paper presented at the EARLI conference, Amsterdam, The Netherlands.

Kyriakides, L., Creemers, B.P.M. and Antoniou, P. (2009) 'Teacher behaviour and student outcomes: Suggestions for research on teacher training and professional development', *Teaching and Teacher Education*, 25(1): 12–23.

Levine, D.U. and Lezotte, L.W. (1990) *Unusually effective schools: A review and analysis of research and practice*, Madison, WI: National Centre for Effective Schools Research and Development.

MacDonald, B. (1991) 'Critical introduction from innovation to reform – a framework for analysing change', in J. Rudduck (ed.) *Innovation and change: Developing involvement and understanding*, Milton Keynes: Open University Press.

Madaus, G.G., Kellagham, T., Rakow, E.A. and King, D. (1979) 'The sensitivity of measures of school effectiveness', *Harvard Educational Review*, 4: 207–30.

Marsh, H.W., Wen, Z. and Hau, K.-T. (2006) 'Structural equation models of latent interaction and quadratic effects', in G. R. Hancock and R.O. Mueller (eds) *Structural equation modelling: A second course*, Greenwich, CT: Information Age Publishing, pp. 225–65.

Monk, D.H. (1992) 'Education productivity research: An update and assessment of its role in education finance reform', *Educational Evaluation and Policy Analysis*, 14(4): 307–32.

Mortimore, P., Sammons, P., Stoll, L., Lewis, D. and Ecob, R. (1988) *School matters: The junior years*, Somerset: Open Books.

Murphy, J.F., Weil, M., Hallinger, P. and Mitman, A. (1982) 'Academic press: Translating high expectations into school policies and classroom practices', *Educational Leadership*, 40(3): 22–6.

Muthén, B.O. (1997) 'Latent growth modelling with longitudinal and multilevel data', in A. E. Raftery (ed.) *Sociological methodology*, Boston: Blackwell, pp. 453–80.

Opdenakker, M.C. and Van Damme, J. (2000) 'Effects of schools, teaching staff and classes on achievement and well-being in secondary education: Similarities and differences between school outcomes', *School Effectiveness and School Improvement*, 11(2): 65–196.

Opdenakker, M.C. and Van Damme, J. (2006) 'Differences between secondary schools: A study about school context, group composition, school practice, and school effects with special attention to public and Catholic schools and types of schools', *School Effectiveness and School Improvement*, 17(1): 87–117.

Pustjens, H., Van de Gaer, E., Van Damme, J. and Onghena, P. (2004) 'Effect of secondary schools on academic choices and on success in higher education', *School Effectiveness and School Improvement*, 15(3–4): 281–311.

Ralph, J.H. and Fennessey, J. (1983) 'Science or reform: Some questions about the effective schools model', *Phi Delta Kappan*, 64(10): 689–94.

Reynolds, D., Creemers, B., Stringfield, S., Teddlie, C. and Schaffer, G. (eds) (2002) *World class schools: International perspectives on school effectiveness*, London: RoutledgeFalmer.

Rogosa, D.R., Brand, D. and Zimowski, M. (1982) 'A growth curve approach to the measurement of change', *Psychological Bulletin*, 90: 726–48.

Rosenshine, B. (1983) 'Teaching functions in instructional programs', *The Elementary School Journal*, 83(4): 335–51.

Rutter, M., Maughan, B., Mortimore, P., Ouston, J. and Smith, A. (1979) *Fifteen thousand hours: secondary schools and their effects on children*, Cambridge, MA: Harvard University Press.

Sammons, P., Hillman, J. and Mortimore, P. (1995) *Key characteristics of effective schools: A review of school effectiveness research*, London: Office for Standards in Education and Institute of Education.

Sammons, P., Power, S., Elliot, K., Campbell, C., Robertson, P. and Whitty, G. (2003) *New community schools in Scotland: Final report – national evaluation of the pilot phase*, Edinburgh: Scottish Executive Education Department.

Sammons, P., Thomas, S. and Mortimore, P. (1997) *Forging links: Effective schools and effective departments,* London: Paul Chapman.

Scheerens, J. (1992) *Effective schooling: research, theory and practice,* London: Cassell.

Scheerens, J. and Bosker, R.J. (1997) *The foundations of educational effectiveness,* Oxford: Pergamon.

Scheerens, J. and Creemers, B.P.M. (1989) 'Conceptualizing school effectiveness', *International Journal of Educational Research,* 13: 691–706.

Schmuck, R.A. (1980) 'The school-organization', in J.H. McMillan (ed.) *The social psychology of school learning,* New York: Academic Press.

Schon, D.A. (1971) *Beyond the stable state,* Harmondsworth: Penguin.

Silins, N. and Mulford, B. (2002) 'Leadership and school results', in K. Leithwood and P. Hallinger (eds), *Second international handbook of educational leadership and administration,* Norwell, MA: Kluwer Aacademic Publishers, pp. 561–612.

Squires, D.A., Hewitt, W.G. and Segars, J.K. (1983) *Effective schools and classrooms: A research based perspective,* Alexandria, VA: Association for Supervision and Curriculum Development.

Stringfield, S.C. and Slavin, R.E. (1992) 'A hierarchical longitudinal model for elementary school effects', in B.P.M. Creemers and G.J. Reezigt (eds) *Evaluation of educational effectiveness,* Groningen: ICO, pp. 35–69.

Taggart, B. and Sammons, P. (1999) 'Evaluating the impact of raising school standards initiative', in R.J. Bosker, B.P.M. Creemers and S. Stringfield (eds) *Enhancing educational excellence, equity and efficiency: Evidence from evaluations of systems and schools in change,* Dordrecht: Kluwer Academic Publishers, pp. 137–66.

Teddlie, C. (1994) 'The integration of classroom and school process data in school effectiveness research', in D. Reynolds, B. Creemers, P.S. Nesselrodt, E.C. Shaffer, S. Stringfield and C. Teddlie (eds) *Advances in school effectiveness research and practice,* Oxford: Pergamon, pp. 111–33.

Teddlie, C. and Reynolds, D. (2000) *The international handbook of school effectiveness research,* London: Falmer Press.

Teddlie, C. and Stringfield, S. (1993) *Schools make a difference. Lessons learned from a 10 year study of school effects,* New York: Teachers College Press.

Tizard, B., Blatchford, P., Burke, J., Farquhar, C. and Plewis, I. (1988) *Young children at school in the inner city,* Hove: Lawrence Erlbaum.

Willett, J.B. (1988) 'Questions and answers in the measurement of change', *Review of Research in Education,* 15: 345–422.

Chapter 2

Methodological issues in Educational Effectiveness Research

Introduction

In this chapter, we analyse the current (fourth) phase of EER, examine the main research questions that form the foci of educational effectiveness enquiry and analyse methodological issues that should be taken into account when designing studies, as well as in analysing quantitative and qualitative data. These issues are presented to show the contribution research methodology has made and can make to the development of EER, before further clarification of the methodologies themselves and how they can be used is presented in the second part of the book. As mentioned in the introductory chapter, the current phase of EER is concerned with promoting a better understanding of the complex and dynamic nature of educational effectiveness. Thus, this chapter is concerned with methodological issues that have important implications, especially for modelling effectiveness, and the next chapter discusses issues associated with the design of studies that search for causal relations. More specifically, causality is a general issue in EER, and almost all effectiveness studies deal in one way or another with hypothesized (or implied) cause-and-effect relations by searching for factors that explain (in a statistical sense) variation in student outcomes. Further, this is usually in terms of academic achievement tests or measures of some kind. However, EER also encounters frequent difficulties in claiming cause-and-effect relations due to the non-experimental nature of most EER designs. In the last chapter of the first part of this book we acknowledge that the emphasis given by the current phase of EER to the dynamic perspective of educational effectiveness draws attention to the importance of searching for predictors of the processes of school improvement. This implies that researchers should not restrict themselves when describing effective practices to only those features that can be observed in schools. Instead, EER should also contribute to the design of theory-driven improvement strategies and in developing measures of their impact on changes in the effectiveness of teachers and schools over time. Since this shift in the research agenda of EER raises specific methodological issues, it is discussed in more detail in Chapter 4, which is concerned with establishing links between EER and policy and practice.

The methodological issues that are presented in the next section of this chapter refer to the contribution of research methodology in modelling effectiveness. Within this, it is taken as essential that researchers should attempt to search for more complex relations (direct, indirect and reciprocal) between different student, classroom/teacher and school factors and change in student achievement or other outcomes. Further, it is also taken as necessary for researchers to explore potential relations among factors operating at the same or at different levels in order to describe the complex nature of educational effectiveness. As such, this section therefore discusses the methodological issues that are associated with the need to search for generic and differential factors. It is acknowledged that during the current phase of EER there is a need to make a distinction between generic and differential factors and identify those that are common across different educational settings and those that are differential or specific, where the size of their effect depends on the setting in which they are operating (Campbell *et al.* 2004; Kyriakides 2007). Thus, a methodological issue stemming from this is not only how differential effectiveness can be investigated but also how the results of such studies can be incorporated into our attempts to establish generic and more context-specific models. Finally, an argument is made that researchers should also attempt to conceptualize the dynamic nature of education, which includes the need to look at ongoing changes in the functioning of teachers and schools and how these are related to changes over time in their effectiveness.

The emphasis that is given to the dynamic perspective of educational effectiveness also implies that the stability of effects related to teachers and schools over time cannot be seen as a necessarily clear measure of the reliability of these concepts (as was assumed during the second and third phases of EER; Kyriakides and Creemers 2008a). Thus, this chapter also discusses methodological issues concerned with the research that should be conducted to search not only for short but also for long-term effects of teachers and schools. These issues are then compared with the processes that should be used in analysing data that is collected for these different types of studies.

The last two sections of this chapter refer to some ongoing methodological questions that have not yet been solved. Specifically, there is an initial discussion of the possibility of research methodology enabling researchers to use different outcomes of schooling as the criteria of effectiveness. Special emphasis is given not only to the valid measurement of these outcomes but also to how they relate to each other. This issue also brings to attention the importance of using appropriate instruments to collect data. Thus, the last section of this chapter is concerned with advances in measurement theory in order to improve the quality of instruments that are used to measure not only student outcomes but also the nature and functioning of different effectiveness factors.

The contribution of research methodology in modelling educational effectiveness

Modelling educational effectiveness was an important research issue during the last (third) and current phases of EER. Moreover, the increasingly important role of this modelling was already evident in the second phase since here it became clear that EER should look at both classroom and school factors and that thus only multilevel models were appropriate to describe educational effectiveness. Following on from this during the third phase of EER, a number of studies were conducted that tried to test the validity of the early theoretical models of EER (Driessen and Sleegers 2000; Kyriakides *et al.* 2000; Reezigt *et al.* 1999). These revealed a number of methodological issues that should be taken into account in developing the theoretical framework of EER. These issues are analysed below and were also partially products of studies that had searched for the effect of school factors and especially factors such as leadership (Leithwood and Jantzi 2006; de Maeyer *et al.* 2007; Robinson *et al.* 2008) and quantitative syntheses of both school (Witziers *et al.* 2003; Scheerens and Bosker 1997) and teacher effectiveness (Monk 1994; Seidel and Shavelson 2007). More specifically, these studies made clear that both the direct and indirect effects on student achievement of such factors should be examined.

Searching for direct and indirect effects of factors on student achievement

In order to search for the relationships between significant educational factors and student achievement, researchers have considered the use of multilevel SEM models. These allow the specification of cross-level relationships by employing multivariate multilevel modelling techniques, which allow the use of more than one dependent variable. For example, the testing of a relationship between a factor concerned with school policy on the quantity of teaching and the management of time by the teacher can be conducted by treating the school factor (that is, school policy on quantity of teaching) as an explanatory variable and treating both the classroom factor (that is, management of time) and student achievement as simultaneous dependent variables.

Searching for relations between factors operating at the same level

The methodological procedure used in multilevel modelling techniques to search for cross-level relationships can also be used to search for relationships between factors that are operating at the same level. Obviously such relations can also be investigated through path analytic models. Searching for relations among factors operating at the same level is also an issue that needs further attention for the theoretical development of EER. This is not only due to different theoretical models referring to particular groups of factors but also because research on instructional effectiveness has developed specific teaching approaches consisting of combinations of particular teaching factors (for example, direct instruction, active teaching, new learning) that are seen as more effective than others.

Searching for nonlinear relations between factors and student achievement

Meta-analyses of the effect of some effectiveness factors upon student achievement has revealed that although they have been conceived of as having an impact on teacher or school effectiveness, the research evidence for their role remains problematic. For example, teacher subject knowledge is widely perceived as a factor that affects teacher effectiveness (Scriven 1994), but teachers' subject knowledge, regardless of how it is measured, has only rarely been correlated with student achievement in practice (Borich 1992; Darling-Hammond 2000). The explanation may be, as Monk (1994) reported, that the relationship is curvilinear. In other words, a minimal level of knowledge is necessary for teachers to be effective, but beyond a certain point, there may be a negative relation. Similar findings have been reported for the association of self-efficacy beliefs with teacher effectiveness (Schunk 1991; Stevenson *et al.* 1993) and for the impact of classroom emotional climate and teacher management upon effectiveness. These findings imply that models of educational effectiveness should acknowledge that nonlinear relations might exist and therefore that a search is needed for the optimal values of factors that are nonlinearly related with achievement (Creemers and Kyriakides 2006).

The challenge of this for modelling educational effectiveness has implications for both the design and the analysis of effectiveness studies since the investigation of nonlinear relations implies that more complex statistical techniques should be used in analysing the data and that more emphasis should be given to ensuring the quality of the measures that are used.

As far as an analysis of data is concerned, two issues need attention. Since models of educational effectiveness refer to factors operating at different levels, it is important to use multilevel modelling techniques that are able to identify the variables at the student, teacher, school, and system levels that are associated with student outcomes of interest. However, as noted above, an issue that has to be taken into account is that some variables may not be linearly related with student achievement. In the case of education, we have already considered the likely existence of inverted-U curvilinear relations since these reveal that there is an optimal point for the impact of a specific factor. After the optimal point, a flattened or negative relation with achievement can exist, and thereby the identification of the optimal point has important implications for improving educational practice. Therefore, in analyses where researchers search for inverted-U relations, the effect of both the various explanatory variables (X_i) and the effect of the second power of these variables (that is, X_i^2 values) upon student achievement have to be identified. This approach may allow us to identify the optimal value of this predictor factor (that is, the values of X for which Y has a maximum value). Of course, other forms of nonlinear relations might also exist. In cases where more than one optimal point can be identified, a question can be raised about the efficiency of application of a certain factor after the first optimal point is reached.

The second issue needing further attention is the issue of measurement errors of variables, because these act as significant obstacles in establishing the existence of possible nonlinear relations. In turn, this implies that researchers should give more emphasis to measurement issues in order to increase the quality of the data collected. Because the investigation of nonlinear relations is based on searching to see whether the second (or even higher) power of a factor is able to explain any additional variation in student achievement, it is important to reduce measurement error as this is magnified in power calculations. In this case, instead of dealing with the measurement error of a factor, you have to deal with this error raised to the relevant power. As a consequence, it is much more difficult to identify statistically significant relations. By giving more emphasis to measurement issues, both the quality of the data collected and their statistical power (that is, reducing the type II error) would be increased. Thus, when a particular study fails to evidence nonlinear relations, this does not necessarily imply that the relationships are truly linear because the finding may instead simply be an artefact of the relatively high measurement error of the particular effectiveness factor in question.

Finally, a failure to demonstrate nonlinear relations also may be attributed to the difficulties of establishing enough variation in the functioning of some factors, especially since almost all the effectiveness studies have been conducted in a single country. Primarily, there are two alternative approaches in the search for nonlinear relations. First, experimental studies can be conducted to create enough variance in the functioning of each factor before then searching for optimal values. However, research on the impact of changes in class sizes reveals that there may be practical and ethical difficulties in attempts that concern the manipulation of school or classroom conditions. Thus attention should be given to the ecological validity of experimental studies as well as to the ethical issues associated with the experimentation (Miller 1984; Robson 1993). On the other hand, comparative studies can be conducted that allow the validity of EER models to be tested, especially when searching for the possible existence of nonlinear relations. For example, international longitudinal studies are more likely to tap the full range of variation in school and classroom quality measures and therefore also variation in potential school and classroom effects. Thus, these studies could help us identify nonlinear relations since within national studies the lack of a significant effect might be due to difficulties in identifying enough variation in either the student outcomes or, more likely, in the explanatory variables studied.

Searching for differential effects of factors on different groups of students

An important aspect of the unidimensionality of the teacher and school effect concepts is whether general effectiveness should be separated from the notion of differential effectiveness (Sammons 1996). During the first three phases of EER, studies investigating teacher and school effectiveness were mainly based on the assumption that the effectiveness of schools or teachers was measured by their effectiveness for the average student (that is, the average with respect to aptitude, socio-economic status, and so on) and other predictors (Campbell *et al.* 2003). Despite the fact that a large number of effectiveness studies had been conducted in many countries, very little attention had been paid to the extent to which teachers and schools perform consistently across differing schools, subjects and outcomes (Bryk and Raudenbush 1992; Campbell *et al.* 2004; Kyriakides 2004; Sammons *et al.* 1993; Sammons *et al.* 1997). Moreover, although evidence concerning differential effectiveness that is related to pupil gender and to ethnic differences shows little overall consensus (Nuttall *et al.* 1989), there is even less consistency concerning differential school effectiveness for groups of pupils and for different levels of prior attainment (Sammons *et al.* 1993). As a result, the issue of differential school effectiveness is clearly of importance, and this can be seen in three areas.

First, research into differential educational effectiveness may provide a new perspective on educational equality and the critics could be answered who argue that EER has not given consideration to equity and justice (Kyriakides 2007). Fielding (1997: 141) acknowledged the early work of EER as 'a necessary corrective to an overly pessimistic, even deterministic, view of the influence of social and political factors on the efficacy of schools'. By contrast, current findings concerning differential school effects have emerged from studies conducted in the United States and suggest that schools matter most for the underprivileged and/or initially low-achieving students (Scheerens and Bosker 1997). This implies that school choice is a critical issue for pupils from disadvantaged backgrounds and policymakers should provide relevant information to parents in this group because they are likely not to take this issue into account as much as parents of privileged students. This also points to the importance of improving schools that are at the low end of the effectiveness spectrum, especially if they serve higher numbers of disadvantaged students (Sammons 2008).

Second, research into differential educational effectiveness may raise issues regarding the development and implementation of policy on educational equality. If schools differ significantly in terms of their effectiveness for particular groups of pupils, or in promoting different outcomes, issues concerning which school effectiveness factors are associated with promoting the progress of specific groups of pupils should be examined. The identification of these factors may be useful for policymakers in order to attempt to design and implement policies on equal opportunities. An investigation into differential school effectiveness might also help the evaluation of national and school policy on equality of opportunities in education. For example, research on different teaching approaches has suggested that low SES and low-ability students may benefit from more direct and traditional strategies rather than from more recent constructivist approaches (van der Werf 2006).

Third, findings concerning factors associated with school effectiveness that promote the progress of specific groups of pupils may have significant implications for theory-building in EER, especially since a distinction between generic and differential factors should be made. However, the concept of differential teacher and school effectiveness ought not to be polarized against a generic concept. Rather, teacher effectiveness should be incorporated as a refinement of the effectiveness of schools. In this context, the 'dynamic model' (Creemers and Kyriakides 2008) is based on the assumption that one of the dimensions used to define factors of effectiveness is that of differentiation. Looking at only a frequency dimension (for example, the quantity at which an activity associated with effectiveness is present in a system/school/classroom) does not help us identify the functioning of a factor that facilitates student achievement. By contrast, it is considered important to see whether different groups of teachers, schools and systems respond to each other's learning needs. This is because an adaptation to the specific needs of each subject or group is more likely to increase the successful implementation of a factor associated with effectiveness and thereby ultimately maximize its effect on student learning outcomes.

Two methodological issues arise from investigating differential effectiveness. First, EER has focused on identifying differential effects for specific groups of students through a single variable – for example, differential effectiveness in relation to social class or in relation to gender. However, even in the few studies where these two factors are evaluated simultaneously, interactions between these are rarely made explicit (Mortimore *et al.* 1988; Sammons *et al.* 1993). Thus, one way of raising the importance of the systematic investigation of differential effectiveness is by looking at interaction effects between different groups of students. This implies that using existing static dualisms such as girl/boy or black/white as categories of analysis may mask other interrelating categories such as socio-economic group (Weiner 1995). Instead, this new perspective suggests that it might be fruitful to investigate differential effectiveness in relation to different groups of students who are defined not by a single variable but through interactions between those background variables that are associated with achievement. In turn, this then obliges larger sample sizes, as these would be needed in such complex interactive models.

Second, beyond looking at the existence of differential teacher and school effectiveness in relation to different groups of students, it is also important to search for interactions among these and student characteristics. This is an approach adopted by Campbell *et al.* (2004), who investigated differential effectiveness in relation to such student characteristics (that is, personality type and thinking styles). In order to examine whether teachers were differentially effective in relation to the personal characteristics of their students, random regression slopes at level two (teacher) were specified for each type of personality and each thinking style that was associated with student progress. For both mathematics and Greek language ability, a significant random slope of 'openness to experience' at level two was found (that is, mathematics: $X^2 = 7.6$; degrees of freedom, $df = 2$; $p < 0.001$; and Greek language: $X^2 = 5.9$; $df = 2$; $p < 0.001$) whereas for the achievement of affective aims, the significant random slope was found for conscientiousness at level two ($X^2 = 6.3$; $df = 2$; $p < 0.001$). Further to the point, Snijders and Bosker (1999: 74) argued that 'if a researcher finds a significant random slope variance she may be led to think of level-two variables that could explain the random slope' and that therefore it is not contradictory to look for a specific cross-level interaction even if no significant random slope has been found. It was upon this basis that Campbell et al. (2004) examined cross-level interactions between variables associated with the quality of teaching, personality type and thinking style. For mathematics, it was found that the cross-level interaction between the student's possession of an executive thinking style and the ability of a teacher to provide practice and application opportunities was significantly related. Specifically, the effect of the executive style on mathematics achievement gain was higher when teachers provided more practical and application opportunities to their students. A further statistically significant cross-level interaction was also found in the analysis of teaching Greek language, and this featured a liberal teaching style and the ability of a teacher to provide information. In this case, the effect of the liberal style of teaching on student achievement gains in the Greek language was found to be higher when the teachers spent less time providing information. This study seems to reveal the importance of searching not only for differential effects but also for interaction effects between teacher (or school) level factors and student factors. The results also justify the treatment of differentiation as a dimension for measuring the functioning of factors that have been found to have a statistically significant interaction with background factors in relation to outcomes.

The contribution of research methodology to measuring the long-term effects of teachers and schools

During the first three phases of EER, little attention was given to the question of the continuity of school and teacher effects that were measured at different stages of a student's school career (Bressoux and Bianco 2004; Goldstein and Sammons 1997; Hill and Rowe 1998). Moreover, the results of studies on the long-term effects of teachers and/or schools that have been conducted in different countries (Bressoux and Bianco 2004; Goldstein and Sammons 1997; Mendro et al. 1998; Tymms et al. 2000) revealed that there was a considerable amount of inconsistency concerning their existence and magnitude. Specifically, some authors argued that an experience of a highly effective (or, by contrast, a highly ineffective) teacher or school can have a critical effect because both factors are thought to affect one's entire schooling and even subsequent work/careers. By contrast, other authors have found only moderate effects, which tend to dissipate over time, or have even concluded that long-term effects do not exist at all and that the effect of a particular teacher or school is quickly cancelled out by the effects of those subsequent. Yet other researchers have also argued that rather than one teacher, a succession of poor teachers may cause a major longer term impact on a student's growth trajectory (Tymms 1995).

During the current phase of EER, the issue of the long-term effect of teachers and schools has become more important due to the emphasis given to exploring the dynamic perspective of educational effectiveness (Creemers and Kyriakides 2008). This has suggested that changes in the effectiveness of schools are likely to be observed and thereby more attention should be given to the long- rather than short-term effects of schools. Moreover, in the current phase of EER, carefully designed longitudinal studies that last for more than two years are needed not only for understanding the process of effectiveness but also for measuring the long-term effects associated with schools. Further, it has also been argued that the inconsistent results of previous studies investigating such effects can be attributed to the fact that most were incapable of taking later occurring effects into account (Kyriakides and Creemers 2008a). For example, one of the main criticisms of studies on long-term teacher effects are their failure to take into account the fact that teachers follow the individual whose long-term impact is being evaluated and, as such, effects may be carried over from the teachers the student has had in the meantime.

In studying the potential long-term effects of primary schools in particular, it is insufficient to show that there is a relationship between the primary school that has been attended and the achievement level at the end of high school because primary- and secondary-school effects may be correlated (positively or negatively). Students who attend effective primary schools may be more likely to attend effective secondary schools (that is, there is a positive correlation between the primary- and the secondary-school effects), and a study investigating the short-term effect of secondary schools may thus *over*estimate the effect of school on student achievement. On the other hand, if there is a negative correlation between primary- and secondary-school effects, then a study investigating the long-term effect of primary schools may *under*estimate the effect of school on student achievement. A study that demonstrates this point was conducted by Goldstein and Sammons (1997). 'Secondary school attended' was included in a multilevel random crossed model where it was found that primary school had an impact on secondary-school GCSE scores at age 16 and that the primary-school effect on GCSE scores was greater than the secondary-school effect. It was therefore argued that there is a deficiency in studies that assess the added value of (secondary) schools after controlling for the students' initial level but not for their past school attendance.

While Goldstein and Sammons' study can be seen as a criticism of studies investigating immediate school effects that do not take past schools into account, the reverse criticism can be directed at studies that look at long-term teacher and school effects using models that include past teachers and schools but not interim teachers. In a longitudinal study that followed students for four years (Kyriakides and Creemers 2008a), all of the teachers a student had during the period under consideration were seen to have an impact on achievement at the end of the study. By analysing data without taking into account the effects of all the teachers that a student has, the long-term effects of teachers and schools can be underestimated and their short-term effects overestimated. In particular however, two methodological issues need attention when measuring the long-term effect of teachers and schools.

First, longitudinal studies that last for at least three years should be conducted and data on student achievement and on all the teachers that students have during this period should be collected. In regard to designing longitudinal studies, other issues should also be considered and an extensive analysis of this type of research design is given in Chapter 5.

Second, modelling the long-term effect of schools and teachers requires a combination of growth curve (Goldstein 1979, 1986; Maas and Snijders 2003; Singer and Willett 2003) and cross-classified multilevel models (Goldstein 2003; Meyers and Beretvas 2006; Rasbash and Goldstein 1994; Raudenbush 1993). The cross-classified structure takes account of the fact that an individual can belong to different hierarchical groups. Specifically, not all students from one class at a certain school year move into the same class in the next grade, and conversely not all students in a given class in a certain year came from the same class in the previous. As far as the use of growth modelling is concerned, the time of measuring student achievement (measurement occasion) constitutes level one with students constituting level two. Statistically, the level one model is a set of separate linear regressions, one for each student in the sample. Through these equations, student achievement scores are regressed on their grade levels. Therefore, the resultant statistical model is rather complex; it contains four hierarchical levels (measurement occasion, students, teachers and schools) with the third level (teachers) having a random crossed structure (see Chapter 11).

The contribution of research methodology to defining effectiveness through different criteria

During the second and third phases of EER, studies on educational effectiveness were mainly focused on attainment in language or mathematics, and this was seen as one of the most significant weaknesses of EER. Although studies investigating the affective outcomes of schooling (Knuver and Brandsma 1993; Kyriakides 2005; Mortimore *et al.* 1988; Opdenakker and Van Damme 2006) and in subjects other than mathematics and language (Kyriakides and Tsangaridou 2008) have been conducted during the last two decades, researchers have not yet been able to monitor student progress across the full range of the school curriculum. Moreover, they have not examined educational effectiveness in relation to the newer goals of education, such as the development of meta-cognitive skills (Campbell *et al.* 2003). Thus, EER has been accused of an over-emphasis on the cognitive domain and a restricted set of outcomes by focusing too heavily on basic knowledge and skills. As a consequence, opponents of EER have criticized it for having too narrow a scope by reducing school learning to discrete, assessable and comparable fragments of academic knowledge (Slee and Weiner 1998: 2). Such arguments can be countered by referring to studies that have used multiple measures of schooling outcomes (Bosker 1990; Knuver and Brandsma 1993; Kyriakides 2005; Mortimore *et al.* 1988; Opdenakker and Van Damme 2000; Sammons *et al.* 2008). However, this argument also reveals the important contribution that advances in research methodology can make to EER since one of the main reasons for not measuring effectiveness in relation to educational outcomes such as affective, psychomotor, social, and new-learning outcomes has been the difficulty of developing appropriate instruments.

Nevertheless, it has become evident from recent studies (such as those just mentioned) that it is possible to measure a broad range of outcomes in a valid and reliable way using conventional methods of assessment. A typical example is the Torrance Tests of Creativity Thinking (TTCT), which has been translated into more than 35 languages and has become highly recommended in the educational field for measuring creativity (Clapham 1998; Kim 2006) and designing intervention programmes (Garaigordobil 2006). This has demonstrated the need to develop psychometrically appropriate tests that measure a broad range of educational outcomes by making use of advances in measurement theory, and these are discussed in the next section. In doing so, it is important to consider practicality and especially the process of administering the tests. For example, Kyriakides and Tsangaridou (2008) designed a study measuring school effectiveness in relation to Physical Education and developed a performance test. However, administering this in a large number of schools was very costly in terms of time taken from schools and the added research time of administering the test to pairs of students. Another issue of practicality is that such studies cannot be conducted unless sufficient funding is available. Although policymakers in different countries may claim the need for a broad curriculum, this will not broaden the scope of EER unless they are also concerned with measuring educational effectiveness across the curriculum and not just in the core subjects. Nevertheless, using different criteria to measure effectiveness enables the development of theory and research in EER by answering the following issues.

First, we can examine the extent to which effectiveness factors are generic in nature, meaning that they are able to explain variations between different outcomes of schooling. By such illustration one can show the robustness of the theory behind the models of EER that refer to these factors, for example, by illustrating that the generalizability of the factors concerned with teacher behaviour in the classroom (such as time management or structuring) and the theory behind this model explain variation in achievement in various subjects of the school curriculum. At the same time, results showing that specific factors have differential effects raise new questions concerning the reasons for which these are able to explain variation in one outcome but not in another (Kyriakides 2007). In order to deal with such questions, EER can benefit from the use of advanced quantitative research methods such as the use of multivariate multilevel modelling techniques, which are discussed in Chapter 11.

Second, we can find out whether teachers and/or schools are equally effective in different areas. Such studies may help to test the reliability of teacher and school effects and aid in classifying subjects into different clusters according to their effectiveness for different outcomes. Thus, not only could specific feedback be given to them, but researchers would then also better understand the concept of consistency, which has been included in theoretical models (Creemers 1994) but has yet to be sufficiently evidenced (Driesen and Sleegers 2000). This issue has significant implications for the development of methodology, especially since the earlier use of cluster analysis was not helpful when searching for consistency in the behaviour of teachers and/or schools and the links between them and outcomes. This can be attributed to the serious methodological limitations of cluster analysis and especially its difficulties in demonstrating that one specific cluster solution is more appropriate than any other (Marcoulides and Drezner 1999; Romesburg 1984). Instead, the use of Generalizability Theory or Confirmatory Factor Analysis (CFA) as part of wider SEM approaches might be more useful. More information on how researchers can employ Generalizability Theory is provided in Chapter 10.

Third, finding ways to relate different outcomes is important since the relation between cognition and other domains, such as the affective and meta-cognitive outcomes of schooling, is not clear (Brandsma and Knuver 1993; Kyriakides 2005; Opdenakker and Van Damme 2000). By using different criteria of effectiveness, one could find out whether schools that give emphasis to the achievement of cognitive outcomes also manage to improve outcomes in other areas. At the moment, there have been studies that have shown that schools that are effective in promoting cognitive outcomes tend also to be effective in affective outcomes because they help students develop positive attitudes toward schooling (Knuver and Brandsma 1993; Kyriakides 2005). It is also important to note that there has been no study to date that has suggested a negative relationship between promoting academic effectiveness and social or affective outcomes. Moreover, using advanced quantitative methods such as SEM can help determine the extent to which achievement in other domains, such as motivation and well-being, is influenced by achievement in cognitive domains and allows reciprocal relationships to be tested. In doing so though, we obviously do not suggest that education should be restricted to cognitive objectives, since only a partial relationship between achievement of cognitive and non-cognitive domains may emerge. However, such results may indicate how achievement in cognitive outcomes can help us promote the non-cognitive aims of education. At the same time, schools should act as institutions within societies and contribute not only to the cognitive but also to the non-cognitive domains of learning. For example, schools are expected to provide a positive social and aesthetic environment in which social behaviour and aesthetic attitude can be developed.

Fourth, so far we have referred to effectiveness in schools by looking at the extent to which specific outcomes of schooling are achieved. However, it is also possible to examine the effectiveness of a school by investigating how far each school managed to reduce the variation between students. This is called an 'equity dimension', whereas looking at the achievement of outcomes is treated as a 'quality dimension' (Creemers and Kyriakides 2008). The equity dimension results in another set of criteria for measuring educational effectiveness, which are not related to achievement of specific outcomes of schooling but are related to different groups of students in relation to one another. The underlying idea is that education can contribute to social justice and democracy by closing the gap between students regarding their background, especially their abilities and the socio-cultural status of their families. As a consequence, early school effectiveness research and school improvement projects led to the idea of creating effective schools for the urban poor (Edmonds 1979). In the 1980s, there was quite a lot of criticism of this kind of school improvement and its research, which featured conspicuous sampling biases (Firestone and Herriot 1982; Good and Brophy 1986, Purkey and Smith 1983; Ralph and Fennessey 1983; Rowan *et al.* 1983). Based on knowledge about quality education, although effective schools are able to promote the learning of all their students they may not especially lift those disadvantaged (Kyriakides 2004). However, no systematic research has yet been conducted looking at the relation between these two dimensions (Creemers and Kyriakides 2010). Moreover, a study that found that school effects are larger (positive or negative) for disadvantaged groups (Bryk and Raudenbush 1992) indicated that the equity dimension also warranted further investigation. This question raises significant implications for EER methodology since it reveals the need to use multilevel modelling techniques to measure both equity and the factors that may promote this. Moreover, searching for consistency in the criteria that are related to the two dimensions of measuring effectiveness is another issue that has implications for multilevel modelling techniques given that, ideally, schools should be equally effective in both dimensions.

The contribution of research methodology to measuring outcomes and factors

A major methodological advance in EER is the creation of instruments that will sensitively measure the functioning of school and classroom factors. This is an advance because most current instruments provide data that mainly refer to how frequently actions associated with a factor take place in classrooms/schools/educational systems. Nevertheless, studies looking at other characteristics have shown that there are factors associated with achievement when qualitative characteristics are considered instead of the frequency dimension (Kyriakides and

Creemers 2008b). This implies that theoretical models of EER should refer not only to factors associated with achievement but also to other different measurement dimensions. Moreover, researchers should develop instruments measuring the functioning of factors that provide data about both qualitative *and* quantitative characteristics. To do so, not only should the construct validity of the instruments be examined but also the validity of the measurement framework, and this should be done by making use of Classical Test Theory and/or the Item Response Theory (IRT).

Another issue that needs further investigation is the argument that different sources of data should be used in order to measure the functioning of effectiveness factors in a valid and reliable way. To some extent, this argument is supported by studies that have looked at factors associated with quality of teaching, since both students and external observers have been found to produce reliable and valid data (Kyriakides and Creemers 2008b; Marsh and Roche 1997; Stronge 1997). However, it is still not clear how these different sources of data can be combined. In turn, this reveals a need for researchers in the area of EER to make good use of both Generalizability Theory and IRT in order to improve the quality of their data and to identify ways of combining different sources in a meaningful way. The possibilities of using these two measurement theories are discussed in Chapters 9 and 10, respectively.

Concluding comments

In this chapter, we discussed the possibilities of using advances in research methodology to improve EER. Specifically, emphasis was given to issues associated with: (a) modelling educational effectiveness, (b) investigating the long-term effect of schools, (c) using different criteria to measure effectiveness and (d) establishing appropriate instruments to measure outcomes and the functioning of different process factors. It was argued that EER can benefit from the advances made in the following areas of research methodology (which are discussed in the second part of the book): conducting longitudinal studies (see Chapter 5), using IRT to measure outcomes and factors (Chapter 8), using Generalizability Theory (Chapter 10), using multilevel modelling (Chapter 11) and using Structural Equation Modelling (Chapter 12). Making use of the knowledge base of EER together with the presented methodological orientations might facilitate progress with respect to addressing the key questions of EER and thereby establish, develop, and empirically test its theoretical frameworks.

References

Borich, G.D. (1992) *Effective teaching methods,* 2nd edn, New York: Macmillan Publishing Company.

Bosker, R.J. (1990) 'Theory development in school effectiveness research: In search for stability of effects', in P. van de Eedem, J. Hox and J. Hauer (eds) *Theory and model in multilevel research: convergence or divergence?*, Amsterdam: SISWO, pp. 77–98.

Bressoux, P. and Bianco, M. (2004) 'Long-term teacher effects on pupils' learning gains', *Oxford Review of Education*, 30(3): 327–45.

Bryk, A.S. and Raudenbush, S.W. (1992) *Hierarchical linear models: Applications and data analysis methods*, Newbury Park, CA: SAGE.

Campbell, R.J., Kyriakides, L., Muijs, R.D. and Robinson, W. (2003) 'Differential teacher effectiveness: Towards a model for research and teacher appraisal', *Oxford Review of Education*, 29(3): 346–62.

Campbell, R.J., Kyriakides, L., Muijs, R.D. and Robinson, W. (2004) *Assessing teacher effectiveness: A differentiated model*, London: RoutledgeFalmer.

Clapham, M.M. (1998) 'Structure of figural forms A and B of the Torrance tests of creative thinking', *Educational and Psychological Measurement*, 58(2): 275–83.

Creemers, B.P.M. (1994) *The effective classroom*, London: Cassell.

Creemers, B.P.M. and Kyriakides, L. (2006) 'A critical analysis of the current approaches to modelling educational effectiveness: The importance of establishing a dynamic model', *School Effectiveness and School Improvement*, 17(3): 347–66.

Creemers, B.P.M. and Kyriakides, L. (2008) *The dynamics of educational effectiveness: A contribution to policy, practice and theory in contemporary schools*, London: Routledge.

Creemers, B.P.M. and Kyriakides, L. (2010) 'Can schools achieve both quality and equity? Investigating the two dimensions of educational effectiveness', paper presented at the American Educational Research Association (AERA) 2010, Denver, Colorado, May 2010.

Darling-Hammond, L. (2000) 'Teacher quality and student achievement: A review of state policy evidence', *Education Policy Analysis Archives*, 8(1). Online. Available at: http://epaa.asu.edu/epaa/v8n1/ [accessed 17 January 2010].

De Maeyer, S., Rymenans, R., Van Petegem, P., van den Bergh, H. and Rijlaarsdam, G. (2007) 'Educational leadership and pupil achievement: The choice of a valid conceptual model to test effects in school effectiveness research', *School Effectiveness and School Improvement*, 18(2): 125–45.

Driessen, G. and Sleegers, P. (2000) 'Consistency of teaching approach and student achievement: An empirical test', *School Effectiveness and School Improvement*, 11(1): 57–79.

Edmonds, R.R. (1979) 'Effective schools for the urban poor', *Educational Leadership*, 37(1): 15–27.

Fielding, M. (1997) 'Beyond school effectiveness and school improvement: Lighting the slow fuse of possibility', in J. White and M. Barber (eds) *Perspectives on school effectiveness and school improvement*, London: Institute of Education, pp. 137–60.

Firestone, W.A. and Herriott, R.E. (1982) 'Prescriptions for effective elementary schools don't fit secondary schools', *Educational Leadership*, 40: 51–3.

Garaigordobil, M. (2006) 'Intervention in creativity with children aged 10 and 11 years: Impact of a play program on verbal and graphic-figural creativity, *Creativity Research Journal*, 18(3): 329–45.

Goldstein, H. (1979) *The design and analysis of longitudinal studies: their role in the measurement of change*, London: Academic Press.

Goldstein, H. (1986) 'Efficient statistical modelling of longitudinal data', *Annals of Human Biology*, 13: 129–42.

Goldstein, H. (2003) *Multilevel statistical models*, 3rd edn, London: Edward Arnold.

Goldstein, H. and Sammons, P. (1997) 'The influence of secondary and junior schools on sixteen year examination performance: A cross-classified multilevel analysis', *School Effectiveness and School Improvement*, 8(2): 219–30.

Good, T.L. and Brophy, J.E. (1986) 'School effects', in M.C. Wittrock (ed.) *Handbook of research on teaching, third edition*, New York: Macmillan, pp. 570–602.

Hill, P.W. and Rowe, K.J. (1998) 'Modeling student progress in studies of educational effectiveness', *School Effectiveness and School Improvement*, 9(3): 310–33.

Kim, K.H. (2006) 'Can we trust creativity tests? A review of the Torrance tests of creative thinking (TTCT)', *Creativity Research Journal*, 18(1): 3–14.

Knuver, A.W.M. and Brandsma, H.P. (1993) 'Cognitive and affective outcomes in school effectiveness research', *School Effectiveness and School Improvement*, 13: 187–200.

Kyriakides, L. (2004) 'Differential school effectiveness in relation to sex and social class: some implications for policy evaluation', *Educational Research and Evaluation*, 10(2): 141–61.

Kyriakides, L. (2005) 'Extending the comprehensive model of educational effectiveness by an empirical investigation', *School Effectiveness and School Improvement*, 16(2): 103–52.

Kyriakides, L. (2007) 'Generic and differentiated models of educational effectiveness: Implications for the improvement of educational practice', in T. Townsend (ed.) *International handbook of school effectiveness and improvement*, Dordrecht, The Netherlands: Springer, pp. 41–56.

Kyriakides, L., Campbell, R.J. and Gagatsis, A. (2000) 'The significance of the classroom effect in primary schools: An application of Creemers' comprehensive model of educational effectiveness', *School Effectiveness and School Improvement*, 11(4): 501–29.

Kyriakides, L. and Creemers, B.P.M. (2008a) 'A longitudinal study on the stability over time of school and teacher effects on student learning outcomes', *Oxford Review of Education*, 34(5): 521–45.

Kyriakides, L. and Creemers, B.P.M. (2008b) 'Using a multidimensional approach to measure the impact of classroom level factors upon student achievement: A study testing the validity of the dynamic model', *School Effectiveness and School Improvement*, 19(2): 183–205.

Kyriakides, L. and Tsangaridou, N. (2008) 'Towards the development of generic and differentiated models of educational effectiveness: A study on school and teacher effectiveness in physical education', *British Educational Research Journal*, 34(6): 807–83.

Leithwood, K. and Jantzi, D. (2006) 'Transformational school leadership for large scale reform: Effects on students, teachers, and their classroom practices', *School Effectiveness and School Improvement*, 17: 201–27.

Maas, C.J.M. and Snijders, T.A.B. (2003) 'The multilevel approach to repeated measures for complete and incomplete data', *Quality and Quantity*, 37: 71–89.

Marcoulides, G. and Drezner, Z. (1999) 'A procedure for detecting pattern clustering in measurement designs', in M. Wilson and G. Engelhard, Jr (eds) *Objective measurement: Theory into practice (5)*, New Jersey: Ablex.

Marsh, H.W. and Roche, L.A. (1997) 'Making students' evaluations of teaching effectiveness effective', *American Psychologist*, 52: 1187–97.

Mendro, R.L., Jordan, H.R., Gomez, E., Anderson, M.C. and Bembry, K.L. (1998) 'Longitudinal teacher effects on student achievement and their relation to school and project evaluation', paper presented at the Annual Meeting of the American Educational Research Association, San Diego, CA.

Meyers, J.L. and Beretvas, S.N. (2006) 'The impact of inappropriate modelling of cross-classified data structures', *Multivariate Behavioral Research*, 41(4): 473–97.

Miller, S. (1984) *Experimental design and statistics*, 2nd edn, London: Routledge.

Monk, D.H. (1994) 'Subject matter preparation of secondary mathematics and science teachers and student achievement', *Economics of Education Review*, 13(2): 125–45.

Mortimore, P., Sammons, P., Stoll, L., Lewis, D. and Ecob, R. (1988) *School matters: The junior years*, Somerset: Open Books.

Nuttall, D., Goldstein, H., Prosser, R. and Rasbach, J. (1989) 'Differential school effectiveness', *International Journal of Educational Research*, 13: 769–76.

Opdenakker, M.C. and Van Damme, J. (2000) 'Effects of schools, teaching staff and classes on achievement and well-being in secondary education: Similarities and differences between school outcomes', *School Effectiveness and School Improvement*, 11(2): 65–196.

Opdenakker, M.C. and Van Damme, J. (2006) 'Differences between secondary schools: A study about school context, group composition, school practice, and school effects with special attention to public and Catholic schools and types of schools', *School Effectiveness and School Improvement*, 17(1): 87–117.

Purkey, S.C. and Smith, M.S. (1983) 'Effective schools: A review', *The Elementary School Journal*, 83(4): 427–52.

Ralph, J.H. and Fennessey, J. (1983) 'Science or reform: Some questions about the effective schools model', *Phi Delta Kappan*, 64(10): 689–94.

Rasbash, J. and Goldstein, H. (1994) 'Efficient analysis of mixed hierarchical and cross-classified random structures using a multilevel model', *Journal of Educational and Behavioral Statistics*, 19: 337–50.

Raudenbush, S.W. (1993) 'A cross random effects model for unbalanced data with applications in cross-sectional and longitudinal research', *Journal of Educational Statistics*, 18: 321–49.

Reezigt, G.J., Guldemond, H. and Creemers, B.P.M. (1999) 'Empirical validity for a comprehensive model on educational effectiveness', *School Effectiveness and School Improvement*, 10(2): 193–216.

Robinson, V.M.J., Lloyd, C.A. and Rowe, K.J. (2008) 'The impact of leadership on student outcomes: An analysis of the differential effects of leadership types', *Educational Administration Quarterly*, 44(5): 635–74.

Robson, C. (1993) *Real world research*, Oxford: Blackwell.

Romesburg, H.C. (1984) *Cluster analysis for researchers*, Belmont, CA: Lifetime Learning Publications.

Rowan, B., Bossart, S.T. and Dwyer, D.C. (1983) 'Research on effective schools. A cautionary note', *Educational Researcher*, 12(4): 24–32.

Sammons, P. (1996) 'Complexities in the judgement of school effectiveness', *Educational Research and Evaluation*, 2(2): 113–49.

Sammons, P. (2008) 'Zero tolerance of failure and new labour approaches to school improvement in England', *Oxford Review of Education*, 34(6): 651–64.

Sammons, P., Nuttall, D. and Cuttance, P. (1993) 'Differential school effectiveness: Results from a reanalysis of the Inner London Education Authority's Junior School Project data', *British Educational Research Journal*, 19(4): 381–405.

Sammons P., Sylva, K., Melhuish, E., Siraj-Blatchford, I., Taggart, B., Hunt, S. and Jelicic, H. (2008) *Influences on children's cognitive and social development in year 6*, Effective Pre-School and Primary Education 3–11 Project (EPPE 3–11), 6; DCSF-RB048-049.Online. Available at: www.dcsf.gov.uk/research/data/uploadfiles/DCSF-RB048-049.pdf [accessed 17 January 2010].

Sammons, P., Thomas, S. and Mortimore, P. (1997) *Forging links: Effective schools and effective departments*, London: Paul Chapman.

Scheerens, J. and Bosker, R.J. (1997) *The foundations of educational effectiveness*, Oxford: Pergamon.

Schunk, D.H. (1991) 'Self-efficacy and academic motivation', *Educational Psychologist*, 26(3): 207–31.

Scriven, M. (1994) 'Duties of the teacher', *Journal of Personnel Evaluation in Education*, 8: 151–84.

Seidel, T. and Shavelson, R.J. (2007) 'Teaching effectiveness research in the past decade: The role of theory and research design in disentangling meta-analysis results', *Review of Educational Research*, 77(4): 454–99.

Singer, J.D. and Willett, J.B. (2003) *Applied longitudinal data analysis: Modeling change and event occurrence*, New York: Oxford University Press.

Slee, R. and Weiner, G. with Tomlinson, S. (eds) (1998) *School effectiveness for whom? Challenges to the school effectiveness and school improvement movements*, London: Falmer Press.

Snijders, T. and Bosker, R. (1999) *Multilevel analysis: An introduction to basic and advanced multilevel modelling*, London: Sage.

Stevenson, H.W., Chen, C. and Lee, S.Y. (1993) 'Mathematics achievement of Chinese, Japanese and American children: Ten years later', *Science*, 259: 53–8.

Stronge, J.H. (1997) *Evaluating teaching: A Guide to current thinking and practice*, Thousand Oaks, CA: Corwin Press.

Tymms, P. (1995) 'The long-term impact of schooling', *Evaluation and Research in Education*, 9(2): 99–108.

Tymms, P., Merrell, C. and Henderson, B. (2000) 'Baseline assessment and progress during the first three years at school', *Educational Research and Evaluation*, 6(2): 105–29.

Van der Werf, M. (2006) 'General and differential effects of constructivist teaching', lecture presented at ICSEI 2006 conference, Fort Lauderdale, FL, USA.

Weiner, G. (1995) 'Ethnic and gender differences', in C. Desfordges (ed.) *An introduction to teaching – Psychological perspective*, Oxford: Blackwell, pp. 237–55.

Witziers, B., Bosker, J.R. and Kruger, L.M. (2003) 'Educational leadership and student achievement: The elusive search for an association', *Educational Administration Quarterly*, 39(3): 398–425.

Chapter 3

Theory and research

The problem of causality

Introduction

An ongoing question that arises from the current state of educational effectiveness concerns the nature of the relationships between so-called 'effectiveness factors' and student learning outcomes. Although the intention of many studies may be to show causal relations between such factors and student achievement, most reveal only *associations* between very specific factors and student achievement, the extent that certain factors can predict *variation* in student outcomes and, in longitudinal studies, how such factors predict change over time. Because the topic of causality is rarely addressed explicitly, in this chapter we discuss its meaning by looking at different orientations within the research methodology and examine the potential importance of searching for causality within EER. Causality is seen as related to the need to establish appropriate theoretical models of educational effectiveness and the use of them for improvement purposes.

To discuss the main methodological issues associated with the problem of demonstrating causality, specific types of research designs, such as experimental and cross-sectional studies, are explored in the second section of this chapter, along with the current state in EER in relation to demonstrating causality and the testing of the validity of theoretical models. By contrast, in the third section, we argue that theories within education can play a significant role in helping to demonstrate causality. Finally, we then argue that theory-driven evaluation studies could help demonstrate causal relations. More information on using this approach is also given in the next chapter because this is concerned with the relationships between EER and matters of educational policy and practice.

Searching for causality to understand the concept of educational effectiveness

To further clarify the claim that EER needs research designs that will enable the identification of potential causal relations, it is important to define the terms 'cause' and 'effect'. Locke (1975) argues that a cause is any construct that makes any other variable change its functioning over time. For instance, in the case of EER, cause can be attributed to a specific school factor that is shown to make schools more effective (that is, helping students improve their achievement in relation to specific learning aims). At the same time an 'effect' is seen as a variable that is influenced by another construct (typically an earlier construct within EER theory). Returning to the above example, the improvement of student outcomes is deemed to be due to the functioning of the hypothetical school factor. However, Shadish *et al.* (2002) claim that we very rarely know all of the potential causes of our observed effects or, indeed, how they may relate to one another. Moreover, Holland (1986) argues that a cause can never be determined unequivocally, and it is likely that some effects represent the result of combinations of factors or interactions between them. For EER, this implies a need to try to identify the probability that particular effects will occur. Estimating the *likelihood* that an effect will occur gives the opportunity for researchers to explore why certain effects seem to occur in some situations but not in others. This also fits well with the kind of statistical approaches used in EER models that typically identify the proportion of variance in outcomes that can be statistically explained or accounted for by different combinations of predictors. This is an important issue that needs to be considered by researchers within EER for whom the ultimate aim is to improve practice through modelling variations in effectiveness over time and the factors that predict such variation in student outcomes (Creemers and Kyriakides 2006).

Further to the issues of causality and statistical modelling, Hedges (2007) points out that it is helpful to distinguish between the inference model that is used to specify the relationship between a hypothesized causal factor and its predicted effect and the statistical procedures that are used to determine the strength of this relationship. Following on from this, the first issue that researchers should thus attempt to answer is whether the focus of their study concerns identifying the effect of a cause or the cause of an effect. For example, if we wish to know whether the use of certain teaching approaches that arise from the constructivist approach to learning (Schoenfeld 1998) are more effective in increasing the mathematics achievement of year-six students compared to more traditional alternatives (often termed 'direct teaching' approaches; Joyce *et al.* 2000), then an experiment can be designed in which the effects of each teaching approach are compared by using some appropriate measures of student learning. If children who are exposed to one teaching approach score higher (on average) in the mathematics assessment than do those exposed to the other and if the students in the two groups are equivalent in all respects other than their assignment to groups adopting each teaching approach (as can often be achieved by randomization), the researcher can conclude that the higher mathematics scores are likely to be the result of the use of one teaching approach rather than the other and therefore that this teaching approach is generally more effective. This argument implies that when correctly implemented, the randomized controlled experiment is a powerful design for detecting the treatment effects of interventions. A random assignment of participants to treatment conditions assures that treatment group assignment is independent of the pre-treatment characteristics of group members. Therefore, differences between the groups can be attributed to treatment effects rather than to the pre-treatment characteristics. It is, however, also important to acknowledge that randomized experiments indicate only whether there are treatment effects and the magnitude of those effects; they do not help us understand the underlying mechanisms (that is, why treatments differ in their impacts) that are contributing to such effects. In turn, this necessitates a role for theory. For example, when there is a strong reason to believe that one treatment may be more effective than another, an experimental approach is warranted for detecting such likely treatment effects (for example, as in research on the impact of reductions in class size where it is hypothesized that student attainment should be higher in smaller classes). That said, although randomized controlled experiments are designed to detect average differences in the effects of different treatments on outcomes of interest, researchers need to recognize that there are a series of important and necessary steps that precede the design of an experiment, and these are discussed in the second section of this chapter. It should also be acknowledged that an experimental study is not always the best approach for demonstrating causality. For example, if we already have valid evidence in favour of one treatment, it would be unethical to administer the old treatment to a group of students simply because we want to measure the size of the effect of this treatment. Thus, methodological issues associated with longitudinal and cross-sectional studies are also here discussed.

In this chapter, it is argued that the ultimate aim in any science is the production of cumulative knowledge (see the more detailed discussion of this topic in Chapter 13). Ultimately, this means the development of theories that explain the phenomena that are of interest. One example are theories that identify school factors associated with student achievement where it is hypothesized that some schools are more effective than others for specific and identifiable reasons. For EER, this implies that its role is to explain the phenomena of variations in school or teacher effectiveness by revealing causal relations between factors related to school and classroom processes and subsequent variation in student outcomes. Although this is a complex task, demonstrating causal relations can contribute significantly to the theoretical development of EER since science proceeds on the assumption that causal relations can eventually be uncovered and understood and that events (that is, EER reaching effectiveness) are explicable in terms of their antecedents (that is, what changes took place in the functioning of factors). Moreover, searching for causality is based on the assumption that there is regularity in the way a specific phenomenon can be observed (Cohen *et al.* 2000), and this is linked to a post-positivist and realist epistemology that uses quantitative measurement. In the case of EER, it is assumed that there are generic and measurable factors that are likely to have a stable impact on effectiveness and that operate similarly in different educational settings (Creemers 1994). However, it is also acknowledged that in some cases there may be important interactions between effectiveness and contextual factors. In this book it is therefore argued that the ultimate aim of EER is to develop valid theories to account for the processes underlying effectiveness in schools that are consistent across different settings and that thereby give a basis for the prediction of variations in this effectiveness (in terms of cause–effect relations). In the end, such cause-and-effect relations should then be translated into means–ends relations. In this way EER would contribute significantly to reforms of policy and practice at both macro and micro levels and thereby help to improve the quality of education (Creemers and Kyriakides 2006).

Different designs used to demonstrate causality in EER: methodological advantages and limitations

In this section, we refer to research methods that have been used to demonstrate causal relations within EER and seek to identify their various strengths and methodological limitations. In the first phase of EER (as described in Chapter 1) the main interest was to show that teachers and schools could make a difference to students' lives in terms of promoting better academic progress and the development of positive attitudes towards schooling. In this phase, there was little interest in describing or trying to explain why some teachers and schools were more effective than others. Thus, searching for causality was not an important feature in the agenda of this first phase.

Demonstrating causality through outlier studies

During the second phase of EER, special attention was given to conducting outlier studies. By statistically identifying and comparing less effective with more effective schools, significant differences in the specific characteristics of these two groups were revealed. These characteristics were treated as factors associated with the effectiveness status of schools, and gradually these became seen as the reasons for the differences in measured effectiveness, which implied a causal relationship. Such an approach is methodologically problematic for several reasons but especially since differences between outlier schools in terms of effectiveness may not necessarily be relevant to the origin of differences in student outcomes. This is because the characteristics of these 'effective' schools may also be observed among typical schools and schools that were less extreme in terms of their effectiveness, and these would not have been studied when only outliers were of interest. We can also raise questions concerning the internal validity of this type of investigation as well as with the generalizability of the results to the whole range of schools that were operating in the countries where such outlier studies took place (because many earlier outlier studies focused on only particular groups of schools that were often in disadvantaged communities). Finally, in some instances one could even claim that the direction of the hypothesized causal relationships may actually have been the opposite of that hypothesized. For instance, the fact that effective schools were found to have more orderly and safe climates than less effective schools (Edmonds 1979) may not necessarily imply that the orderly and safe climate is the reason for greater effectiveness, but instead that this type of school climate may be a consequence (or reflection) of the fact that in this group of schools, students had higher achievement than in the other. It is possible that students attending more effective schools have good reasons to behave better (for example, they realize that their schools offer them something), which means that the establishment of such a climate was not the cause but rather an associated effect of the students attending a more effective school. It is also possible that such factors are reciprocal, with better behaviour first helping better attainment, which in turn promotes better behaviour and so on in a virtuous upward spiral. Such alternative views can only be explored by studies of the factors linked to changes in effectiveness status of schools over time (see Chapter 5).

Demonstrating causality through cross-sectional studies

During the second and, especially, the third phase of EER, emphasis was given to conducting cross-sectional and longitudinal studies. Researchers within EER made especial use of studies involving multi-sample comparisons since several international comparative studies were being (or had been) conducted, such as Progress in International Reading Literacy Study (PIRLS) and TIMSS. It is acknowledged that some of the most important theoretical and methodological work in educational research has resulted from data analyses using large-scale national data sets such as the Early Childhood Longitudinal Study (ECLS) and the National Education Longitudinal Study (NELS) of 1988–2000. In addition, the number of dissertations, articles in refereed journals, and other publications that have been written from these national data sets is also extremely high. This can be attributed to the fact that large-scale data sets that are drawn from multistage probability samples allow for predictive analyses and thereby tentative causal inference. With such data, researchers can therefore estimate the probable effects of certain conditions for specific populations over time. In instances where there are data elements about school or pedagogical practices, analytic techniques can estimate the likelihood of what would happen if certain organizational, institutional or instructional reforms were implemented on a larger scale. In some cases, such data sets can also be used to approximate randomized controlled experiments. For example, matched sampling can be used to assess the causal effects of interventions when randomized experiments cannot be conducted (Rubin 2006). In relation to EER, such a study might concern the effect of teacher behaviour on student outcomes by using data from large-scale studies, especially since experimental studies can only be conducted when teachers agree to co-operate and are willing to change their behaviours in specific ways. Over the past three decades in particular, statisticians (Rosenbaum 1986; Rubin 1974, 1978) and econometricians (Heckman 1976, 1979) have developed several methods of analysis for making causal inferences with observational data such as that found in large-scale national data sets.

There are several advantages to using large-scale, nationally representative data sets to search for factors associated with differences in student achievement. As one would expect, such studies are based on nationally representative samples of students, their parents, schools and teachers. This contrasts sharply with randomized controlled experiments that are designed to yield valid causal results but often have limited generalizability in establishing the impact of specific interventions rather than which aspects of an intervention are most important. By comparison, large-scale national educational studies are typically designed to be generalizable to specific populations of students and allow changes in the outcomes of interest (for example, in overall educational standards). This permits large-scale data sets to be seen as rich sources of descriptive information on students, teachers and schools.

Because they are based on large, nationally representative samples, large-scale national data sets are also useful in studying the characteristics and achievement of subgroups, such as minority and low-income students, groups that are often targeted for educational interventions that aim to improve school effectiveness (Kyriakides 2007). In addition, such data sets are often longitudinal, which makes it possible to measure achievement gains at both the individual and group levels over time (de Fraine *et al.* 2007). They can also be used to develop plausible hypotheses regarding the likely causes of differences in student achievement gains and can inform the design of subsequent randomized controlled trials for hypothesis-confirming purposes. For example, these data sets can be used to identify promising interventions and to target subgroups that are thought to be most likely to benefit. They may also suggest potential causal mechanisms that may explain why the functioning of a school factor may have positive effects on student achievement, such as a school's policy on parental involvement. Moreover, when randomized controlled trials are not feasible (for example, for measuring the absolute effect of schooling), large-scale, nationally representative studies may provide the best source of data on which to base studies that seek to explore the existence of possible causal relations using alternative approaches, such as regression discontinuity (Kyriakides and Luyten 2009).

Despite the strengths of these studies, however, one can also identify some serious methodological weaknesses in attempts by researchers to claim causality by using cross-sectional data and searching for correlations between the functioning of specific factors at different levels (for example, teacher, school, country) and variation in student achievement outcomes (Gustafsson 2007; Kyriakides and Charalambous 2005). The main problem with this approach is that large-scale observational data sets do not typically feature a random assignment of individuals or schools to treatment and control groups. Therefore, researchers must be aware of the tradeoffs that are involved in choosing experimental versus non-experimental designs when both can be used to address a particular research question and both are logistically and ethically feasible. The most important weaknesses of the cross-sectional approach are outlined below.

First, however, an issue that needs further attention is the measurement of effectiveness based only on a measure of student outcomes without controlling for differences in prior achievement. For example, the inclusion of aptitude variables in International Association for the Evaluation of Educational Achievement (IEA) studies could lead to more coherent conclusions since the effect of this variable in effectiveness studies that have collected data on various background characteristics (for example, aptitude/prior attainment level, gender, SES) has consistently revealed that the effect of aptitude/prior attainment is stronger than the effect of student SES (Kyriakides 2006; Mortimore *et al.* 1988; Sammons and Ko 2008; Sammons *et al.* 1993; Sammons *et al.* 1997). Moreover, studies that do not take into account aptitude are not able to explain significant proportions of the variance in later student achievement situated at the student level, and so such models lack appropriate statistical control (or these are under- or mis-specified). From this perspective, it can be argued that the inclusion of variables such as prior attainment in future comparative and cross-sectional studies should be taken into account. To this end, the use of value-added forms of assessment may not only help us 'correct' simple evaluations of schools and educational systems but may also help develop better models of educational effectiveness (Fitz-Gibbon 1997; Goldstein 1997; Sammons 1996). However, even if such measures are taken into account, there are still important problems in arguing that the results of the usually employed multilevel modelling procedure reveal a causal relation between the explanatory variables situated at different levels and student outcome measures, which are treated as dependent variables.

A typical effectiveness study following a cross-sectional design usually measures the achievement outcomes of students in a set of schools within a country. Information is collected about specific factors situated at different levels, such as student characteristics (for example, SES, gender), teacher characteristics (for example, teacher reported policy or behaviour in the classroom, teacher experience/knowledge) and school characteristics (for example, school policy on teaching, school learning environment). Using different kinds of statistical analyses (such as regression analysis) these background and contextual factors are treated as independent variables and their statistical influence on achievement (ability to predict variation in achievement) is determined. However, it is possible to confuse the direction of causality in cross-sectional data and so caution should be exercised before attempting to make causal statements based on analyses of such data. For example and illustrating the role of theory, when researchers have correlated the time students spent on homework with achievement, some have found a significant negative correlation, meaning that students who spend more time doing their homework tend to obtain lower grades. However, it does not seem reasonable to interpret the negative correlation to mean that the more homework students are asked to do, the lower the level of achievement obtained. A more reasonable explanation for the negative correlation would be that students with lower levels of aptitude or achievement take more time to do their homework, especially when the same amount and type of homework is given to all students of each classroom. Their attainment might actually be even lower if they were not set any homework or chose not to do it. Moreover, other studies have generally found a positive effect at the secondary level.

The problem of confusion over the direction of causality is well known in virtually every social science. In econometrics, this difficulty in drawing causal relations from cross-sectional data is called an 'endogeneity' problem, whereas sociologists and psychologists refer to this difficulty as the problem of 'reversed causality'. Yet another term for it is 'selection bias', which means that the levels of performance of the different groups in the sample may not have been comparable before they received a treatment and this has then biased subsequent results. A typical example of this problem is provided by Lazear (2001) who has developed a model to account for the effects of variation in class size. This model shows that there is a selection bias in studies searching for the effect of class size since it is demonstrated that larger-sized classes tend to be populated by higher performing students (because in many schools lower ability students may be taught in smaller groups as a form of support). However, irrespective of the term that is used to describe this problem, one should be aware that this difficulty is very likely to occur in cross-sectional studies, especially when a study is conducted at the individual/student level. One way to minimize this problem is to control statistically for the differences between students that existed before a treatment was applied. This approach requires the measurement of pre-existing differences, but in cross-sectional studies, such measures are usually not taken into account. However, during the third and fourth phases of EER, longitudinal designs have come to be used more frequently and thereby data has become available on prior achievement and/or other aptitude variable(s), as well as on these measures after treatment (that is, at the end of a school year or a specific period of schooling). This implies that it is now possible for researchers in the area of educational effectiveness to use such designs and so draw stronger arguments about likely cause-and-effect relationships.

Before we move to the discussion of other methodological problems that tend to arise from using cross-sectional studies to search for causal relations, it should also be acknowledged that national data sets are now available and researchers within EER should make use of the different procedures that have been developed in order to adjust for selection bias. One of the earliest and best known of these techniques was developed by Heckman (1979). In a two-step procedure, a multiple regression model is first estimated for an outcome of interest (for example, mathematics achievement) before a selection model is then estimated that compares those who participated in a programme against those who did not. If differences between participants and non-participants are detected, then adjustments are made to the first model to correct for these. However, there are limitations to the procedures used to correct for selection bias. These mainly arise from the fact that the selection model used to detect and correct for selection differences may be mis-specified, such as when important variables are missing (Stolzenberg and Relles 1997; Winship and Mare 1992). Another method that can be used to try to correct for selection bias is adjusting outcomes for relevant observed variables that are correlated with both the outcome and the independent variables of interest (termed 'observable selection bias'; Barnow *et al.* 1980). Nonetheless, it should still be acknowledged that unobserved characteristics may continue to bias estimates of programme effects even when this method is employed.

From the notion of observable selection bias comes the observation that a potential source of erroneous causal inference from cross-sectional data is the problem of omitted variables. For example, when an independent variable is related to a dependent variable in a statistical model and the estimated relation is interpreted in causal terms, it is assumed that there are no other independent variables associated with the independent variable being studied (no multi-colinearity). However, if such omitted variables do exist, they will lead to bias in the estimated causal relations if they are correlated with the regression residual associated with the dependent variable, possibly leading researchers to ascribe causality to variables other than the ones that are really involved. Theoretically, one approach to solve this problem would be to measure and analyse all potential variables. However, it is practically impossible to include all relevant variables even if a strong theory is available to help researchers select all of these. Therefore, the problem of omitting variables may lead researchers to consider some independent variables as causes whereas, in practice, the independent variables that are really involved in a cause-and-effect relationship may have been ignored because they were either not measured or not included in a statistical model.

Further to the point of omitted variables, social scientists have developed several methods to adjust for observed and/or omitted variables when making comparisons across groups using observational data. The following three methods are mainly used: (a) fixed-effects models (see Chapter 5), (b) propensity score matching and (c) regression discontinuity designs (see Chapter 11). Winship and Morgan (1999) provide a useful overview of these methods and advocate that researchers within EER should consider their use to explore potential cause-and-effect relations. While propensity score matching is presented in this chapter, the other two methods are discussed in Chapters 5 and 11 respectively. Of note here, however, is that some studies within EER that have used the regression discontinuity design have indicated the possibility of measuring the effect of schooling in specific contexts, such as in countries where the entry to primary school is based on date of birth (Kyriakides and Luyten 2009).

Concerning propensity score matching however, this is a technique aimed at estimating the predicted probability that individuals with certain characteristics will be assigned to a treatment group when assignment is non-random (Rubin 1997). The advantage of using propensity score matching is that it aggregates a number of characteristics that individually would be very difficult to match among those in the treatment and the control groups. For example, if researchers are interested in measuring the impact of remedial teaching on student achievement, one could assume that students from disadvantaged families are much more likely to attend this type of provision in schools. On the other hand, students of upper middle-class families might have a relatively smaller probability of attending such provision because of the link between SES and achievement level. To approach a random assignment trial, a comparison should be made between individuals who have a reasonable probability of being chosen to be in either the treatment (for example, remedial teaching programme) or the control group. Students with similar propensities to be in the treatment group (whether they are actually in the treatment group or not) can then be matched on the basis of their propensity scores. As a consequence, the difference in subsequent achievement scores would then be closer to the difference we would expect in a random assignment of these students to the two groups.

There are a number of ways propensity scores can be used to match students in treatment and control groups. The most common way is to sort students from each group into 'bins' or strata based on the distribution of propensity scores. Within each bin, the characteristics of students in the two treatment conditions are similar on a weighted composite of observed covariates. If the average characteristics of students within a bin are not equal, a more refined model is developed, using additional bins or strata until a balance in the characteristics of students in each group is achieved. In some cases, there may be 'bins' in which there is no overlap between the treatment and control groups, indicating that students have almost no probability of either obtaining or missing out on a treatment. Because these students have no matching counterparts in the other group, they are then excluded from any further analysis. This technique approximates randomized assignment since students within each of the remaining bins or strata have a roughly equal probability (based on their aggregate characteristics) of being selected into either the treatment or control condition.

It can be argued that propensity scores address an important issue in empirical research, namely providing estimates of effects for certain groups when randomization is not possible (for example, remedial teaching) and where sample elements have self-selected themselves into treatment or control conditions (for example, when teachers decide by themselves which in-service training (INSET) programmes they will attend). However, it is important to note that propensity score matching adjusts only for *observed* characteristics. Because a large number of background characteristics are used in calculating propensity scores, the probability that a relevant variable has been omitted from analysis, although reduced, is not eliminated. Nevertheless, it is also possible to test the sensitivity of subsequent results to hypothesized omitted variables (Rosenbaum 1986, 2002). Because an aggregate of characteristics is used to compute propensity scores and analytic samples are restricted to individuals (or schools) that can be matched across treatment conditions, propensity scores are more effective at approximating randomized assignment when large, nationally representative data sets are used. In such cases, the samples on which these data sets are based are sufficiently large to allow for the analyses of a sub-sample and contain comprehensive information on the background characteristics of students and schools.

If selection into the analysis is unbiased (for example, exclusions due to missing data do not result in differences between the analysis sample and the larger sample), subsequent results may also be generalizable back to the population of students or schools. However, it should be acknowledged that by following this approach, the size of the two groups involved in any study is likely to be decreased, and this might cause major problems for demonstrating causality due to the fact that statistical power has been significantly reduced.

Finally, it is important to make clear to the reader that from our discussion of the strengths and weaknesses of using cross-sectional data to search for causal relations, one can easily see that there are important limits to survey analysis even when adjustments for selection bias and multiple levels of analysis are used. Since populations are heterogeneous, estimates of the relationship between an effectiveness factor and student outcomes (that have been corrected for selection bias) may not be applicable to groups that have a low probability of falling into either the treatment or control group. However, it should also be acknowledged that in the last few years, analyses of large-scale data sets using the methods described above have produced several important findings concerning educational effectiveness, some of which have implications for causal inference and for the design of randomized experiments. For example, Hong and Raudenbush (2005) draw data from the Early Childhood Longitudinal Study (ECLS) and by using propensity score matching to construct treatment groups, they evaluated the effect of kindergarten policy on children's cognitive growth in mathematics and reading. Similarly, longitudinal research from the Effective Provision of Pre-School, Primary, and Secondary Education (EPPSE) project in England has demonstrated the impact of both duration and quality of pre-school on young children's cognitive and social behavioural development and on reducing the likelihood of identifying subsequent special educational needs (SEN) (Anders *et al.* 2009; Sammons *et al.* 2008; Sammons *et al.* 2005; Taggart *et al.* 2006).

Demonstrating causality through experimental studies

The foregoing discussion about the advantages and limitations of cross-sectional and longitudinal studies reveals the need to consider the possibility of carrying out experimental studies in order to demonstrate causal relations between certain factors of interest and changes in student achievement. However, it should be acknowledged that, so far, only a few experimental studies within EER have been conducted to identify cause-and-effect relations between school factors and improvements in school effectiveness (Antoniou 2009; Demetriou 2009; Tymms and Merrell 2009). This can be attributed to practical reasons, such as funding and obtaining consent to allocate students randomly into experimental and control groups but also to the initial interest of EER in *describing* practices that are effective rather than trying to create effective practices based on theory. As previously mentioned, when conducting experimental studies, attention should be given to the ecological validity of the experiment as well as to associated ethical issues (Miller 1984; Robson 1993), while threats to internal validity should also be taken into account. However, in this chapter, it is argued that further careful use of well constructed experimental studies may yet provide strong evidence for hypothesized cause-and-effect relations and contribute both to the testing of theoretical models and to the establishment of stronger links between EER and improvement practices.

Another issue we would like to raise in this chapter is the importance of using *group randomization* to study the effects of teacher- and school-level factors on student achievement. Readers are reminded that interventions aimed at changing teacher behaviour and/or school factors are designed to affect the behaviour of groups of interrelated people rather than of disparate unconnected individuals (in the case of teacher factors, the students in their classroom and the teacher; in the case of school factors, the teachers and/or students in the school). Therefore, it is generally not feasible to measure the effectiveness of these interventions in an experiment by randomly assigning each student to each of the groups. Instead, by randomizing at the level of groups (that is, teachers or schools) researchers can still reap most of the methodological benefits afforded by random assignment. Further, the use of group randomization to study the effects of reform policies is now spreading across many fields in the social sciences. Over the past decade, this approach has been used to evaluate various interventions in education, such as 'whole-school' reforms (Cook *et al.* 2000), as well as community health promotion campaigns (Murray *et al.* 2000), school-based drinking prevention programmes (Flay 2000) and community employment initiatives (Bloom and Riccio 2005). The main reasons why a research team might choose to study the impact of an intervention programme in a place-based design using group randomization are mentioned below. It is argued that this approach is useful in demonstrating causal relations between teacher and/or school factors and changes in student achievement.

However, problems in implementing experiments can also present substantial threats to their validity, and some of these, especially those faced in using experimental approaches to evaluate reforms in education, are discussed in Chapter 6. Readers are reminded that the ideal example of an experimental study assumes that an innovative programme is implemented with fidelity, that students do not move between treatment and control groups and that they remain in their assigned groups for the duration of the study. This is because the statistical solution to the fundamental problem of causality relies on an assumption of independence between pre-treatment characteristics and treatment group assignment. However, this independence is also very difficult to achieve in non-randomized studies. As a result, statistical models are typically used to adjust for potentially confounding variables (that is, characteristics of students, classrooms or schools that predict treatment group assignment and also predict outcomes) when outcomes for different groups are compared. However, as Raudenbush points out, 'No matter how many potential confounders [analysts] identify and control, the burden of proof is always on the [analysts] to argue that no important confounders have been omitted' (2005: 28). By contrast, because randomized assignment to treatment groups takes into account observed and unobserved characteristics, such control is not deemed necessary. This is why randomized field trials are often considered as the 'gold standard' for making causal inferences. Nevertheless, implementing experiments with randomized assignment can also present problems for researchers, such as breakdowns in randomization, treatment noncompliance, attrition and variation in fidelity of programme implementation. To counter these, methodologists have developed a number of procedures, although such solutions are not always adequate. Some of these problems are discussed below, and the ways of addressing them in randomized field trials are presented.

Breakdowns in randomization

There is sometimes resistance to randomization, particularly when a promising new treatment (for example, the use of technology in teaching) is being tested. For example, parents may lobby to have their children included in a promising new treatment programme. Such problems can be avoided by monitoring both the randomization process and the actual treatment received by each participant following randomization. Another strategy to minimize breakdowns in randomization is to isolate the units under study. For example, when different treatments are given to different schools (high isolation of units), it is less likely that breakdowns in randomization will occur than when different treatments are given to different classrooms within the same school (low isolation of units). However, when schools or other groups are assigned to treatment conditions, randomization occurs at the group rather than at the individual level (that is, group or cluster randomization). Therefore, the assumption that individual responses are independent ceases to be valid because individuals within the same group are more likely to provide similar responses than individuals in different groups. At the same time, this problem can be dealt with by the use of multilevel modelling techniques (see Chapter 11), which can simultaneously provide estimates of causal effects at both the individual and group levels. In terms of EER, this approach has been used in experimental studies aiming to identify the impact of using the dynamic model of educational effectiveness to improve teacher and school effectiveness (Antoniou 2009; Demetriou 2009).

Treatment noncompliance

Individuals who are randomly assigned to treatment and control conditions may not actually receive treatment as some may simply fail to show up for the particular programme to which they have been assigned. For example, randomly assigning teachers to receive different teacher professional development courses does not mean that they will attend these (Antoniou 2009). There are several practical ways to encourage participation, however, such as providing incentives, removing obstacles (for example, providing the courses at convenient times) and including only those individuals who are willing to participate. However, even when such steps are taken, some of those selected for participation in a study may still fail to participate.

Three statistical strategies have been used in cases where there is participant noncompliance. In the first approach, known as the 'intention-to-treat analysis', the mean responses of those assigned to the treatment condition (regardless of whether they actually received treatment) are compared with the mean responses of those assigned to the control condition. Assuming that the treatment has positive effects, the mean for the treatment group will typically be found to be lower than it would if all individuals assigned to the treatment condition had actually received treatment. Therefore, this analysis usually yields conservative estimates of treatment effects and this might be seen as its main limitation. The second approach eliminates individuals assigned to the treatment condition who do not actually receive the treatment. However, unless it can be shown that those who drop out of the treatment condition are a random sample of the participants in that condition, this analysis will yield a biased estimate of the treatment effect. The third strategy focuses on estimating the intention–to-treat effect for the subset of participants who are 'true compliers'. True compliers are those who will take the treatment or the control when assigned it. Noncompliers are those who will not take what they are assigned, whether it is the treatment or the control condition (Angrist et al. 1996; Little and Yau 1998). Noncompliers are of three possible types: (a) never-takers (who never take treatment no matter what condition they are assigned to); (b) always-takers (who always take treatment no matter what condition they are assigned to); and (c) defiers (who always do the opposite of what they are assigned). Because only the true compliers can be observed both taking and not taking treatment, they are the only subgroup for which we can learn about the effect of taking a treatment versus being in a control group. An additional assumption of this strategy yields the 'instrumental variable estimate' for the noncompliers, where there is no effect of the assignment on what would be observed. That is, the 'exclusion restriction' says that if the assignment to treat versus the control cannot affect which condition a participant will take (that is, the noncompliers will do what they want regardless of the condition to which they are assigned), it cannot affect the participants' outcome.

Attrition

In many cases, individuals who are selected for study initially participate but later drop out. It is not always possible to maintain contact with all participants, and those who are contacted may refuse to continue their participation. As such, researchers have developed strategies for estimating the effect of attrition on outcomes of interest. Little and Rubin (2002) reviewed several techniques for dealing with missing data, including data missing due to attrition. Three categories of missing-data mechanisms were identified: missing completely at random (MCAR), missing at random (MAR) and missing not at random (MNAR). Data are said to missing completely at random if the probability of having missing data on an outcome variable Y is not dependent on Y or on any of the variables included in analysis. If data are MCAR, estimates of treatment outcomes are unbiased. Data are said to be missing at random if the likelihood of having missing data is related to the observed values of other variables included in the analysis. In this case, the missing data are unrelated to Y after controlling for other variables. In cases where data are missing not at random, the probability of having missing data is dependent on both observed and unobserved values of the outcome Y. For example, attrition may depend on values that were recorded after dropout. If only individuals with incomes below a certain level drop out of the study, and data on income are available only for those who remain in the study, then estimates of treatment effects will be biased. However, it is important to note that in any given situation, the actual missing data mechanism remains unknown. The researcher has to assess the plausibility of each alternative assumption based on what he/she knows about the population included and what they reveal about how the missing data were generated.

In cases of attrition from randomized experiments, researchers typically have information on the pre-treatment characteristics of participants as well as their treatment group assignments and can conduct analyses to determine whether there are significant differences in initial measures between those who dropped out of the study and those who remained. Significant differences between leavers and stayers indicate that the characteristics of those who left differ from the characteristics of those who remained, and this suggests that the study findings may not be generalizable to the population of interest. Furthermore, when the characteristics of participants who drop out of the treatment group differ from the characteristics of those who drop out of the control group, the estimate of the treatment effect may again be biased. In such cases, researchers are advised cautiously to explore techniques for adjusting for potential bias (for example, imputing missing values, modelling the effects of attrition on responses or estimating maximum and minimum values to bracket the treatment effect).

Another issue in implementing a true experiment given significant attrition is the issue of statistical power. In the context of experimentation, *power* refers to the ability of a statistical test to detect a *true* treatment effect (Cohen 1988). Existing reviews of the literature indicate that insufficient power for making appropriate statistical judgments is a problem with studies across several fields (Cuijpers 2003; Dignam 2003; Halpern *et al.* 2002; Rossi 1990; West *et al.* 2000). This is a serious problem for EER, given both the cost of conducting randomized experiments and the failure of underpowered studies to yield consistent answers. Fortunately, there are several methods for increasing statistical power. Increasing original sample size is the most obvious, but practical considerations such as cost, available resources and access to populations of interest (for example, children with learning disabilities) may restrict this option for many researchers. Instead, the following approaches may be more practical when increasing statistical power: (a) using more reliable measures, (b) minimizing participant attrition, (c) increasing the fidelity of treatment implementation and (d) measuring and adjusting for characteristics related to the outcome of interest. Again in relation to EER, studies investigating the use of the dynamic model have successfully made use of these approaches to evaluate the effects of improvement interventions (Antoniou 2009; Demetriou 2009).

Finally, it is acknowledged that while experiments provide the best evidence with respect to treatment effects, they may yield results that are local and particular with issues for generalizability. Statistically, the only formal basis for ensuring the generalization of causal effects is to sample randomly from a well-defined population. Although formal probability sampling is viewed as the ideal with respect to generalizing to populations and settings, it is also extremely difficult to implement in practice (and in education especially) when participation in the experiment is voluntarily. Randomly selecting settings (for example, schools), while possible, may be difficult to implement in practice due to the cost of studying more than a few sites. Because of the practical difficulties of implementing random sampling, researchers have often relied on study replication to generalize results from single studies to other outcomes, populations or settings (Raudenbush and Liu 2000). In this context, the next part of this section refers to the importance of conducting meta-analysis of effectiveness studies in order to demonstrate cause-and-effect relations.

Demonstrating causality through meta-analysis

One approach to demonstrating causality in EER is the use of quantitative syntheses of effectiveness studies. Meta-analyses integrate the findings of studies and reveal simpler patterns of relationships that underlie research literatures and, as such, provide a basis for theory development and empirical testing. Moreover, meta-analysis can help to correct for the distorting effects of sampling error, measurement error and other artefacts that can produce the illusion of conflicting findings (Hunter and Schmidt 2004). Furthermore, in the case of using meta-analyses to search for causal relations between prospective factors and student achievement, researchers are able to examine whether the prospective factor could be considered generic or differential. The extent to which variables (such as the country where each study was conducted or the age range of the students involved in each study) explain variation in the effect sizes of prospective factors helps to identify those factors that should be treated as differential and those that are generic in nature.

However, there are also limitations in using meta-analyses to demonstrate causal relations between factors and student achievement, and these are discussed in Chapter 13. One of the most significant limitations is that the results of a quantitative synthesis are strongly dependent on the characteristics of the available studies. For example, if all studies are cross-sectional or correlational then it is not possible to draw strong conclusions about the existence of causal relations.

However, we do not support the idea that only studies using true experimental approaches should be selected or given more emphasis than studies using other designs, such as longitudinal or cross-sectional, as proposed by the 'best evidence' approach (Slavin 1986, 1987). This is because reliance on 'perfect studies' does not provide a solution to researchers when they are confronted with the problem of conflicting research findings. On the contrary, the characteristics of studies used to conduct a meta-analysis (for example, research design employed, statistical techniques employed) can be taken into account and attempts made to find out the extent to which these characteristics can predict variation in the observed effect sizes of interest. Where it can be shown that the particular research design employed does not predict variation in the observed effect sizes, one can more easily claim the existence of causal relations between these factors and student achievement. Further information on the development of this research approach is given in Chapter 13, especially since there have been recent methodological advances in this area and some multilevel meta-analyses of effectiveness studies using this approach have already been conducted (Creemers and Kyriakides 2008; Scheerens and Bosker 1997; Scheerens *et al.* 2005).

The role of theory in demonstrating causality

In the first section of this chapter, we showed that there has been a gradual change in the focus of EER from trying to identify the characteristics associated with better student outcomes, to a concern with making claims about factors that were seen to be important in terms of inducing effectiveness, and then to studies that seek to identify factors that can statistically explain variation in student outcomes. Due to these changes in the agenda of EER, there has been a greater emphasis on the development of theoretical models during the third and the fourth phases of development of this field. These models do not refer to single factors and their relation to student outcomes, but instead the newer models look at multiple factors operating at different levels. The choice of these factors is determined by the theoretical perspective under which educational effectiveness has been conceptualized (see also Chapter 1). As a result of this theoretical development, a number of important studies testing the validity of models of EER have been conducted. Although these studies expected to demonstrate causal relations, (as implied in the models) there have been methodological difficulties in doing so. Nonetheless, they have a significant advantage over those preceding in that they have been guided by theory and they attempt to test the validity of these theories rather than searching for relations that may exist for several reasons other than a hypothesized causal relation between specific factors and student achievement. This has been especially true for studies where researchers have tried to claim that causal relations were identified by collecting data through cross-sectional studies and using Structural Equation Modelling (SEM) procedures to analyse them (see Chapter 12).

The argument about conducting studies that are guided by theory in order to demonstrate or reject causal relations brings attention to another issue. The successful use of such studies depends on following strict procedures in the analysis of data (in line with the confirmatory nature of this design) and with difficulties that researchers may face in transforming theoretical concepts into meaningful instruments measuring these. This argument suggests another reason for developing appropriate instruments to measure the function of hypothesized effectiveness factors, such as different dimensions of teacher behaviour or school climate (Kyriakides *et al*. 2009; Sammons and Ko 2008; Teddlie *et al*. 2006). As was mentioned in Chapter 2, advances in EER partly depend on the appropriate use of measurement theories in designing effectiveness studies, details of which are further presented in Chapters 9 and 10. These measurement theories can help us develop more appropriate instruments to carry out studies driven by theoretical models that are better placed to demonstrate causality and thereby confirm or deny the validity of these models.

Concluding comments

In this chapter, the advantages and limitations of using different research designs to demonstrate causal relations between factors that relate to specific features of school or classroom processes and variation in student outcomes have been discussed.

First, a reliance only on comparisons via outlier studies was criticized and researchers were encouraged to make greater use of experimental designs (especially group-randomization studies) and longitudinal investigations (see also Chapter 5). Moreover, mixed-method research can investigate the difficulties of demonstrating causal-effect relations in specific contexts. For example, rather than noting that schools in low SES contexts do less well even when student level intake factors are controlled, such studies may illuminate why and how low SES context affects school and classroom processes and climate and thus affects student outcomes (see Chapter 7).

Second, the limitations of cross-sectional studies and of studies involving multi-sample comparisons – such as in international studies of educational achievement – in demonstrating causality were discussed. Although the use of experimental studies was recommended in this chapter, the practical difficulties in carrying out such studies were also acknowledged. Finally, in the third section of this chapter, the potential of using theory (based on emerging EER models) in demonstrations of causality was stressed. It was argued that special emphasis should be given to the use of cross-sectional studies and/or studies involving multi-sample comparisons guided by theoretical developments within the field and making use of Structural Equation Modelling in analysing their data to demonstrate causality. The latter can also be seen as a more practical way to search for causality than conducting expensive, large-scale experimental and longitudinal studies to demonstrate cause-and-effect relations. However, this approach can only be carried out under strict conditions and by operationalizing theoretical concepts into instruments that will provide reliable and valid data. In this context, we argue that researchers should not only make use of cross-sectional studies that are guided by theories, but should also attempt to conduct theory-driven evaluation studies. In the next chapter we show that such theory-driven evaluation studies could also help us demonstrate causal relations. Moreover, detailed consideration of how to use this approach in conducting evaluation studies is provided, as it also concerned with the relation of EER to policy and practice.

References

Anders, Y., Sammons, P., Sylva, K., Melhuish, E., Siraj-Blatchford, I. and Taggart, B. (2009) 'Special educational needs at age 10 assessed by teachers: A longitudinal investigation of the influence of child, family, home factors and preschool education on the identification of SEN', revised version of paper presented at the AERA Conference 2008, submitted to the *British Educational Research Journal*.

Angrist, J.D., Imbens, G.W. and Rubin, D.B. (1996) 'Identification of causal effects using instrumental variables (with commentary)', *Journal of the American Statistical Association*, 91: 444–72.

Antoniou, P. (2009) 'Using the dynamic model of educational effectiveness to improve teaching practice: Building an evaluation model to test the impact of teacher professional development programs', unpublished doctoral dissertation, University of Cyprus, Cyprus.

Barnow, B., Cain, G. and Goldberger, A. (1980) 'Issues in the analysis of selectivity bias', in E. Stromsdorfer and G. Farkas (eds) *Evaluation studies, 5*, Beverly Hills, CA: Sage, pp. 43–59.

Bloom, H.S. and Riccio, J.A. (2005) 'Using place-based random assignment and comparative interrupted time-series analysis to evaluate the Jobs-Plus employment program for public housing residents', *The ANNALS of the American Academy of Political and Social Science*, 599(1): 19–51.

Cohen, D., Manion, L. and Morrison, K. (2000) *Research methods in education*, 5th edn, London: RoutledgeFalmer.

Cohen, J. (1988) *Statistical power analysis of the behavioural sciences*, 2nd edn, New York: Academic Press.

Cook, T.D., Murphy, R.F. and Hunt, H.D. (2000) 'Comer's school development program in Chicago: A theory-based evaluation', *American Educational Research Journal*, 37(2): 535–97.

Creemers, B.P.M. (1994) *The effective classroom*, London: Cassell.

Creemers, B.P.M. and Kyriakides, L. (2006) 'A critical analysis of the current approaches to modelling educational effectiveness: The importance of establishing a dynamic model', *School Effectiveness and School Improvement*, 17(3): 347–66.

Creemers, B.P.M. and Kyriakides, L. (2008) *The dynamics of educational effectiveness: A contribution to policy, practice and theory in contemporary schools*, London: Routledge.

Cuijpers, P. (2003) Examining the effects of prevention programs on the incidence of new cases of mental disorders: The lack of statistical power', *American Journal of Psychiatry*, 160(8): 1,385–91.

de Fraine, B., Van Damme, J. and Onghena, P. (2007) 'A longitudinal analysis of gender differences in academic self-concept and language achievement: A multivariate multilevel latent growth approach', *Contemporary Educational Psychology*, 32(1): 132–50.

Demetriou, D. (2009) 'Using the dynamic model to improve educational practice', unpublished doctoral dissertation, University of Cyprus, Cyprus.

Dignam, J. (2003) 'From efficacy to effectiveness: Translating randomized controlled trial findings into treatment standards', paper presented at the invitational conference 'Conceptualizing Scale-Up: Multidisciplinary Perspectives, Data Research and Development Center', Washington, DC, November 2003.

Edmonds, R.R. (1979) 'Effective schools for the urban poor', *Educational Leadership*, 37(1): 15–27.

Fitz-Gibbon, C.T. (1997) *The value added national project: Final report: Feasibility studies for a national system of value added indicators*, London: School Curriculum and Assessment Authority.

Flay, B.R. (2000) 'Approaches to substance use prevention utilizing school curriculum plus social environment change', *Addictive Behavior*, 25: 861–85.

Goldstein, H. (1997) 'The methodology of school effectiveness research', *School Effectiveness and School Improvement*, 8(4): 369–95.

Gustafsson, J.-E. (2007) 'Understanding causal influences on educational achievement through analysis of differences over time within countries', in T. Loveless (ed.) *Lessons learned: What international assessments tell us about math achievement*, Washington, DC: The Brookings Institution, pp. 37–63.

Halpern, S.D., Karlawish, J.H. and Berlin, J.A. (2002) 'The continuing unethical conduct of underpowered clinical trials', *Journal of the American Medical Association*, 288: 358–62.

Heckman J.J. (1976) 'The common structure of statistical models of truncation, sample selection and limited dependent variables and a simple estimator for such models', *Annals of Economic and Social Measurement*, 5: 475–92.

Heckman, J.J. (1979) 'Sample selection bias as a specification error', *Econometrica*, 47(1): 153–61.

Hedges, L.V. (2007) 'Effect sizes in cluster-randomized designs', *Journal of Educational and Behavioral Statistics*, 32(4): 341–70.

Holland, P.W. (1986) 'Statistics and causal inference', *Journal of the American Statistics Association*, 81: 945–70.

Hong, G. and Raudenbush, S.W. (2005) 'Effects of kindergarten retention policy on children's cognitive growth in reading and mathematics', *Educational Evaluation and Policy Analysis*, 27(3): 205–24.

Hunter, J.E. and Schmidt, F.L. (2004) *Methods of meta-analysis: Correcting error and bias in research findings*, 2nd edn, Thousand Oaks, CA: Sage.

Joyce, B., Weil, M. and Calhoun, E. (2000) *Models of teaching*, Boston: Allyn & Bacon.

Kyriakides, L. (2006) 'Using international comparative studies to develop the theoretical framework of educational effectiveness research: A secondary study of TIMSS 1999 data', *Educational Research and Evaluation*, 12: 513–34.

Kyriakides, L. (2007) 'Generic and differentiated models of educational effectiveness: Implications for the improvement of educational practice', in T. Townsend (ed.) *International handbook of school effectiveness and improvement*, Dordrecht, The Netherlands: Springer, pp. 41–56.

Kyriakides, L. and Charalambous, C. (2005) 'Using educational effectiveness research to design international comparative studies: Turning limitations into new perspectives', *Research Papers in Education*, 20(4): 391–412.

Kyriakides, L., Creemers, B.P.M. and Antoniou, P. (2009) 'Teacher behaviour and student outcomes: Suggestions for research on teacher training and professional development', *Teaching and Teacher Education*, 25(1): 12–23.

Kyriakides, L. and Luyten, H. (2009) 'The contribution of schooling to the cognitive development of secondary education students in Cyprus: An application of regression discontinuity with multiple cut-off points', *School Effectiveness and School Improvement*, 20(2): 167–86.

Lazear, E.P. (2001) 'Educational production', *Quarterly Journal of Economics*, 116(3): 777–803.

Little, R.J. and Rubin, D.B. (2002) *Statistical analyses with missing data,* New York: John Wiley.

Little, R.J. and Yau, L.H.Y. (1998) 'Statistical techniques for analyzing data from preventive trials: Treatment of no-shows using Rubin's causal model', *Psychological Methods,* 3: 147–59.

Locke, J. (1975) *An essay concerning human understanding,* Oxford: Clarendon Press. (Original work published in 1690.)

Miller, S. (1984) *Experimental design and statistics,* 2nd edn, London: Routledge.

Mortimore, P., Sammons, P., Stoll, L., Lewis, D. and Ecob, R. (1988) *School matters: The junior years,* Somerset: Open Books.

Murray, D.M., Feldman, H.A. and McGovern, P.G. (2000) 'Components of variance in a group-randomized trial analysed via a random-coefficients model: The Rapid Early Action for Coronary Treatment (REACT) trial', *Statistical Methods in Medical Research,* 9(2): 117–33.

Raudenbush, S.W. (2005) 'Learning from attempts to improve schooling: The contribution of methodological diversity', *Educational Researcher,* 34(5): 25–31.

Raudenbush, S.W. and Liu, X. (2000) 'Statistical power and optimal design for multisite randomized trials', *Psychological Methods,* 5(2): 199–213.

Robson, C. (1993) *Real World Research,* Oxford: Blackwell.

Rosenbaum, P.R. (1986) 'Dropping out of high school in the United States: An observational study', *Journal of Educational Statistics,* 11(3): 207–24.

Rosenbaum, P.R. (2002) *Observational studies,* 2nd edn, New York: Springer.

Rossi, J.S. (1990) 'Statistical power of psychological research: What have we gained in 20 years?', *Journal of Consulting and Clinical Psychology,* 58: 646–56.

Rubin, D.B. (1974) 'Estimating causal effects of treatments in randomized and nonrandomized studies', *Journal of Educational Psychology,* 66: 688–701.

Rubin, D.B. (1978) 'Bayesian inference for causal effects: The role of randomization', *Annals of Statistics,* 6: 34–58.

Rubin, D.B. (1997) 'Estimating causal effects from large data sets using propensity scores', *Annals of Internal Medicine,* 127(8): 757–63.

Rubin, D.B. (2006) *Matched sampling for causal effects,* New York: Cambridge University Press.

Sammons, P. (1996) 'Complexities in the judgement of school effectiveness', *Educational Research and Evaluation,* 2(2): 113–49.

Sammons, P., Anders, Y., Sylva, K., Melhuish, E., Siraj-Blatchford, I., Taggart, B. and Barreau, S. (2008) 'Children's cognitive attainment and progress in English primary schools during Key Stage 2: Investigating the potential continuing influences of pre-school education', *Zeitschrift für Erziehungswissenschaften,* 10, Jahrg, Special Issue (Sonderheft) 11/2008: 179–98.

Sammons, P. and Ko, J. (2008) 'Using systematic classroom observation schedules to investigate effective teaching: Overview of quantitative findings', Effective Classroom Practice (ECP) ESRC Project Report, School of Education, University of Nottingham, Ref. no. RES-000-23-1564.

Sammons, P., Nuttall, D. and Cuttance, P. (1993) 'Differential school effectiveness: Results from a reanalysis of the Inner London Education Authority's Junior School Project data', British Educational Research Journal, 19(4): 381–405.

Sammons, P., Siraj-Blatchford, I., Sylva, K., Melhuish, E., Taggart, B. and Elliot, K. (2005) 'Investigating the effects of preschool provision: Using mixed methods in the EPPE research', International Journal of Social Research Methodology: Theory & Practice, 8(3): 207–24.

Sammons, P., Smees, R., Thomas, S., Robertson, P., McCall, J. and Mortimore, P. (1997) The impact of background factors on pupil attainment, progress and attitudes in schools, London: ISEIS, Institute of Education, University of London.

Scheerens, J. and Bosker, R.J. (1997) The foundations of educational effectiveness, Oxford: Pergamon.

Scheerens, J., Seidel, T., Witziers, B., Hendriks, M. and Doornekamp, G. (2005) Positioning and validating the supervision framework, University of Twente: Department of Educational Organisation and Management.

Schoenfeld, A.H. (1998) 'Toward a theory of teaching in context', Issues in Education, 4(1): 1–94.

Shadish, W.R., Cook, T.D. and Campbell, D.T. (2002) Experimental and quasi-experimental designs for generalized causal inference, Boston: Houghton-Mifflin.

Slavin, R.E. (1986) 'Best-evidence synthesis: An alternative to meta-analytic and traditional reviews', Educational Researcher, 15(9): 5–11.

Slavin, R.E. (1987) 'Ability grouping and student achievement in elementary schools: A best-evidence synthesis', Review of Educational Research, 57: 293–326.

Stolzenberg, R.M. and Relles, D.A. (1997) 'Tools for intuition about sample selection bias and its correction', American Sociological Review, 62(3): 494–507.

Taggart, B., Sammons, P., Smees, R., Sylva, K., Melhuish, E. and Siraj-Blatchford, I. (2006) 'Early identification of special educational needs and the definition of "at risk": The Early Years Transition and Special Educational Needs (EYTSEN) project', British Journal of Special Education, 33(1): 40–5.

Teddlie, C., Creemers, B.P.M., Kyriakides, L., Muijs, D. and Fen, Y. (2006) 'The international system for teacher observation and feedback: Evolution of an international study of teacher effectiveness constructs', Educational Research and Evaluation, 12(6): 561–82.

Tymms, P. and Merrell, C. (2009) 'Improving attainment across a whole district: Peer tutoring in a randomized control trial', paper presented at the AERA 2009 Conference, San Diego, CA.

West, S.G., Biesanz, J.C. and Pitts, S.C. (2000) 'Causal inference and generalization in field settings', in H.T. Reis and C.M. Judd (eds) Handbook of research methods in social and personality psychology 40–84, Cambridge: Cambridge University Press.

Winship, C. and Mare, R.D. (1992) 'Models for sample selection bias', Annual Review of Sociology, 18: 327–50.

Winship, C. and Morgan, S.L. (1999) 'The estimation of causal effects from observational data', Annual Review of Sociology, 25: 659–706.

Chapter 4

Theory-driven evaluation studies

Establishing links between research, policy and practice

Introduction

During the fourth phase of EER, it was acknowledged that the ultimate aims of the field were not only the identification of associative and stronger cause-and-effect relations and the development of plausible empirically supported theories explaining the processes of educational effectiveness, but also to have a positive impact by informing policy and practice (Creemers and Kyriakides 2006). Since EER was previously mainly concerned with searching for evidence of existing effective practices rather than making use of a knowledge base to improve practice, this is an important shift in the research agenda and we here deal with methodological issues that have arisen from this. In this chapter, it is argued that theory-driven evaluation studies can be used to provide new links between EER and policy and practice. For this reason, the main features of this approach are described and it is demonstrated how EER creates such new linkages. Moreover, it is shown that EER can influence the design of different types of evaluation studies so that in-depth answers concerning why specific reform policies are more or less effective can be provided to policymakers (Creemers and Van der Werf 2000). This can help us establish an evidence-based approach in policymaking and a theory-driven approach in improving education (see also Chapter 6). Finally, it is claimed that evaluation studies should contribute to the development of a theoretical framework of educational effectiveness since data emerging from such studies will help us understand better its complex and dynamic nature. In order to design theory-driven evaluation studies that can achieve the main purposes described, the methodological orientations presented in the second part of the book should be taken into account by both researchers and evaluators.

Designing theory-driven evaluation studies

Theory-driven evaluation is a collection of different methodological approaches that can be used by evaluators in trying to understand the impact of a reform policy evaluation, such as those of programme theory, theories-of-change, and realism (Bledsoe and Graham 2005; Rosas 2005). In all of these perspectives, social programmes are regarded as products of the human imagination; they are hypotheses about social betterment (Bickman 1985). Programmes chart out a perceived course where wrongs might be put right, deficiencies of behaviour corrected and inequalities of condition alleviated. Programmes are thus shaped by a vision of change and social justice and they succeed or fail according to the veracity of that vision. In respect to these, evaluation has the task of testing out the underlying programme theories (Chen and Rossi 1987) but also of identifying unintended consequences, which may or may not be beneficial. When one evaluates, one must always return to the core theories about how a programme is supposed to work and then interrogate it by asking whether the basic plan is sound, plausible, durable, practical and, above all, valid.

Evaluation projects that are theory-driven take into account the needs and issues raised by the various stakeholders associated with an innovation, such as the practitioners and the policymakers. However, the evaluation agenda behind these projects are also not entirely defined by the stakeholders. The overall agenda is expanded in such a way as to allow evaluators not only to provide answers to the questions raised by stakeholders but also to help them understand the reasons why a reform is more or less effective (Weiss 1997). In this chapter, it is argued that in order to provide such answers, evaluators in education should make use of the growing knowledge base of EER as it is concerned with the correlates of effective practice and provides theories about their relationships with each other and with student outcomes. Educational effectiveness can be seen as a theoretical foundation upon which can be built better evaluation studies in education. Further, programmes are embedded in social systems as they are delivered (Shaw and Replogle 1996). As a result, it is through the workings of entire systems of social relationships in and outside the classroom and/or the school that any changes in behaviours, events and social conditions in education are put into effect. Serving to aid an understanding of variation within an effective implementation of a reform, theories of educational effectiveness can help evaluators identify factors most closely associated with the effective implementation. Moreover, in making use of these theories evaluators may also contribute to the development of the knowledge base of EER itself.

A typical example of a theory-driven evaluation is the evaluation of a 1998 Cypriot reform that concerned the use of schema theory in teaching mathematics (Kyriakides *et al.* 2006). Five years after the introduction of the reform, an evaluation study was conducted in order to determine its current implementation. The study aimed to examine the main stakeholders' (that is, teachers and student) reaction to the reform and the factors influencing its effectiveness. The study not only provided answers to policymakers but also revealed that student achievement was determined by a number of factors related to teachers' and students' personal characteristics and teachers' reaction to the reform itself. The research verified the decisive role of teachers in implementing any reform. Based on the findings of this study and drawing on the theoretical assumptions of the 'emergent design' research model, a conceptual framework for conducting programme evaluations was proposed that attributes a central role to teachers' classroom behaviour. It was claimed that teacher effectiveness research could be a foundation upon which to design studies regarding the evaluation of reforms. In turn, this study revealed that EER can be seen as a foundation upon which a theory-driven evaluation project can be designed. Furthermore, this study reveals that it is possible to combine theoretical models of EER with evaluation projects that have their agendas defined by different stakeholders for political and practical reasons. Such projects contribute to the development of the knowledge base of EER and provide more elaborate and better answers to the questions posed by the various stakeholders of education.

The last part of this section provides more guidelines for conducting theory-driven evaluation studies that are based on educational effectiveness models, and a theoretical framework is offered (see Figure 4.1) that leads to the following observations.

First, we recommend that evaluators reformulate the research questions that policymakers may have in relation to a reform process. In doing so, the theory upon which a reform is based and the main characteristics of the theoretical model that they consider as appropriate should be taken into account. The chosen model should meet the following criteria based on the current knowledge base of EER. First, the model should be multilevel in nature and refer to factors operating at different levels such as students, teachers/classes/departments, schools and various features of the local and national context. It should outline hypothesized relationships between factors and student outcomes (for example, linear or nonlinear) and should refer to relationships among factors that exist both within and across levels. Second, the model should provide a clear framework for measuring the functioning of factors. Finally, the model should have sufficient empirical support. This implies that the multilevel structure of education and the factors that operate at different levels should at least be considered. For example, a reform programme implementing a reduction in class size could investigate its impact on the quality of teaching, factors describing teacher and student behaviour in the classroom and only then, finally, student outcomes. Therefore, the reformulation of the evaluation questions of the stakeholders can be seen as a starting point for the design of the evaluation plan.

After the reformulation of policy questions, the second step should be to design an evaluation plan. Evaluators should not only attempt to achieve the summative purpose of evaluation but also address formative purposes. The latter are closely related to the implementation of the reform, whereas the summative aspect of evaluation is expected to study both short- and long-term effects of the reform on student outcomes. Given that variation in the implementation of reforms is expected, we propose that evaluators need to focus their attention on the behaviour of those expected to make use of it. Data concerning the impact of the reform on teachers' and students' behaviours as well as on the behaviours of other stakeholders may help to identify factors associated with its effective implementation. The chosen evaluation model may even be of use in identifying

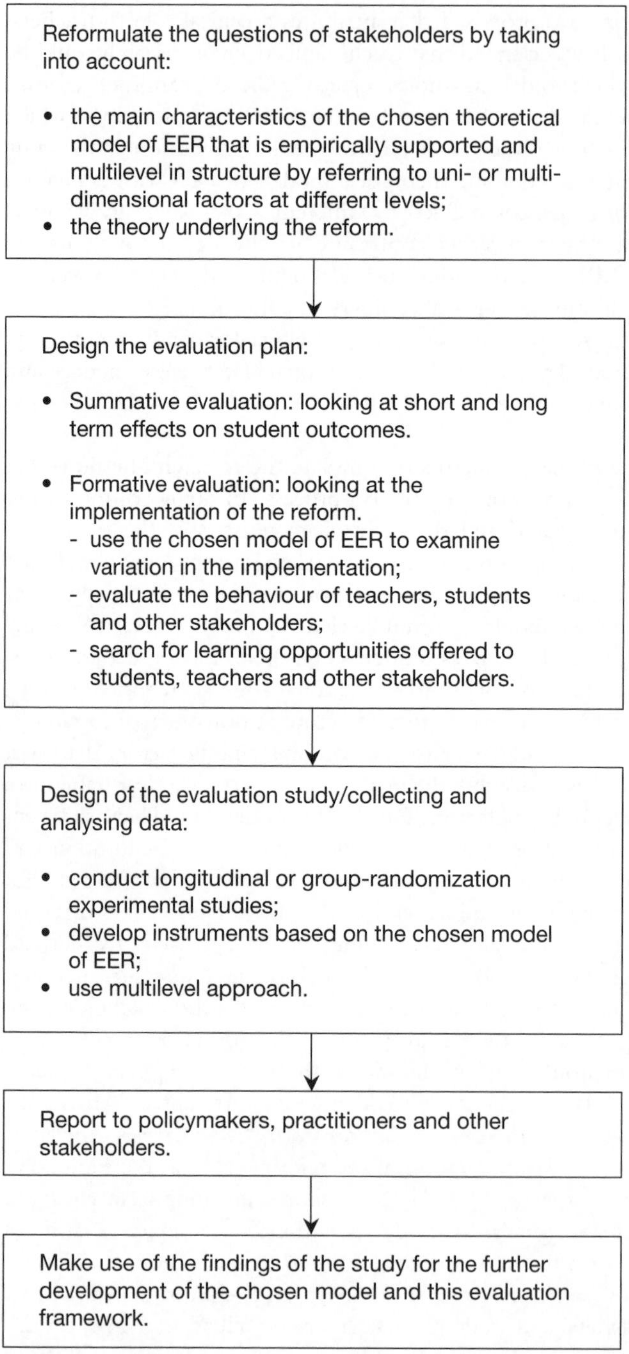

Reformulate the questions of stakeholders by taking into account:

- the main characteristics of the chosen theoretical model of EER that is empirically supported and multilevel in structure by referring to uni- or multi-dimensional factors at different levels;
- the theory underlying the reform.

Design the evaluation plan:

- Summative evaluation: looking at short and long term effects on student outcomes.

- Formative evaluation: looking at the implementation of the reform.
  - use the chosen model of EER to examine variation in the implementation;
  - evaluate the behaviour of teachers, students and other stakeholders;
  - search for learning opportunities offered to students, teachers and other stakeholders.

Design of the evaluation study/collecting and analysing data:

- conduct longitudinal or group-randomization experimental studies;
- develop instruments based on the chosen model of EER;
- use multilevel approach.

Report to policymakers, practitioners and other stakeholders.

Make use of the findings of the study for the further development of the chosen model and this evaluation framework.

Figure 4.1 A framework for conducting theory-driven evaluation studies in educational effectiveness

the impact of such effectiveness factors and may also suggest how the reform could be redesigned in such a way that it would provide further support to those who need it. Rather than discussing issues related to the existence of prescribed plans for implementing reforms, there is a need to examine how teachers use and modify these plans in order to meet the needs of students and promote learning. Finally, instead of giving too much emphasis to students' reactions to a reform, it is important to examine what learning opportunities students and other stakeholders (for example, teachers and headteachers) have been provided with by participating in the reform.

The third step is the design of the study and should feature the collection and analysis of data. The framework proposed here suggests that beyond examining student progress in terms of learning outcomes, we also need to collect longitudinal data for both teachers and students. Namely, it is worth examining both short-term and long-term effects on students since there is evidence that reforms and intervention programmes may not have enduring effects on student learning (Plewis 2000). This framework also suggests that evaluators should examine whether teachers improve their practices throughout the years as a consequence of implementing the reform (that is, the reform itself could be considered as a force able to bring about change in teacher practice). In order to achieve these purposes, either an experimental study should be conducted by following the group randomization approach mentioned earlier or a longitudinal design should be used (see also Chapters 5 and 6). The choice of this design depends not only on practicality issues but also on whether the reform programme is implemented in the same way across the participating teachers/schools or by offering different treatments to different groups (Kyriakides *et al.* 2006). The chosen model of EER and the way that factors are defined are both expected to help evaluators design appropriate instruments, although they are also expected to investigate the properties of these before conducting the main evaluation. In this book, Chapters 8, 9 and 10 detail how different measurement theories can be used for this purpose. Finally, the multilevel structure of the data to be collected should also be taken into account through the use of appropriate analysis techniques, such as multilevel modelling techniques (see Chapter 11) or SEM techniques (see Chapter 12).

In the fourth phase, evaluators are expected to report the results to different stakeholders. If a participatory model is adopted, then different reports for policymakers and teachers, but also for parents and students, should be produced. However, beyond providing answers to the specific questions raised by the policymakers and other stakeholders concerning the impact of the reform and possibilities for its development, evaluators are also expected to draw implications for the further development of the chosen model of EER and for the development of the proposed evaluation framework presented above.

The framework proposed here does not aim to provide a *comprehensive* model for evaluating educational reforms however. Rather, it instead aims to incorporate different theoretical frameworks into a single model, acknowledging the fact that each theoretical framework could illuminate different aspects of the reform under scrutiny. It is argued that the theoretical models of EER could have an important role in this process. However, further research is needed to refine and elaborate this framework, especially since it did not arise from empirical evidence or the results of evaluation studies. Again, we underline that the evaluation framework is offered as a set of hypotheses that need to be tested further; we believe though that it provides a framework for developing a dynamic rather than a static model of evaluating educational reforms.

Establishing a theory-driven and evidence-based approach to improving education

Although the responsibility for, and the improvement of, educational practice cannot be dictated by educational theory and research, it is a major objective of educational science to contribute to the effectiveness and improvement of education by providing a knowledge base for practice and by helping schools develop effective intervention programmes (Creemers and Kyriakides 2006). However, the relationship between general practice in education, science and, specifically, EER has not always been successful. There are many publications that spell out problems in attempts to create better links between theory and practice in education. In fact, these publications point out differences in approach, implementation problems and differences between teachers and schools that should make it almost impossible to use existing theoretical 'knowledge' in school improvement (Creemers and Reezigt 1997; Scheerens and Bosker 1997; Teddlie and Reynolds 2000). By contrast, it would be reasonable to expect that there might be a good link between EER (which aims to develop knowledge about what works in education and why) and the school improvement orientation, which aims to improve and develop education in classrooms and schools. The explicit purpose of those who initiate research on the effectiveness of classrooms, schools and educational systems is, after all, that the results of this research could be used in practice. For example, one of the major aims of the 1988 establishment of the International Congress for School Effectiveness and Improvement (ICSEI) was to bring together researchers, practitioners and policymakers in productive co-operation for the benefit of education in general and for the development of the participating 'disciplines'.

In recent years, there have been several examples of productive co-operation between school effectiveness and school improvement and new ways of merging the two traditions/orientations have been attempted (Creemers and Reezigt 2005; Gray et al. 1999; MacBeath and Mortimore 2001; Reynolds and Stoll 1996; Reynolds et al. 2000; Stoll et al. 1996). However, after two decades one might conclude that the link between EER and school improvement is still problematic. Research on school effectiveness has strongly focused on student outcomes and the characteristics (factors) of classrooms, schools and systems associated with these outcomes without looking at the processes that are needed to change the underlying situation and processes (Teddlie and Reynolds 2000). By contrast, school improvement has mainly been concerned with the process of change in classes (and to a larger extent in schools) without looking too much at the consequences for student outcomes and without criteria to identify what processes were linked to positive effects. This was under the assumption that if the processes were good, positive outcomes would surely follow (Creemers and Reezigt 2005). However, in several publications, the reasons for this disappointing situation have been analysed in order to provide ways for a more productive co-operation between the two endeavours (Creemers and Reezigt 1997; Reynolds *et al.* 2000). After a careful analysis of the failure to link research and improvement effectively, strategies for school improvement that attempt to combine the strongest elements of research and improvement have since developed. Major elements of this combination are an emphasis on the evidence stemming from theory and research and the need to collect multiple data sources about the achievement of students. Moreover, further major elements of this combination concern classroom and school *processes*, the context of individual schools, and thereby also the development and implementation of programmes for classes and schools by schools themselves.

In practice, however, there remains sparse evidence in terms of contribution to student achievement outcomes associated with such an approach. In many cases, concentrating on processes at the level of individual schools almost necessarily implies losing a clear focus on the research evidence. For example, in the Effective School Improvement (ESI) project, which attempted to combine the knowledge base of EER with knowledge about school improvement, the final framework still reflected the different orientations (Creemers 2006). One can easily observe that achievement outcomes do not belong to the core of the improvement process, which encompasses the improvement of school culture and school process (Mijs *et al.* 2005). Therefore, there are clearly still serious problems in connecting the effectiveness and improvement traditions of enquiry. The question persists of how best to apply the knowledge base of effectiveness in practice, or in other words, how to get valid and useful information about school improvement out of EER (Creemers and Kyriakides 2006).

In this section, we claim that conducting theory-driven evaluation studies on educational effectiveness contributes to the establishment of a dynamic perspective on improvement (Creemers and Kyriakides 2008) and helps to establish stronger links between EER and policy and practice. This perspective gives emphasis to the use of theory-driven and evidence-based approaches to the development of improvement strategies and action plans. The importance of such approaches is discussed below by showing that a valid theory of educational effectiveness and evaluation data should guide the design of improvement efforts.

Establishing clarity and consensus about the aims of school improvement

The first step of any school improvement effort is based on the assumption that it is important to start with a clear understanding of the intended destination and how one is seeking to improve the quality of education. This could be considered 'a purposeful task analysis' (Wiggins and McTighe 1998: 8) and suggests a planning sequence, while a commitment to collaborative work also needs to be established. However, Fullan (1991) points out that people have different perceptions of change, meaning that it is difficult to reach consensus among the participants of school reform efforts, although this may be crucial for their success. Therefore, it is important to establish procedures to ensure clear understanding among stakeholders as to the aims of any school improvement programme. To this end, results of theory-driven evaluation studies based on EER can be a useful tool for helping stakeholders realize that the ultimate aim of any school reform effort should be an improvement in student achievement across the school. This is the basic assumption upon which theory-driven evaluation studies in EER are based. For this reason, a major emphasis is given to measuring the short- and long-term effects of reforms on student outcomes (see Figure 4.1). It can also be argued that unless learning and learning outcomes are improved, any school improvement effort could not be considered truly successful no matter how much it has managed to improve any aspect of the climate of the school. This is due to the fact that learning is the mission of the school and so the main emphasis should be given to improving learning outcomes. An example of such an approach is the evaluation of the impact of network learning communities in England or New Community Schools in Scotland where a range of positive impacts were reported by teachers and head teachers but where little impact on student attainment was found (Sammons *et al.* 2007; Sammons *et al.* 2003).

Addressing school factors that are able to influence learning and teaching to improve and/or maintain the quality of schools

Beyond providing support to school stakeholders in the design of improvement programmes, the results of theory-driven evaluation studies in EER suggest that school stakeholders should attempt to build whole school reform efforts that are able to improve the functioning of school level factors that have been included in the chosen effectiveness model (see Figure 4.1). This is due to the fact that the chosen model has to be multilevel in nature and thereby refers to school factors that are expected to be related to student learning outcomes. Therefore, designing improvement efforts focusing on only the classroom-level factors may improve the teaching practice of individuals but may not necessarily improve the functioning of the school-level factors also included in the chosen model. In such cases, teachers who may manage to improve aspects of their teaching practice that have been addressed by a specific improvement programme will need at some stage some other type of support to improve other teaching skills. However, in cases where a reform does not aim to improve school factors, such support may not be available when needed and the long-term effect of a programme aiming to improve teaching practice could be questioned. At the same time, it is also acknowledged that school stakeholders should develop interventions/improvement efforts that will not only improve the functioning of the school-level factors but will ultimately promote the quality of teaching and eventually raise student achievement. Therefore, results emerging from theory-driven evaluation studies will ideally demonstrate that efforts at school improvement give emphasis to improving not only the teaching practice but have improved practice through improved functioning of school-level factors as well. In this way, not only are new learning opportunities offered to different stakeholders, as is supported by the proposed evaluation framework (see Figure 4.1), but also the conditions are provided that enable them to improve their teaching practice continuously.

Collecting evaluation data and identifying priorities for improvement

The use of a valid theory to design an improvement effort cannot in itself ensure that the aims of a proposed reform will be achieved even if it is implemented in the way it was designed (Kyriakides *et al.* 2006). In this section, a theory-driven approach to improve the quality of schools is suggested and emphasis is given to using empirical evidence to identify the strengths and weaknesses of a school and design relevant improvement efforts. The importance of using an evidence-based approach to school improvement arises from the fact that several studies have revealed that the evaluation of school policy is an important factor operating at the school level (Creemers and Kyriakides 2008; de Jong *et al.* 2004; Scheerens and Bosker 1997). Therefore, based on the results that emerge from theory-driven evaluation studies, the strengths and weaknesses of teachers/schools/systems should be identified. Moreover, stakeholders may also identify priorities for improving the functioning of specific factors and/or grouping of factors. Furthermore, evaluation data may reveal more than one improvement priority for each teacher/school/educational system, although the identification of more than one weakness is not always helpful for identifying how a particular teacher can develop professionally. However, due to the dynamic nature of models of EER, different priorities for professional development for each teacher/school/educational system can also emerge from such theory-driven evaluation studies.

Establishing a developmental evaluation strategy

The suggestions for theory-driven evaluation studies provided in the previous section may also help stakeholders establish a developmental evaluation strategy in their attempt to improve the effectiveness status of teachers and schools. However, it is important to note that effectiveness studies support the use of a *continuous* model of evaluation since such a model allows teachers/schools/ systems to adapt their policy decisions in relation to the needs of different groups of school stakeholders. It can therefore be claimed that the results of theory-driven evaluation studies will eventually show that a developmental evaluation strategy should be established at either the macro or micro level. This strategy should ultimately contribute to the improvement of the effectiveness of teachers and schools.

One example of this might be a situation where a developmental evaluation strategy of the school policy and of the actions taken for improving relations between school and parents can be used (Kyriakides 2005). In such a case, the evaluation process is expected to follow a linear sequence that starts with the development of a plan for school policy on partnership and from which priorities and targets then emerge along with associated performance indicators. At the next stage, evaluation questions that follow from the targets and performance indicators will be established to provide the criteria for data collection. Next, the data will be collected and analysed and fed back into the formative process of evaluation. In this way, stakeholders will be able to find out what is happening during the implementation of the school policy on partnership.

This strategy for improving effectiveness has a number of significant features. The evaluation process is expected to assist the implementation and development of a school policy since the establishment of targets and performance indicators may specify the developmental process of the partnership policy. Moreover, evaluation data may be related to the aims of the policy through the evaluation questions. As a consequence, a logical chain of action that relates aims to targets, evaluation questions, and to particular information sources can then be established. However, although this evaluation process is linear, it is very likely to be less tidy in practice. Once the evaluation process is underway, different working groups of stakeholders (for example, co-ordinators of partnership policy, teachers of different subjects) may implement parts of the policy at different rates (Kyriakides 2005). However, the extent to which there is a gap between the implementation of a reform policy and the design of an intervention could be identified. Thus, the results of theory-driven evaluation studies, especially those addressing the formative aim of evaluation, may help stakeholders take decisions on how to improve school policy or how to provide additional support to those working groups that may need it (Kyriakides *et al.* 2006). However, new research is needed to investigate the impact that the use of theory-driven evaluation studies may have on establishing a dynamic perspective on school improvement, as described above.

The contribution of theory-driven evaluation studies to establishing theoretical models of EER

In the last section of this chapter, it is argued that results of theory-driven evaluation studies can contribute to the further theoretical development of EER. This is because the procedure followed in these evaluations is such that data are collected on factors included in the theoretical models of EER and student achievement gains. Moreover, the design of these studies is expected to be made more rigorous by using appropriate methodological approaches. Therefore, more valid and reliable data on the functioning of factors and on the effectiveness status of teachers and schools are likely to be collected and can then be used for testing the relationships included in effectiveness models. In addition, these studies might also be concerned with the longer term effects of a reform and thereby data would be collected that could further elaborate on the dynamic perspective of educational effectiveness. For example, changes in the effectiveness status of teachers and schools could be observed and linked to changes in the functioning of factors operating at different levels (Kyriakides and Creemers 2009). Furthermore, these studies may also refer to variables that are strongly related to the theory upon which a reform is designed but which may not yet be included in the chosen model of effectiveness. In cases where the results of such studies reveal that these variables are associated with student achievement (and thereby should be treated as effectiveness factors), the underlying theoretical model could then be expanded to test this assumption further. Finally, since these studies follow a specific framework, experiences gained from conducting them could help the further development of the framework itself and the establishment of stronger links between EER and the evaluation of reform policies. Furthermore, in the previous section it was also argued that these studies could contribute to the establishment of a theory-driven and evidence-based approach to the improvement of policy and practice. Thus, the extent to which such an approach can improve the quality of education at macro and micro levels may also be investigated by the theory-driven evaluation studies discussed here.

Our argument that theory-driven evaluation studies based on EER could contribute in the development of this field is also supported by the fact that previous evaluation studies have already helped researchers to test the validity of various theoretical models (Kyriakides and Tsangaridou 2008; Reezigt *et al.* 1999; Van der Werf *et al.* 2001) and to identify which of the models' assumptions are most useful for understanding the impact that reforms have on learning outcomes. At the same time, results from these studies could help to identify possible reasons why specific assumptions are not supported by available empirical evidence and would thereby contribute to refining or further developing these models. For example, the study by Reezigt *et al.* (1999) raised doubts about the relevance of the concept of consistency developed in the comprehensive model (Creemers 1994) and also provided a basis for not including this concept in the dynamic model (Kyriakides 2008) Thus, the dynamic model is partly based on the comprehensive model, but at the same time encourages researchers to look at consistency through the introduction of stage as a measurement dimension. This development was found to be useful in understanding the functioning of factors and describing the dynamic nature of effectiveness (Kyriakides and Creemers 2008).

Finally, results of theory-driven evaluation studies that are based on a model of EER can help us test the generalizability of results from other studies in order to test the validity of the chosen model (Kyriakides 2008). As mentioned above, the model chosen should have enough empirical support to warrant this. Therefore, results of theory-driven evaluation studies based on such a model may further support its validity and could be taken into account by quantitative syntheses of effectiveness studies that search for evidence of the generic nature of the model. At the same time, in cases where the model is not supported by the results of a theory-driven evaluation study, one should be careful in drawing conclusions concerning the invalid character of the model. In order to establish such arguments, replication studies should be conducted to help us identify the extent to which (or under which conditions) the factors of the model are not useful in predicting variation in student learning outcomes. In this way, we can further specify the differential character of the chosen model and thereby contribute significantly to the theoretical development of the field.

Main conclusion emerging from Part A

In Part A of this book, readers have been provided with an account of the state of the art of EER, which has explicitly shown that EER has benefitted greatly from applying gradually more methodologically rigorous approaches in conducting effectiveness studies. For example, some of the studies conducted during the third and fourth phases of EER were only made possible due to further advances in research methodology, such as the use of advanced multi-level modelling and SEM techniques. As a result, one can identify reciprocal improvements in both the methodology of EER and in the establishment of the knowledge base of the field. Part of this improvement was also a movement from descriptive questions concerned with the characteristics of effective and ineffective schools to searching for direct and indirect associative and causal relations between factors and learning outcomes. As a consequence of this shift in the research agenda of EER, the methodological issue of causality is becoming a critical one for the future development of the research methods used. Moreover, a stronger emphasis has emerged for establishing theories explaining the process of effectiveness. However, this again implies the need for further development of EER methodology in order to test the validity of these and expand the theoretical models further.

In terms of methodological issues that need to be addressed in designing such studies, this chapter mentioned that the design and analysis of data should be improved in order to enable researchers to better understand the relations between factors and outcomes, and the relations among factors. Moreover, the need to consider the use of different criteria for measuring effectiveness was raised and issues associated with how we can relate these criteria were discussed. The use of two different dimensions of measuring effectiveness (namely, quality and equity) is of particular interest and should be addressed in future studies. However, searching for relations in measuring school effectiveness by using each of these two dimensions implies that further methodological development in analysing data is needed. Furthermore, the use of different criteria for measuring effectiveness reveals the need to measure effectiveness in relation to student achievement in broader domains of educational outcomes, such as affective, psychomotor, social, and new-learning outcomes. However, in doing so, issues associated with measurement should be considered to allow the development of instruments to collect valid and reliable data on such outcomes. At the same time, practicality issues arising from administering these instruments should be taken into account. In this context, measurement theories should guide our attempt to establish appropriate instruments for exploring student outcomes in these broader educational domains. Measurement theories should also be considered in designing and investigating the psychomotor properties of instruments measuring the function of different effectiveness factors.

In the last chapter of Part A, it has been argued that EER should ultimately attempt to influence policy and practice by establishing theory-driven and evidence-based approaches to school improvement. In the past, efforts to establish links between EER and improvement took place, but their success was very limited. Part A shows that EER could have a greater impact on policy and practice if theory-driven evaluation studies based on theoretical models of EER are conducted. The use of this kind of evaluation study draws attention to specific methodological issues, which were discussed in this chapter. Moreover, a framework for conducting such studies was then provided using methodological advances that are also useful for conducting basic research on effectiveness. It was made explicit that theory-driven evaluation studies will not only provide different stakeholders with a better picture of the impact of a reform policy and how it can be improved, but their results will also contribute to the further theoretical development of the field.

In Part A of the book, it has also been shown that EER needs to use and apply different types of research design and especially longitudinal and experimental studies. It was shown that each research method can address specific research questions in an appropriate way and contribute not only to developing and testing the theoretical framework of EER but also to establishing better links between EER and the improvement of practice. However, beyond collecting data through a specific empirical study, researchers can also undertake quantitative syntheses of effectiveness studies and test the generic nature of factors included in the theoretical models. Thus, in Part B of this book, we illustrate how different types of research design can be conducted (such as longitudinal, experimental and mixed methods – see Chapters 5, 6 and 7), and we also refer to advancements made in conducting meta-analyses (Chapter 13). The importance of conducting secondary analyses of data from major international comparative studies is also raised. In different chapters of this second part, it is shown that two measurement theories (Classical Test Theory and Item Response Theory) can significantly contribute to the further development of EER (Chapters 8, 9 and 10). In particular, this development is achieved by improving the quality of instruments used to collect data and by allowing us to search for relations in measuring effectiveness by using different criteria. Thus, Chapters 8, 9 and 10 refer to these two different measurement theories and show how Item Response Theory and Generalizability Theory can be used for developing and testing the validity of psychometrically appropriate research instruments. Finally, due to the complexity of the nature of educational effectiveness and the need to elaborate on it by drawing on empirical data that can emerge from any kind of study (from basic research to evaluation), the use of advanced techniques in analysing data is apparent. Thus, Chapters 11 and 12 refer to advanced techniques in analysing data. More specifically, Chapter 11 refers to the use of multilevel modelling techniques whereas SEM techniques are discussed in Chapter 12.

References

Bickman, L. (1985) 'Improving established statewide programs – a component theory of evaluation', *Evaluation Review*, 9(2): 189–208.

Bledsoe, K.L. and Graham, J.A. (2005) 'The use of multiple evaluation approaches in program evaluation', *American Journal of Evaluation*, 26(3): 302–19.

Chen, H.T. and Rossi, P.H. (1987) 'The theory-driven approach to validity', *Evaluation and Program Planning*, 10(1): 95–103.

Creemers, B.P.M. (1994) *The effective classroom*, London: Cassell.

Creemers, B.P.M. (2006) 'The importance and perspectives of international studies in educational effectiveness', *Educational Research and Evaluation*, 12(6): 499–511.

Creemers, B.P.M. and Kyriakides, L. (2006) 'A critical analysis of the current approaches to modelling educational effectiveness: The importance of establishing a dynamic model', *School Effectiveness and School Improvement*, 17(3): 347–66.

Creemers, B.P.M. and Kyriakides, L. (2008) *The dynamics of educational effectiveness: A contribution to policy, practice and theory in contemporary schools*, London: Routledge.

Creemers, B.P.M. and Reezigt, G.J. (1997) 'School effectiveness and school improvement: Sustaining links', *School Effectiveness and School Improvement*, 8: 396–429.

Creemers, B.P.M. and Reezigt, G.J. (2005) 'Linking school effectiveness and school improvement: The background and outline of the project', *School Effectiveness and School Improvement*, 16(4): 359–71.

Creemers, B.P.M. and Van der Werf, G. (2000) 'Economic viewpoints in educational effectiveness: Cost-effectiveness analysis of an educational improvement project', *School Effectiveness and School Improvement*, 11(3): 361–84.

De Jong, R., Westerhof, K.J. and Kruiter, J.H. (2004) 'Empirical evidence of a comprehensive model of school effectiveness: A multilevel study in mathematics in the 1st year of junior general education in the Netherlands', *School Effectiveness and School Improvement*, 15(1): 3–31.

Fullan, M. (1991) *The new meaning of educational change*, New York: Cassell.

Gray, J., Hopkins, D., Reynolds, D., Wilcox, B., Farrell, S. and Jesson, D. (1999) *Improving schools: Performance and potential*, Buckingham: Open University Press.

Kyriakides, L. (2005) 'Evaluating school policy on parents working with their children in class', *The Journal of Educational Research*, 98(5): 281–98.

Kyriakides, L. (2008) 'Testing the validity of the comprehensive model of educational effectiveness: A step towards the development of a dynamic model of effectiveness', *School Effectiveness and School Improvement*, 19(4): 429–46.

Kyriakides, L., Charalambous, C., Philippou, G. and Campbell, R.J. (2006) 'Illuminating reform evaluation studies through incorporating teacher effectiveness research: A case study in mathematics', *School Effectiveness and School Improvement*, 17(1): 3–32.

Kyriakides, L. and Creemers, B.P.M. (2008) 'Using a multidimensional approach to measure the impact of classroom level factors upon student achievement: A study testing the validity of the dynamic model', *School Effectiveness and School Improvement*, 19(2): 183–205.

Kyriakides, L. and Creemers, B.P.M. (2009) 'Explaining stability and changes in schools: A follow-up study testing the validity of the dynamic model', paper presented at the EARLI Conference, Amsterdam, August 2009.

Kyriakides, L., Demetriou, D. and Charalambous, C. (2006) 'Generating criteria for evaluating teachers through teacher effectiveness research', *Educational Research*, 48(1): 1–20.

Kyriakides, L. and Tsangaridou, N. (2008) 'Towards the development of generic and differentiated models of educational effectiveness: A study on school and teacher effectiveness in physical education', *British Educational Research Journal*, 34(6): 807–83.

MacBeath, J. and Mortimore, P. (2001) *Improving school effectiveness*, Buckingham: Open University Press.

Mijs, D., Houtveen, T., Wubells, T. and Creemers, B.P.M. (2005) 'Is there empirical evidence for school improvement', paper presented at the ICSEI 2005 Conference, Barcelona, January 2005.

Plewis, I. (2000) 'Evaluating educational interventions using multilevel growth curves: The case of reading recovery', *Educational Research and Evaluation*, 6(1): 83–101.

Reezigt, G.J., Guldemond, H. and Creemers, B.P.M. (1999) 'Empirical validity for a comprehensive model on educational effectiveness', *School Effectiveness and School Improvement*, 10(2): 193–216.

Reynolds, D. and Stoll, L. (1996) 'Merging school effectiveness and school improvement: The knowledge base', in D. Reynolds, R. Bollen, B. Creemers, D. Hopkins, L. Stoll and N. Lagerweij (eds) *Making good schools: Linking school effectiveness and school improvement*, London: Routledge, pp. 94–112.

Reynolds, D., Teddlie, C., Hopkins, D. and Stringfield, S. (2000) 'Linking school effectiveness and school improvement', in C. Teddlie and D. Reynolds (eds) *The international handbook of school effectiveness research*, London: Falmer Press, pp. 206–31.

Rosas, S.R. (2005) 'Concept mapping as a technique for program theory development – An illustration using family support programs', *American Journal of Evaluation* 26(3): 389–401.

Sammons, P., Mujtaba, T., Earl, L., Gu, Q. (2007) 'Participation in network learning community programmes and standards of pupil achievement: Does it make a difference?', *School Leadership and Management*, 27(3): 213–38.

Sammons, P., Power, S., Elliot, K., Campbell, C., Robertson, P. and Whitty, G. (2003) *New Community Schools in Scotland: Final report – national evaluation of the pilot phase*, Edinburgh: Scottish Executive Education Department.

Scheerens, J. and Bosker, R.J. (1997) *The foundations of educational effectiveness*, Oxford: Pergamon.

Shaw, K.M. and Replogle, E. (1996) 'Challenges in evaluating school-linked services – toward a more comprehensive evaluation framework', *Evaluation Review*, 20(4): 424–69.

Stoll, L., Reynolds, D., Creemers, B. and Hopkins, D. (1996) 'Merging school effectiveness and school improvement: Practical examples', in D. Reynolds, R. Bollen, B. Creemers,

D. Hopkins, L. Stoll and N. Lagerweij (eds) *Making good schools*, London/New York: Routledge, pp. 113–47.

Teddlie, C. and Reynolds, D. (2000) *The international handbook of school effectiveness research*, London: Falmer Press.

Van der Werf, G., Creemers, B.P.M. and Guldemond, H. (2001) 'Improving parental involvement in primary education in Indonesia: Implementation, effects and costs', *School Effectiveness and School Improvement*, 12(4): 447–66.

Weiss, C.H. (1997) 'How can theory-based evaluation make greater headway', *Evaluation Review*, 21(4): 501–24.

Wiggins, G. and McTighe, J. (1998) *Understanding by design*, Alexandria, VA: ASCD.

Part B

The contribution of different methodological orientations

The development of educational effectiveness research

Chapter 5

Longitudinal designs

Jan-Eric Gustafsson

University of Gothenburg, Sweden

Introduction

As has been made clear in the previous chapters of this book, there are many good reasons to use longitudinal designs in EER, and these have been used much more frequently during the last two decades. However, there are many different types of longitudinal designs and these are not always easily implemented. It is therefore necessary to have a firm grasp of the advantages and disadvantages of the different types of design. The main aim of the current chapter is to provide a basis for understanding the benefits and disadvantages of longitudinal studies. However, the field is enormously large and of great complexity so no claims of completeness are made. Rather, this chapter is a conceptually oriented introduction to the use of longitudinal designs in EER, with references for further reading.

What is special about longitudinal designs?

One fundamental characteristic of a longitudinal design is that it involves observations of the same units (for example, students) at more than one point in time. It is thus different from the cross-sectional (or survey) design, in which the units are only observed once. Another fundamental characteristic of longitudinal design is that it is observational; it does not involve manipulations, such as assigning different groups of subjects to different treatments. In this way it is different from the experimental design, which does exactly this.

However, the characterization of longitudinal design as involving repeated observations of the same units is much too simplified to carry any important information, and further complexities are needed to fill out the picture. However, it must also be stressed that it is possible to combine experimental and longitudinal designs in a large variety of ways. For example, one can create longitudinal intervention designs (Antoniou 2009; Demetriou 2009).

One may also ask what it means to observe units at more than one point in time. Suppose that we conduct a survey at the end of grade nine, in which we include questions about which school marks the students obtained in mathematics in grades six and nine. Given that we have information about the students' level of school performance at two time points, it could be claimed that this is a longitudinal study. Such a design is commonly referred to as a *retrospective longitudinal design*, but it is considered to generate data of lower quality than a study with a *prospective longitudinal design*, which in our example would involve starting in grade six and following the students through to grade nine. There are two reasons why the prospective design is superior. One is that the retrospective design relies on memory, and it is a well known fact that human memory is unreliable and often systematically biased. The other is that the grade nine sample is likely to be a biased non-representative sample because of processes of attrition due, for example, to movement, non-promotion and grade-skipping. For these reasons, retrospective longitudinal designs should be avoided. However, it must be realized that prospective longitudinal designs often also include certain elements of retrospection in questionnaire items as well.

Even if it is agreed that there should be repeated observations of the same units at more than one point in time, one may still ask if there should be a certain minimum number of time points for a design to qualify as longitudinal. It has been observed (Rogosa *et al.* 1982) that when there are only two time points, the amount of information available for studying individual change and development is very limited, and that it is therefore usually desirable to have observations from more time points. There is, however, general agreement among methodologists that a design with observations at two points still qualifies as longitudinal.

Another part of the definition of a longitudinal design that lacks clarity is the meaning of the term 'unit'. One of the characteristics of EER is that it operates with several different 'units', such as students, teachers, classroom, schools, school-districts and school-systems, and these are typically hierarchically nested. One obvious research design is to apply repeated measurements to the students along with observations of characteristics of their teachers, classrooms and schools. Such designs, in which the micro-level units are followed over time, correspond to our intuitive notions of the meaning of longitudinal research, and these are referred to with different labels. Keeves (1988) refers to such designs as 'time series designs', while others call them 'panel designs' or just longitudinal designs.

It is also possible to conduct longitudinal research in which there are new micro-level units at each wave of measurement. Consider, for example, research in which we are interested in the stability and consistency over time of achievement differences between schools. This research issue has the school as a unit, and to investigate it empirically would require that we conduct repeated measurements of a set of schools by observing the level of achievement of, for example, their grade nine students at each measurement. However, for each of these measurements, there will be a new set of grade nine students in each school, so the design is longitudinal with respect to the schools but not with respect to the students.

Another example of a design that is longitudinal at a macro-level but not a micro-level is the design adopted by many of the international investigations of educational achievement (for example, PIRLS, PISA and TIMSS) in which studies are repeated every third, fourth or fifth year. The repetition is done in such a way that samples are drawn from the same population and the achievement tests are linked so that results are expressed on the same scales. This provides a basis for investigating trends in the levels of achievement for those countries that participate repeatedly. Thus, this design is longitudinal at the level of school systems, but not at the student level. Keeves (1988) refers to this kind of longitudinal research as a 'trend design', and while this kind of design has not been common in previous educational research, it has been used more frequently within other disciplines (such as political science) under labels such as 'time-series cross-sectional designs'.

From the discussion above, it is clear that even though the basic idea of the longitudinal design is simple, there are many different versions and possibilities. This is one of the reasons why this is such a useful tool in EER. The benefits of such longitudinal research in EER will now be discussed.

Benefits of the longitudinal approach

The longitudinal approach provides several benefits, but discussing these more explicitly will provide a clearer understanding of when and why the extra cost and trouble involved in adopting such a design is worthwhile.

The first and most obvious benefit of the longitudinal approach is that it allows investigation of issues that have to do with stability and change over time. There are many important questions within EER along these lines, such as the development of effects of schools and teachers over time, the constancy and consistency of effects over time and long-term versus short-term effects. As was pointed out in Chapter 1, much of the recent EER has directed attention to such issues, and this has necessitated adoption of longitudinal research approaches because alternative cross-sectional approaches offer very limited possibilities to investigate such issues.

The second benefit of longitudinal research is that it provides a better basis for inference about causality than do cross-sectional designs. It must be emphasized, however, that compared to experimental approaches, the longitudinal approach is considerably weaker when it comes to causal inference (see also Chapter 3). As a result, it is therefore necessary to bring in strong substantive theory to support causal inferences when conducting longitudinal research. Furthermore, there are also several different ways in which longitudinal designs can improve their basis for causal inference.

First, one necessary requirement for causal inference is that a putative independent variable precedes the outcome in time. With a longitudinal design, the time ordering of events is often relatively easy to establish, while in cross-sectional designs this is typically impossible. It must be emphasized, however, that even though we may have established a relation between an independent variable that precedes the dependent variable in time, this is not in itself sufficient evidence that the relation is causal. The reason for this is that there may be another variable that influences both the putative independent and the dependent variables. If there is no information in the study about theoretically possible third variables we do not have any possibility to investigate their possible causal roles, and so run the risk of making an incorrect causal inference.

Such omitted variables may be regarded as the most common and serious threat against valid causal inference in non-experimental designs. Often 'selection bias' is mentioned as a special category of problems in causal inference (Gustafsson 2007), but selection bias may be seen as just a particular case of the omitted variable problem. For example, a study reported by Mullis *et al.* (1993) used a cross-sectional design and found a significant negative correlation between the amount of instruction that students had obtained and their reading performance. Thus, the students who had obtained more teaching were concluded to have had a lower level of reading achievement. However, it does not seem reasonable to interpret this relationship as meaning that more direct teaching of reading had caused the students to read more poorly. Instead, a more reasonable explanation for the negative correlation is that direct teaching of reading was part of a compensatory educational strategy, in which poorer readers were provided with more teaching resources, either in regular education or in special education. This is an example of selection bias, because the levels of performance of the groups of students who received different amounts of instruction were not comparable before they received the instruction. However, we may also conceive of this as an omitted variable problem, because if we had had information about the students' levels of reading performance before they received the differing amounts of instruction, the differences in initial level of reading performance could have been controlled for and a correct determination of the effects of the extra teaching could have been achieved.

With longitudinal designs, it is possible to obtain information about initial, intermediate and final levels of achievement and to use this information in 'value-added' analyses of for example schools and teachers. Such studies are of great interest to effectiveness researchers and are also of great practical interest in correctly determining the education contributions of particular schools for purposes of school choice, accountability and development. Furthermore, there has lately been a great amount of focus on the development of designs and analytical models that feature this 'value-added' modelling (for example, OECD 2008; McCaffrey *et al.* 2004). One of the conclusions from this research is that controlling for baseline student socio-economic and demographic factors is insufficient in proxying for initial level of achievement and that measures of prior performance are needed (OECD 2008: 128).

However, initial levels of achievement may not be the only omitted variable. Indeed, the great challenge of the omitted variable problem is that potentially there are an infinite number of omitted variables and no empirical study can ever aspire to represent more than a small fraction of those relevant. Fortunately, one of the great benefits of the longitudinal approach is that it offers possibilities for dealing with at least certain aspects of this problem. Because we may choose to analyse longitudinal data in such a way that we only focus on change over time, omitted variables that stay constant do not exert any influence on the results. This is an abstract idea that is not easily captured, so a concrete example is presented below to support an intuitive understanding.

The example is a simple one taken from Gustafsson (2007), who investigated relations between the mean age of students in different countries in the TIMSS study and the country's mean level of performance. There are quite large differences in the mean age of the students in the countries that participate in international studies of student achievement, and this is potential source of bias in the between-country comparisons of achievement. However, the relationship between age and achievement for 22 countries participating in the TIMSS 1995 study (Beaton *et al.* 1996) was only 0.19. Furthermore, for the same set of countries the correlation in the TIMSS 2003 study was equally low (0.16). These results seem to indicate that age differences between students participating in international studies do not have any effect on the outcomes. This is an unexpected result that is difficult to understand and accept as valid, particularly given the amount of attention that age differences are given in the discussions of outcomes in these studies. Inspection of the scatter plot of the relation between age and mathematics score provides no obvious explanation, except perhaps that there is a tendency towards curvilinearity: with high-performing Asian countries having an age close to the mean, and average-performing countries being found at both extremes of the age variable.

However, a cross-sectional correlation only provides a snapshot of relations among variables at a particular point in time, and this relation is influenced by a large number of other variables that are not included in the analyses. For example, the 'school-start' age varies among countries, and this means that students of the same age may have gone to school for a different number of years. Given that the number of years of schooling influences achievement, this variable obviously needs to be taken into account. Further, it is easy to conceive of many other variables – such as rules for promotion from one grade to another – that are also correlated with both the mean age of the students and with achievement but which were omitted from these studies.

One of the most important features of the TIMSS study is that the results of successive repetitions, which are done every fourth year, are expressed on the same scale. This makes it possible to investigate trends in the development of country levels of achievement. Referring back to the above example, change scores between 1995 and 2003 were computed for both mathematics achievement and age. The correlation between the mathematics change variable and the age change variable was 0.58 ($p < 0.005$). A regression analysis of mathematics change on age change then yielded an unstandardized regression coefficient of 37.8, implying that a one-year increase in age was associated with an increase in mathematics achievement of close to 38 score points.

The two example analyses thus yield dramatically different results, which illustrates that analysis of cross-sectional data is something quite different from analysis of longitudinal data. As has already been pointed out, the cross-sectional results provide a static snapshot of how the variables happen to relate at a particular point in time. The change score, in contrast, captures the dynamic relation between age and achievement. The reason it does this is that those omitted variables that stay constant over time do not influence the relation between age and achievement. Rules for 'school-start' age and grade promotion are characteristics of school systems that tend to be very stable. Furthermore, the variability in age that we observe is largely determined by incidental circumstances, such as when holidays make it practical to carry out the assessments within a particular country. The incidental character of the variability in age change does not prevent it from being related to mathematics achievement, but it does reduce the likelihood that it is correlated with any omitted variable.

We can thus conclude that longitudinal designs can offer ways to reduce the impact of omitted variables on relations between independent and dependent variables. This is a major benefit of the longitudinal approach, but it must be realized that it does not come regularly and automatically. Depending upon how the study is designed and data are analysed, researchers may or may not be able to take advantage of this benefit.

Challenges of the longitudinal approach

The advantages of the longitudinal approach do not come without a price. The main problem associated with it is that of attrition, or a successive increase of missing data over the course of a study. This may be even more of a problem in EER because of the complex multilevel nature of the phenomenon of education. For example, students, teachers and school-leaders sometimes relocate from one school to another, or they are unable to participate in one or more of the waves of measurement even though they still remain in the study. What may be even more of a problem is that in many school systems, students are expected to change teachers (and sometimes classmates and school) when moving from one grade to another. Thus, what starts out as a simple and neat longitudinal design of students, teachers and schools is after a few years often a design with large amounts of missing data and a complex cross-classified design structure. However, even though these complexities offer great challenges to the researcher, it should be added that they may offer benefits as well. This is because changes in combinations of students, teachers and schools sometimes make it possible to tease out the effects contributed by such different categories, which would not be possible if they were completely confounded over time.

It also should be mentioned that, recently, sophisticated analytical tools have been developed that allow the researcher to deal with these complexities. Software is now available that allows the researcher to explore complex, multilevel and cross-classified designs. Further, new approaches for dealing with missing data that are particularly well suited to dealing with longitudinal data have also been developed.

Concerning missing data and its treatment in more detail, the simplest method for dealing with 'missingness' is to apply list-wise deletion. However, unless the information is missing completely at random (MCAR), this method creates bias and causes loss of power. There are also sophisticated methods for imputing missing data based on the data that is not missing (Schafer and Graham 2002). These methods make better use of the available data, but they carry other disadvantages, such as disturbing the covariance matrix among the measures. However, methods for dealing with partial missingness (based on weaker assumptions) are now available in many programs for analysing longitudinal and multilevel data. One class of methods, which is often implemented in the current programs for Structural Equation Modelling (SEM) and multilevel analysis, is based on maximum likelihood estimation. These methods will not introduce bias, providing that the data is missing at random (MAR). While this assumption may sound restrictive, it must be not be confused with the assumption that the data is MCAR. The latter assumes that cases with partially missing information should not be different in any other way from those with complete data. This is a very restrictive assumption that is unlikely to be met by the data typically analysed in EER. However, the assumption that MAR is weaker is conditional upon available data such that the missing information is not *systematically* different from the non-missing information. This allows for the fact that missing information for weaker students, for example, may be different from missing information for stronger students. Given that much information is typically available about the participants in longitudinal design, this makes this kind of missing-data modelling particularly useful for this research.

Another challenge that may prove difficult for longitudinal studies, especially those over longer periods of time, is having appropriate measures of development to capture both a *wide range* of individual differences at any particular wave of measurement and also a great deal of the development from the first to the last wave of measurement. Given that certain methods of analysis (especially growth-curve modelling) require that the repeated measures be expressed on the same scale, utilized measurement instruments need to be developed into several different versions with different levels of difficulty that are vertically equated to yield scores on the same scale. This can be accomplished with modern psychometric methods (Item Response Theory – see Chapters 8 and 9), but it may require great effort and careful planning when the study is designed.

Approaches to the design and analysis of longitudinal studies

The design of longitudinal studies and the analyses of the data they yield are two highly interrelated issues. It is therefore necessary to be aware of the restrictions on and the possibilities that are offered by different analytical approaches, so that the study can be designed appropriately.

There are a wide range of methods available to analyse longitudinal data, which is partly due to the fact that longitudinal designs are used in a wide variety of disciplines within both the natural and social sciences. This also has caused a considerable confusion with respect to terminology, and different traditions for analysing longitudinal data have evolved in different disciplines. These different traditions and terminologies may at times also cause confusion, but advantages may also be gained by profiting from the different experiences that have been gained. The brief review of designs and analytical methods presented below therefore covers approaches that have a background in educational research, as well as approaches that are more frequently used in other disciplinary fields, such as economics.

We consider five main approaches to analysing longitudinal data: fixed-effects regression models, mixed-effects regression models, multilevel regression models, growth models and structural models. These are briefly introduced below, and their use is demonstrated through examples.

Fixed-effects regression

It has been realized for quite some time that many statistical techniques, such as analysis of variance, SEM and multilevel analysis are applications of regression analysis (Cohen *et al.* 2003) via the statistical 'family' that they belong to: General Linear Models (GLMs). The linear additive model that regression analysis is based upon is very versatile and the fixed-effects regression model for longitudinal data is a demonstration of this.

Assume that we have a dependent variable (y) for a set of N individuals at T occasions, along with a set of K independent variables (x). For individual i at occasion t we denote the dependent variable observation y_{it} and the observations of the independent variables $x_{it\cdot1}, \ldots, x_{it\cdot K}$. The fixed-effects regression model then is:

$$y_{it} = \alpha_i + \beta_1 x_{it\cdot1}, \ldots, + \beta_K x_{it\cdot K} + \varepsilon_{it} \qquad (1)$$

In this model, α denotes the intercept, and β represents the effects of the respective independent variables on y. The β coefficients represent fixed population parameters that are the same for all individuals, and it is these that are the parameters we are primarily interested in estimating and interpreting.

Model (1) thus looks like an ordinary regression model. However, there is a subtle but very important difference, namely that the intercept parameter has the index i (α_i), which means that each individual has a different intercept. In general we are not interested in interpreting these parameters, and they are often referred to as nuisance parameters. However, these are necessary when accounting for the often very substantial variability we find between individuals. Here, this is done under the assumption that a fixed effect is associated with each individual and is captured by α_i.

There is another difference between an ordinary regression model and the model in (1), which is perhaps not immediately obvious. In an ordinary regression analysis, the number of observations is N, but to estimate the parameters of model (1) we use NT observations. Thus, for each individual, there are as many observations as there are occasions of measurement.

Model (1) may be estimated in several different ways, but the most natural approach within the regression framework is to estimate the fixed α_i parameters using a dummy variable approach. Let us illustrate this with the data on 22 countries participating in TIMSS 1995 and TIMSS 2003 analysed by Gustafsson (2007), which was previously referred to. We first create a data set with 44 lines by putting the TIMSS 2003 observations after the TIMSS 1995 observations. The mathematics results for the two occasions are put in the same column (Math), and we also put the mean age for the two occasions in the same column (Age). We create one dummy variable (Time) representing occasion of measurement (TIMSS 1995 = 0, TIMSS 2003 = 1) and 21 dummy variables representing country. In the last step we perform the regression analysis using Math as the dependent variable, and Age, Time and the 21 country dummies as independent variables.

The regression analysis shows that the unstandardized regression coefficient (β) for Age on Math is 37.8. Interestingly enough, this is exactly the same estimate as was obtained when change in mathematics score was regressed on change in age! This demonstrates that the interpretation of the fixed-effects regression model specified above is to be made in terms of relations between changes in independent and dependent variables. While this may not be immediately obvious from (1) it follows from the fact that we allowed α_i to capture the variability among the units (that is, countries) and that the other part of the model estimated the factors related to change between the two occasions.

It should be emphasized that even though the unstandardized regression estimate for age that was obtained with the fixed-effects regression model is identical to the unstandardized regression coefficient obtained when we regressed change in mathematics score to change in age, the standardized regression coefficients (β) are not identical. In the latter analysis the standardized co-efficient was 0.58, while in the former analysis the partial standardized regression coefficient was 0.30. This is because the variances of the independent and dependent variables are different in the two models. The standardized coefficient of 0.58 tells us that we can account for 33.6 per cent of the variance in change over time for the 22 countries from the differences in mean age at the two occasions of measurement. The standardized coefficient of 0.30 from the fixed-effects regression model tells us that 9 per cent of the total amount of variance between countries can be accounted for by the differences in mean age. Thus, these estimates are not in contradiction; they just describe different aspects of the empirical results.

As has already been mentioned, one of the main advantages of certain types of longitudinal designs is that they control for the effects of omitted variables that are constant over time. The fixed-effects regression model enjoys this property, and this is why we get a sensible estimate for the effects of age on achievement with the specification used here (see Gustafsson 2007, for a more extended discussion). The two cross-sectional estimates of the relations between age and achievement that we can compute from these data (and which both are close to zero) are, by contrast, influenced by correlations with omitted variables and cannot therefore be interpreted. However, it must be emphasized that even though the fixed-effects regression estimate is more interpretable, it is necessary to be careful about causal inferences and these must be supported by strong, substantive theory (see Chapter 3 for more on causality).

In the example above, the units were school systems, and it seems reasonable to treat these units as a fixed set rather than as a random sample. However, given the desirable properties of the fixed-effects regression model, it may be asked what the limits are for its use. Even though we cannot give a general answer to this question, there is much published research, particularly in the economics of education literature, that makes extensive use of fixed-effects regression specifications.

In one such study, Sund (2009) used a large longitudinal database of students to investigate peer effects on student achievement in Swedish upper secondary schools (that is, grades 10–12). There has been a considerable amount of research on peer effects and quite a few studies have reported on their existence. However, this is a controversial and difficult area of research and offers great challenges in correctly estimating effects. In particular, the problem of selection bias is a difficult one because there are many mechanisms that can cause positive selection of students into classes and schools. Furthermore, teachers are also not randomly allocated to classes and schools, which only increases this bias.

In order to control for these selection effects, Sund (2009) specified a fixed-effects regression model that included fixed effects for students, teachers and schools. This was possible because the database allowed the matching of teachers and peers with every student for every course. The database included 82,896 students enrolled in upper secondary school between 1998 and 2004, 27 schools and 4,181 classes. The main independent variable was the mean achievement level of the classmates (with the standard deviation also being entered). Without any controls, the value-added effect of the peer mean achievement level was 0.42, and when time, school and teacher effects were added the effect was reduced to 0.32. Adding student fixed effects then reduced this to 0.16. These decreases indicated that there was selectivity that would have caused bias if not taken into account. However, the remaining effect was still highly significant, and corresponded to an effect of 0.08 times the standard deviation for a 1 standard deviation increase in mean peer performance. There was also a significant effect, although smaller, from the heterogeneity of the peer group. In further analyses, Sund (2009) then showed that this peer effect was larger for those students with a lower level of initial performance. This study demonstrates that it is possible to estimate fixed-effects regression models for extremely large and complex longitudinal data sets, and it would seem that this kind of analytical method could be taken advantage of in EER to a greater extent than has been done so far.

Mixed-effects regression models

Even though the above-discussed Sund (2009) study demonstrates that it is possible to apply the fixed-effects regression approach with a very large numbers of observations, it is a tedious approach to estimate one intercept parameter for each observation. Another approach is to consider the α_i in (1) not as a set of fixed parameters, but as a random variable with an assumed normal distribution (we will refer to this random variable as α_{0i}). The estimation problem then becomes one of estimating the mean and standard deviation of this random variable. This is a so-called *random effect* and if we assume that in accordance with (1), we also want to estimate fixed effects for the independent variables, then we have a so called *mixed-effects model*. When interpreted in this way, model (1) is often referred to as a *random intercepts* model (model 2).

We may estimate this mixed-effects model for the same TIMSS data as were used to illustrate the fixed-effects model through one of the many statistical software packages that are available. Here we use the Mixed Models program available in SPSS (statistical package for the social services) (Bickel 2007). We use the same data arrangement as before, with 44 'cases' and each country appearing twice in the data file. Here, however, we do not identify the countries with dummy variables, but with a unique identifier. We also enter two independent variables into the model, namely Time and Age.

The estimated unstandardized regression coefficient for Age in this model was 35.2 ($t = 3.19$, $p < 0.004$), and this estimate is slightly lower than obtained in the fixed-effects model (37.8). For Time, the estimate was −7.08, which is also close to that obtained in the fixed-effects model (−7.37).

Thus in this case, the fixed-effects and the mixed-effects models give quite similar results, even though there are slight differences that raise the question, are there any general principles that may be relied on for model choice? One such principle is whether we regard our set of observations as a sample from a population or not. If we do, the random-effects model is a natural choice. In this case, however, the countries cannot be regarded as a sample and so the fixed-effects model is the most reasonable choice. Another principle is whether we are interested in obtaining estimates for individual cases or not. If we are, then again the fixed-effects model should be used.

Although the above example of a mixed-effects model is trivially simple, exceedingly complex mixed-effects model can also be specified and this is extremely useful given the great complexity of educational phenomena and particularly when these are investigated longitudinally. McCaffrey *et al.* (2004) proposed a multivariate, mixed-effects model for longitudinal student outcomes designed to capture teacher and school effects. This is a general model of which several previously presented models may be regarded as special cases. The great complexity of this model prevents us from presenting it in full detail, but it is instructive to consider its basic structure.

The model considers results for students in schools in successive grades. Given that the results achieved in one grade carry over to later grades (to a smaller or larger extent) this must be reflected in the model. For grade 0 (that is, the first grade considered) it is assumed that there are random school and teacher effects. The model also includes student characteristics that may be either fixed (for example, gender, race) or time-varying (for example, special accommodations at testing). Classroom-level characteristics may also be included.

For grade 1 and following grades, it is necessary to take into account the fact that students change teachers and that students are not necessarily grouped together in the same class. This is done through explicitly modelling the effects of the previous grades, teachers and schools on current year scores using a cross-classification model. Thus in this model, the influence of prior grade teachers and schools on current results is estimated empirically, while in other models it is often assumed that these effects persist (undiminished) over time. The model can also be extended to deal with multiple subjects and multiple teachers within each grade.

This model has many interesting characteristics and it clearly demonstrates the complexities involved in modelling longitudinal data in school settings. The estimated teacher and school effects are assumed to be interpretable as causal contributions to student achievement, even though the grade 0 effects must be interpreted cautiously because the model does not completely represent the student's history prior to the grade of testing.

McCaffrey et al. (2004) demonstrated that the model can be estimated on empirical data of at least moderate size (678 students, five schools and three grades) and also presented results estimated from simulated data. These results indicated that the model yields reasonable results for teacher effects and that it is reasonably robust to deviations from some of the model assumptions. However, the results also indicated that the estimates of teacher effects are biased when estimated from schools serving distinctly different student populations.

Multilevel regression models

As has been repeatedly emphasized, one of the fundamental characteristics of education is that there are units at multiple levels of observation, such as students, classrooms, schools and school systems. As is made clear in other chapters of this volume (and in Chapter 11 in particular) special multilevel statistical models have been developed to make it possible to deal with such hierarchical data. This is true for longitudinal designs as well, and as we shall see below, such designs generate a particular kind of multilevel data where observations at different time points are nested under different individuals.

There are two main reasons why hierarchical data require special statistical techniques. One is that units that belong to a higher level unit (for example, students within classrooms) tend to be more similar than randomly drawn units. This violates the assumption of independently observed units that is made in most statistical techniques, and if the intraclass correlation (a measure of the amount of mean differences between the higher level units) is higher than 0.05, a rule of thumb says that something needs to be done about the resulting bias. This bias does not generally pertain to the parameter estimates themselves, but to the estimates of the degree of uncertainty of the parameter estimates (that is, the standard errors). The bias always causes the standard errors to be *under*estimated or (equivalently) the precision to be *over*estimated.

The other main reason why special techniques are required to deal with multilevel data is that the substantively interesting variables are observed at different hierarchical levels (for example, student achievement at the student level, teacher experience at the teacher level, and instructional quality at the classroom level). One way to investigate relations between variables observed at different levels is to aggregate all the variables to the highest level of observation (for example, the classroom or school-system level), but this typically entails loss of information because variability between lower-level units is not taken into account. Another way is to disaggregate all the variables to the lowest level of observation (for example, the student level) but this causes the number of observations and the statistical precision to be overestimated. Yet another way is to conduct a full-fledged multilevel analysis, which involves estimation of mixed-effects regression models of the kind introduced above.

Intuitively, a multilevel regression model may be thought of in the following way (a more complete presentation is given in Chapter 11). Once a random intercept of the kind defined in model (2) has been estimated, the α_{0i} random variable may be taken to be a dependent variable, the variation of which may be accounted for in a regression model with one or more independent variables. Suppose that we are investigating a set of schools and their students and that we capture the variation in school means with α_{0i}. We may then investigate how much of the variation in α_{0i} is accounted for by, for example, an aggregated measure of school SES and a measure of school climate as estimated by the principals. This model may then be fitted to data with general-purpose software that estimates mixed-effects regression models or with special programs for multilevel analysis (see Chapter 11). Such a model is sometimes referred to as an 'intercepts-as-outcomes' model, and this is a simple multilevel model that may be extended in many different ways.

Suppose then that within each of the schools, we regress student achievement on student SES using a mixed-effects approach in which we capture the distribution of within-school regression coefficients with a random variable (β_{1i}). Should the slope be shallow within some schools yet also steep within others then this is an interesting phenomenon that indicates that schools vary in the degree to which they support achievement for students with different SES. If we can then account for this variation with different school characteristics then this would be even more interesting. We can investigate this issue if we extend the multilevel model by also making β_{1i} a dependent variable, and estimating how much of the variation in the slopes can be accounted for by the two independent variables: school-level SES and school climate. Such a model is sometimes referred to as a 'slopes-as-outcomes' model.

The multilevel model may also be extended to encompass more than two levels. One possibility is to add, below the student level, another level that comprises observations at different time-points in a longitudinal design. We discuss this extension at greater length below. Another possibility is to extend the multilevel model by adding units at levels above the student, such as classroom, school and municipality levels.

Having introduced the challenges created by hierarchically nested layers of observation and multilevel modelling as a set of tools to meet these challenges, it is interesting to consider the advantages and disadvantages of the fixed-effects approach described above. One striking characteristic of the TIMSS example is that the analysis was conducted at the highest level of aggregation possible, namely the school-system level. As was pointed out above, aggregation may entail loss of precision and there is also suspicion that aggregation may be a source of bias. For example, Hanushek *et al.* (1996) observed that studies of effects of resources on student achievement tended to yield higher effect estimates when conducted with highly aggregated data (for example, state level rather than classroom level data). They argued that this is because aggregation magnifies omitted variable bias, and that the results that are obtained with highly aggregated data are therefore not to be trusted. However, it may also be observed that many of the mechanisms that generate omitted-variable bias are operating at lower levels within the school system. For example, compensatory resource allocation (which is a major source of omitted variable bias) typically operates at both the classroom and school levels (Lazear 2001). However, in data aggregated to higher levels, such as the school district or school system, no effects of the bias created by compensatory resource allocation at lower levels are seen (Wößmann and West 2006). Thus, the question of whether aggregation amplifies omitted variable bias or contributes to solving the aggregation bias problem seems to be an open one in need of further research. However, what is more important in this context is that with longitudinal designs, time-invariant omitted variables do not cause any bias, and to obtain this advantage individual-level longitudinal designs are not necessary. As has already been observed, many of the international studies of educational achievement are longitudinal at the school-system level, and within countries there are many data sets that are longitudinal at the school or school-district level. These aggregated longitudinal data sets form rich sources of information that are so far largely untapped by EER (Kyriakides and Creemers 2009).

It is of course not necessary to limit the analysis to the aggregated level. Even though a study may not be longitudinal at the individual, classroom or school level there may be reason to involve variables observed at these levels of observation in order to increase power and to study interactive effects. When this is done, the data will have a multilevel structure and it will be necessary to take into account the clustered nature of the observations. One way to do this is to use multilevel modelling and estimate full-fledged mixed-effects models. It is thus possible to extend the fixed-effects model (1) with data from students in schools and estimate a mixed-effects model. However, such models may be unnecessarily complex and, as was pointed out above, clustered data generally biases standard errors rather than parameter estimates themselves. In cases when we are not interested in micro-level relations, there is also an alternative approach to correct the standard errors for the underestimation caused by the clustering of data, namely to use what is called by programs 'clustering robust standard errors'. For example, this option is offered for the ordinary regression command in Stata and causes the clustering of the data to be taken into account when computing the standard errors.

Growth models

One approach to the analysis of longitudinal data that has gained much attention during the last couple of decades is growth curve modelling. This is partly due to the fact that over time, methods suitable for dealing with individual change, such as multilevel analysis, have increasingly become available. Another reason for this growing interest is that it has been realized that traditional methods for dealing with longitudinal data suffer from both conceptual and statistical limitations.

Growth modelling is fundamentally based on the idea of analysing change over time. However, one of the reasons that there was reluctance to adopt such approaches in educational and psychological research was that measures of change over time were viewed with suspicion. Much research had a focus on two waves of measurement, and within such designs a difference score was simply computed to measure this change. However, difference scores are also seen as problematic for psychometric reasons. For example, Cronbach and Furby (1970) argued in a classic paper that residual gain scores could be estimated, but that generally researchers are better advised to reformulate the research question so as to avoid change measures.

One of the problems with change scores is that they often have a low reliability. The reliability of difference scores are low when the correlation between the two waves is high, and vice versa. One problem with a low correlation between two waves of measurement is that this may indicate that the same construct is not measured. The problem with the reliability being inversely related to the amount of between-wave correlation is sometimes seen as a conflict between validity and reliability. However, Rogosa et al. (1982) noted that the correlation coefficient is a measure that expresses constancy of rank-ordering of individual differences and that it need not be relevant in the study of change. Thus, whether the variable being studied retains its meaning over time cannot be resolved by the value of the correlation between the two measures alone.

However, a main point made by Rogosa *et al.* (1982) was that to study change over time with precision, we need more than two time points and we need to analyse change within the framework of explicit models. They therefore proposed that a growth curve approach should be adopted to analyse change over time. Since this plea was made there has since been a virtual explosion of longitudinal research using such approaches, along with the development of analytic techniques and tools (Muthén 1997; Raudenbush and Bryk 2002; Singer and Willett 2003).

One frequently used approach to growth modelling is multilevel analysis. Suppose that we have administered an instrument measuring achievement at four different occasions one year apart to a group of persons. We may represent these data in such a way that for each individual, we plot the score for each of the four waves in a scatter diagram. In a further step we may (for each individual) compute a linear regression of achievement on wave of measurement (or time) to obtain one intercept parameter representing initial achievement and one slope parameter representing change over time. Thus, in this approach, we explicitly involve time as a variable in the analysis, and through using data from multiple waves of measurement, we can achieve a higher degree of stability in the parameter estimates than if we had used a simple difference score. We can also improve estimation by relying on data for all persons and use a mixed-effects model to estimate the mean and variance of the distributions of the parameters of the regression model rather then estimate the regression models individually. This means that we are adopting a multilevel approach where the individuals are at level two and the observations at the different time-points are at level one. This model can then be extended in many different ways, such as by adding level two variables representing antecedents and consequences of growth, and by adding further levels (for example, classrooms, schools, school district). If there are more than three waves of measurement, we may also consider using models other than the linear model for representing change over time, such as different kinds of curvilinear trends and functions.

One example of a multilevel growth model is de Fraine *et al.* (2005) who fitted several different models to a large longitudinal data set in which the development of well-being in school was investigated from grade 1 in secondary school (age 12) to grade 6. There were four occasions of measurement (grades 1, 2, 4 and 6) and the study included only those students who remained in the same school throughout the study. The sample originally comprised 3,788 students in 53 schools. Of these, 54 per cent participated at all four occasions, while the other students participated at one, two or three. However, the analysis included all students in the sample because the authors took advantage of the missing-data modelling capability of the multilevel model. In their investigation, several different models were fitted and were of two main types. One type was the growth approach, where different trajectories over time for the students were modelled. The other type was a fixed-effects approach, in which the different time-points were represented with dummy variables and in which there were random effects for students and schools. This approach, which was referred to as the 'multivariate approach', imposes no restrictions on the pattern of change over time for the students. We will here focus on the growth-model approach.

The favoured growth model was a three-level model. At the first level students' well-being was described as a quadratic function of time. By comparison, the second level described the variability in the individual growth curves, while the third level described differences between schools.

The fixed part of the model described the average growth trajectory by means of three parameters: the average intercept (β_0), the average linear growth parameter (β_1) and the average quadratic growth parameter (β_2). The trajectory of each individual was described by three parameters: a student-specific intercept (β_{0i}), a student-specific linear growth parameter (β_{1i}) and a student-specific quadratic growth parameter (β_{2i}). In addition, the model comprised student-specific residuals that were assumed to be generated by a trivariate normal distribution with an unrestricted covariance matrix.

The average growth curve indicated a continuous decline in the well-being of students from grade 1 to grade 6 but with a diminishing rate over time. However, the results also showed that there were large individual differences in both initial level of well-being and in the trajectories over time. Thus, for a majority of the students the growth trajectory had a linear decline, but some trajectories were characterized by a linear increase in well-being. Assessment of the fit of the quadratic growth curve model for individual students showed that it fitted well in many cases, but there were also students for whom the model did not seem to fit well at all. However, the limited number of observations for each student made it difficult to assess individual level fit. When the quadratic model was tested against the unrestricted model, it was also found to fit somewhat more poorly.

The amount of school variance for the intercept parameter was significant, but the parameter estimate was small, indicating that there was a small influence of school on student well-being. The parameter estimates for the linear and quadratic components at the school level were also small.

The model could have been extended with student-level characteristics specified as independent variables to account for the variation in student trajectories over time, but this was not a purpose of the study. Where differences in growth patterns are of interest as independent variables to account for other outcomes, it is also easy to envision research problems. However, the standard multilevel algorithms do not allow specification of growth models where parameters are used as independent variables.

Another way to estimate growth models is to set the model up as a latent growth model within the framework of SEM (Gustafsson 2004; Muthén 1997; Willett and Sayer 1994). With this approach, the problem is regarded as a multivariate problem, and the vector of observations from different points in time is modelled by specifying relations with latent variables that express intercepts, linear components, quadratic components and so on. These latent variables may be described as 'container' variables, which express characteristics of the random coefficients through their mean and variance. The SEM approach brings several advantages to growth modelling. One advantage is that it is possible to take advantage of the full range of SEM techniques for estimating models and evaluating their fit. Another advantage is that the SEM approach is very flexible and allows models to be specified where variables are both dependent and independent variables at the same time. This makes it possible to use latent variables that are part of the growth model both as independent and dependent variables in relation to other variables.

One example comes from Bub *et al.* (2007) who investigated change in internalizing and externalizing behaviour problems from 24 months of age to school start at age six and studied relations between the trajectories of behaviour problems and cognitive variables in grade 1. The original sample consisted of 1,364 children and families, and of these, 882 children had complete data. The analysis was restricted to the latter group even though it would have been possible to include all cases through using the missing data techniques implemented in current SEM programs (such as Amos, LISREL and Mplus). The children were assessed at five different time points, with scales capturing internalizing and externalizing behaviour problems, and in grade 1 tests were administered measuring cognitive abilities and school achievement. Linear growth models were fitted separately to the scales measuring internalizing and externalizing behaviour problems, and the intercept and slope parameters of these models were related to cognitive ability and achievement in grade 1. The intercept parameters for internalizing and externalizing behaviour problems were both significantly negatively related to the level of cognitive performance in grade 1. In contrast, the slope parameter for internalizing problems was related to cognitive performance showing that children with increases in the amount of behaviour problems between 24 months and grade 1 had lower cognitive abilities in grade 1.

Structural models

In the example presented above, SEM was used to estimate a growth model, and it is easily demonstrated that when these can be estimated by software both for multilevel regression analysis and for SEM, identical results are achieved (de Fraine *et al.* 2007). However, these two approaches also have their unique advantages. For example, with multilevel regression it is, in principle at least, possible to specify models with an unlimited number of levels, and it also is possible to set up so called cross-classified models that take into account changing group membership over time. In comparison, SEM allows models in which variables have the double role of being both dependent and independent variables, which makes it possible to set up chains of variables influencing each other in direct and indirect fashions (allowing for tests of hypotheses of mediation). Such models must be formulated on the basis of substantive theory, previous results and knowledge about the nature of the empirical data. In this context, longitudinal data is also a great asset because knowledge about the time ordering of variables is important in specifying directions of influence among variables. Another great advantage of SEM is that multiple fallible observed variables may be used as indicators of a limited set of latent variables, which allows for a parsimonious analysis of variables that are typically closer to the theoretical constructs under investigation than are the observed variables.

As has already been observed, SEM may be used to estimate growth models and several other types of models for investigating change over time (see Chapter 12 for an extended presentation). However, there are also other SEM models that have classically been used to analyse longitudinal data. The most important among these are different kinds of autoregressive models in which a variable is regressed upon an earlier measurement of itself. For example, suppose that we have measured achievement at four different time points (y_1, . . ., y_4). Such a univariate series of repeated measures often results in what is called a simplex model (Jöreskog 1970). Simplex models can easily be estimated, and under certain assumptions it also is possible to estimate the amount of error variance in each of the measures (see Figure 5.1).

A bivariate series of repeated measures typically requires a model with both autoregressive and cross-lagged relations, as shown in Figure 5.2.

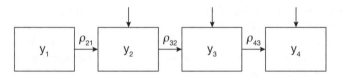

Figure 5.1 An autoregressive model for repeated measures

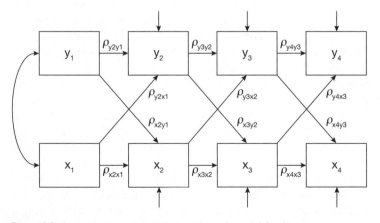

Figure 5.2 An autoregressive and cross-lagged model for bivariate measures

Such cross-lagged panel models have attracted quite a lot of attention in research aiming to determine the relative importance of mutually influencing factors. For example, it has been shown that school achievement influences academic self-concept positively and vice versa. These results provide the basis for what has been called the 'reciprocal effects model', which argues that two factors are reciprocally related and mutually reinforcing (Marsh *et al.* 2002). Attempts also have been made to determine if either of the two directions of influence is stronger than the other, but no consistent results have been found.

However useful the models, SEM has also faced criticism. For example, the autoregressive approach has been criticized in comparison with growth curve approaches (Rogosa and Willett 1985) where it has been observed that the model focuses on variances and covariances, while means are typically not included. Another criticism is that even though multiple waves of measurement may be dealt with, the autoregressive model basically focuses on change between any two points in time. Yet another problem is that change that does not affect rank ordering of individuals can typically not be captured with the autoregressive approach.

However, in spite of these criticisms it may be noted that there are many longitudinal research problems for which the autoregressive approach is well suited, and the growth curve and autoregressive approaches may be regarded as complementary rather than conflicting (Bollen and Curran 2004). One example of an interesting application of the autoregressive approach is in a study by Francis *et al.* (1989), the aim of which was to investigate changes in the relationship of verbal and non-verbal skills to reading ability in kindergarten, second grade and fifth grade. The subjects were 220 boys who at the three occasions were given a battery of tests designed to measure verbal and non-verbal abilities, while at second and fifth grades reading achievement was also measured. An autoregressive model was then fitted to these data, as shown in Figure 5.3.

At each of the three occasions, latent variables representing non-verbal (NV) abilities and verbal (VS) abilities were specified from three indicators. The autoregressive relations over time for these abilities were close to 0.90 for NV and higher than 0.95 for VS. The kindergarten measures of VS and NV both predicted second grade reading achievement, VS being the somewhat stronger predictor. However, fifth grade reading achievement was only predicted by second grade reading achievement and VS, there being no relation to NV. Thus, these patterns of relations gave evidence of important changes over time in the roles of verbal and non-verbal abilities in the development of early reading skills.

In combining the approaches of SEM and multilevel modelling, it must be noted that traditionally SEM has assumed independently sampled observations and so the basic model is not appropriate for dealing with multilevel data. However, Muthén (1989, 1997) has extended the basic model into a two-level model, which can analyse variability between groups in one model and variability among individuals within groups in another model. This is done through decomposing the total covariance matrix into one between-level and one

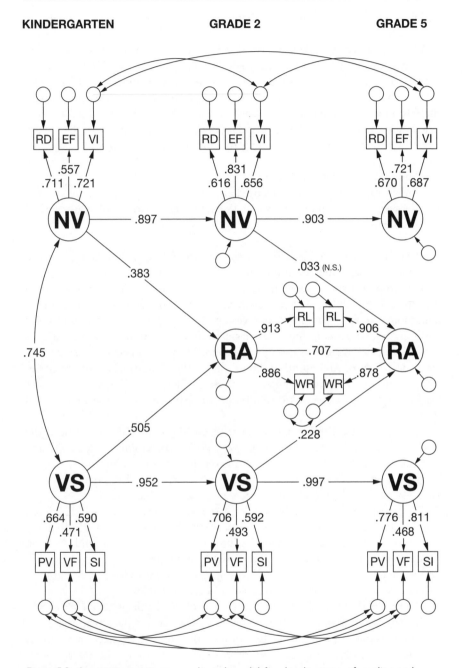

Figure 5.3 An autoregressive, cross-lagged model for development of reading and cognitive abilities

Source: Francis *et al.* 1989

within-level matrix to which the between- and the within-level models are simultaneously fitted.

We present here a study using two-level SEM to investigate effects of teacher content knowledge (CK) and pedagogical content knowledge (PCK) in mathematics on quality of teaching and student progress (Baumert *et al.* in press). This study is based on previous work designed to conceptualize and measure the CK and PCK dimensions by Krauss *et al.* (2008). CK was conceptualized as a profound mathematical understanding of the curricular content to be taught, while PCK was defined as comprising three different dimensions:

- knowledge of mathematical tasks as instructional tools;
- knowledge of students' thinking and assessment of understanding;
- knowledge of multiple representations and explanations of mathematical problems.

Confirmatory Factor Analysis (CFA) showed the CK and PCK dimensions to be empirically separable, even though they were highly correlated.

This empirical study was conducted as an extension of the German part of the 2003 PISA study, which transformed the cross-sectional design into a longitudinal design spanning a one-year period. At the end of the ninth and tenth grades, students in the PISA classes were administered achievement tests as well as questionnaires assessing background data and aspects of their mathematics instruction. Among other things, the mathematics teachers of the classes were administered tests designed to measure CK and PCK. A total of 181 teachers with 194 classes and 4,353 students participated in the longitudinal study.

In order to assess the quality of instruction, the tests and examinations the teachers had set in the school year were coded for cognitive demands and curricular level. The students were also asked to rate the amount of individual learning support on six different scales. Both students and teachers also were asked to rate the degree of effectiveness of classroom instruction.

The two-level latent variable model was mainly focused on the class level. The model controlled for selective intake to the classes, with ninth grade achievement being measured and the influence of teachers' CK and PCK on learning outcomes at the class level in the tenth grade being investigated. Furthermore, models were fitted to investigate the extent to which CK and PCK effects were mediated by the instructional quality variables.

The results showed that both teacher CK and PCK influenced the class-level mathematical progress but that the effect of PCK was stronger than the effect of CK. The mediation models also showed that the PCK effect came about because PCK influenced the level of cognitive activation, the instructional alignment with the curriculum and the individual learning support. By contrast, the mediation model did not apply to CK. However, Baumert *et al.* (in press) argued that these results should not be interpreted as showing that CK is unimportant or that lack of CK can be compensated for by an increased emphasis on PCK in teacher training. Instead, they concluded that CK may be regarded as a necessary but not sufficient condition for development of PCK.

Conclusions

As is described in Chapters 1 and 2, EER is currently in a phase in which the development of theoretical models aiming to explain the intricate relations among different levels and components of the educational system has a high level of priority. This cannot be completed unless the dynamic and changing nature of educational phenomena are adequately captured, and it also requires insight into the fundamental causal mechanisms of educational systems. In turn, this makes it necessary to adopt longitudinal research as one of the main approaches in EER.

As we have seen in this chapter, there are a wide variety of designs that may be regarded as belonging to the longitudinal category, including designs in which schools and educational systems are followed over time rather than individual students. Given that there are large numbers of high-quality databases with such information and that have often been created for administrative purposes rather than for the purposes of research, these may prove to be a valuable asset for the field of EER. It is, however, a great challenge to analyse such data in such a way that the relationships are properly teased out. Several of the examples presented in this chapter have, however, demonstrated that this can be done.

Not only are existing databases an important source of information, but research studies designed to provide knowledge about different research problems are even more important. Even though the challenges involved in conducting longitudinal research are typically greater than those involved in conducting cross-sectional research, it would seem that the amount and quality of information that may be obtained with the longitudinal designs makes the extra effort worthwhile. The insights into how longitudinal studies should be designed to provide maximum information have also increased as a function of the increasing sophistication in analysing longitudinal data. Of particular importance in this context is the recognition that development over time should be analysed with explicit models and that observations at several time points is often needed to get sufficient information about the patterns of change.

References

Antoniou, P. (2009) 'Using the dynamic model of educational effectiveness to improve teaching practice: Building an evaluation model to test the impact of teacher professional development programs', unpublished doctoral dissertation, University of Cyprus, Cyprus.

Baumert, J., Kunter, M., Blum, W., Brunner, M., Dubberke, T., Jordan, A., Klusman, U., Krauss, S., Neubrand, M. and Tsai, Y-M. (in press) 'Teachers' mathematical knowledge, cognitive activation in the classroom, and student progress', *American Educational Research Journal*.

Beaton, A.E., Mullis, I.V.S., Martin, M.O., Gonzalez, E.J., Kelly, D.L. and Smith, T.A. (1996) *Mathematics achievement in the middle school years: IEA's Third International Mathematics and Science Study*, Chestnut Hill, MA: Boston College, TIMSS International Study Centre.

Bickel, J. (2007) *Multilevel analysis for applied research: It's just regression!*, New York: The Guildford Press.

Bollen, K.A. and Curran, P.J. (2004) 'Autoregressive Latent Trajectory (ALT) models: A synthesis of two traditions', *Sociological Methods and Research*, 32(3): 336–83.

Bub, K.L., McCartney, K. and Willett, J.B. (2007) 'Behavior problem trajectories and first grade cognitive ability and achievement skills: A latent growth curve analysis', *Journal of Educational Psychology*, 99: 653–70.

Cohen, J., Cohen, P., West, S.G. and Aiken, L.S. (2003) *Applied multiple regression/ correlation analysis for the behavioral sciences*, 3rd edn, Mahwah, NJ: Lawrence Erlbaum Associates.

Cronbach, L.J. and Furby, L. (1970) 'How should we measure "change" – or should we?', *Psychological Bulletin*, 74: 68–80.

de Fraine, B., van Landeghem, G., Van Damme, J. and Onghena, P. (2005) 'An analysis of well-being in secondary school with multilevel growth curve models and multilevel multivariate models', *Quality and Quantity*, 39(3): 297–316.

de Fraine, B., Van Damme, J. and Onghena, P. (2007) 'A longitudinal analysis of gender differences in academic self–concept and language achievement: A multivariate multilevel latent growth approach', *Contemporary Educational Psychology*, 32(1): 132–50.

Demetriou, D. (2009) 'Using the dynamic model to improve educational practice', unpublished doctoral dissertation, University of Cyprus, Cyprus.

Francis, D.J., Fletcher, J.M., Maxwell, S.E. and Satz, P. (1989) 'A structural model for developmental changes in the determinants of reading achievement', *Journal of Clinical Child Psychology*, 18(1): 44–51.

Gustafsson, J.-E. (2004) 'Modelling individual differences in change through latent variable growth and mixture growth modelling: Basic principles and empirical examples', in A. Demetriou and A. Raftopolous (eds) *Emergence and transformations in the mind*, New York: Cambridge University Press, pp. 379–402.

Gustafsson, J.-E. (2007) 'Understanding causal influences on educational achievement through analysis of differences over time within countries', in T. Loveless (ed.) *Lessons learned: What international assessments tell us about math achievement*, Washington, DC: The Brookings Institution, pp. 37–63.

Hanushek, E.A., Rivkin, S.G. and Taylor, L.L. (1996) 'Aggregation and the estimated effects of school resources', *The Review of Economics and Statistics*, 78(4): 611–27.

Jöreskog, K.G. (1970) 'Estimation and testing of simplex models', *British Journal of Mathematical and Statistical Psychology*, 23: 121–45.

Keeves, J. (1988) 'Longitudinal designs', in J. Keeves (ed.) *Educational research, methodology and measurement: An international handbook*, Oxford: Pergamon Press.

Krauss, S., Brunner, M., Kunter, M., Baumert, Blum, W., Neubrand, M. and Jordan, A. (2008) 'Pedagogical content knowledge and content knowledge of secondary mathematics teachers', *Journal of Educational Psychology*, 100(3): 716–25.

Kyriakides, L. and Creemers, B.P.M. (2009) 'Explaining stability and changes in schools: A follow-up study testing the validity of the dynamic model', paper presented at the EARLI Conference, Amsterdam.

Lazear, E.P. (2001) 'Educational production', *Quarterly Journal of Economics*, 116(3): 777–803.

Marsh, H.W., Kong, C.K. and Hau, K.T. (2002) 'Multilevel causal ordering of academic self-concept and achievement: Influence of language of instruction (English vs. Chinese) for Hong Kong students', *American Educational Research Journal*, 39: 727–63.

McCaffrey, D.F., Lockwood, J.R., Koretz, D.M., Louis, T.A. and Hamilton, L. (2004) 'Models for value-added modelling of teacher effects', *Journal of Educational and Behavioral Statistics*, 29(1): 67–101.

Mullis, I., Campbell, J. and Farstrup, A. (1993) *NAEP 1992 Reading Report Card for the Nation and the States*, Washington, DC: National Centre for Education Statistics.

Muthén, B. (1989) 'Latent variable modelling in heterogeneous populations', *Psychometrika*, 54: 557–85.

Muthén, B. (1997) 'Latent variable modelling with longitudinal and multilevel data', in Raftery (ed.) *Sociological methodology*, Boston: Blackwell Publishers, pp. 453–80.

OECD (2008) *Measuring improvements in learning outcomes: Best practices to assess the value-added by schools*, Paris: OECD publishing.

Raudenbush, S.W. and Bryk, A.S. (2002) *Hierarchical linear models: Applications and data analysis methods*, 2nd edn, Newbury Park, CA: Sage Publications.

Rogosa, D.R., Brandt, D. and Zimowski, M. (1982) 'A growth curve approach to the measurement of change', *Psychological Bulletin*, 92(3): 726–48.

Rogosa, D. and Willett, J.B. (1985) 'Satisfying a simplex structure is simpler than it should be', *Journal of Educational and Behavioral Statistics*, 10(2): 99–107.

Schafer, J.L. and Graham, J.W. (2002) 'Missing data: Our view of the state of the art', *Psychological Methods*, 7(2): 147–77.

Singer, J.D. and Willett, J.B. (2003) *Applied longitudinal data analysis: Modeling change and event occurrence*, New York: Oxford University Press.

Sund, K. (2009) 'Estimating peer effects in Swedish high school using school, teacher, and student fixed effects', *Economics of Education Review*, 28: 329–36.

Willett, J.B. and Sayer, A.G. (1994) 'Using covariance structure analysis to detect correlates and predictors of change', *Psychological Bulletin*, 116: 363–81.

Wößmann, L. and West, M. (2006) 'Class-size effects in school systems around the world: Evidence from between-grade variation in TIMSS', *European Economic Review*, 50(3): 695–736.

Chapter 6

Experimental studies in education

Robert E. Slavin

Johns Hopkins University and University of York

Throughout the twentieth century, in fields such as medicine, agriculture, transportation and technology, processes of development, rigorous evaluation and dissemination have produced a pace of innovation and improvement that is unprecedented in history (Shavelson and Towne 2002). These innovations have transformed the world. Yet education has failed to embrace this dynamic, and as a result, education moves from fad to fad. Educational practice does change over time, but the change process more resembles the pendulum swings of taste characteristic of art or fashion rather than the progressive improvements characteristic of science and technology (Slavin 1989, 2003).

At the dawn of the twenty-first century, education is finally being dragged into the twentieth century. The scientific revolution that utterly transformed medicine, agriculture, transportation, technology and other fields early in the twentieth century almost completely bypassed the field of education. It is not that we have not learned anything about effective education. It is rather that applications of the findings of educational research, and especially of EER, remain haphazard, and that evidence is respected only occasionally, and only if it happens to correspond to current educational or political fashions.

Early in the twentieth century, the practice of medicine was at a similar point. For example, research had long since identified the importance of bacteria in disease, and by 1865 Joseph Lister had demonstrated the effectiveness of antiseptic procedures in surgery. In the 1890s, William Halsted at Johns Hopkins University introduced rubber gloves, gauze masks and steam sterilization of surgical instruments, and demonstrated the effectiveness of these procedures. Yet it took thirty years to convince tradition-bound physicians to use sterile procedures. If he dropped his scalpel, a physician in 1910 was as likely as not to give it a quick wipe and carry on.

Today, of course, the linkage between research and practice in medicine is so tight that no physician would dream of ignoring the findings of rigorous research. Because medical practice is so closely based on medical research, funding for medical research is vast, and advances in medicine take place at breathtaking speed.

The most important reason for the extraordinary advances in medicine, agriculture and other fields is the acceptance by practitioners of evidence as the basis for practice. In particular, it is the randomized clinical trial more than any single medical breakthrough that has transformed medicine (Doll 1998). In a randomized clinical trial, patients are assigned at random to receive one treatment or another, such as a drug or a placebo. Because of random assignment, it can be assumed with an adequate number of subjects that any differences seen in outcomes are due to the treatment, not to any extraneous factors (see Chapter 3 for more on the establishment of causality). Replicated experiments of this kind can establish beyond any reasonable doubt the effectiveness (or lack thereof) of treatments intended for applied use (Boruch 1997).

Experiments in education

In education, experiments are not uncommon, but they are usually brief, artificial experiments on topics of theoretical more than practical interest, often involving hapless college sophomores. Far rarer are experiments evaluating treatments of practical interest studied over a full school year or more. I write an educational psychology textbook (Slavin 2009) that is full of research findings of all kinds, findings that are valuable in advancing theory and potentially valuable to teachers in understanding their craft. Yet the brief experiments, correlational studies and descriptive studies that yield most of the information presented in any educational psychology text do not collectively add up to school reform. They are suggestions about how to think about daily teaching problems, not guides to the larger questions educators and policymakers must answer. Imagine that research in cardiology described heart function and carried out small-scale laboratory studies, but never developed and tested an artificial heart valve. Imagine that agricultural research studied plant growth and diseases, but never developed and tested new disease-resistant crops. Educational research has produced many rigorous and meaningful studies of basic principles of practice, but few rigorous studies of programmes and practices that could serve as a solid base for policy and practice, and has had little respect for the studies of this kind that do exist. Because of this, policymakers have rarely seen the relevance of research to the decisions they have to make and therefore have provided minimal funding for research. This has led to a declining spiral, as inadequate investments in research lead to a dearth of the kind of large-scale, definitive research that policymakers would feel to be valuable, making these policymakers unwilling to invest in large-scale, definitive research.

Shifting policy perspectives

Changes in federal education policies in the United States could potentially reverse this declining spiral. New funding is flowing into experimental research. If this produces some notable successes, we could have an ascending spiral:

rigorous research demonstrating positive effects of replicable programmes on important student outcomes would lead to increasing funding for such research, which could then lead to more and better research and therefore more funding. More importantly, millions of children would benefit. Once we establish replicable paradigms for development, rigorous evaluation, replication and dissemination, these mechanisms could be applied to any educational intervention or policy. Imagine that there were initiatives under way all the time to develop, evaluate and disseminate new programmes in every subject and every grade level, as well as programmes on school-to-work transitions, special education, gifted programmes, dropout prevention, programmes for English language learners, race-relations programmes, drug abuse prevention, violence prevention and so on. Every one of these areas lends itself to a development–evaluation–dissemination paradigm, as would many more. Over time, each area would likely experience the step-by-step, irreversible progress characteristic of medicine and agriculture, because innovations would be held to strict standards of evaluation before being recommended for wide scale use.

Research designs

The scientific revolution in education will only take hold and produce its desired effects if research in fact begins to focus on replicable programmes and practices central to education policy and teaching, and if it in fact employs research methods that meet the highest standards of rigour.

This begs an important question: what kinds of research are necessary to produce findings of sufficient rigour to justify faith in the meaning of their outcomes?

Of course, all sorts of research designs are appropriate for various purposes, from description to theory building to hypothesis testing. However, many educational researchers throughout the world (Angrist 2004) have been arguing that nothing less than *randomized* experiments will do for evaluations of educational interventions and policies. When we want to know the outcome of choosing programme X instead of programme Y, there is no substitute for a randomized experiment.

Randomized experiments

The difference in the value of randomized and well-matched experiments relates primarily to the problem of selection bias. In a matched experiment, it is always possible that observed differences are due not to treatments, but to the fact that one set of schools or teachers was willing to implement a given treatment while another was not, or that a given set of students selected themselves or were selected into a given treatment while others were not (see also Chapter 3).

When selection bias is a possibility at the student level, there are few if any alternatives to random assignment, because unmeasured (often, unmeasurable) pre-existing differences are highly likely to be alternative explanations for study findings. For example, consider studies of after-school or summer-school programmes. If a researcher simply compared students attending such programmes to those not attending who were similar in pre-test scores or demographic factors, it is very likely that unmeasured factors such as student motivation, parental support for education or other consequential factors could explain any gains observed, because the more motivated children are more likely to show up. Similarly, studies comparing children assigned to gifted or special education programmes to students with similar pre-test scores are likely to miss key selection factors that were known to whoever assigned the students but not measured. If one child with an IQ of 130 is assigned to a gifted programme and another with the same IQ is not, it is likely that the children differ in motivation, conscientiousness or other factors. In these kinds of situations, use of random assignment from within a selected pool is essential.

In contrast, there are situations in which it is teachers or schools or local educational authorities that elect to implement a given treatment, but there is no selection bias that relates to the children. For example, a researcher might want to compare the achievement gains of children in classes using co-operative learning, or schools using comprehensive reform models, to the gains made by control groups. In such cases, random assignment of willing teachers or schools is still far preferable to matching, as matching leaves open the possibility that volunteer teachers or staffs are better than non-volunteers. However, the likely bias is much less than in the case of student self-selection. Aggregate pre-test scores in an entire school, for example, would indicate how effective the current staff has been up to the present, so controlling for pre-tests in matched studies of existing schools or classes controls out much of the potential impact of having more willing teachers.

In practice, it is the case that in a wide range of educational experiments, effect sizes for randomized experiments are very similar to those for large, well-matched quasi-experiments (Slavin and Smith 2008; Cook *et al.* 2008). Randomized experiments are still preferable, but it is important to be aware that other alternatives can produce similar findings.

The importance of this discussion lies in the fact that randomized experiments of interventions applied to entire classrooms can be difficult and expensive to do, and are sometimes impossible. Sometimes a randomized experiment is no more difficult than a matched one, but in many cases the cost of doing one randomized study can be two or three times that of an equally large-scale matched study. It is at least arguable that replicated matched studies, done by different investigators in different places, might produce more valid and meaningful results than one definitive, once-in-a-lifetime randomized study.

In Chapter 3, various difficulties of conducting randomized experiments were discussed. However, it is advocated that in most areas of policy-relevant programme evaluation, and whenever they are possible, randomized experiments should be used. Beyond the benefits for reducing selection bias, there is an important *political* reason to prefer randomized over matched studies at this point in history. Because of political developments in the US, we have an opportunity to reverse the 'awful reputation' that educational research has among policymakers (Kaestle 1993; Lagemann 2002). Over the longer run, I believe that a mix of randomized and rigorous matched experiments evaluating educational interventions may be healthier than a steady diet of randomized experiments, but right now we need to establish the highest possible standard of evidence – on a par with standards in other fields – to demonstrate what educational effectiveness research can accomplish.

Is random assignment feasible in Educational Effectiveness Research?

Having said that randomized designs are desirable, are they feasible? The fact is, educators, parents and students hate to be assigned at random. It goes against human nature. Therefore, incentives are usually needed. Randomized experiments can only be used when a treatment can be assigned to schools, teachers or students who have not had it before, so treatments in randomized studies are always in their first year, a serious problem if the treatments are difficult to implement or take time to work. Further, education has one characteristic that makes random assignment very difficult: students are usually taught in groups. Unlike other human service fields, such as medicine, social services and clinical psychology, education takes place in schools to which it is rarely possible to randomly assign children.

In designing randomized experiments, there are several characteristics of samples, treatments and theories of action that facilitate or rule out particular designs. In particular, answers to the following seven key desiderata largely determine what design to choose (or whether randomization is practical at all):

I WHAT IS THE UNIT OF INTERVENTION?

The unit of intervention is a major factor in research design. For statistical analysis, a rule of thumb might be that with a good pre-test, a sample size of about 100 experimental and 100 control children is necessary to find a significant difference with an effect size of 0.20 (20 per cent of a standard deviation), often thought of as the lower bound for educational significance. Because aggregate scores are more stable than individual ones, a sample size of, say, 25 experimental and 25 control schools or classrooms might be needed to find the same effect size. However, it is usually far easier to find 200 *children* than to find 50 *schools* or *classrooms* (50 schools might involve 25,000 to 100,000 children!). For this reason, a randomized study of one-to-one tutoring, after-school programmes or gifted programmes, in which children can (in principle) be assigned one at a time to one treatment or another, may be much easier to do than one in which the classroom or teacher is the unit of intervention, or (worse yet) where the school is the unit of intervention.

Implied in this discussion is the important principle that the level of random assignment should dictate the level of analysis. The principle is frequently violated and is in fact more important in some circumstances than in others, but clearly a study in which, say, just one school is 'randomly' assigned to treatment A while another is randomly assigned to treatment B cannot be considered a valid randomized experiment, because treatment would be completely confounded with characteristics of the schools.

2 HOW LONG IS THE INTERVENTION?

If a planned intervention is expected to show its effects in one academic year or less, a powerful design element can be introduced: a delayed treatment control. That is, a group of students, teachers or schools might be invited to implement a given treatment, with an understanding that they have a 50–50 chance of receiving the treatment now or (say) in the next school year. The next-year group serves as a control group this year. There are two major advantages to this. First, all participants are equally (and positively) motivated to participate. The only necessary 'incentive' is the treatment itself. Further, the control group is likely to be motivated to participate in testing and to have a stake in the entire process. Also, sometimes it is possible to have the delayed treatment group, in the year it receives the treatment, serve as an experimental group in a matched (non-randomized) experiment.

However, some treatments only make sense over multiple years, and few participants would be willing to wait that long for their delayed treatment.

3 IS THERE EXCESS DEMAND FOR THE INTERVENTION? (FOR EXAMPLE, IS THERE A WAITING LIST?)

It is enormously helpful in randomized experiments in education to have an ongoing service or programme that is so sought after that there is an extensive waiting list. For example, imagine that a school district has a very popular technology magnet school and wants to evaluate it. Because it is a magnet school, selection artifacts make a matched study out of the question (because there is no way to match students who went to the trouble of applying to a magnet school with those who did not). Yet instead of 'first come, first served' or some sort of test or application, the district could decide to select randomly from the pool of qualified applicants. Willingness to participate in testing could be a criterion for having an opportunity to be selected. This type of design has been used, for example, in studies of vouchers, where children who applied for vouchers to attend private schools were randomly selected to receive them or not, but could not even be considered unless they agreed to participate in the study.

4 IS THERE LIKELY TO BE A SPILLOVER EFFECT FROM THE TREATMENT?

A very efficient design in educational research is one in which children are randomly assigned to classes within a school, or where teachers or classes are randomly assigned. However, designs of this type cannot be used when it is likely that teachers within a school will exchange ideas and materials, so that the 'control' group might be implementing parts of the experimental programme. This is called the 'spillover' effect. In contrast, consider the Tennessee class-size experiment (Finn and Achilles 1999). Children were individually assigned to large or small classes, or to large classes with an aide. In this case, there was little reason to worry that the large-class teachers would get ideas or 'small classness' from the small-class teachers.

Sometimes spillover effects can be minimized in within-school designs by taking advantage of organization or spatial features of schools. For example, middle schools are often organized in separate 'houses', so treatments randomly assigned to one house or another may cause less contamination than would be likely in other circumstances. Multi-track year-round schools often have different, self-contained 'tracks' to which students may be assigned at random (Chambers et al. 2008, for an example).

While the possibility of spillover is always there in within-school designs, it at least tends to work against finding experimental–control differences. In experimental design, it is essential that any potential design flaws be conservative; ones that might enhance experimental–control differences are to be avoided particularly.

5 DO TEACHERS HAVE MULTIPLE CLASSES?

One very efficient design, if it makes sense, involves randomly assigning classes taught by the same teachers. For example, if secondary teachers teach several mathematics classes each day, each might randomly assign some classes to one treatment or another. The problem of 'spillover' is great with this design, but it can work if the treatment is a resource or set of materials difficult to transport from one class to another. For example, a study of the use of technology could work with the same teachers, teaching technology and no-technology classes, because it is unlikely that they would sneak computers into their control classes. If the treatment is intended to affect teachers' ideas or teaching strategies, this design is not appropriate, however, because ideas are sure to affect teachers in all of their classes.

6 IS THE TREATMENT EXPENSIVE?

Obviously, if the treatment is very expensive, providing it for free to a delayed-treatment group may be impractical. However, there is also a problem in not providing something to the control group, as it may be that the provision of resources, not the treatment itself, could account for any effects observed. When a delayed-treatment control group is impossible, researchers often give control schools cash or other resources to make up for the lack of the treatment.

7 TO WHAT SHOULD THE EXPERIMENTAL GROUP BE COMPARED?

In education, a control group is rarely receiving 'no treatment.' As long as children are in school, they are receiving a treatment. This treatment might just be 'traditional instruction', but what does that mean in practice?

The question of what the control group should be depends on the questions being asked in the experiment. Most often, in a study of a large-scale, practical intervention, the researchers want to know what the experimental group would have experienced had the experiment not taken place. This means that some classes might be using alternative programmes and some might be doing nothing in particular. The researchers should study and describe what the comparison groups did, but might not want to affect it in any way. Alternatively, researchers might want to have a more conceptually 'pure' comparison. They often compare treatments both to a business-as-usual group and to an alternative treatment. For example, many years ago I did an experiment in which teachers were randomly assigned to use a form of co-operative learning or a treatment that used an identical schedule of teaching, practice and assessment (without co-operative groups) that I called 'focused instruction' (Slavin 1980). This treatment standardized the comparison with the co-operative learning group, so that the only differential factor was co-operative learning itself. I also included a matched external 'business as usual' control group. To my surprise, while the co-operative learning group made the greatest gains, the 'focused instruction' group also did very well in comparison to the untreated control group. The focused instruction treatment could be thought of as an antidote to a Hawthorne Effect (because those teachers were also in an experimental group), but more likely there were elements in both the co-operative learning and the focused instruction groups that were genuinely effective, such as a clear focus on well-specified instructional objectives. The larger point here is that both the focused-instruction control and the untreated control were appropriate, but outcomes for each comparison had different meanings. The comparison with the untreated group told educators and researchers how much gain to expect if they implemented the entire co-operative learning package. The focused-instruction comparison told educators and researchers how much of that gain was uniquely due to co-operative learning itself.

Based on these seven desiderata, it is possible to describe generic designs for randomized experiments, as follows:

- **Delayed treatment control**
  Students, classes or schools are assigned at random to immediate and delayed intervention conditions. The delayed group serves as the control group during the experiment, and then receives its training and materials (for

example) at the end of the formal experiment. This works whenever the treatment duration is not longer than the delayed group's patience would permit, and when there is little interest in long-term or lasting effects.

An important variation of delayed treatment is a 'waiting list control', when more students or schools want a given programme than can have it. In this case, students or schools can be randomly assigned to receive a treatment now or go on a waiting list (and agree to be tested while they are waiting), knowing that they will get the treatment within a reasonable time period.

- **Within-school/within-teacher comparisons**
  Students or classes are randomly assigned to experimental or control groups within a given school, or, in departmentalized schools, a given teacher's classes could be randomly assigned. This design is appropriate only if spillover is unlikely (that is, the treatment is not likely to affect the control classes).

- **Random assignment of individuals**
  Individual students can be randomly assigned to one treatment or another. This is most possible when the treatment is given to individuals (for example, tutoring) or where a service is inherently limited to some but not all students (for example, summer school).

- **Alternative treatment comparison**
  A variation possible with all designs is provision of a specific alternative treatment as a comparison to an experimental group, rather than a comparison to 'traditional instruction'.

When are matched experiments 'close enough'?

Of course, there are circumstances in which it is not practical to do randomized experiments on important interventions. For example, early in their development, few interventions are operating at a large enough scale, or have enough training capacity, to carry out a randomized experiment of sufficient size. Because of the need either to provide intervention at no cost to participants or to provide incentives, randomized experiments can be very expensive. Sometimes it is unethical or illegal to withhold treatments to which students are entitled, as in the case of special education or Title I services, making randomized experiments impossible.

Conceptually, matched studies cannot completely rule out the possibility of selection bias. Schools using a given intervention are likely to be more motivated, cohesive or have more resources to spend than other, similar schools, or contrarily, they may be more desperate. Besides the obvious possibilities for selection bias, any number of less obvious biases could operate. Yet there are clearly ways to reduce bias and to have matched studies approach the 'gold standard' of randomization even if they can never reach it.

One key requirement for a quality matched study is to have a close match on key variables from within an underlying similar population. For example, if you have a study with ten low-achieving schools using a given programme and ten matched schools of very similar demographics and prior test scores, the results are likely to resemble those of a randomized experiment (Slavin and Smith 2008). If you tried to match the ten lowest-achieving schools in a high achieving district to the highest-achieving schools in a low-achieving district, this would not be legitimate, as the two sets of schools are from distributions with underlying population means that are very different. They would tend to regress to different means, and would not be equivalent in terms of their local standings and reputations, among other things. In addition, it is critical that the matching criterion is as highly correlated as possible with the post-test. For example, matching on free-lunch count in a study of achievement is not as good as matching on pre-tests, preferably the same test as the one used as the post-test. Finally, it is important to reduce selection bias as much as possible by choosing as controls similar schools that could not have selected the treatment rather than those that had the option to do so but declined. Providing alternative treatments (such as 'focused instruction') may also help, as the controls at least had to be willing to implement something.

Non-experimental research

Forms of research other than experiments, whether randomized or matched, can also be of great value. Correlational and descriptive research are essential in theory building and in suggesting variables worthy of inclusion in experiments. Our 'Success for All' comprehensive reform programme, for example, owes a great deal to correlational and descriptive process–product studies of the 1970s and 1980s (Slavin et al. 2009). As components of experiments, correlational and descriptive studies can also be essential in exploring variables that go beyond overall programme effects. In some policy contexts, experiments are impossible, and well-designed correlational or descriptive studies or longitudinal studies may be sufficient (see also Chapters 3 and 5).

The experiment, however, is the design of choice for studies that seek to make causal conclusions, and particularly for evaluations of educational innovations.

Basing educational policy on evidence

Historically, the impact of education research on education practice has been tenuous at best. Innovation takes place, but it is based on fads and politics rather than evidence. At best, education policies are said to be 'based on' scientific evidence, but are rarely scientifically evaluated. This distinction is critical. The fact that a programme is based on scientific research does not mean that it is, in fact, effective. For example, imagine an instructional programme whose materials are thoroughly based on scientific research, but that is so difficult to implement that, in practice, teachers do a poor job of it, or that is so boring that students do not pay attention, or that provides so little or such poor professional development that teachers do not change their instructional practices. Before the Wright brothers, many inventors launched airplanes that were based on exactly the same 'scientifically based aviation research' as the Wright brothers used at Kitty Hawk, but the other airplanes never got off the ground. Worse, any programme or policy can find some research somewhere that suggests it might work.

Given the current state of research on replicable programmes in education, it would be difficult to require that government funds be limited to programmes that have been rigorously evaluated, because there are so few such programmes. However, programmes that do have strong, rigorous evidence of effectiveness should be emphasized over those that are only based on valid principles, and there needs to be a strong effort to invest in development and evaluation of replicable programmes in every area, so that eventually legislation can focus not on programmes '*based* on scientifically based research' but on programmes that have actually been successfully evaluated in rigorous experiments.

Potential impact of evidence-based policies on educational research

If evidence-based policies take hold, this will be enormously beneficial for all of educational research, not just research involving randomized or matched experiments. First, I am confident that when policymakers perceive that educational research and development is actually producing programmes that are shown in rigorous experiments to improve student outcomes, they will fund research at far higher levels. This should not be a zero-sum game, in which new funds for experiments will be taken from the very limited funds now available for educational research (Shavelson and Towne 2002). Rather, making research relevant and important to policymakers will make them more, not less, willing to invest in all forms of disciplined inquiry in education, be it correlational, descriptive, ethnographic or otherwise. The popularity of medical research depends totally on its ability to cure or prevent diseases, but because randomized experiments routinely identify effective treatments (and protect us from ineffective treatments), there is vast funding for *basic* research in medicine, including epidemiological, correlational and descriptive studies. Researchers and developers will be able to argue convincingly that basic research is essential to tell us what kinds of educational programmes are worth evaluating.

A climate favourable to evidence-based reform will be one in which individual researchers working on basic problems of teaching and learning will be encouraged and funded to take their findings from the laboratory or the small-scale experiment, or from the observation or interview protocol, and to develop and then rigorously evaluate educational treatments themselves. Education is an applied field. Research in education should ultimately have something to do with improving outcomes for children.

Conclusion

Issues related to experimental designs in research and the relation to evaluation are also dealt with in Chapters 3 and 4. This chapter is, therefore, mainly concerned with the importance of experiments for evidence-based policy. It is argued in this chapter that evidence-based policies have great potential to transform the practice of education, as well as research in education. Evidence-based policies could also set education on the path toward progressive improvement that most successful parts of our economy and society embarked on a century ago. With a robust research and development enterprise and government policies demanding solid evidence of effectiveness behind programmes and practices in our schools, we could see genuine, generational progress instead of the usual pendulum swings of opinion and fashion.

This is an exciting time for educational research and reform. We have an unprecedented opportunity to make research matter, and then to establish once and for all the importance of consistent and liberal support for high-quality research. Whatever their methodological or political orientations, educational researchers should support the movement toward evidence-based policies, and then set to work to generate the evidence that will be needed to create the schools our children deserve.

Acknowledgements

Portions of this paper are adapted from Slavin, R.E. (2003) 'Evidence-based policies: Transforming educational practice and research', *Educational Researcher*, 31(7): 15–21. This paper was written under funding from the US Department of Education (grant no. R305A040082). However, any opinions expressed are those of the author and do not necessarily represent Department of Education positions or policies.

References

Angrist, J.D. (2004) 'American education research changes tack', *Oxford Review of Economic Policy*, 20(2): 198–212.

Boruch, R.F. (1997) *Randomized experiments for planning and evaluation: A practical guide*, Thousand Oaks, CA: Corwin.

Chambers, B., Slavin, R.E., Madden, N.A., Abrami, P.C., Tucker, B.J., Cheung, A. and Gifford, R. (2008) 'Technology infusion in Success for All: Reading outcomes for first graders', *Elementary School Journal*, 109(1): 1–15.

Cook, T., Shadish, W.R. and Wong, V.C. (2008) 'Three conditions under which experiments and observational studies produce comparable causal estimates: New findings from within study comparisons', paper presented at the annual meetings of the Society for Research on Effective Education, Crystal City, VA.

Doll, R. (1998) 'Controlled trials: The 1948 watershed', *British Medical Journal*, 317: 1217–20.

Finn, J.D. and Achilles, C.M. (1999) 'Tennessee's class size study: Findings, implication, misconceptions', *Educational Evaluation and Policy Analysis*, 21(2): 97–110.

Kaestle, C.F. (1993) 'The awful reputation of educational research', *Educational Researcher*, 22(1): 23, 26–31.

Lagemann, E.C. (2002) 'An elusive science: The troubling history of education research', paper presented at the annual meeting of the American Educational Research Association, New Orleans, April 2002.

Shavelson, R.J. and Towne, L. (eds) (2002) *Scientific research in education*, Washington, DC: National Academy Press.

Slavin, R.E. (1980) 'Effects of student teams and peer tutoring on academic achievement and time on-task', *Journal of Experimental Education*, 48: 252–57.

Slavin, R.E. (1989) 'PET and the pendulum: Faddism in education and how to stop it', *Phi Delta Kappan*, 70: 752–8.

Slavin, R.E. (2003) 'Evidence-based education policies: Transforming educational practice and research', *Educational Researcher*, 31(7): 15–21.

Slavin, R.E. (2009) *Educational psychology: Theory into practice*, 9th edn, Boston: Allyn & Bacon.

Slavin, R.E. and Smith, D. (2008) 'Effects of sample size on effect size in systematic reviews in education', paper presented at the annual meetings of the Society for Research on Educational Effectiveness, Crystal City, Virginia, March 2008.

Slavin, R.E., Madden, N.A., Chambers, B. and Haxby, B. (eds) (2009) *Two million children: Success for All*, Thousand Oaks, CA: Corwin.

Chapter 7

Applications of mixed methods to the field of Educational Effectiveness Research

Charles Teddlie and Pam Sammons

Louisiana State University and University of Oxford (respectively)

The following chapter has four sections. In the first section, a summary of the characteristics of mixed methods research (MMR) is provided. The relationship between EER and MMR is discussed in the second section. Examples of effectiveness studies using mixed methods are provided in the third section. Finally, in the fourth section, we draw conclusions concerned with the application of mixed methods to the field of EER.

Summary of the characteristics of mixed methods research

The emergence and value of mixed methods research

We are pleased that MMR has been included in this volume as one of the methodological orientations that is important for the further advancement of EER. Its inclusion is particularly important since it is the only methodological orientation in this volume that is not primarily quantitative (QUAN) in nature. Even longitudinal studies, which often involve the gathering of both qualitative (QUAL) and QUAN data, are presented here (see Chapter 5) using primarily QUAN applications, such as value-added indices and growth-curve modelling. Since we believe that future methodological and conceptual advances in EER necessarily entail QUAL and MMR applications (in addition to QUAN techniques) this chapter is important in explaining why these applications are crucial to the further development of EER.

MMR has emerged as an alternative to the dichotomy of the QUAL and QUAN traditions in the social and behavioural sciences over the past 20 years (Brannen 1992; Bryman 1988; Creswell 1994; Tashakkori and Teddlie 1998, 2003). A handful of studies have recently looked at the incidence rates of QUAN, QUAL and MMR studies in the social sciences (Alise 2008; Hart *et al.* 2009; Hutchinson and Lovell 2004; Niglas 2004). The incidence rates varied widely across the studies according to several factors. Overall, there was a preference for QUAN studies (51 per cent of total empirical research studies averaged across the four studies) compared to 16 per cent classified as mixed method studies.

Nevertheless, an incidence rate of 16 per cent is impressive given the late arrival of MMR as the third methodological approach.

MMR has roots going back some 50 years with the advent of the multitrait–multimethod matrix and the first triangulation techniques (Campbell and Fiske 1959; Denzin 1978; Webb *et al.* 1966). Also, many classic studies in the social sciences were mixed in nature, even though the terminology and typologies associated with MMR had not been developed (Lipset *et al.* 1956; Roethlisberger and Dickson 1939; Warner and Lunt 1941, as summarized in Hunter and Brewer 2003).

The popularity of MMR is due largely to its flexibility in simultaneously addressing multiple and diverse research questions through integrated QUAL and QUAN techniques as described in the following quote from an international development researcher:

> The question of whether quantitative research is preferable to qualitative research creates a false divide for researchers . . . [T]he most persuasive policy research includes both of these elements: *numbers* that define the scope and patterns of the problem, and a *story* that shows how the problem works in daily life and provides for empathetic understanding. These two elements stem from quantitative and qualitative research.
>
> (Spalter-Roth 2000: 48, italics in original)

'Numbers and a story' succinctly illustrate the appeal of MMR, because the combination of both general numeric findings and specific cases exemplifying those findings generate a synergy that neither can alone. It is the generation of new knowledge that goes beyond the sum of the QUAL and QUAN components that makes MMR so valuable in understanding social phenomena, such as educational effectiveness.

General characteristics of MMR

A standard definition of MMR is 'research in which the investigator collects and analyses data, integrates the findings, and draws inferences using both qualitative and quantitative approaches or methods in a single study or program of inquiry' (Tashakkori and Creswell 2007: 4). Key to this definition of MMR is the notion of *integration*, which Bryman (2007: 8) characterizes as the extent to which 'mixed methods researchers analyse, interpret, and write up their research in such a way that the quantitative and qualitative components are mutually illuminating'.

'Mutual illumination' implies that the QUAN and QUAL components are specifically designed by MMR researchers to complement one another in generating new insights about a particular phenomenon of interest. The inductive–deductive research cycle (cycle of research methodology) depicted in Figure 7.1 illustrates this process. The nature of this process signifies that research on any social phenomenon is cyclical rather than linear; that is,

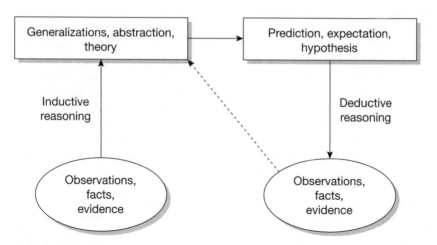

Figure 7.1 The inductive–deductive research cycle (cycle of scientific methodology)

researchers are constantly looking for deeper understandings of what they study, rather than being satisfied with static, constant, linear 'truths' or 'laws' about that phenomenon.

A defining characteristic of MMR is a set of unique (that is, different from either QUAL or QUAN) research designs that it employs. QUAN, QUAL and MMR designs are distinct from one another in the following ways:

1   QUAN designs are well-established, with the best known typologies describing experimental, quasi-experimental, correlational and survey research, which have evolved over the past 50 years (Campbell and Stanley 1963; Cook and Campbell 1979; Shadish *et al.* 2002).
2   Standardized QUAL research designs are virtually non-existent, except in a broadly generic sense (for example, ethnographic research designs, case study research designs). The major reason for this appears to be the emergent nature of much of QUAL research, which mitigates against the a priori specification of distinct typologies of research designs (Patton 2002).
3   MMR designs combine elements of both the QUAN and QUAL orientations and require creativity and flexibility in their construction and implementation. While there are several competing typologies of MMR designs, Teddlie and Tashakkori (2006, 2009) contend that methodologists cannot create a complete taxonomy of those designs due to their (the designs') capacity to mutate into other, diverse forms. Similarly, Maxwell and Loomis (2003: 244) conclude that 'the actual diversity in mixed methods studies is far greater than any typology can adequately encompass'.

In this chapter, we use the typology of MMR designs presented by Teddlie and Tashakkori (2006, 2009), but we encourage readers to investigate alternative typologies as well (Creswell and Plano-Clark 2007; Greene 2007; Maxwell and Loomis 2003). While there is variation among these, there is also considerable agreement in terms of basic types (for example, parallel or concurrent, sequential). Teddlie and Tashakkori's (2006, 2009) MMR design typology consists of five 'families' of designs: parallel mixed, sequential mixed, conversion mixed, multilevel mixed, and fully integrated. These designs are defined in Table 7.1, which also lists the types of MMR data analysis techniques associated with each.

Extended discussion of these designs is not possible in this volume due to space limitations. The following points summarize the most important information about these families of MMR design, which are referred to later in this chapter when examples are presented.

Table 7.1 Typology of mixed methods research designs and analytic techniques

MMR design 'family'	Definition of design 'family'	Analytic techniques used with this design 'family'
Parallel mixed designs	Designs in which mixing occurs in an independent manner either simultaneously or with some time lapse; QUAL and QUAN *strands* are planned/implemented in order to answer related aspects of same questions	Parallel track analysis; cross-over track analysis
Sequential mixed designs	Designs in which mixing occurs across chronological phases (QUAL, QUAN) of the study; questions or procedures of one *strand* emerge from or are dependent on the previous strand; *research questions* are built upon one another and may evolve as the study unfolds	Sequential QUAL → QUAN analysis; Sequential QUAN → QUAL analysis; iterative sequential mixed analysis
Conversion mixed designs	Designs where mixing occurs when one type of data is transformed and then analysed both qualitatively and quantitatively	Quantitizing narrative data; qualitizing numeric data (for example, profile formation); inherently mixed data analysis
Multilevel mixed designs	Designs where mixing occurs across multiple levels of analysis; Mixing occurs as QUAN and QUAL data from different levels are analyzed and integrated to answer aspects of the same or related questions	Analysing data from each level separately, then integrating them vertically
Fully integrated mixed designs	Family of mixed methods designs in which mixing occurs in an interactive manner at all *stages* of the study; at each *stage*, one approach affects the formulation of the other	Combinations of all those above

Adapted from Teddlie and Tashakkori 2006, 2009

- **Parallel mixed designs** evolved from the concept of methodological triangulation, which is the concurrent use of both QUAL and QUAN methods to study a single problem (Patton 2002).
- Parallel mixed designs can be challenging for a single investigator to conduct because they involve at least two concurrent independent research strands, one of which is QUAL in nature and one of which is QUAN. (See Box 7.1 for the definition of a 'strand').
- Meta-inferences can be drawn from parallel mixed designs (and the other types of mixed designs described in this chapter) by integrating the inferences from the QUAL and QUAN strands of a mixed methods study.
- The defining characteristic of **sequential mixed designs** is that they involve chronological phases of a study (for example, QUAL → QUAN or QUAN → QUAL) in which a QUAN strand is followed by a QUAL strand, or vice versa. The questions and/or procedures of one strand are dependent on inferences from the previous strand. Figure 7.2 presents an illustration of a sequential mixed design. (Box 7.1 defines the elements in Figure 7.2.)
- The most basic sequential mixed design involves only two strands, one QUAL and one QUAN. Iterative sequential mixed designs have more than two strands. They can range from simple applications to increasingly more complex ones (such as QUAN → QUAL → QUAN → QUAL → QUAN).

Box 7.1 Description of the elements contained in Figure 7.2

The rectangles and ovals in Figure 7.2 represent either a QUAL or a QUAN stage of a research strand. For example, if the sequential mixed design presented in this figure was a QUAN → QUAL design, then the rectangles on the left side would represent the stages of the QUAN strand, while the ovals on the right side would represent the stages of the QUAL strand.

Each research strand found in Figure 7.2 has three stages (conceptualization, experiential, inferential). The experiential stage is broken into two components (methodological and analytical) to allow for conversion designs (that is, designs in which QUAL data are converted into QUAN data or vice versa). In a QUAL strand, all stages are QUAL in nature (that is, qualitatively orientated questions, employing QUAL methods and data analysis procedures, with conclusions based on a QUAL inference process); in a QUAN stand, all stages are QUAN in nature.

There is a broken line arrow in Figure 7.2 going from the inferential stage to the methodological component of the experiential stage. This indicates that conclusions emerging from the inferential stage of a study may lead to further data gathering and analysis in the same study.

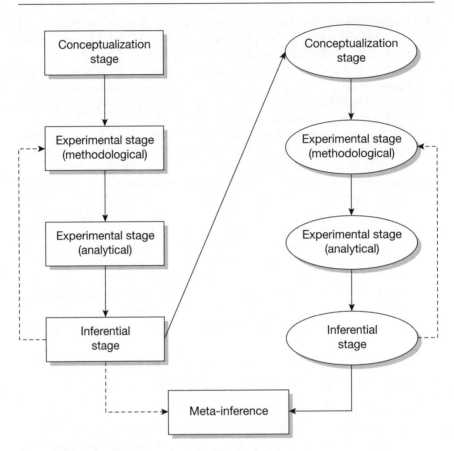

Figure 7.2 Graphic illustration of sequential mixed designs

- **Conversion mixed designs** are those in which one type of data is transformed into another and then analysed both qualitatively and quantitatively.
- 'Quantitizing' refers to the process of converting QUAL data into numerical codes that can be analysed statistically (Miles and Huberman 1994).
- 'Qualitizing' refers to the process of converting QUAN data into data that can be analysed qualitatively (Tashakkori and Teddlie 1998).
- **Multilevel mixed designs** are specialized designs that can be used to examine organizations that have a hierarchical structure, such as schools or hospitals (Tashakkori and Teddlie 1998).
- **Fully integrated mixed designs** are the most complete manifestation of MMR designs, in which the mixing of the QUAL and QUAN approaches occurs in an interactive manner across all stages of a study (Holbrook and Bourke 2004; Schulenberg 2007).

EER and MMR

Definition of Educational Effectiveness Research

Creemers and Kyriakides (2008: 4) defined EER as follows:

> ... we are using the term 'educational effectiveness' rather than the terms 'teacher' and/or 'school effectiveness' to emphasize the importance of conducting joint school and teacher effectiveness research which can help us identify the interactions between the school, classroom, and individual student levels, and their contributions to student learning. Finally, it is important to note that EER refers to the functioning of the system as a whole, and can therefore be used to develop models of effectiveness ...

Creemers and his colleagues have long advocated for the use of the term 'educational effectiveness' (see Chapter 1 in this volume), arguing convincingly that researchers must examine effectiveness factors (and their interactions) at all levels of the process in order truly to understand effectiveness in educational settings (Creemers and Reezigt 1991, 1996; Creemers and Scheerens 1994; Scheerens and Bosker 1997). This idea has gained more support over the past several years primarily because Creemers, Kyriakides and their colleagues have developed two 'generic' theories of educational effectiveness (first the comprehensive model, then the dynamic model – again, see Chapter 1) and have since gathered empirical evidence to support them (Creemers and Kyriakides 2006, 2008; De Jong *et al.* 2004; Kyriakides 2005). These theoretical models have gone a long way toward dispelling the criticism that school/educational effectiveness research needs more of a theoretical base (Teddlie and Reynolds 2000; Sammons 1999).

While the comprehensive and dynamic models are the most ambitious of those proposed for EER, other models have also incorporated the school and teacher levels (Scheerens 1992; Slater and Teddlie 1992; Stringfield and Slavin 1992). Another sophisticated example of the use of theory in school effectiveness research is the employment by Muijs *et al.* (2004) of three theoretical frameworks (contingency theory, compensation hypothesis, additivity hypothesis) in their review of the literature on 'improving schools in socioeconomically disadvantaged areas'.

Methods currently used in EER

For the purposes of this chapter, we consider the contemporary field of EER to be composed of the extensive school effectiveness research (SER) and teacher effectiveness research (TER) literatures, plus theory and a limited amount of empirical work conducted recently under the inclusive umbrella of EER. This section contains a discussion of the methods that are commonly used in SER, TER and EER, which sets the stage for further consideration of how MMR can contribute to the development of EER.

Most SER studies have traditionally been concerned with phenomena that occur throughout the school, while most TER studies have been concerned with processes that occur within the classroom (Teddlie 1994). There are three distinct traditions of SER (Reynolds *et al.* 2000), which include:

- **School effects research.** This research is concerned with the study of the *foundational properties* of school effects (for example, the magnitude of school effects). These studies are almost exclusively QUAN in nature, evolving from regression-based input–output research (Coleman *et al.* 1966) under the general label of the educational production function to more mathematically complex multilevel and SEM research studies (see Chapters 11 and 12).
- **Effective schools research.** This research is concerned with the processes of effective schooling and, in its initial phases, involved the generation of case studies of outlier schools that produced high achievement scores for students living in poverty (Edmonds 1979; Weber 1971). Cumulative results from effective school research have resulted in detailed descriptions of effective school characteristics across a variety of contexts (James *et al.* 2006; Marzano 2003; Reynolds and Teddlie 2000; Sammons 1999). These studies are primarily QUAL in nature, although several have used QUAN descriptive statistics to supplement the case study narratives.
- **Theory based school improvement research.** Harris and Chrispeels (2006: 7) have identified examples of school improvement models that 'draw upon … robust evidence . . . to produce interventions that were solidly based on tried and tested practices'. These include *Improving the quality of education for all* (Hopkins *et al.* 1996) and High Reliability Schools (Stringfield *et al.* 2008). Studies based on these school improvement projects have focused on QUAN results, but some have also included QUAL themes that emerged from interviews and observations (Stringfield *et al.* 2008), thereby resulting in MMR.

In summary, SER can be described as having three separate traditions, each of which can be characterized as predominantly QUAN or QUAL; there has been relatively more overall emphasis in SER on the former (QUAN) than the latter (QUAL). There has also been limited MMR conducted in SER in large-scale studies involving complex sets of research questions (Brookover *et al.* 1979; Mortimore *et al.* 1988; Sammons *et al.* 1997; Teddlie and Stringfield 1993).

TER is an area of research that attempts to identify those teacher behaviours that are related to student learning or achievement. Creemers (2008) recently discussed the evolution of TER through the 'lens' of the four editions of the *Handbook of research on teaching*. His analysis and that of others (Rosenshine 1996) led to the following conclusions regarding the use of methods in that field:

- TER began in the United States and elsewhere in the 1950s, with notable early studies including Medley and Mitzel (1959) and Flanders (1960). The initial studies were correlational in nature and evolved into more complex process–product studies and experimental/quasi-experimental research.

- **The first handbook (Gage 1963).** According to Creemers (2008: 474), the 'most important message of the first handbook was the plea for empirical evidence for theories about teaching, which concentrates on process–product relations'. The empirical evidence was QUAN in nature and emphasized the statistical testing of the relationships between teaching processes and student learning.
- **The second handbook (Travers 1973).** The emphasis on theory-based empirical QUAN-orientated research continued; some initial criticism of this research surfaced. Rosenshine (1996) concluded that the largest number of QUAN-orientated TER studies were produced in the 1970s.
- **The third handbook (Wittrock 1986).** This volume was notable for the inclusion of two extensive reviews of TER (Brophy and Good 1986; Rosenshine and Stevens 1986) and an influential review and critique of SER (Good and Brophy 1986). Between the publication of the third and fourth handbooks, there was increasing criticism in the United States and elsewhere of the process-product model and the dominance of QUAN methods in TER (Gage and Needels 1989). The first *Handbook of qualitative research* edited by Denzin and Lincoln appeared in 1994, challenging the traditional postpositivist QUAN research model. The paradigm wars were in full bloom during this period (Gage 1989).
- **The fourth handbook (Richardson 2001).** This handbook took a decidedly different approach to research on teaching, with an emphasis on QUAL methods and the postmodernist point of view. Creemers (2008) noted that only two of the 51 chapters in this handbook focused on the traditional QUAN-orientated TER approach.

In summary, there are two distinct and separate traditions of TER. The traditional QUAN orientation dominated during most of the last half of the twentieth century, while the QUAL approach has gained some influence over the past 20 years. There is little tradition of MMR in TER, which is interesting since several teacher observational systems exist that combine both QUAN and QUAL data gathering and analysis techniques (Teddlie and Tashakkori 2009).

Recent advancements in EER are directly related to the work of Creemers and his colleagues regarding the comprehensive and dynamic models of educational effectiveness. Creemers and Kyriakides (2008) presented studies from Cyprus and the Netherlands testing the 'validity' of the comprehensive model (de Jong *et al.* 2004), plus a comparative study that utilized a secondary analysis of the TIMSS 1999 study. These studies were QUAN in nature, employing large numeric databases to estimate statistically school and classroom effects on student achievement. Similarly, Kyriakides and Creemers (2008) reported the results of a recent QUAN analysis of the validity of the classroom-level factors in the dynamic model.

As noted at the beginning of this chapter, all the methodological orientations presented in this volume on EER are QUAN in nature, with the exception of this chapter on MMR. There is little or no discussion of QUAL data collection or analysis either in this volume, Creemers and Kyriakides (2008) or any of the studies that validated components of the EER models. This leads to the conclusion that the emerging area of EER, as exemplified in this volume and in Creemers and Kyriakides (2008), is clearly situated within the postpositivist QUAN-orientated tradition (for example, see Chapter 6).

On the other hand, it has been documented throughout this section that there are distinct traditions of both QUAL and QUAN research in TER and SER, with a limited number of studies (primarily in SER) that use MMR techniques. This leads to a couple of key questions: *are MMR techniques applicable to EER, and if so, what can they contribute to its further development?*

Are MMR techniques applicable to EER?

In a way, this is a rhetorical question, but it is important to take a slight digression, before addressing those applications, to consider some philosophical differences between 'postpositivistic' EER and 'pragmatic' MMR, as described by Tashakkori and Teddlie (1998, 2003) and many others.

We do not want to rehash the paradigm wars any more than is necessary, since we agree with the following paraphrased sentiment: 'most researchers (have) become bored with philosophical discussions and (are) more interested in getting on with the task of doing their research' (Smith 1996: 163). Nevertheless, we feel that it is valuable to consider a few differences in postpositivism and pragmatism, since those differences may better inform us with regard to how pragmatic MMR can enhance postpositivistic EER.

Paradigm contrast tables (Lincoln and Guba 1985) contain contrasts on several dimensions between philosophical viewpoints held by different researchers. In the following section, we compare postpositivists and pragmatists on three dimensions particularly relevant to the application of mixed methods to EER:

- Methods – postpositivists utilize QUAN methods primarily, as opposed to pragmatists who utilize both QUAN and QUAL methods.
- Logic – postpositivists emphasize deductive logic, especially through the use of the hypothetico-deductive model as opposed to pragmatists, who ascribe to the inductive/deductive research cycle presented in Figure 7.1.
- The possibility of generalizations – postpositivists sometimes make nomothetic statements (context- and time-free generalizations) under highly prescribed circumstances, while pragmatists are more inclined toward ideographic statements (context- and time-bound generalizations).

The use of methods in EER

With regard to methods, we described EER as primarily (actually, almost entirely) QUAN based on the information presented in this volume and in Creemers and Kyriakides (2008). We believe that individuals conducting EER will also use mixed methods if they see the value of adding QUAL methods to their research; otherwise, their orientation will stay primarily QUAN.

It should be noted, in fairness, that the tendency of some EER researchers to emphasize QUAN methods is due to the extreme positions that some individuals professing a QUAL orientation (often self-described as postmodernists) take toward empirical research. Gorard and Taylor (2004: 161, italics added) described this orientation as follows:

> Research is here merely the deconstruction of meaning rather than the search for the truth (or preference) or practicality (what works). And so, 'Post-modern theorizing alternates between banality and absurdity, between triviality posing as revelation and bizarre claims that conflict with common sense' (Bailey 1999: 162) . . . [B]y denying the possibility that there is any means of judging knowledge claims to be more or less true, *postmodernism makes research a completely pointless activity.*

Fortunately, most QUAL and MMR researchers believe in the efficacy of empirical research. MMR evolved to a large degree from methodological triangulation, which refers to 'the use of multiple methods to study a single problem' (Patton 2002: 247).

Methodological triangulation is often valued for generating *convergent results* (Greene and Caracelli 1997), but its value in terms of producing *divergent results* is as important (Arnon and Reichel 2009; Erzberger and Kelle 2003). Divergent findings are valuable in that they lead to a re-examination of the conceptual frameworks and the assumptions underlying each of the two components.

For instance, let's consider a hypothetical mixed methods study of the existence and characteristics of cross-level interactions within EER (for example, school leadership style interacting with some aspect of teaching quality). Such a study might yield convergent or divergent results; in either case, the hypothetical mixed methods study would yield more robust and interesting findings than a QUAN (or QUAL) stand-alone study. 'Numbers and a story' generate a synergy that neither could alone, and the research reports involving both are inherently more engaging.

The methodology issue, therefore, boils down to whether QUAN-orientated researchers working within EER believe that QUAL methods are valuable to the further development of their field. We believe that many researchers working within EER appreciate the value of QUAL methods, since postpositivists have long recognized the merit of those methods. As Patton (2002: 586) concluded: 'When eminent measurement and methods scholars such as Donald Campbell and Lee J. Cronbach began publicly recognizing the contributions that qualitative methods could make, the acceptability of qualitative/naturalistic approaches was greatly enhanced'.

The use of logic in EER

With regard to logic, we characterized postpositivists as employing the hypothetico-deductive model (H-DM), while pragmatists are more likely to use both induction and deduction in their research.

Creemers and Kyriakides (2008) were intent on 'testing the validity', first of the comprehensive model and then of their proposed dynamic model. These models are based on literally hundreds of studies conducted in TER and SER over the past 40–50 years. Creemers and Kyriakides (2008) tested their models through QUAN-orientated empirical studies that followed the deductive logic of the H-DM. If results from those studies were consistent with their hypotheses, then these 'validity tests' of their models were affirmative. If the data were not consistent, then 'the theory must either be discarded in favour of a better theory or modified to accommodate the newly acquired facts' (Schwandt 1997: 66).

MMR techniques, on the other hand, can be used in a variety of situations, including theory verification, but they are best utilized when both theory-based research hypotheses and novel research questions are being considered. MMR techniques employ the cycle of research methodology (Figure 7.1), which entails the use of inductive and deductive logic in an iterative manner.

Differences in the use of induction and deduction in research may be conceptualized in terms of William Whewell's distinction (Fisch 1991) between what would later (Reichenbach 1938; Schickore and Steinle 2006) be called:

- **The context or logic of justification**. The process associated with the testing of theories and hypotheses.
- **The context or logic of discovery**. The process associated with the generation of theories and hypotheses.

Before Whewell's distinction, these two components of the scientific method were both presumed to be part of what was then called the inductive method of science. While emphasizing the logic of justification as a key part of the scientific method, Whewell also pointed out the importance of the context of discovery, which involves creative insight and possibly leads to new knowledge (Teddlie and Johnson 2009).

MMR involves using both the logics of discovery and justification in the same research studies, which is exemplified by those studies having both research hypotheses (testing of theories) and research questions (involving the discovery of new knowledge). MMR in educational effectiveness would, therefore, typically involve some hypotheses related to a theoretical position, plus some research questions about aspects of schools or of teacher behaviour about which little is known.

Creemers and Kyriakides (2008) make extensive use of the context or logic of justification in testing their models of educational effectiveness, but they do not appear to have employed the logic of discovery. (Our comments here refer to Creemers and Kyriakides' work as described in this volume and in their 2008 book. Both have been involved in other EER studies that actively employed QUAN and MMR methods, such as Reynolds *et al.* 2002; Teddlie *et al.* 2006.) The logic of discovery is an area where MMR could enhance future EER.

How does new knowledge emerge in educational research? Some new knowledge can emerge when hypotheses are rejected and 'new facts' materialize, but these facts are typically limited to the topic(s) that the hypothetical propositions addressed. We believe that most new knowledge in educational research comes from asking innovative questions about the phenomena under study, or from the serendipitous emergence of novel insights that occurs during fieldwork. Mixed methodologists generate 'new' knowledge through answering innovative research questions using inductive logic.

The logic issue, therefore, reduces to whether researchers working within EER want to generate new knowledge about a phenomenon of interest, as well as test the validity of their *a priori* theoretical propositions. We believe that many educational effectiveness researchers want to do both, and MMR techniques are appropriate for their use.

The possibility of generalizations in EER

With regard to the possibility of generalizations, we indicated that postpositivists believe there are some highly prescribed circumstances in which nomothetic statements are possible, while pragmatists are more inclined toward making ideographic statements.

Creemers and Kyriakides (2008) are intent on developing what they call 'generic theory' in EER, as opposed to 'differentiated theory'. These generic factors operate across all settings, although there is an acknowledgment that 'their impact on different groups of students or teachers or schools may vary' (Creemers and Kyriakides 2008: 82). Despite this, differential educational effects 'should be incorporated as a refinement' to generic theory (Creemers and Kyriakides 2008: 82).

A similar sentiment is made in Chapter 3 of this volume: '. . . it is assumed that there are generic and measurable factors that have a stable impact on effectiveness and operate similarly in different educational settings'. This position is a consistent one, going back to earlier writings by Creemers (1994) on the characteristics of the 'effective classroom'. Forty to 50 years of relatively consistent TER and SER results constitute the 'highly prescribed circumstances' that allow Creemers and Kyriakides (2008) to promote the generalizability of the dynamic model across different educational contexts.

MMR researchers, on the other hand, are more concerned about the 'fallibility' of their knowledge and are unsure that 'context- and time-bound generalizations' are indeed possible. To these researchers, context- and time-bound ideographic statements are not only more defensible, but they are often more interesting since they focus on the particularization or uniqueness of individual cases (Stake 1995). In fact, the study of the *context* (that is, the particular social and environmental characteristics) of school effects is a clearly delineated sub-area within SER (Sammons *et al.* 1997; Teddlie 1994; Teddlie *et al.* 2000), the origin of which goes back to studies of the 'balance effect' (Willms 1985) and differential 'peer group influence' (Murnane 1975).

This difference of opinion on the issue of generalizability is a fundamental one that has no easy resolution, which is reminiscent of many of the paradigm war debates. This issue may be reframed in terms of the relative importance of particularization to a case (Stake 1995) versus generalization to a theory (Yin 2003).

One caution that mixed methodologists can make concerning the issue of generalizations is that an overemphasis on 'generic theory' may result in our missing important context-specific educational phenomena. A recent MMR study (Teddlie and Liu 2008) was conducted in China to determine if characteristics of effective schools and teachers derived from US literature would also be important in China. The researchers translated instruments developed in the United States to measure school and teacher effectiveness into Mandarin Chinese. Chinese researchers then conducted all data gathering activities in the research project. Results indicated that teacher and school effectiveness factors based on research findings from the United States successfully differentiated between Chinese elementary schools that were categorized a priori into more-effective and less-effective categories. Thus, there was strong evidence to support the researchers' hypotheses that the effectiveness factors developed in the United States were 'universals' (Reynolds *et al.* 2002) that would also be important in China.

The researchers also conducted case studies of six schools, which were guided by very general research questions aimed at the discovery of unique effectiveness factors: What effective teaching practices observed in China are different from those described in the international teacher effectiveness literature? What effective schooling practices observed in China are different from those described in the international school effectiveness literature?

The Chinese researchers utilized QUAL techniques to identify unique Chinese factors related to educational effectiveness. For example, they discovered three types of teachers in the Chinese schools for whom there are no equivalents in the United States or western Europe: *banzhuren*, *daduifudaoyuan*, and *daike* (Teddlie and Liu 2008). The activities of these different types of teachers were crucial in determining the effectiveness of their schools.

If this research study had been limited to the QUAN procedures used to assess the research hypotheses, then these three types of Chinese teachers would not have been 'discovered' through the case study research. The discovery of new knowledge regarding educational effectiveness in China was made possible through QUAL-orientated research associated with broad research questions unrelated to theories of educational effectiveness.

Why MMR techniques may be particularly useful in EER

The following section presents a brief summary of the attributes of MMR that might make its application particularly valuable in EER.

MMR CAN SIMULTANEOUSLY ADDRESS A RANGE OF BOTH CONFIRMATORY AND EXPLORATORY QUESTIONS USING BOTH QUAL AND QUAN APPROACHES

Combining QUAN and QUAL methods may be the best way to answer comprehensively important EER questions related to both causal effects and causal mechanisms, thereby allowing the further development of theoretical models. Teddlie and Tashakori (2009: 128–9, bold and italics in original) described this strength:

> While both QUAL and QUAN researchers are interested in studying causal relations, the two types of research have different strengths in terms of specifying those relationships . . . Many QUAN oriented researchers believe that QUAN (methods) are better positioned to examine **causal effects** (i.e., *whether* X caused Y), because these research designs can better control for the impact of extraneous variables. On the other hand, many QUAL oriented researchers believe that QUAL methods are better positioned to answer questions related to **causal mechanisms** or processes (i.e., *how* did X cause Y). Through a skillful mixture of both QUAL and QUAN methods, MMR researchers can address both causal effects and causal mechanisms questions simultaneously . . .

MMR PROVIDES BETTER (STRONGER) META-INFERENCES DUE TO THE USE OF DIFFERENT TYPES OF DATA SOURCES

Many authors have commented on this strength of methodological triangulation from the mid-1960s through contemporary writing. A classic combination of methods leading to stronger meta-inferences involves the use of closed-ended questionnaires (through mail, internet, and so on,) together with personal one-on-one interviews, resulting in a mixed methods database with both breadth and depth of information.

MMR PROVIDES THE OPPORTUNITY FOR A GREATER ASSORTMENT OF DIVERGENT VIEWS

Divergent results may lead to (1) quality audits to be sure that methodological techniques were used appropriately in all phases of the research; (2) additional conceptual work required to make the inconsistency understandable; and (3) the design of a new study or phase for further investigation.

MM MANUSCRIPTS ARE OFTEN MORE ENGAGING AND CONVINCING THAN THOSE BASED ON ONE METHODOLOGICAL APPROACH ALONE

The appeal of 'numbers and a story' was noted earlier in this chapter. Sandelowski (2003) discussed methods for creating powerful combinations of 'tables and tableaux' in MMR reports.

Examples of SER and TER using mixed methods

In the following section we provide details on four studies that used mixed methods to examine educational effectiveness: two of these come from the SER tradition (Jang *et al.* 2008; Teddlie and Stringfield 1993) and two from the TER tradition (Day *et al.* 2008; Teddlie *et al.* 2006). These examples were selected because they demonstrate one or more of the advantages of MMR that were noted previously.

Examples of MMR studies within the SER tradition

Results from the first study described in this section (Teddlie and Stringfield 1993) were published while the initial MMR literature was emerging (Brannen 1992; Bryman 1988; Creswell 1994; Greene *et al.* 1989; Morse 1991). This study was designed and partially implemented before there were published typologies of mixed methods designs and analytical procedures, but it used techniques that would later become 'standard' in MMR.

The second study in this section (Jang *et al.* 2008) successfully utilized design, sampling and analysis techniques from the formal mixed methods literature in a study of 'schools that were succeeding from socioeconomically disadvantaged areas', which is a defined sub-area within SER (James *et al.* 2006; Muijs *et al.* 2004). The literature review for Jang *et al.* (2008) contained an interesting mix of references from both MMR and EER.

The Louisiana School Effectiveness Study (LSES) (Teddlie and Stringfield 1993)

The LSES was composed of a series of five interrelated phases: an initial pilot study (LSES-I, 1980–82), a macro-level 76-school process–product study (LSES-II, 1982–84), and a three-phase micro-level 16-school longitudinal mixed methods study (LSES III, IV, and V with extensive data gathering in 1984–85, 1989–90 and 1995–96). This synopsis focuses on longitudinal MMR from LSES-III and LSES-IV, which involved eight matched pairs of schools initially classified as either more effective or less effective using baseline achievement data.

We discuss the following components of the LSES in this section:

- the composition of the interdisciplinary team that conducted the LSES;
- the combination of research hypotheses and questions that guided the study;

- the fully integrated mixed methods design of the study;
- results based on both the logics of justification and of discovery.

Members of this research team had a wide variety of educational, methodological and experiential backgrounds, as recommended by Shulha and Wilson (2003). All of the team members were comfortable working on a mixed methods study, although some of them were selected specifically for their QUAN or QUAL methodological expertise. Research meetings involved discussion of all data sources, resulting in case studies for all 16 schools investigated during LSES-III and LSES-IV. Six of those case studies were published in Teddlie and Stringfield (1993), along with numerous statistical tables comparing the more-effective with the less-effective schools.

LSES-III and LSES-IV were guided by several complementary research hypotheses and questions. The hypotheses included the following:

Research hypothesis 1: Schools originally classified as either more effective or as less effective will remain in those effectiveness classifications during LSES-III and LSES-IV. This hypothesis predicted that school effects would be stable from the initial classification (baseline data from 1982–84) through LSES-III (1984–85) and LSES-IV (1989–90).
Research hypothesis 2: Teachers in more-effective schools will generate higher time-on-task rates than will teachers in less-effective schools.
Research hypothesis 3: Teachers in more-effective schools will display more effective teaching behaviours in their classrooms than teachers in less-effective schools.

These and other hypotheses were tested using primarily QUAN data gathered in the schools and classrooms. While the QUAN analyses of these hypotheses were important to the researchers, they were also interested in how the processes of effective schooling and teaching evolve over time. The researchers examined those processes more closely by investigating several research questions, including the following:

QUAL research question 1: What are the themes associated with changes in school effectiveness (improvement, decline) over time, if such changes occur?
QUAL research question 2: How are teachers selected and socialized at more-effective schools as opposed to less-effective schools?
QUAL research question 3: What are the differences in school-level leadership in more-effective schools as opposed to less-effective schools?

These and other research questions evolved over the course of the study and were tested using primarily QUAL data gathered in the schools and classrooms.

The LSES employed a fully integrated MMR design in which the mixing of the approaches occurred in an interactive manner across all stages of the study. The fully integrated mixed methods design was first presented formally in the

MMR literature by Tashakkori and Teddlie (2003), but it was employed more than a decade earlier in the LSES. Steps in the fully integrated MMR design employed in the LSES included the following:

- At the conceptualization stage, the formulation of the QUAN-orientated questions informed the formulation of the QUAL-orientated questions, and vice versa. The complementary nature of the initial research hypotheses and questions are demonstrated in Research hypothesis 1, which predicted *stability* of school effects, and Research question 1, which addressed the emergence of new themes *if changes occurred*.
- At the experiential (methodological/analytical) stage, QUAL data were quantitized and analysed statistically, and QUAN data were qualitized and profiles of schools were generated. The results of these statistical and profile analyses affected the formulation of additional QUAL and QUAN analyses.
- Quantitizing QUAL teacher data led to analyses demonstrating differences in standard deviations of teaching behaviour exhibited in differentially effective schools. This led to new questions, such as 'What reduced the variance in teaching behaviours in more-effective schools?' Socialization experiences, among other phenomena, were examined (Kirby 1993).
- Qualitizing QUAN data led to four profiles of schools, including declining and improving schools. This led to more focused questions, such as 'Are there differences and similarities in the themes associated with school improvement or decline?'
- Results from the two major QUAN and QUAL strands, and their crossover analyses (quantitizing, qualitizing), resulted in meta-inferences, which were expressed in a dozen or so major conclusions.

Results from LSES-III and LSES-IV were based on both the logics of justification and of discovery. Supporting evidence for Research hypotheses 1 through 3 was based on the logic of justification. For instance, schools originally classified as either more effective or as less effective remained in those effectiveness classifications in LSES-III. On the other hand, half of the matched pairs of schools experienced changes in effectiveness status by the time of LSES-IV, thus leading to emergent themes based on the logic of discovery. Other examples of LSES-III and LSES-IV results based on the logic of discovery included:

- There were no district effects on school effectiveness. The investigators were surprised by the lack of meaningful influences from the district offices on school effectiveness across all phases of the LSES. This result has been recently replicated by Tymms *et al.* (2008) and others.
- The emergence was seen of what the researchers called the process of 'stable adaptability', where the principal of one of the case study schools was able to maintain an effective school despite significant context changes at the school.

- Differences were seen between 'naturally occurring' school improvement (for example, caused by pressures from the local community) and improvement efforts that were led by external agents.

Jang et al. (2008) study of schools in challenging circumstances

One of the advantages of MMR is that it provides stronger meta-inferences due to the use of different types of data sources. A common question asked of MMR researchers is 'How do you integrate the inferences from your separate QUAL and QUAN data sources into integrated meta-inferences?' A typical response is that MMR researchers look for common themes across the two types of data and interpret those to be the integrated themes. Simple convergence across QUAL and QUAN data sources, however, may not generate the most fully realized and integrated meta-inferences.

Jang *et al.* (2008) employed a parallel mixed methods design in which the QUAL and QUAN strands were analysed independently using thematic and factor analyses, respectively. After these traditional analyses were completed, the authors applied four additional integrative strategies to enhance the quality of their meta-inferences: parallel integration for member checking, data transformation for comparison, data consolidation for emergent themes and case analysis for the generation of refined school profiles.

Parallel integration for member checking typically involves having participants verify the investigators' initial interpretations of QUAL data. In this study, Jang *et al.* (2008) had principals check the researchers' preliminary interpretations of three types of data: their QUAL thematic analysis of 11 themes from the interview and focus group data, their QUAN analysis (with graphic displays) of the nine QUAN factors from the survey analysis, and their description of the school context. Such member checks can help clarify and contextualize the data from different research strands before final meta-analyses are made.

Data transformation for comparison in the Jang *et al.* study involved *qualitizing* the nine QUAN factors into narrative descriptions, which were then compared with the QUAL themes. Overlapping and non-overlapping aspects of school improvement were ascertained based on comparison of the two sets of QUAL factors.

Data consolidation for emergent themes was a third technique used by Jang *et al.* In this study, eight integrated themes emerged from comparisons of original and reorganized QUAL and QUAN data. Three of those themes were common across the original thematic and factor analyses, but the other five consolidated themes emerged based on additional integrative strategies.

Case analysis for the generation of refined school profiles was the final integrative strategy employed by Jang *et al.* based on earlier work by Caracelli and Greene (1993). The investigators took the case study schools from their research, generated narrative profiles for each of them and then compared the narratives with regard to the eight consolidated themes that had emerged from the previous step of the analysis. An iterative analytic process then examined the different ways schools coped with the integrated themes (for example, high versus low parental involvement in successful schools).

The Jang *et al.* (2008) study is important methodologically because it points to new directions for fully integrating QUAN and QUAL themes beyond merely looking for commonalities across the original thematic and statistical analyses. Jang *et al.* (2008: 43) quoted one of their graduate researchers' conclusions about being involved in the study:

> My participation in a mixed methods project expanded my horizons from research methodology as a debate between paradigms that dealt with 'people versus numbers' and from an understanding that abstract debates between 'either-or' actually, and quite compellingly, dialectically resolve into an 'and'.

This qualitatively orientated graduate researcher had originally been concerned about how she could contribute to the QUAN part of the study. She commented that her 'rich' understanding of the QUAL data led her to seek a better understanding of the statistical analyses and graphic displays, which she discovered to be 'full of life'.

Examples of MMR studies within the TER tradition

The first study described in this section is a four-year national study – Variations in Teachers' Work and Lives and their Effects on Pupils (VITAE; Day *et al.* 2006; Day *et al.* 2007). This study adopted a longitudinal MMR design that can be described as complex, iterative and sequential (Sammons *et al.* 2007; Day *et al.* 2008), although the initial conception involving several linked QUAN and QUAL phases did not envisage the extent of iterative integration that evolved over the course of the research.

The second study in this section involves the development of the International System for Teacher Observation and Feedback as described by Teddlie *et al.* (2006). This study employed a complex, iterative sequential mixed methods design, with a series of inductive/deductive steps.

From integration to synergy in a mixed study of teachers' lives, work, and effectiveness (Day et al. 2008)

The VITAE study was commissioned to inform education policy development in England by the Department for Children, Schools and Families (DCSF) on the basis that '. . . any attempts to sustain initiatives aimed at raising standards in schools and classrooms and to retain high quality teaching are unlikely to succeed without a more comprehensive understanding of teacher effectiveness, its complex configuration and its antecedents' (DfES Tender No: 4/RP/173/99: 6–7). The project was intended to address several areas of particular policy concern at the time, including improving the quality of teaching, raising standards of pupil attainment and supporting retention to the teaching profession.

Although the project research team was independent of government, the design itself had to relate to the tender document requirement that 'teacher effectiveness should be assessed in relation to outcomes', and that 'robust and reliable quantitative data, and in-depth qualitative data from a representative sample of LAs [Local Authorities – the equivalent of school districts] and schools should be collected'. The project funders' requirements indicated they expected a mixed methods approach to the topic, and this concurred with the method-ological preference of the research team. The VITAE research was conducted between 2001 and 2005 with a nationally representative sample of 300 primary (Key stage 1 and 2) and secondary (Key stage 3 English and mathematics) teachers working in 100 schools across seven LAs. The schools were selected to be representative of those in England in terms of levels of social disadvantage of pupil intakes and current attainment level of the schools because it was hypothesized that context factors were likely to be relevant.

The research sought to describe and analyse influences on teachers' profes-sional and personal lives, their identities and effectiveness, and explore their interconnections. It also investigated associations between the school contexts in which teachers worked and these features. The study approximates to a complex sequential iterative MMR design (Tashakkori and Teddlie 2003) involving several linked phases to create case studies of 300 teachers working with classes of pupils in years 2, 6 and 9. The field work was conducted over three consecutive academic years and collected a wide range of data through interviews, questionnaire surveys and assessment data on pupils' attainments in English and mathematics. The focus on teachers working with pupils in years 2, 6 and 9 was deliberate because these are the years when pupils in England undertake national assessments in three 'core' areas of the curriculum: English, mathematics and science (at ages 7, 11 and 14 years).

The research sought to examine variations among the 300 teachers in their relative effectiveness in promoting pupils' academic progress. The research team was able to collect pupil-level attainment outcome data from central DCSF databases and link this with other data on individual pupils in the classes taught by the teacher sample, including additional pupil baseline data on English and mathematics tests selected by the project staff. This strategy of using national datasets to obtain outcome measures had the advantage of reducing the research demands on teachers and schools, an important pragmatic consideration in a longitudinal study involving fieldwork with teacher participants (see Chapter 5 for more on longitudinal research). Even so, the project requirements over three consecutive years involved a considerable commitment from participants. By the third year some teachers and schools reduced their participation in the survey and testing component, leading to incomplete data for some aspects of the 300 individual teacher case studies. The higher demands in terms of data collection that may be required by longitudinal mixed methods designs in terms of participants' involvement and resources required in EER studies need to be balanced against the additional opportunities to examine both potential causal effects and potential causal mechanisms as described earlier.

Detailed accounts of the research findings are presented in a number of publications (Day *et al.* 2006; Day, Stobart *et al.* 2006; Day *et al.* 2007), and an overview of the study and mixed methods approach to the research design is given by Sammons *et al.* (2007). This section provides a detailed examination of the use of mixed methods in the VITAE research and how the study sought to move beyond integration of QUAN and QUAL approaches to contribute to new knowledge of variations in teachers' work, lives and effectiveness that can be termed 'synergistic understanding'. It is argued that the strength of integrated approaches that result in synergy is that they 'hold the potential for enabling the consideration and combination of a greater range of differential data, thus potentially providing opportunities for more nuanced, authentic accounts and explanations of complex realities' (Day *et al.* 2008: 330).

The use of mixed methods enabled investigation of a range of direct and indirect contributory influences on teachers' perceived effectiveness, how they managed these influences in different contexts and whether there were associations between these and the measurable progress of their students – rather than seeking only to identify particular cause-and-effect relationships. The study shows how a mixed methods design and integration of data analyses and interpretation through the combination of QUAN and QUAL approaches allowed the team to explore both possible causal effects and causal mechanisms. Day *et al.* (2008) demonstrate how the MMR team attempted to move from conceptual and methodological integration to more synergistic understandings, which enabled the discovery and delineation of key findings that were both more enlightening and more robust than would have been the case if one method or another (QUAN or QUAL) had dominated.

The main aim of the VITAE study was outlined in the tender specification by DCSF: 'To assess variations over time in teacher effectiveness, between different teachers and for particular teachers, and to identify factors that contribute to variations.' It thus recognized the need for a longitudinal approach and conceptualized teacher effectiveness as a dynamic concept. It also entailed an assumption that teachers become more effective during their careers because the tender document indicated that the DCSF wanted to understand how teachers become *more effective over time*. This was an assumption that required testing since previous research has suggested that neither teacher age nor years of experience are necessarily predictive of teacher effectiveness in promoting pupils' academic outcomes.

Key questions addressed were:

• Does teacher effectiveness vary from one year to another and in terms of different pupil outcomes and do teachers necessarily become more effective over time?

- What are the roles of biography and identity?
- How do school and/or department leadership influence teachers' practice and their effectiveness?
- What particular kinds of influence does continuing professional development (CPD) have on teachers' effectiveness?
- Are teachers equally effective for different pupil groups or is there differential effectiveness relating (for example) to pupils' gender or socio-economic status?
- Do the factors that influence effectiveness vary for teachers working in different school contexts, or for different kinds of outcomes?
- Do factors influencing teachers' effectiveness vary across different sectors (primary and secondary) and different age groups (Key stage 1, 2 and 3)?

An extensive literature review was used to develop a clearer conceptual understanding of the dimensions of teacher 'effectiveness' at the start of the study. This initial examination was extended to include other areas that emerged as important themes as the analysis of the empirical data progressed, including the concepts of: teacher well-being, professional life phases, identity, resilience and commitment. These concepts became central to the research team's understanding of the nature of different influences on and outcomes of variations in teachers' work and lives.

Data collection within VITAE brought together research in two areas: mainly QUAN research on teacher (and school) effectiveness on the one hand, and mainly QUAL research on teachers' work and lives on the other. VITAE sought to integrate these different perspectives in order to address better the central research questions. It chose to focus on following the same teachers over three successive years, with QUAN-derived measures of student outcomes (academic and affective), relating to three successive classes/teaching groups. The issue of change over time in various aspects (teacher effectiveness, job satisfaction, motivation and commitment) was explored using student attainment outcome measures, students' views, and teachers' perceptions and accounts in initial questionnaires and regular in-depth interviews. Figure 7.3 outlines the sample design.

Two dimensions of effectiveness were investigated: **perceived effectiveness** (relational) and **relative effectiveness** (value added). The main data concerning perceived effectiveness were collected through twice yearly semi-structured, face-to-face teacher interviews. Measures of teachers' relative effectiveness were derived from statistical analyses of pupil progress and attainment by matching baseline test results at the beginning of the year, with pupils' national curriculum results at the end and exploring the influence of pupil background characteristics. This enabled differences in the relative 'value added' to be analysed, using multilevel contextual models that included adjustment for individual pupil background factors (for example, age, gender, prior attainment and numerous other variables). Pupil surveys were also conducted each year to gather their views of their schools

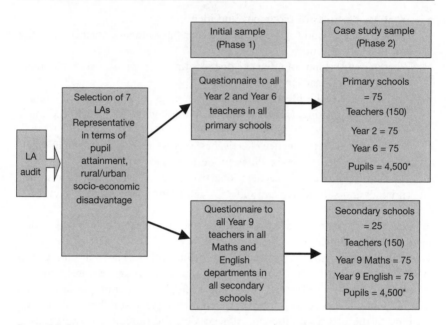

Figure 7.3 Summary of VITAE sampling design (Day *et al.* 2006, 2007). Data on pupils' views were collected by survey on a class or teaching group of pupils for each teacher for three successive school years

and teachers, including features of school and classroom climate as well as attitudes to school and learning. Data reduction techniques – Exploratory Factor Analysis and Confirmatory Factor Analysis (CFA, see Chapter 12) – identified underlying dimensions in the pupil questionnaire data. These were tested in multilevel models to investigate the relationships between pupil attitudes and dimensions related to school and classroom processes and variations in pupils' academic progress in each of the three years.

ATTEMPTING METHODOLOGICAL SYNERGY

The demands of the VITAE research aims and questions necessitated an integrated, sequential mixed methods approach involving the combination of a range of research techniques, including approaches traditionally associated with both post-positivist/QUAN and interpretive/QUAL paradigms. A longitudinal perspective was needed to investigate variation over time with three years of data collection. The main QUAL data collection were semi-structured, face-to-face interviews, supplemented at various stages of the research by document analysis and interviews with school leaders and groups of pupils, among others (see Box 7.2). The data were collected and analysed in an iterative and evolving process consistent with the use of grounded theory methods. So, for example, guided

Box 7.2 Summary of data collection methods by participant group

Focus	Method	Participants
Teachers	Questionnaire survey	Year 2, 6 and 9 (maths and English) teachers in all schools in sample LAs
	Semi-structured interview	300 case study teachers
	Hierarchically-focused interview	300 case study teachers
	Narrative approach interview and teacher worklines	300 case study teachers
	Telephone interview	300 case study teachers
School leaders	Semi-structured interview	Headteachers, heads of department, key stage leaders
Pupils	Baseline and outcome measures: NFER tests in English and mathematics	Years 6 and 9 (maths and English) pupils in classes or sets (year 9) taught by case study teachers
	Baseline and outcome measures: National test data	Years 2, 6 and 9 (maths and English) pupils
	Attitudinal survey	Years 2, 6 and 9 (maths and English) pupils in classes or sets (year 9) taught by case study teachers
	Focus group interview	Sub-sample of years 2, 6 and 9 (maths and English) pupils

by a critical examination of the literature, an initial questionnaire for teachers was developed. The analysis of data collected from this questionnaire plus the literature review informed the development of first-round interview schedules and further follow-up interviews. Group interviews with pupils added a QUAL element to the study of pupil views to complement and extend the survey strand. Here, focus groups were identified in 30 classes taught by teachers in the study (approximately 10 per cent of the participating teachers). The focus groups provided the opportunity to follow up findings from analyses of the first year QUAN analysis of the main pupil attitudinal questionnaire.

Additional narrative interviews were constructed drawing on the emerging analyses of the first two rounds of QUAN and QUAL data to explore teachers' retrospective perceptions of changes in their effectiveness and their interpretations of the various factors that shape this over the longer course of their teaching careers. Teachers were asked to construct a timeline indicating critical influences on their perceived effectiveness, looking back over their career histories. This retrospective element was necessary in order to gather the range of information needed to address all the complex and potentially interrelated issues and concerns of the study, and to provide a detailed and methodologically robust, rigorous account of teachers' work, lives and effectiveness. So while 300 individual teacher case studies were the prime focus of the study, these were constructed using

four main sources of evidence: teacher interviews, teacher and pupil questionnaires, and pupil assessment data. This combination of approaches provided
greater opportunities for mapping, analysis and interpretation to provide more
holistic understandings of the research area than would have been gained if relying
on a single paradigm.

The development of the teacher case studies involved qualitizing QUAN
evidence and quantitizing QUAL evidence, and allowed the integration and
eventual attempts at synthesis of the two in various ways, including full individual teacher case studies, summary teacher profiles and 'cameos or pen portraits'
via the creation of an overall teacher matrix for further exploration of associations
between key attributes (for example, teacher professional life phase, school
context, sector) and other concepts, including effectiveness (perceived and value
added), commitment, resilience and identity. The strengths of the mixed methods
strategy included the professional learning of team members being enabled
through the iterative process of data collection, ongoing analysis, tentative
hypothesis generation and testing and interpretation of results.

The study faced various challenges, including the inevitable time lag on the
collection and analysis of cognitive outcome data; the capacity of the NVivo
computer package to handle the large amounts of qualitative data generated;
and the lack of complete data sets due to the voluntary nature of participation
and demands over three years. The pupil attitude and value-added data required
teachers to administer special baseline tests and pupil questionnaire surveys in
each year of three years of study. By the third year the teacher response rate to
these additional requests was reduced, reflecting the extra demands of involvement in a longitudinal study and thus analyses of these data laid greater weight
on the first two cohorts of pupil data.

An illustration of the iterative nature of the ongoing integration of the QUAN
and QUAL mixed methods design is illustrated by the way VITAE changed its
conceptualization in response to emerging findings. The initial conceptual
framework was based on a model where teacher effectiveness was considered
central and was understood to relate to pupil attitudes, achievements and attainments and to be affected by policy, pupils, and teachers' personal and practice
factors. Following the analysis of an initial survey of all teachers in schools in
the seven LAs and the first round of interviews with the teacher sample (discussed
in more detail in Day *et al.* 2008), the team reassessed the initial conceptualization
and instead decided that teachers themselves should be seen as central to the
study. A second conceptual framework grounded in the emerging QUAN and
QUAL empirical data was thus developed, with teachers' identities and professional life phases viewed as key factors that might moderate their commitment
and both perceived and relative effectiveness (see Figure 7.4).

The results from the multilevel statistical analyses (QUAN) of teachers' relative
effectiveness were gained independently at first from the QUAL analyses of interview data, but were later incorporated into the teacher case study profiles. These
were then used as one of several important attributes in subsequent QUAL

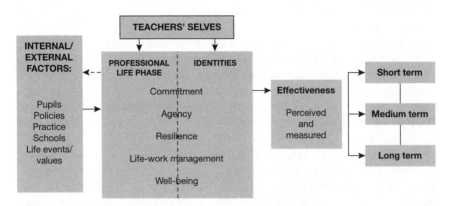

Figure 7.4 Teachers' selves as factors influencing effectiveness

analyses in order to understand the potential influences on variations in effectiveness more fully. Discussion of this integration of data (not the integration itself) led to the identification of two key features of teachers' work and lives – professional life phase and identity – that, together, contributed positively and negatively to variations among teachers in relation to these features. Discussion of the interaction between these led to hypotheses about their association with teachers' *perceived effectiveness* and, later in the research process, between teachers' commitment and their *relative effectiveness* (measured by value-added analyses).

Three claims that emerged from the research illustrated the processes of moving first to methodological integration and then attempts at conceptual and methodological synergy. Day *et al.* (2008) argue that neither QUAL nor QUAN analyses in isolation could have led to these new understandings of the links between teachers' professional life phase, identity, commitment and their perceived and value-added effectiveness:

Claim 1: Teachers in later phases of their professional lives are more vulnerable in terms of sustaining their commitment to teaching.
Claim 2: Pupils of teachers who are sustaining or continuing to build their commitment are more likely to attain results at or above the level expected, regardless of school context.
Claim 3: Teachers do not necessarily become more effective in promoting their students' academic outcomes over time. A higher proportion of teachers in later career phases, though still a minority, are likely to be relatively less effective in promoting students' academic outcomes.

The significant statistical results in the QUAN analyses of the VITAE research supported the QUAL analyses of interview data on variations in teachers' work and lives over the three years of the field study and in the longer term from narrative. When integrated, the data showed differences in commitment and effectiveness between teachers in different phases of their professional lives. The further association of these findings with those of teachers' relative effectiveness, however, suggested that not only are teachers in their late career phase at greater risk of becoming less effective, but that effectiveness is closely associated with commitment to teaching. Taken together, these three linked findings shed new light on the ways in which teacher effectiveness, commitment and professional life phase interact, and this drew attention to the important concept of teacher resilience.

The longitudinal nature of the VITAE research also posed some challenges in terms of continuity of project staffing and expertise as well as maintaining the interest and participation of schools and teachers over an extended (four-year) period. A further limitation of this study was a lack of funding for a proposed classroom observation component, which meant that it was unable to explore variations in this central dimension of teachers' work and lives (see the discussion of the ISTOF research below for an illustration of this important topic in studying teacher effectiveness).

Despite the limitations, the VITAE team found benefits from the mixed methods approach adopted. These included the development of research relationships and understandings within the team through regular workshops that focused on building shared understandings of data analyses, interpretation and emergent themes and contained, within it, members with QUAL and QUAN expertise and experience. The building of good will and mutual support and learning proved to be key factors supporting the processes of conceptual and methodological integration and synergy.

Development of the International System for Teacher Observation and Feedback (Teddlie et al. 2006)

One of the families of MMR designs listed in Table 7.1 is sequential mixed designs, which has a subfamily, iterative sequential mixed designs. These iterative designs range from simple three stage designs (for example, QUAL → QUAN → QUAL) to increasingly more complex ones such as the International System for Teacher Observation and Feedback (ISTOF), which had seven stages.

In developing ISTOF, Teddlie *et al.* (2006) used what has been called the internet-based iterative sequential mixed methods design (IBIS-MM; Teddlie *et al.* 2008). The particular IBIS-MM design used in this study was QUAL-QUAN-QUAL-QUAN-QUAL-QUAN-MM in nature.

The research team came from 20 countries, and the study was conducted from January 2004 through to August 2006. Pilot tests of the final version of this instrument (Sammons and Ko 2008) are still ongoing in various participating countries. Instead of a set of complementary research hypotheses and questions, ISTOF consisted of a series of stages (with activities) that could be classified as QUAN, QUAL or both. There were also three 'organizational stages' in ISTOF that could not be characterized as having a particular methodological orientation: a preliminary stage, which involved assembling the international group of researchers and developing the committee structure; developing a conceptual framework for ISTOF; and generating the initial and final versions of ISTOF (Teddlie *et al.* 2006).

Table 7.2 describes the activities (and the methodological approaches) for each of the stages in ISTOF.

Seven stages and six internet queries were used to generate, in order, the components, indicators and items associated with ISTOF:

- Stage 1: Query 1 asked the country teams to generate a list of *components* of effective teaching with definitions. QUAL data were generated and analysed using content analysis.
- Stage 2: Query 2 asked teams to rate (on 5-point scales) and rank order the potential *components* generated through Query 1 in terms of importance. QUAN data were generated and analysed using generalizability analysis.
- Stage 3: Query 3 asked the teams to generate a list of *indicators* (with comments) associated with the components generated in the previous stage. QUAL data were generated and analysed using content analysis.
- Stage 4: Query 4 asked teams to rate (5-point scales) the potential *indicators* generated through Query 3 in terms of importance. QUAN data were generated and analysed using generalizability analysis.
- Stage 5: Expert panels generated a bank of potential *items* for ISTOF. QUAL data were generated.
- Stage 6: Query 5 asked the teams to rank order the potential *items* generated through the work of expert panels in terms of relevance to the underlying indicators. QUAN data were generated and analysed using generalizability analysis.
- Stage 7: Query 6 asked the teams to comment on the structure and content of the initial version of the teacher observation protocol using closed-ended and open-ended responses. Mixed methods data were generated and analysed. (See Table 7.2 for more details on these steps.)

IBIS-MM designs have a number of strengths due to the characteristics of internet research and the iterative nature of sequential designs. The IBIS-MM, as exemplified by the ISTOF study, had several particular strengths:

1   IBIS-MM designs provide an excellent opportunity for participants to work with one another in situations where they cannot meet as a group. This allows for more international research among scholars who would not normally be able to convene at one location. The responses from multiple countries in ISTOF resulted in TER meta-inferences that were more valid internationally than previous research.

Table 7.2 An example of iterative sequential mixed methods designs: the ISTOF QUAL-QUAN-QUAL-QUAN-QUAL-QUAN-MM design

Stage	Activity	Methodological orientation
Preliminary stage	1 Assemble international group of researchers; establish committee structure 2 Select country co-ordinators, country team members, chairs of committees	Not applicable
Stage 1 17 countries	1 Generation of potential *components* of effective teaching – Query 1 2 QUAL analysis of narrative data – content analysis	QUAL
Stage 2 17 countries; 257 individual responses	1 Ranking and 5-point scale rating of potential *components* of effective teaching using Query 2 data 2 QUAN analysis of numeric data – generalizability analysis	QUAN
Interim stage – Activities of deductive committee	1 Develop a conceptual framework for ISTOF 2 Refine components generated by Queries 1 and 2	Not applicable
Stage 3 16 countries	1 Generation of potential *indicators* of effective teaching – Query 3 2 QUAL analysis of narrative data – content analysis	QUAL
Stage 4 19 countries 213 individual responses	1 5-point scale ranking of potential *indicators* of effective teaching – Query 4 2 QUAN analysis of numeric data – generalizability analysis	QUAN
Stage 5 Activities of expert panels	Generation of potential *items* to assess effective teaching (item bank)	QUAL
Stage 6 20 countries	1 Ranking of potential *items* to assess effective teaching – Query 5 2 QUAN analysis of numeric data – generalizability analysis	QUAN
Development of protocol by ISTOF committees	Generate initial version of the teacher observation protocol	Not applicable
Stage 7 19 countries	Query 6 1 Overall 5-point scale rating of first version of teacher observation protocol 2 Rating of items on initial version of teacher observation protocol 3 Final suggestions for altering items 4 QUAN and QUAN analyses of numeric and narrative data	Mixed
Development of protocol by ISTOF committees	Generate the final version of the teacher observation protocol	Not applicable

2   IBIS-MM designs are designed to capitalize on a characteristic 'ebb and flow' process in which inductive and deductive logic are used iteratively and in sequence (that is, the cycle of research). This design type allows research studies to evolve spontaneously on the basis of participants' responses from the previous round.

3   The IBIS-MM design employed in the ISTOF study allowed countries and individuals who typically cannot participate in an international study to do so, especially those from less developed or isolated locations. ISTOF included participants from countries such as Argentina, Belarus, Chile, India, Malaysia and Nigeria, whose points of view were heard on the international stage in TER for the first time.

4   IBIS-MM designs can yield high participation rates, such as that recorded for ISTOF. The participation rate across all phases of the project was excellent, because the 20 research teams could respond online at their convenience.

5   An unexpected side-effect of the ISTOF study was the increased communication among team members within the same country. This serendipitously allowed for the further development of research traditions in countries where they had not existed before.

The ISTOF pilot instrument developed by the MMR process described above sought to address an important topic of both theoretical and practical importance, namely the extent to which 'more effective' teaching practices can be described and how generalizable or, by contrast, how differentiated they may be in different contexts. By piloting an international instrument in a wide range of international contexts it sought to establish what features of effective practice seem to 'travel' across countries and whether certain features are more evident in specific contexts. It thus offers the prospect of furthering understanding of potential causal mechanisms related to classroom practice, a key advantage of mixed methods designs. Moreover, the instrument was intended to offer potential as a feedback system that would be of practical value for teachers involved in its use and thus can be seen as a valuable addition to future school improvement project designs.

Conclusions

This chapter argued that mixed methods approaches offer a valuable strategy for incorporating greater use of QUAL methods into EER. This is seen as important because there is a strong postpositivist QUAN orientation to much of the current EER field. The use of mixed methods designs offers an alternative to the existing QUAN or QUAL dichotomy, which still tends to divide the school effectiveness and school improvement fields. Song, Sandelowski and Happ (2010) describe a similar process in public health settings in which mixed methods intervention programmes introduce various types of QUAL research into what had been exclusively QUAN-orientated experimental research (see also Chapter 6).

Early seminal SER studies such as *Fifteen thousand hours* (Rutter *et al.* 1979) and *School matters* (Mortimore *et al.* 1988) used both QUAN measures to identify and define the magnitude of school effects and also used QUAL approaches to describe schools and classrooms in the research. However, it is argued that these studies did not have access to the more recently developed mixed methods approaches outlined in this chapter and thus did not fully integrate the QUAN and QUAL elements, which were largely conducted in parallel. They thus did not provide the kinds of meta-inferences and deeper understandings developed in later mixed methods SER studies such as the LSES (Teddlie and Stringfield 1993) or the *Forging links* research (Sammons *et al.* 1997).

We suggest that one of the advantages of well-designed MMR is that it offers the prospect of making stronger meta-inferences where QUAL and QUAN components are specifically designed to complement each other and provide 'mutual illumination'. Combining numbers and narratives illustrates the appeal of mixed methods approaches, and this chapter provides a summary of different mixed methods designs and the way mixed methods approaches can extend existing knowledge bases through producing convergent and/or divergent results and by combining the logic of justification (testing theories and hypotheses) with the logic of discovery (to develop new theories and hypotheses). Illustrations are provided of EER studies that have adopted mixed methods approaches to achieve powerful new insights that move beyond integration of QUAL or QUAN findings by a cyclical, iterative process that combines inductive and deductive reasoning to achieve deeper, synergistic understandings of teachers, teaching and learning processes and educational effectiveness.

Nonetheless, we recognize that there are potential weaknesses and limitations involved in MMR. In particular, such studies are likely to involve greater expense and often take longer to conduct. Moreover, they require QUAN and QUAL researchers to develop their own understanding and knowledge of different approaches and take time to work together to integrate findings and engage in cyclical reviews of results in order to investigate phenomena more deeply, identify convergent and divergent results and produce new insights.

While there is an important need in EER to test further existing and new educational effectiveness models and the extent to which EER concepts and theories are generalizable, we also argue the case for a 'third way' involving pragmatic approaches that explore the extent to which relationships and concepts may be context and time bound (differentiated). However, we believe that the greater use of mixed methods designs offers interesting possibilities for the further advancement and bringing together of the effectiveness and improvement traditions.

References

Alise, M. (2008) 'Disciplinary differences in preferred research methods: A comparison of groups in the Biglan classification scheme', unpublished doctoral dissertation,

Louisiana State University, Baton Rouge. Online. Available at: http://etd.lsu.edu/docs/available/etd-02222008-085519/unrestricted/alisediss.pdf [accessed 17 January 2010].

Arnon, S. and Reichel, N. (2009) 'Closed and open-ended question tools in a telephone survey: An example of a mixed method study', *Journal of Mixed Methods Research* (3)2: 172–96.

Bailey, R. (1999) 'The abdication of reason: Postmodern attacks upon science and reason', in J. Swann and J. Pratt (eds) *Improving education: Realist approaches to method and research*, London: Cassell.

Brannen, J. (1992) *Mixing methods: Quantitative and qualitative research*, Aldershot: Avebury.

Brookover, W., Beady, D., Flood, P., Schweitzer, J. and Wisenbaker, J. (1979) *School social systems and student achievement: Schools can make a difference*, New York: Praeger.

Brophy, J. and Good, T.L. (1986) 'Teacher behaviour and student achievement', in M.C. Wittrock (ed.) *Handbook of research on teaching*, 3rd edn, New York: Macmillan.

Bryman, A. (1988) *Quantity and quality in social research*, London: Unwin Hyman.

Bryman, A. (2007) 'The research question in social research: What is its role?', *International Journal of Social Research Methodology Theory and Practice*, 10(1): 5–20.

Campbell, D.T. and Fiske, D.W. (1959) 'Convergent and discriminant validation by the multitrait-multimethod matrix', *Psychological Bulletin*, 56: 81–105.

Campbell, D.T. and Stanley, J. (1963) 'Experimental and quasi-experimental designs for research on teaching', in N. L. Gage (ed.) *Handbook of research on teaching*, Chicago: Rand McNally; also published as *Experimental and quasi-experimental designs for research* (1966), Chicago: Rand McNally, pp. 171–246.

Caracelli, V.J. and Greene, J.C. (1993) 'Data analysis strategies for mixed-method evaluation designs', *Educational Evaluation and Policy Analysis*, 15(2): 195–207.

Coleman, J.S., Campbell, E., Hobson, C., McPartland, J., Mood, A., Weinfeld, R. and York, R. (1966) *Equality of educational opportunity*, Washington, DC: Government Printing Office.

Cook, T.D. and Campbell, D.T. (1979) *Quasiexperimentation: Design and analysis issues for field settings*, Boston: Houghton Mifflin Company.

Creemers, B.P.M. (1994) *The effective classroom*, London: Cassell.

Creemers, B.P.M. (2008) 'The AERA handbooks of research on teaching: Implications for educational effectiveness research', *School Effectiveness and School Improvement*, 19(4): 473–7.

Creemers, B.P.M. and Kyriakides, L. (2006) 'Critical analysis of the current approaches to modelling educational effectiveness: The importance of establishing a dynamic model', *School Effectiveness and School Improvement*, 17(3): 347–66.

Creemers, B.P.M. and Kyriakides, L. (2008) *The dynamics of educational effectiveness: A contribution to policy, practice and theory in contemporary schools*, London: Routledge.

Creemers, B.P.M. and Reezigt, G.J. (1991) *Evaluation of educational effectiveness*, Groningen: ICO.

Creemers, B.P.M. and Reezigt, G.J. (1996) 'School level conditions affecting the effectiveness of instruction', *School Effectiveness and School Improvement*, 7(3): 197–228.

Creemers, B.P.M. and Scheerens, J. (1994) 'Developments in the educational effectiveness research programme', in R.J. Bosker, B.P.M. Creemers and J. Scheerens (eds) *Conceptual and methodological advances in educational effectiveness research*, Special issue of *International Journal of Educational Research*, 21(2): 125–40.

Creswell, J.W. (1994) *Research design: Qualitative and quantitative approaches*, Thousand Oaks, CA: Sage Publications.

Creswell, J. and Plano-Clark, V. (2007) *Designing and conducting mixed methods research*, Thousand Oaks, CA: Sage Publications.

Day, C., Kington, A., Stobart, G. and Sammons, P. (2006) 'The personal and professional selves of the teachers: Stable and unstable identities', *British Educational Research Journal*, 32(4): 601–16.

Day, C., Sammons, P. and Gu, Q. (2008) 'Combining qualitative and quantitative methodologies in research on teachers' lives, work, and effectiveness: From integration to synergy', *Educational Researcher*, 37(6): 330–42.

Day, C., Sammons, P., Stobart, G, Kingston, A. and Gu, Q. (2007) *Teachers matter*, Milton Keynes: Open University Press.

Day, C., Stobart, G., Sammons, P., Kingston, A., Gu, Q., Smees, R. and Mujtaba, T. (2006) 'Variations in teachers' work, lives and effectiveness', final report for the VITAE Project, Nottingham: Department for Education and Skills, London.

De Jong, R., Westerhof, D.J. and Kruiter, J.H. (2004) 'Empirical evidence of a comprehensive model of school effectiveness: A multilevel study of mathematics in the 1st year of junior general education in The Netherlands', *School Effectiveness and School Improvement*, 15(1): 3–31.

Denzin, N.K. (1978) *The research act: A theoretical introduction to sociological method*, 2nd edn, New York: McGraw-Hill.

Denzin, N.K. and Lincoln, Y.S. (eds) (1994) *Handbook of qualitative research*, Thousand Oaks, CA: Sage Publications.

Edmonds, R.R. (1979) 'Effective schools for the urban poor', *Educational Leadership*, 37(10): 15–24.

Erzberger, C. and Kelle, U. (2003) 'Making inferences in mixed methods: The rules of integration', in A. Tashakkori and C. Teddlie (eds) *Handbook of mixed methods in social and behavioural research* 457–90, Thousand Oaks, CA: Sage Publications

Fisch, M. (1991) *William Whewell, philosopher of science*, Oxford: Oxford University Press.

Flanders, N.A. (1960) *Teacher influence, pupil attitudes and achievement*, Minneapolis: University of Minnesota; also published under this title as FS 5.225:25040 US Department of Education, US Government Printing Office.

Gage, N.L. (ed.) (1963) *Handbook of research on teaching*, Chicago: Rand McNally.

Gage, N.L. (1989) 'The paradigm wars and their aftermath: A "historical" sketch of research and teaching since 1989', *Educational Researcher*, 18(7): 4–10.

Gage, N.L. and Needels, M.C. (1989) 'Process-product research on teaching: A review of criticisms', *The Elementary School Journal*, 89: 253–300.

Good, T.L. and Brophy, J.E. (1986) 'School effects', in M. Wittrock (ed.) *Handbook of research on teaching*, 3rd edn, 570–602, New York: Macmillan.

Gorard, S. and Taylor, C. (2004) *Combining methods in educational and social research*, Buckingham: Open University Press.

Greene, J.C. (2007) *Mixing methods in social inquiry*, San Francisco: Jossey-Bass.

Greene, J.C. and Caracelli, V.J. (1997) 'Defining and describing the paradigm issue in mixed method evaluation', in J.C. Greene and V.J. Caracelli (eds) *Advances in mixed-method evaluation: The challenges and benefits of integrating diverse paradigms*, New Directions for Evaluation, no. 74, San Francisco: Jossey-Bass.

Greene, J.C., Caracelli, V.J. and Graham, W.F. (1989) 'Toward a conceptual framework for mixed-method evaluation designs', *Educational Evaluation and Policy Analysis*, 11: 255–74.

Harris, A. and Chrispeels, J. (2006) 'Introduction', in A. Harris and J. Crispeels (eds) *Improving schools and educational systems: International perspectives* 3–22, London: Routledge.

Hart, L.C., Smith, S.Z., Swars, S.L. and Smith, M.E. (2009) 'An examination of research methods in mathematics education (1995–2005)', *Journal of Mixed Methods Research*, 3(1): 26–41.

Holbrook, A. and Bourke, S. (2004) 'An investigation of PhD examination in Australia using a mixed method approach', *Australian Journal of Educational and Developmental Psychology*, 4: 153–69. Online. Available at: www.newcastle.edu.au/Resources/Research%20Centres/SORTI/Journals/AJEDP/Vol%204/v4-holbrook-bourke.pdf [accessed 17 January 2010].

Hopkins, D., West, M. and Ainscow, M. (1996) *Improving the quality of education for all*, London: David Fulton.

Hunter, A. and Brewer, J. (2003) 'Multimethod research in sociology', in A. Tashakkori and C. Teddlie (eds) *Handbook of mixed methods in social and behavioural research*, Thousand Oaks, CA: Sage Publications, pp. 577–94.

Hutchinson, S.R. and Lovell, C.D. (2004) 'A review of methodological characteristics of research published in key journals in higher education: Implications for graduate research teaching', *Research in Higher Education*, 45(4): 383–403.

James, C., Connolly, M., Dunning, G. and Elliot, T. (2006) *How very effective primary schools work*, London: Paul Chapman.

Jang, E.E., McDougall, D.E., Pollon, D., Herbert, M. and Russell, P. (2008) 'Integrative mixed methods data analytic strategies in research on school success in challenging circumstances', *Journal of Mixed Methods Research*, 2(2): 221–47.

Kirby, P. (1993) 'Teacher socialization in effective and ineffective schools', in C. Teddlie and S. Stringfield (eds) *Schools make a difference: Lessons learned from a 10-year study of school effects*, New York: Teachers College Press, pp. 187–201.

Kyriakides, L. (2005) 'Extending the comprehensive model of educational effectiveness by an empirical investigation', *School Effectiveness and School Improvement*, 16(2): 103–52.

Kyriakides, L. and Creemers, B.P.M. (2008) 'Using a multidimensional approach to measure the impact of classroom level factors upon student achievement: A study testing the validity of the dynamic model', *School Effectiveness and School Improvement*, 19(2): 183–205.

Lincoln, Y.S. and Guba, E.G. (1985) *Naturalistic inquiry*, Beverly Hills: Sage.

Lipset, S.M., Trow, M. and Coleman, J. (1956) *Union democracy*, Garden City, NY: Anchor Books.

Marzano, R.J. (2003) *What works in schools: Translating research into action*, Alexandria, VA: Association for Supervision and Curriculum Development.

Maxwell, J. and Loomis, D. (2003) 'Mixed methods design: An alternative approach', in A. Tashakkori and C. Teddlie (eds) *Handbook of mixed methods in social and behavioural research*, Thousand Oaks, CA: Sage Publications, pp. 241–72.

Medley, D.M. and Mitzel, H.E. (1959) 'Some behavioural correlates of teacher effectiveness', *Journal of Educational Psychology*, 50: 239–46.

Miles, M. and Huberman, M. (1994) *Qualitative data analysis: An expanded sourcebook*, 2nd edn, Thousand Oaks, CA: Sage.

Morse, J.M. (1991) 'Approaches to qualitative-quantitative methodological triangulation', *Nursing Research*, 40(2): 120–23.

Mortimore, P., Sammons, P., Stoll, L., Lewis, D. and Ecob, R. (1988) *School matters*, Berkeley: University of California Press.

Muijs, D., Harris, A., Chapman, C., Stoll, L. and Russ, J. (2004) 'Improving schools in socioeconomically disadvantaged areas: A review of research evidence', *School Effectiveness and School Improvement*, 15(2): 149–75.

Murnane, R.J. (1975) *The impact of school resources on the learning of inner city children*, Cambridge, MA: Ballinger Publishing Co.

Niglas, K. (2004) 'The combined use of qualitative and quantitative methods in educational Research', Tallinn Pedagogical University Dissertations in Social Sciences 8, Tallinn, Pedagogical University Series, Dissertations on Social Sciences.

Patton, M.Q. (2002) *Qualitative research and evaluation methods*, 3rd edn, Thousand Oaks, CA: Sage Publications.

Reichenbach, H. (1938) *Experience and prediction*, Chicago: University of Chicago Press.

Reynolds, D., Creemers, B., Stringfield, S., Teddlie, C. and Schaffer, E. (2002) *World class schools: International perspectives on school effectiveness*, London: RoutledgeFalmer.

Reynolds, D. and Teddlie, C. (2000) 'The processes of school effectiveness', in C. Teddlie and D. Reynolds (eds) *The international handbook of school effectiveness research*, London: Falmer Press, pp. 134–59.

Reynolds, D., Teddlie, C., with Creemers, B., Scheerens, J. and Townsend, T. (2000) 'An introduction to school effectiveness research', in C. Teddlie and D. Reynolds (eds) *The international handbook of school effectiveness research*, London: Falmer Press, pp. 3–25.

Richardson, V. (ed.) (2001) *Handbook of research on teaching*, 4th edn, Washington, DC: American Educational Research Association.

Roethlisberger, F.J. and Dickson, W.J. (1939) *Management and the worker*, Cambridge MA: Harvard University Press.

Rosenshine, B. (1996) 'Advances in research on instruction', in J.W. Lloyd, E.J. Kameanui and D. Chard (eds) (1997) *Issues in educating students with disabilities*, Mahwah, NJ: Lawrence Erlbaum, pp. 197–221.

Rosenshine, B. and Stevens, R. (1986) 'Teaching functions', in M.C. Wittrock (ed.) *Handbook of research on teaching*, 3rd edn, New York, Macmillan.

Rutter, M., Maughan, B., Mortimore, P., Ouston, J. and Smith, A. (1979) *Fifteen thousand hours: Secondary schools and their effects on children*, Cambridge, MA: Harvard University Press.

Sammons, P. (1999) *School effectiveness: Coming of age in the twenty-first century*, Lisse, The Netherlands: Swets & Zeitlinger.

Sammons, P., Day, C., Kington, A., Gu, Q., Stobart, G. and Smees, R. (2007) 'Exploring variations in teachers' work, lives and their effects on pupils: Key findings and implications from a longitudinal mixed methods study', *British Educational Research Journal*, 33(5): 681–701.

Sammons, P. and Ko, J. (2008) 'Effective classroom practice (ECP) report: Using systemic classroom observation schedules to investigate effective teaching: Overview of quantitative findings', ESRC ECP Project Report 2, Nottingham: University of Nottingham.

Sammons, P., Thomas, S. and Mortimore, P. (1997) *Forging links: Effective schools and effective departments,* London: Paul Chapman Press.

Sandelowski, M. (2003) 'Tables or tableux? The challenges of writing and reading mixed methods studies', in A. Tashakkori and C. Teddlie (eds) *Handbook of mixed methods in social and behavioural research,* Thousand Oaks, CA: Sage, pp. 321–50.

Scheerens, J. (1992) *Effective schooling: Research, theory and practice,* London: Cassell.

Scheerens, J. and Bosker, R. (1997) *The foundations of educational effectiveness,* Oxford: Pergamon Press.

Schickore, J. and Steinle, F. (eds) (2006) *Revisiting discovery and justification: Historical and philosophical perspectives on the context distinction,* The Netherlands: Dordecht.

Schulenberg, J.L. (2007) 'Analyzing police decision-making: Assessing the application of mixed-method/mixed-model research design', *International Journal of Social Research Methodology,* 10: 99–119.

Schwandt, T. (1997) *Qualitative inquiry: A dictionary of terms,* Thousand Oaks, CA: Sage Publications.

Shadish, W., Cook, T. and Campbell, D. (2002) *Experimental and quasi-experimental designs for general causal inference,* Boston: Houghton Mifflin.

Shulha, L. and Wilson, R. (2003) 'Collaborative mixed methods research', in A. Tashakkori and C. Teddlie (eds) *Handbook of mixed methods in social and behavioural research,* Thousand Oaks, CA: Sage, pp. 639–70.

Slater, R.O. and Teddlie, C. (1992) 'Toward a theory of school effectiveness and leadership', *School Effectiveness and School Improvement,* 3(4): 247–57.

Smith, J.K. (1996) 'An opportunity lost?', in L. Heshusius and K. Ballard (eds) *From positivism to interpretivism and beyond: Tales of transformation in educational and social research,* New York: Teachers College Press, pp. 161–8.

Song, M., Sandelowski, M. and Happ, M.B. (2010) 'Current practices and emerging trends in conducting mixed methods intervention studies', in A. Tashakkori and C. Teddlie (eds) *Handbook of mixed methods in social and behavioural research,* 2nd edn, Thousand Oaks, CA: Sage Publications.

Spalter-Roth, R. (2000) 'Gender issues in the use of integrated approaches', in M. Bamberger (ed.) *Integrating quantitative and qualitative research in development projects,* Washington, DC: The World Bank, pp. 47–53.

Stake, R.E. (1995) *The art of case study research,* Thousand Oaks, CA: Sage Publications.

Stringfield, S., Reynolds, D. and Schaffer, E. (2008) 'Improving secondary students' academic achievement through a focus on reform reliability: 4- and 9-year findings from the High Reliability Schools project', *School Effectiveness and School Improvement,* 19(4): 409–28.

Stringfield, S.C. and Slavin, R.E. (1992) 'A hierarchical longitudinal model for elementary school effects', in B.P.M. Creemers and G.J. Reezigt (eds) *Evaluation of educational effectiveness,* Groningen: ICO, pp. 35–69.

Tashakkori, A. and Creswell, J. (2007) 'The new era of mixed methods', *Journal of Mixed Methods Research,* 1(1): 3–7.

Tashakkori, A. and Teddlie, C. (1998) *Mixed methodology: Combining the qualitative and quantitative approaches,* Thousand Oaks, CA: Sage Publications.

Tashakkori, A. and Teddlie, C. (eds) (2003) *Handbook of mixed methods in social and behavioural research,* Thousand Oaks, CA: Sage Publications.

Teddlie, C. (1994) 'Integrating classroom and school data in school effectiveness research', in D. Reynolds, B. Creemers, P.S. Nesselrodt, E.C. Shaffer, S. Stringfield and C. Teddlie (eds) *Advances in school effectiveness research and practice,* Oxford: Pergamon, pp. 111–32.

Teddlie, C., Creemers, B., Kyriakides, L., Muijs, D. and Yu, F. (2006) 'The International System for Teacher Observation and Feedback: Evolution of an international study of teacher effectiveness constructs', *Educational Research and Evaluation*, 12: 561–82.

Teddlie, C. and Johnson, B. (2009) 'Methodological thought before the twentieth century', in C. Teddlie and A. Tashakkori (eds) *The foundations of mixed methods research: Integrating quantitative and qualitative techniques in the social and behavioural sciences*, Thousand Oaks, CA: Sage Publications, pp. 40–61.

Teddlie, C. and Liu, S. (2008) 'Examining teacher effectiveness within differentially effective primary schools in the People's Republic of China', *School Effectiveness and School Improvement*, 19(4): 387–407.

Teddlie, C. and Reynolds, D. (2000) *The international handbook of school effectiveness research*, London: Falmer Press.

Teddlie, C. and Stringfield, S. (1993) *Schools make a difference: Lessons learned from a 10-year study of school effects*, New York: Teachers College Press.

Teddlie, C., Stringfield, S. and Reynolds, D. (2000) 'Context issues within school effectiveness research', in C. Teddlie and D. Reynolds (eds) *The international handbook of school effectiveness research* 160–85, London: Falmer Press.

Teddlie, C. and Tashakkori, A. (2006) 'A general typology of research designs featuring mixed methods', *Research in the Schools*, 13(1): 12–28.

Teddlie, C. and Tashakkori, A. (2009) *The foundations of mixed methods research: Integrating quantitative and qualitative techniques in the social and behavioural sciences*, Thousand Oaks, CA: Sage Publications.

Teddlie, C., Tashakkori, A. and Johnson, B. (2008) 'Emergent techniques in the gathering and analysis of mixed methods data', in S. Hesse-Biber and P. Leavy (eds) *Handbook of emergent methods in social research*, New York: Guilford Publications, pp. 389–413.

Travers, R.M.W. (ed.) (1973) *Handbook of research on teaching*, 2nd edn, Chicago: Rand McNally.

Tymms, P., Merrell, C., Heron, T., Jones, P., Albone, S. and Henderson, B. (2008) 'The importance of districts', *School Effectiveness and School Improvement*, 19(3): 261–74.

Warner, W. and Lunt, P.S. (1941) 'The social life of a modern community', *Yankee city series*, 1, New Haven, CT: Yale University Press.

Weber, G. (1971) *Inner city children can be taught to read: Four successful schools*, Washington, DC: Council for Basic Education.

Webb, E.J., Campbell, D.T., Schwartz, R.D. and Sechrest, L. (1966) *Unobtrusive measures: Nonreactive research in the social sciences*, Chicago: Rand McNally.

Willms, J.D. (1985) 'The balance thesis – contextual effects of ability on pupils' O-grade examination results', *Oxford Review of Education*, 11(1): 33–41.

Wittrock, M.C. (ed) (1986) *Handbook of research on teaching*, 3rd edn, New York: Macmillan.

Yin, R.K. (2003) *Case study research: Design and methods*, 3rd edn, Thousand Oaks, CA: Sage Publications.

Chapter 8

Using Item Response Theory to measure outcomes and factors

An overview of Item Response Theory models

Norman Verhelst, CITO, The Netherlands

1 Introduction

In Educational Effectiveness Research, outcomes of educational practice as well as possible factors associated with or influencing these outcomes are usually formulated as rather complex concepts. This implies that EER has to make use of theories of measurement in order to generate valid and reliable measures of student outcomes and of different effectiveness factors that operate at different levels.

The basic problem with educational measurement is that its outcomes – most of the time the performance of students in some subject matter – are never measured in a unitary operation, but come about by an aggregation of small bits of information: the answers to small tasks are scored in a more or less objective way, and the measure of the performance is the sum – weighted or unweighted – of the scores on the constituent tasks, commonly referred to as items. The collection of items administered to the students is referred to as a test, and the sum of the item scores is the test score.

In Classical Test Theory, the basic observation at student level is the test score, and one could say in a fairly general way that the basic objective of EER is to explain – in a statistical way – the variability of the test scores or, even more generally, the covariance structure of the test scores if they are multivariate. As a theory of test scores, however, Classical Test Theory is rather weak since the only concept it uses is the so-called true score, which is of a statistical nature: an observed score is the sum of its average (under an infinitely large sample of equivalent test administrations under the same conditions) and the deviation from the observed score to this average. The average is the true score, and the deviation is the measurement error. However, this decomposition between average and deviation to the average holds for any test, whether its composition (the items) is well considered or completely arbitrary, whether the items measure the same concept or are completely chosen at random from an arbitrary collection of domains. Classical Test Theory, as a statistical theory, is not concerned with the meaningfulness of the composition of a test; it has almost no rules on which a decision to include or exclude a particular item in a test can be based.

In modern test theory, as it is sometimes called, the concept to be measured takes a central place. In many applications it is conceived as a continuous, unbounded variable (that is, running from minus infinity to plus infinity), which is not directly observable – hence the term latent variable. The observable variables, the answers given to the items, are considered as indicators of the latent variable. Roughly formulated, this means that a correct answer to a mathematics item is considered as a sign or indicator of higher mathematics ability than an incorrect one. The precise meaning of the expression 'is an indicator of' is the definition of the models that are studied in the area of Item Response Theory (IRT). In the sections that follow, some examples will be treated in a detailed way. For now, it is important to emphasize that an IRT model is a hypothesis about the behaviour of students, and that such a hypothesis needs an empirical test. To understand the nature of such empirical testing, however, it is necessary that the model itself is understood in a correct way, and that the deductions from the model definition are derived in a correct way. This makes the use of IRT models a non-trivial undertaking. An overview of the logical steps to be taken when using IRT modelling is given below:

- IRT models rest upon a set of assumptions and formulate the 'indicator function' of an item response in a probabilistic way: they express the probability of a correct answer to an item as a mathematical function of the underlying ability. This function is specific for each item, and the dependence on the item is expressed by the use of one or more parameters per item. These functions are referred to as item response functions (IRFs) and usually belong to the same family. It is important to understand that IRT models do not specify the answer to the items, but only the probability of the possible answers – that is, IRT models are probabilistic models.
- In the formulation of the model, parameters are introduced as formal entities, but in any application a value has to be assigned to these parameters. Assigning values to the parameters on the basis of the observed responses is known as parameter estimation. Procedures for parameter estimation are usually quite complicated. In the present chapter, only the most important principles of the estimation procedures are discussed. For technical details, the reader is referred to specialized literature. The important point to be retained from the parameter estimation procedure is that it does not reveal the 'true' value of the parameters, only estimates become available and these estimates have an estimation error. The order of magnitude of these errors is usually expressed by the standard error.
- From the assumptions of the model, a plethora of predictions about the data follow. As an example, take the correlations between the item answers. If the parameters of the model are known, all correlations can be predicted exactly. If the parameters are known approximately, then the correlations are also known approximately. In either case, the observed correlations can be compared to the predicted ones, and the validity of the model is judged by the

correspondence between predicted and observed correlations. The judgment of the quality of the correspondence (is it good or not good enough) is usually done by a statistical test. The generic name for such statistical tests is goodness-of-fit tests. There are two problems associated with the use of goodness-of-fit tests, which should be distinguished carefully:

- Are the statistical tests proposed in the literature genuine statistical tests? Is the real statistical significance level equal or approximately equal to the nominal one? Sometimes the construction of statistical tests is quite complicated, due to the fact that the predicted statistics (the correlations in the above example) are based on parameter estimates, which are in turn estimated from the same data that are used in the statistical test itself. Ignoring this dependence may invalidate the statistical testing procedure. This problem will be touched upon in the next chapter, but the theory will not be explained in much detail, because of its quite complicated technical nature.

- The other problem requires much more involvement from the applied researcher than the first one. Referring to the example above, the important question is why one should pay attention to a good prediction of the item correlation matrix. This question has two sides. If the correspondence between observed and predicted correlations is good, one has some evidence on the validity of the model, but it would be a mistake to think that a good prediction of the correlations is all there is that can be said about the validity of the model. There may exist other defects in the model that are not detected by an investigation of the correlations, but that may appear if other aspects of the data are predicted. In statistical terms, it is said then that the test on the correlations has little or no power to detect these other defects. On the other hand, it may be the case that the goodness-of-fit test detects a poor prediction of the correlations, but that this defect is not important for the purpose of the study. Suppose as an example that the study is set up to find out whether two different instructional methods lead to different outcomes in a mathematics test. In such a case it is hardly imaginable how the poor prediction of the item correlations could invalidate in any serious way the conclusion that method A is better than method B, say. In more general terms, this latter problem is referred to as robustness: to what extent can we tolerate a defect in the model without jeopardizing the conclusions of our research?

• An important logical step in using IRT models (or for that sake, any model) is the decision to accept or to reject the model as a vehicle for drawing substantive conclusions. Although the choice is presented as binary, it is seldom applied in such a rigorous way. Complete rejection may mean complete failure of the research, which is seldom acceptable or justifiable. In many cases, the defect can be repaired by appropriate actions such as deleting part of the items or deleting part of the student sample from the study. Similarly, acceptance is not a synonym of a perfect model: if some evidence can be provided that the substantive conclusions from the study are not affected seriously by an imperfect model, the model could be used anyway. It is important, however, that partial failures or actions such as deleting part of the item material are well documented. Such documentation can be the source for new ideas, be it in the substantive field of the research questions, or in the psychometric modelling.

- Logically, the last step in applying formal models for measurement is to use them in actual measurement. To assess whether the ability in some domain is associated with curricular, personal and external factors, it seems necessary that this ability can be measured in a faithful way. Therefore, the establishment of a trustworthy measurement instrument takes logical precedence over the assessment of the relative influence of all factors of interest.

The application of these five logical steps is not always easy, and may impose some restrictions on the available measurement models. The logical steps represent a separation of the measurement model and the structural model (as in SEM, see Chapter 12), and an important question is whether it is possible to assess the validity of the measurement model without assuming anything about the structural model – that is, without making any substantive assumption about the distribution of the latent variable in the population of interest.

As an example, consider again the case where the main substantive question is to know which of two available instructional methods are associated with the highest level of mathematics ability in two groups of students. As a measurement instrument, a mathematics test is used. The question that is addressed here is whether a thorough analysis of the measurement instrument can be reached without assuming (for example) that the ability in the two populations is normally distributed, or that the ability distribution in both populations has the same variance. Some other important questions are stated below:

- Is it important that the samples from the two populations are simple random samples, or can the sampling be done in several stages (first a sampling of schools and then a sample of students within schools)?
- Will the intra-class correlation influence in a systematic way the outcomes of the measurement analysis?
- What if we use only a convenience sample to analyse the measurement instrument?
- What if there is a difference between the two instructional methods, but there is also a substantial difference due to gender, and on top of that, there might be an important interaction effect of gender and method?

In the preceding paragraphs, a number of serious problems have been raised, but what does one win if the logical steps are followed as described and the outcomes of the analysis are on the whole quite positive? Apart from the general methodological requirements to show the validity of inferences based on test results, there is one big advantage in the use of the IRT methodology: as the concept to be measured is central in the theory, and as the item answers are only indicators, it follows that different indicators (of the same concept) can be used for different students or groups of students. This means that the measurement instrument does not need to be the same for all students, or from the viewpoint of the total collection of items, it means that data can be collected in an incomplete design. In terms of the above example, it means that the mathematics ability in population A can be assessed by a test that is different from the one used in population B, and still yield valid comparisons of the ability in both populations. This invaluable advantage does not hold in the framework of Classical Test Theory.

In this context, Chapters 8 and 9 will roughly follow the logical steps described above. This chapter will be restricted to an overview of IRT models that can be useful in EER. Section 2 is devoted to the most elementary model in IRT, the Rasch model. This offers the possibility to introduce a number of key concepts that appear throughout the IRT literature. Section 3 discusses two generalizations of the Rasch model, the two- and the three-parameter logistic models, and in Section 4 the family of normal ogive models is introduced. All these models were originally introduced to describe responses on binary items. In Section 5, extensions to items with more than two categories are discussed. Section 6, finally, discusses the relationship between IRT models and factor analysis. Parameter estimation and statistical testing of the goodness-of-fit of IRT models are rather involved and technical. They are treated in some detail in the next chapter. Using the results of an IRT analysis in actually doing EER is complicated as well. Thus, Chapter 9 also provides some suggestions on how researchers in the field of educational effectiveness can make use of IRT to develop further not only the methodology of EER but also its theoretical framework.

2 Basic concepts

2.1 Guttman's scalogram

A basic idea of IRT models is that the answer of a student v to an item i reflects in some respect a relation between the student and the item. If the answer is correct, this is an indication that the student dominates the item. If the item is about mathematics, then a correct answer indicates that the student has more ability than required by the item; if the answer is incorrect, the item dominates the student, meaning that the student has less ability than required by the task. Using terms such as 'more' and 'less' implies an order relation, and a geometric representation of this order is the use of a directed line or dimension, where the terms of the comparison are represented as points. This idea is due to Guttman (1950) and is the basis of scalogram analysis. The idea is displayed graphically in Figure 8.1: the horizontal line represents the ability continuum,

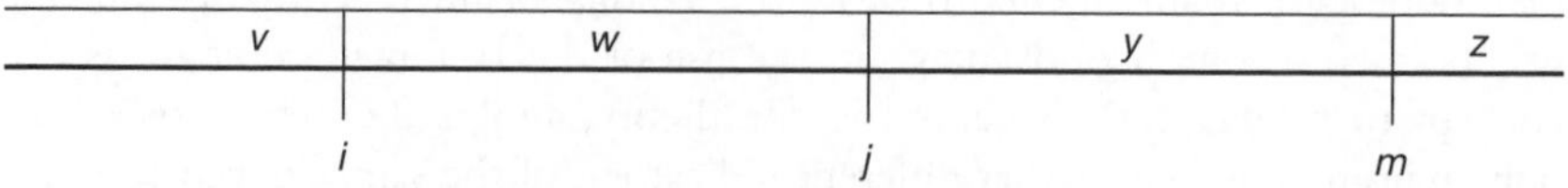

v	w	y	z

i   j   m

Figure 8.1 Graphical representation of scalogram analysis

the vertical lines correspond to the position of the items *i*, *j* and *m* and the letters *v*, *w*, *y* and *z* represent the positions of four students. The relative positions of the letters to each other represent the dominance relation: the right-most position reflects the higher ability.

The theory of scalogram analysis amounts to the following:

- If the positions of student and item points are known, then the behaviour – the item answer – is known: if a student position dominates the item position, then the answer is correct; otherwise it is incorrect. This means that Guttman's model is deterministic.

- Items and students are positioned on the same continuum. From the viewpoint of the student the position reflects his ability; the position of the item reflects its difficulty, but unlike in Classical Test Theory, the difficulty does not represent a proportion of correct answers in some population; it reflects the required ability to grant a correct response.

- The theory is testable. In Figure 8.1, there is no point on the continuum that dominates the position of item *j* and that at the same time is dominated by the position of item *i*. Or, in behavioural terms, it is not possible to give a correct answer to a difficult item and an incorrect answer to an easier item. With a test of three items, it follows that there are only four response patterns possible: $(0,0,0)$, $(1,0,0)$, $(1,1,0)$ and $(1,1,1)$, represented in Figure 8.1 by the letters *v*, *w*, *y* and *z* respectively. In the general case with a test of *k* items, only $k + 1$ different response patterns are allowed, while the number of possible answers is 2^k. Guttman's theory leaves no room for 'errors', and consequently, it has to be rejected in most of the cases.

- A scalogram analysis amounts to finding the correct order of the items and students from a given data set. The result is an ordinal scale, and scale values given to students can only be used as ordinal numbers. Assigning the values 1, 2, 3 and 4 to the students *v*, *w*, *y* and *z* reflects their ordering in ability, but the same ordering is reflected by the scale values 1, 7, 32 and 107, and there is nothing in the theory that justifies the preference of one above the other.

The vulnerable aspect of Guttmans's theory is its deterministic character. In probabilistic terms, it only uses probabilities of zero and one: if the item dominates the student, the probability of a correct answer is zero; otherwise it is one. Most IRT models in use can be seen as a relaxation of this deterministic feature, as they describe in much detail the probability of a correct answer as a function of the relative position of student and item points on the ability continuum. A simple model is described in the next section.

2.2 The Rasch model

In Figure 8.2 a graphical display of the Rasch model (Rasch 1960) is shown. The horizontal axis represents the ability dimension, named θ, and exactly as in Guttman's model each student is represented by a point on this dimension. For each point on the line, the model expresses the probability of a correct response to each of the items in the test; so for each item there is curve associating the ability point to the probability of a correct answer. This curve is known as the item characteristic curve, or item response curve. (In the older literature, the term 'trace line' is used as well.) Each curve is the graphical display of a function, known as item characteristic function or item response function (IRF). The point on the θ-scale that yields a probability of 0.5 for item i is labeled by a special symbol, β_i. In a general description of the model, the exact position of this point or, equivalently, its value is not known, but has to be estimated from the data. The quantities β_i for each item are referred to as item parameters.

There are a number of features in Figure 8.2 that also appear in other IRT models, or are distinctive for other models. They are discussed in turn:

- The IRFs are monotonically increasing, or in behavioural terms, the higher the ability the higher the probability of a correct response. This seems quite natural in achievement or ability testing, and all IRT models used in this area of research have this feature. In the area of attitude and preference

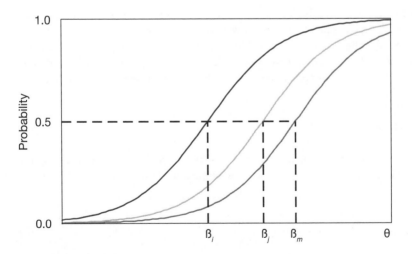

Figure 8.2 Item response functions in the Rasch model

research, single peaked IRFs are used sometimes, that is, functions that are increasing up to some point on the scale and then decrease. Single-peaked functions also appear in the area of achievement testing, and some of these will be discussed in the next section; these functions, however, are not IRFs.

- In the model definition, the scale values are unbounded: they range from minus infinity to plus infinity. This feature is common to all IRT models.
- The probability of a correct answer on any item is different from zero and one, but as θ increases without bound, the probability of a correct answer approaches one, and if it decreases without bound, the probability approaches zero. One says that zero and one are the lower and upper asymptotes respectively. This feature, especially about the lower asymptote, has been a source of a lot of criticism of the Rasch model. It will be discussed in more detail later.
- Item response curves in the Rasch model do not intersect: for all points on the ability scale it holds that item i has the highest probability of a correct response and item m the lowest one. Moreover, all curves in Figure 8.2 have exactly the same form; they differ only in location. Any curve in the figure can be shifted horizontally until it coincides completely with either of the other two.

These features jointly, however, do not define the Rasch model, as there can be many different mathematical functions that have the same features. In the Rasch model, the IRFs are defined as:

$$f_i(\theta) = \frac{\exp(\theta - \beta_i)}{1 + \exp(\theta - \beta_i)}, \tag{1}$$

which is an increasing function of θ that depends on a single parameter β_i. (The expression $\exp(x)$ is just a convenient way to write down the exponential function e^x, where e is the base of the natural logarithms and equals approximately 2.718. Notice that $e^0 = 1$.) The function $f_i(\theta)$ is a conditional probability. If we denote the outcome of an answer to item i as X_i, then the meaning of the IRF becomes clear:

$$f_i(\theta) = P(X_i = 1 | \theta). \tag{2}$$

Since the outcome of an item answer is binary, yielding the value one if the answer is correct and zero otherwise, we immediately deduce from (1) and (2) that

$$P(X_i = 0 | \theta) = 1 - f_i(\theta) = \frac{1}{1 + \exp(\theta - \beta_i)}. \tag{3}$$

There are some interesting ways to look at the IRF defined by (1).

- The curves in Figure 8.2 are very similar to the curves of the cumulative normal distribution, but they are not representing the normal distribution. They represent the cumulative *logistic* distribution, which is similar to the normal distribution: it is symmetric, but has thicker tails than the normal distribution. The standard logistic distribution has a mean of zero and a variance equal to $\pi^2/3$. A normal distribution with a mean of zero and a standard deviation of 1.7 is very similar to the standard logistic distribution. The function in equation (1) is known by the name 'logistic function'. Its *argument* is the difference $\theta - \beta_i$.
- Since the outcome variables X_i are binary, the expected value equals the probability that the outcome equals one:

$$E(X_i|\theta) = 0 \times P(X_i = 0|\theta) + 1 \times P(X_i = 1|\theta) = f_i(\theta).$$

This means that the IRFs are regression functions of the outcome variables X_i on the latent variable θ. The regression is not linear, as can be seen clearly from Figure 8.2.

- An interesting function is the *logit function* or the *log-odds function*. It is given by

$$\ln\frac{P(X_i = 1|\theta)}{P(X_i = 0|\theta)} = \ln\frac{f_i(\theta)}{1 - f_i(\theta)} = \theta - \beta_i,$$

which is linear in θ. Generalizations of the logit function are useful to understand the structure of other, more complicated models.

- The right-hand sides of equations (1) and (3) are fractions with the same denominator, meaning that this denominator does not depend on the specific value of the outcome variable X_i. The denominator is the sum of both numerators; clearly its function it to make sure that the sum of the probabilities of all possible outcomes equals one. This denominator is also called the normalizing constant. Therefore we can write (1) and (3) equivalently as

$$P(X_i = 1|\theta) \propto \exp(\theta - \beta_i) \tag{1a}$$

and

$$P(X_i = 0|\theta) \propto 1, \tag{3a}$$

where the symbol $\propto$ means 'is proportional to'. The normalizing constant is one divided by the sum of the right-hand sides of (1a) and (3a).

Conditional independence

The Rasch model is not completely defined by its IRFs. These functions describe the marginal distribution of the outcome variables X_i, conditional on θ, but from these marginal distributions the joint distributions cannot be derived uniquely. To put it more simply: from (1) one cannot specify the probability $P(X_i = 1$ and $X_j = 1|\theta)$. Therefore, something more has to be added to the model to make it fully defined. This addition has the form of an assumption that is ubiquitous in statistical modelling: the assumption of conditional independence or local stochastic independence, the term 'local' pointing to the fact that the latent variable is fixed. Let a test consist of k items, and let $\underline{X} = (X_1, \ldots, X_k)$ be the vector of outcome variables, also called the response pattern. Let $\underline{x} = (x_1, \ldots, x_k)$ be a realization of $\underline{X}$, that is, $\underline{x}$ is some observable response pattern. The assumption of conditional independence states that

$$P(\underline{X} = \underline{x} \,|\, \theta) = \prod_{i=1}^{k} P(X_i = x_i \,|\, \theta), \qquad (4)$$

for all possible response patterns $\underline{x}$. This assumption is analogous to the axiom of independent measurement errors in Classical Test Theory. Notice that this assumption does not say that item answers are independent and hence correlate zero; it says that item answers are independent in all populations where the latent variable θ is constant, and hence that correlations between item responses are zero in such populations. However, this means also that if, in some population, item responses do correlate, that this correlation is explained (completely) by the variation in the latent variable θ. In this sense, the Rasch model is very similar to the one-factor model. The relation between factor analysis and IRT models will be discussed further in Section 6.

Exponential families

Apart from the conditional independence, there is another principle of independence that applies, namely, experimental independence. This principle says that test performances, given the latent abilities of a group of students, are independent of each other. As an example consider a sample of n students, and denote the latent ability of a single student v by θ_v. The item responses of the n students to a test of k items are collected in an $n \times k$ matrix X with the rows representing students and the columns corresponding to the items. X is a multivariate random variable, which on administration of the test will take particular values or realizations. These realizations are indicated by x. The v-th row of X and x will be denoted as $\underline{X}_v$ and $\underline{x}_v$, respectively, and individual elements as X_{vi} and x_{vi}. The principle of experimental independence states that

$$P(\mathbf{X} = \mathbf{x} \,|\, \theta_1, \ldots, \theta_n) = \prod_{v=1}^{n} P(\underline{X}_v = \underline{x}_v \,|\, \theta_v), \qquad (5)$$

Substituting the right-hand side of equation (4) into equation (5) gives as a result:

$$P(\mathbf{X} = \mathbf{x} \mid \theta_1,\ldots,\theta_n) = \prod_{v=1}^{n} \prod_{i=1}^{k} P(X_{vi} = x_{vi} \mid \theta_v), \qquad (6)$$

and using (1) and (3) one finds that

$$P(\mathbf{X} = \mathbf{x} \mid \theta_1,\ldots,\theta_n) = \frac{\exp\left[\sum_v \theta_v \sum_i x_{vi} - \sum_i \beta_i \sum_v x_{vi}\right]}{\prod_{v=1}^{n} \prod_{i=1}^{k}\left[1 + \exp(\theta_v - \beta_i)\right]}. \qquad (7)$$

The probability of the observed data, considered as a function of the unknown quantities θ_v and β_i, is called the likelihood function. Defining

$$s_v = \sum_{i=1}^{k} x_{vi} \text{ and } t_i = \sum_{v=1}^{n} x_{vi},$$

and taking the logarithm of (7) gives

$$\ln P(\mathbf{X} = \mathbf{x} \mid \theta_1,\ldots,\theta_n) = \sum_{v=1}^{n} s_v \theta_v + \sum_{i=1}^{k} t_i(-\beta_i) - \sum_{v=1}^{n}\sum_{i=1}^{k}\ln\left[1 + \exp(\theta_v - \beta_i)\right]. \qquad (8)$$

The right-hand side of equation (8) consists of two important parts: the two sums that contain functions of the data (s_v and t_i), and the double sum, which is independent of the data. Each term in the first two sums consists of a product, one factor being a function of the unknown quantities in the model (θ_v and $-\beta_i$) and the other factor a function of the data (s_v and t_i). Models for which the log-likelihood function can be written in this form are referred to as 'exponential family models'. Such models have attractive features that are used in the parameter estimation procedures to be discussed in the next chapter.

The quantity s_v is the row total of row v of the observed data matrix x, and t_i is the column total of the i-th column. From (8) we see that the likelihood of the observed data depends on the data only through its marginal sums, or, equivalently, that under the Rasch model, all observed matrices with the same marginal sums are equiprobable. This means also that anything we can learn about the latent ability of student v is contained in this row sum s_v, which is called the 'sufficient statistic' for the unknown quantity θ_v. Similarly, the column sums t_i are the sufficient statistics for the item parameters.

This section is concluded with a general consideration of the notions of independence that have been discussed so far. It may seem that the Rasch model (and, in fact, any of the other models that will be discussed subsequently) is unrealistic, as any researcher in the area of EER knows that test data may show substantial dependence, due, for example, to school or classroom effects. There is, however, no contradiction in this because equation (7) describes a conditional probability, where the condition is the collection of latent values represented in the sample. Roughly formulated, the axiom of conditional independence means that each new item is a new opportunity to show one's ability, and that the probability of success does not depend on failures or successes on other items. The principle of experimental independence means simply that students have to work alone and independently of their classroom peers. The lack of independence often encountered in EER is due to the effect of using a sampling scheme different from simple random sampling, such as cluster sampling. In terms of equation (7), this means that the students and, consequently, their latent abilities are not independent of each other, but this dependence is a dependence in the condition of the conditional probability, not in the outcome variables. Or to put it slightly differently, equation (7) is assumed to hold, no matter how the sample of the n students has been drawn.

3 The two- and three-parameter logistic models

The models to be discussed in this section can be considered as generalizations of the Rasch model, although, historically, they were not developed as such. In many discussions, criticism of the Rasch model mostly points to two severe restrictions in the model, and the two models to be discussed are ways to cope with these criticisms by introducing more complicated models.

3.1 The two-parameter logistic model

In the Rasch model, each item has one parameter β_i, commonly referred to as the difficulty parameter. From elementary techniques in Classical Test Theory it is well known that items do not differ only in difficulty but also in discrimination. In the Rasch model, there is no possibility to make the items differ in discrimination. In Figure 8.3, two response curves are displayed for items i and j, both having the same difficulty, but they differ in discrimination in the following sense: imagine two students with a latent ability in a small neighborhood of the common difficulty parameter of the two items – that is, where the two curves cross, one being a bit lower, the other a bit higher. With item i the difference in probability of success for the two students is quite small (this difference is displayed as the distance between the two dashed lines on the left vertical axis), while with item j the corresponding difference is much larger (refer to the right vertical axis), meaning that item j discriminates better than item i. This difference in probabilities is associated with the steepness of the two curves in the neighborhood of the difficulty parameter.

To grasp this difference in a mathematical expression, one needs an extra parameter. The IRF for this generalized model is given by

$$P(X_i = 1 \mid \theta) = \frac{\exp[\alpha_i(\theta - \beta_i)]}{1 + \exp[\alpha_i(\theta - \beta_i)]}, (\alpha_i > 0). \tag{9}$$

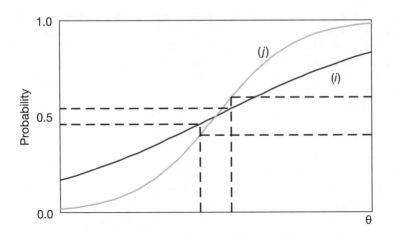

Figure 8.3 Two items with equal difficulty but different discrimination

The larger the parameter α, the steeper the curve is. This parameter is commonly referred to as the discrimination parameter. The function in (9) is also a logistic function; its argument is $\alpha_i(\theta - \beta_i)$. The model with IRFs given by (9) is known as the two-parameter logistic model (2PLM).

It may be interesting to see what happens if the discrimination parameter becomes very large. Taking limits of (9) for $\alpha_i \to \infty$ gives different results, depending on the sign of the difference $\theta - \beta_i$:

$$\lim_{\alpha i \to \infty} P(X_i = 1|\theta) = 1 \text{ if } \theta > \beta_i,$$

$$\lim_{\alpha i \to \infty} P(X_i = 1|\theta) = 0 \text{ if } \theta < \beta_i.$$

This means that with a very large discrimination parameter the item behaves as a Guttman item.

The log-likelihood function for this model is given by

$$\ln P(\mathbf{X} = \mathbf{x}\,|\,\theta_1,\ldots,\theta_n)$$
$$= \sum_{v=1}^{n} w_v \theta_v + \sum_{i=1}^{k} t_i (-\alpha_i \beta_i) - \sum_{v=1}^{n}\sum_{i=1}^{k} \ln\left[1 + \exp[\alpha_i(\theta_v - \beta_i)]\right], \qquad (10)$$

where the sufficient statistic for the difficulty parameters is $t_i = \Sigma_v x_{vi}$, as in the Rasch model, and

$$w_v = \sum_{i=1}^{k} \alpha_i x_{vi},$$

the weighted score – that is, the sum of the discrimination parameters of the correctly answered items by student v. However, this weighted sum is not a mere statistic, that is, a function of the observed data; it also depends on the unknown discrimination parameters, and therefore the 2PLM is not an exponential family model. If one knows the value of these parameters, or treats them as known constants (by hypothesis, for example), then the model becomes an exponential family model. More on this will be said in the section on parameter estimation in the next chapter.

3.2 The three-parameter logistic model

A serious criticism of the Rasch model and the 2PLM is that these models are not capable of describing accurately the behaviour of students in tests where some or all of the items have a forced choice format, such as multiple choice items. If the ability is very low, both models predict a success probability very near zero, but correct answers may come about by some guessing strategy. If the item is a multiple choice item with four alternatives, picking an alternative at random will guarantee a success probability of 0.25. Formally, this is handled by adding another parameter to each item, which changes the lower asymptote from zero to some positive (but unknown) constant c_i. The IRFs for this model are given by

$$P(X_i = 1 \mid \theta) = c_i + (1 - c_i) \frac{\exp[\alpha_i(\theta - \beta_i)]}{1 + \exp[\alpha_i(\theta - \beta_i)]}. \tag{11}$$

The parameter c_i is known as the guessing parameter, and the parameters α_i and β_i are the discrimination and difficulty parameters just as in the 2PLM. This model is known as the three-parameter logistic model (3PLM), although the IRF defined by (11) is not a logistic function. In Figure 8.4 the item response functions are displayed for two items, i and j, having the same discrimination and difficulty, but $c_i = 0$ and $c_j = 0.25$. The location of the difficulty parameter is indicated by the dashed line.

Notice that in this model, the difficulty parameter no longer has the elegant interpretation as the ability that grants a 50 per cent probability of a correct response. If the right-hand side of (11) is evaluated at the point $\theta = \beta_i$, the result is $(1 + c_i)/2$, which, in the figure, yields 0.5 for item i and 0.625 for item j.

When it comes to a choice between the Rasch model, the 2PLM or the 3PLM, the problem seems to be trivial: as the latter model is the most general, it will (by definition) fit the data at least as well as the other two. Along this line of reasoning, it has even been proposed to use the so-called four-parameter logistic model, which has on top of the three parameters per item present in the 3PLM also an extra parameter to shift the upper asymptote away from one. The rationale for this parameter is to explain carelessness errors, for cases where the correct answer is 'known' almost certainly, but for some reason (carelessness, for example) it is not written down. However, the unbridled growth in complexity of models by adding more and more parameters has its price, in at least two respects:

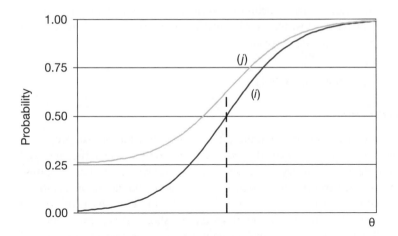

Figure 8.4 Two items in the 3PLM with equal discrimination and difficulty

- Commonly the parameters are estimated from a single data set, which consists just of a table filled with ones and zeros. Adding parameters to the model means adding more sources of insecurity (about their 'true' values), but the amount of information one has available to solve this insecurity remains the same. The consequence will inevitably be that the standard errors of the estimates will increase as the number of parameters increases, and even worse, the correlations between (some) parameter estimates will tend to become very high (in absolute value). This is the case, for example, in the 3PLM, for the guessing parameter and the difficulty parameter of the same item: their estimates show usually a high negative correlation, suggesting a trade-off between guessing and difficulty.
- The second aspect bears more on the construct validity of the model, or formulated more accurately, on the inferences one can make from the model. Here is an example. Suppose the 3PLM is applied with a test of 100 items, and the guessing parameters have estimates all close to 0.25. If some student has answered correctly about one quarter of the items, one might be tempted to say that this student has really guessed on all items. However, there is no direct evidence of this; nobody has 'seen' this student guessing, and maybe the student knew the answer to 25 of the 100 items, has guessed (incorrectly) on some others and had a misconception about the remaining ones, all leading to an incorrect answer. If one sticks to the simple table with ones and zeros as the only observation to be analysed, the processes having led to these answers are caught in a black box, and there is no evidence beyond the match of the model to these data to make further inferences. But, strictly speaking, the model is nothing else than a formal description of the data in statistical terms, and one should not overplay one's hand

in drawing substantive conclusions from such a description; much more convincing evidence would be obtained by an interview of the students on how they came to their answers.

4 Normal ogive models

4.1 Derivation

In the Thurstonian tradition of scaling, the normal distribution has been used extensively to model unexplained variation in responses. When the observed behaviour is discrete or binary, an underlying, not observed continuous response variable is assumed to operate, together with a kind of boundary or threshold. The observed or overt response then is thought to come about by a comparison of the unobserved continuous response to the threshold. This is exemplified in Figure 8.5. When answering an item, a latent response, z, is drawn from a normal distribution with standard deviation equal to one. The mean of this distribution is the ability of the student. The item defines a threshold, β_i, and the overt response is correct if the latent response is greater than the threshold.

The probability that the answer is incorrect is given by

$$P(X_i = 0 \mid \theta) = \frac{1}{\sqrt{2\pi}} \int_{-\infty}^{\beta_i} \exp[-\frac{1}{2}(z-\theta)]^2 \, dz = \Phi(\beta_i - \theta), \tag{12}$$

where $\Phi(.)$ denotes the standard normal distribution function. The IRF for the model is then readily found by using the symmetry of the normal distribution:

$$P(X_i = 1 \mid \theta) = 1 - \Phi(\beta_i - \theta) = \Phi(\theta - \beta_i). \tag{13}$$

The graph of the function $\Phi(.)$ is known as the normal ogive, and it looks very similar to the curves in Figure 8.2.

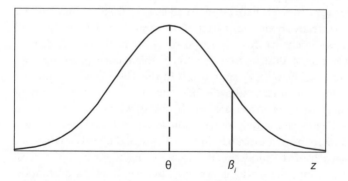

Figure 8.5 The normal ogive model using latent responses

4.2 The one- and two-parameter normal ogive models

When the above derivation applies equally to all items, the one-parameter normal ogive model results. The main feature of this is that it is assumed that for every item the standard deviation of the latent responses is equal. The two-parameter model is obtained when it is assumed that the standard deviations of the latent responses may vary across items. Representing these standard deviations by σ_i, one finds readily that

$$P(X_i = 1 \mid \theta) = \Phi\left(\frac{\theta - \beta_i}{\sigma_i}\right). \tag{14}$$

The graphs of these functions are steeper the smaller the standard deviation is, meaning that the inverse of the standard deviation has the same interpretation as the discrimination parameter in the 2PLM. Defining $\alpha_i = \sigma_i^{-1}$, one finds the standard expression for the two-parameter normal ogive model:

$$P(X_i = 1 \mid \theta) = \Phi[\alpha_i(\theta - \beta_i)]. \tag{15}$$

4.3 Relation between logistic and normal ogive models

The derivation shown for the normal ogive models can also be applied to the Rasch model and the 2PLM, although historically, this does not seem to have been done. The only difference is that the normal distribution is replaced by the logistic distribution. Using the function symbol $\Psi(.)$ for the logistic distribution function, we then find an expression for the 2PLM analogous to (15):

$$P(X_i = 1 \mid \theta) = \Psi[\alpha_i(\theta - \beta_i)]. \tag{16}$$

Although the two distribution functions $\Phi(.)$ and $\Psi(.)$ have very similar graphs, the graphs will be quite dissimilar if in (15) and (16) the same values are used for the parameters α_i and β_i. The reason for this is that the standard logistic distribution does not have a standard deviation equal to one. A close similarity is found if the discrimination parameter in the 2PLM is 1.7 times the discrimination parameter in the two-parameter normal ogive model; the difficulty parameters can be treated as equal. This gives

$$\Phi[\alpha_i(\theta - \beta_i)] \approx \Psi[1.7\alpha_i(\theta - \beta_i)].$$

The scale factor 1.7 is often found in textbooks treating the 2PLM and the 3PLM. In Figure 8.6, a graph of both IRFs is given for the interval $(0, 3)$ with $\beta_i = 0$ for both models; the discrimination parameter for the normal model equals one, and for the logistic model it is 1.7.

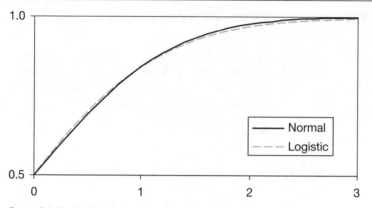

Figure 8.6 Similarity of the normal ogive and the logistic models

As the differences are very small, it might be concluded that the models can be used interchangeably, and for practical purposes this is undoubtedly the case. Nevertheless, models of the logistic family have been more popular than the normal ogive models in the history of modern psychometrics. At least two reasons can be given for this. First, the mathematics needed to study the characteristics of the models are easier and more elegant in the logistic family than with the normal models. A thorough study of the 2PLM and the 3PLM can be found in the influential book by Lord and Novick (1968), especially the contributions of A. Birnbaum. The great attention that IRT has got in Europe is certainly due to the important work of Rasch (1960) and the pioneering work of Fischer. Both these authors have spent a lot of effort demonstrating that the Rasch model follows necessarily from a few requirements that can be attributed to objective measurement. The interested reader is referred to Fischer (1974, 1995) for a detailed (and often quite difficult) discussion on these topics.

In the 1990s, renewed attention was given to the normal ogive models. Estimation techniques based on sampling procedures, such as the Gibbs sampler, became popular and feasible due to the increasing computing speed of modern computers. It appeared that these techniques were easier to implement with the normal ogive models than with models from the logistic family.

5 Models for polytomous item responses

Sometimes observations are categorized in more than two categories, such as correct and incorrect. If the items allow for more than two categories, they are called 'polytomous'. For polytomous data one distinguishes ordered and unordered polytomies. Unordered categories correspond to nominal data. An example is offered by multiple choice items, where each alternative just represents a nominal response category. Instead of merely dichotomizing these categories as either correct or incorrect, one might assume that different alternatives give different information about the underlying ability.

Commonly, however, the different response categories are considered as ordered categories; in that case one has an ordered polytomy, where the categories are usually labelled as 0, 1, 2, . . . The ordering is with respect to the underlying ability: it is assumed that obtaining a '1' is an indication of a higher ability than obtaining a '0'; '2' indicates a higher ability than '1', and so on.

In this section, a model for unordered categories is briefly discussed – Bock's (1972) nominal response model. Two models for ordered categories, the partial credit model and the graded response model will be discussed thereafter.

5.1 The nominal response model (NRM)

The discussion on this model serves two functions. First the model is interesting enough in itself to devote some attention to it. It shows how very unstructured data, just observations in nominal categories, can be treated in a way that allows one to draw quantitative inferences. Second, the model offers a good opportunity to discuss some identifiability problems present in all IRT models that were not mentioned in the previous discussions.

Suppose a test consists of k items, and the responses to each item are classified in a number of categories. This number can differ across items. The number of categories for item i is denoted as m_i, and it is assumed that $m_i \geq 2$. Furthermore, it is assumed that all responses can be considered as indicators for the same latent ability θ. If there are more than two categories, then the concept of an IRF does not make much sense; in such cases models specify the probability that a certain category will be chosen as a function of the underlying variable θ. These functions are called 'category response functions'. In the nominal response model, these functions are given by

$$P(X_i = j|\theta) \propto \exp[\alpha_{ij}(\theta - \beta_{ij})], \, (j = 1, \ldots, m_i), \quad (17)$$

where the expression $X_i = j$ means: the answer to item i belongs to category j. To find the exact probabilities, one has to determine the proportionality constant, which is one divided by the sum of the m_i expressions specified in (17). Notice that in this model, unlike in the 2PLM, there are no positivity restrictions on the α-parameters.

There are three different reasons why this model is not identified as it is specified in (17). One reason applies to each item separately; the other two apply to all items jointly. We discuss them in turn.

If we consider the ratio of the probabilities for two categories of the same item, the normalizing constant cancels, since it is common for all categories. Now consider the ratio of the probability for category j to the probability for some other category r:

$$\frac{P(X_i = j \mid \theta)}{P(X_i = r \mid \theta)} = \frac{\exp[\alpha_{ij}(\theta - \beta_{ij})]}{\exp[a_{ir}(\theta - \beta_{ir})]} = \frac{\exp[(a_{ij} - a_{ir})\theta - a_{ij}\beta_{ij} + a_{ir}\beta_{ir})]}{1}. \quad (18)$$

Defining

$$\alpha^*{}_{ij} = \alpha_{ij} - \alpha_{ir},$$

and

$$\beta^*{}_{ij} = \begin{cases} \dfrac{a_{ij}\beta_{ij} - a_{ir}\beta_{ir}}{a_{ij} - a_{ir}} & \text{if } a_{ij} \neq a_{ir}, \\[2em] \beta_{ij}, & \text{if } \alpha_{ij} = \alpha_{ir}, \end{cases}$$

one finds that

$$\frac{P(X_i = j \mid \theta)}{P(X_i = r \mid \theta)} = \frac{\exp[a^*_{ij}(\theta - \beta^*_{ij})]}{1}, \quad (j \neq r). \tag{19}$$

Together with the restriction that the sum of the probabilities of all m_i equals one, it follows that (19) defines an equivalent NRM as (17). Moreover, for the reference category r, it holds that the denominator of the right-hand side of (19) is no longer dependent on θ, which implies that $a_{ir} = 0$. The reference category can be chosen freely among the categories of the item, and across items this choice is completely arbitrary.

However, if we do this, then we find that $P(X_i = r \mid \theta) \propto 1$, which also means that the location parameter β_{ir} has disappeared completely from all expressions; it simply does not exist anymore. So, for each item, there are only $m - 1$ location parameters β and $m - 1$ weight parameters α. A similar phenomenon is found in the 2PLM: although there are two response categories per item, correct and incorrect, the model has only one discrimination parameter and one difficulty parameter. The reference category for each item is the incorrect response.

The two other indeterminacies have to do with the origin and the unit of the θ-scale. As to the origin of the scale, it will be clear from the right-hand side of (17) that applying the transformations

$$\theta^* = \theta + d \text{ and } \beta^*_{ij} = \beta_{ij} + d,$$

with d being an arbitrary constant, yields $(\theta - \beta_{ij}) = (\theta^* - \beta^*_{ij})$, and thus lets (17) remain unchanged. To solve this indeterminacy one can fix a single arbitrary location parameter β_{ij} ($j \neq r$) to an arbitrary constant (zero, for example) or require that the sum of all location parameters is zero. Likewise, for the unit of the scale, the transformations

$$\theta^* = c\theta, \ \beta^*_{ij} = c\beta_{ij} \text{ and } \alpha^*_{ij} = \alpha_{ij}/c,$$

where c is an arbitrary positive constant, yield $\alpha_{ij}(\theta - \beta_{ij}) = \alpha^*_{ij}(\theta^* - \beta^*_{ij})$ and will not change the value of the right-hand side of (17). This indeterminacy can be solved, for example, by fixing a single α-parameter to one. Notice that if α_{ij} is set to one, the category j must not be the reference category for that item. The specific way in which origin and unit for a model are chosen is called 'normalization' in IRT.

In summary then, the number of free category parameters in the nominal response model is not $\Sigma_i\, m_i$ as may be suggested by (17) but $\Sigma_i(m_i - 1) - 2$.

In Figure 8.7, a graphical display is given for a four-category item. The second category has been chosen as the reference category. The four weight parameters α are -1, 0, 0.5 and 1.2, respectively. The location parameters are -1.5, -0.5 and 0.65 for the categories 1, 3 and 4, respectively. The location parameter for the reference category does not exist.

A general characteristic of the category response functions for this model is visible in the figure: exactly one of the curves is increasing and one is decreasing; the others are single peaked. The increasing one is associated with the category having the largest α-parameter; the decreasing one is associated with the category with the smallest α-parameter. The increasing one approaches the upper asymptote (one) as θ increases without bound, and the decreasing approaches the same asymptote as θ decreases without bound. If there is more than one category with the largest weight parameter, than all the associated curves increase; their asymptotes, however are less than one, but the sum of their asymptotes equals one. This follows similarly for the smallest value.

Now assume that the item in Figure 8.7 represents a multiple choice item, and the category labels 1 to 4 represent the alternatives. From the figure it is clear that the ability level where category 3 is the modal one is higher than the level where category 2 is the modal one. For the NRM it holds that, whatever the distribution of the ability is in the population, the average value of students choosing category 3 is higher than the average for those choosing category 2. So, a valid NRM allows for discriminating between these two categories of students. In working only with binary data (correct or incorrect) the distinction

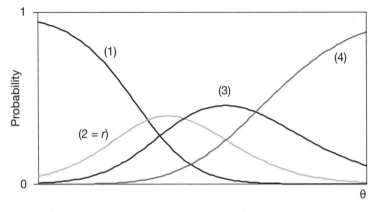

Figure 8.7 Category response functions in the NRM

between students choosing category 2 or 3 is lost, meaning that one has removed useful information about the latent ability.

More in general, it looks as if the four curves in Figure 8.7 are ordered, and most importantly, they are ordered in the same way as the α-parameters. These parameters appear in (17) as the coefficients of the latent variable θ, and they can be interpreted as the score a student gets when a category is chosen. In the example, a score of –1 is given for category 1, a score of zero for category 2, and so on. The score on the test is then the sum of all item scores obtained, meaning that the test score is a weighted sum of the categories chosen. This is the same rationale as in the 2PLM. Notice that in the NRM and the 2PLM, the estimate of θ is not this weighted sum, but it is a monotonic transformation of it.

5.2 The partial credit model (PCM)

This model was introduced formally by Andersen (1977), but the name is due to Masters (1982). It can be understood in several ways, and two of them will be discussed here. In one approach, it will be considered as a special case of the NRM, in the other, it will be characterized as a linear logit model.

As the PCM is a model for ordered categories, this implies that the order of the categories is known, unlike in the NRM. Situations where this can arise are items that can be partially correct, and a partial credit is given for such an answer. Formally, the PCM has the same category response functions as the NRM, but the α-parameters are given a fixed value. It is customary in this model to number the categories starting from zero. If the highest category is m, then there are $m + 1$ response categories. The PCM is equivalent to the NRM with the parameter α_{ij} fixed at j for all items. The zero category is automatically the reference category.

In the parameterization proposed by Andersen (1977), the category response functions are given by

$$P(X_i = j) \propto \begin{cases} 1 & \text{if } j = 0, \\ \exp(j\theta - \eta_{ij}) & \text{if } j > 0. \end{cases} \tag{20}$$

Masters uses another parameterization, where the η-parameters in (20) are cumulative sums:

$$\eta_{ij} = \sum_{g=1}^{j} \beta_{ig}. \tag{21}$$

Such a reparameterization does not change the model, and if one knows the η-parameters, the β-parameters are immediately available:

$$\beta_{i1} = \eta_{i1},$$

$$\beta_{ij} = \eta_{ij} - \eta_{i, j-1}, \, (j > 1).$$

The PCM is an exponential family model. The sufficient statistic for the latent variable θ is the raw score: the sum of the partial item scores obtained, and the sufficient statistic for the category parameters, is just the number of times the category has been obtained.

The β-parameters in the Masters parameterization have a nice interpretation: the parameter β_{ij} is the location on the θ-scale where the categories j and $j-1$ have the same probability, which is shown in Figure 8.8 for two items with three response categories, 0, 1 and 2: in the left-hand panel of the figure it holds that the β-parameters are ordered in the same order as the categories, that is, $\beta_{i1} < \beta_{i2}$; for the right-hand panel, the order is reversed, $\beta_{i2} < \beta_{i1}$. If the parameter values are ordered in the same order as the categories, then for each category there is an interval on the θ-scale where that category is the modal one, that is, the category is the most probable one. In the left-hand panel of Figure 8.8, it is seen that category 1 is the most probable one for $\beta_{i1} < \theta < \beta_{i2}$. In the right-hand panel, category 1 is never the modal one. Sometimes it is claimed that the β-parameters must be ordered in the same way as the categories, but there is nothing in the model definition that prescribes such a rule.

The second derivation of the PCM is one where it is conceived as a possible generalization of the Rasch model. In Section 1 it was shown that the Rasch

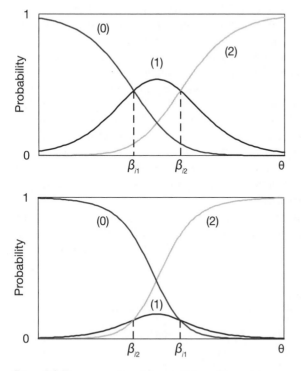

Figure 8.8 Two examples of the partial credit model

model can be viewed as a logit-linear model. For binary outcomes, the logit function is well defined: it is the logarithm of $p/(1-p)$, where p is the probability of a success. With variables with more than two outcomes, however, the logit function is not uniquely determined, although it is used in these contexts, with a suitable modification.

The PCM can be characterized by the adjacent category logits (Agresti 1990) as follows:

$$\ln \frac{P(X_i = j \mid \theta)}{P(X_i = j-1 \mid \theta)} = \theta - \beta_{ij}, \quad (j > 0). \tag{22}$$

Together with the requirement that $P(X_i = 0 \mid \theta) \propto 1$, this defines the PCM in the Masters parameterization. Equation (22) is also equivalent with the following conditional probability:

$$P(X_i = j \mid \theta, X_i = j \text{ or } X_i = j-1) = \frac{\exp(\theta - \beta_{ij})}{1 + \exp(\theta - \beta_{ij})}, \tag{23}$$

that is, the probability that the highest category is obtained, given that the choice is between this category and the preceding one. The right-hand side of (23) has exactly the same structure as the IRF for the Rasch model, but for the interpretation, it is important to look carefully at the left-hand side. It is not easy to imagine what could be a meaningful interpretation of this conditional probability in an educational context. Moreover, the model is not invariant under a collapsing of categories, as will be shown in a simplified example.

Suppose an item i has been scored into four categories, and furthermore that it is applied in a population where the ability of all the test takers is constant, say $\theta = 0$. The probabilities of responding to each category are given in the second row of Table 8.1. Now assume that the PCM is valid for the original categorization. The value of $P(X_i = 2 \mid \theta = 0, X_i = 2 \text{ or } X_i = 1)$ is $0.35/(0.35 + 0.20) = 0.636$, and solving the right-hand side of (21) for β_{i2} gives $\beta_{i2} = -0.56$. Now, suppose one wants to apply the PCM but with one category less: the original categories 0 and 1 are collapsed into a single category, which is the new reference category; the other categories are renumbered from 2 and 3 to 1 and 2 respectively. But applying the PCM rationale to this collapsed table will give $P(X_i = 2 \mid \theta = 0, X_i = 2 \text{ or } X_i = 1) = 0.35/(0.35 + 0.35) = 0.5$ and as

Table 8.1 Collapsing categories

	0	1	2	3
Original categories	0	1	2	3
Probabilities	0.15	0.20	0.35	0.30
Collapsed categories	0	1	2	
Probabilities	0.35	0.35	0.30	

a result $\beta_{i1} = 0$. This means that the β-parameters in the PCM cannot be interpreted as a kind of lower bound of the categories, or as steps or thresholds, because in the example, the definition of the original category 2 (category 1 after collapsing) has not changed by the collapsing of the two lower categories, but the value of the associated β-parameter has changed substantially.

Moreover, if the PCM is the exact model for the original categorization, it cannot be exact for the data after collapsing.

A slight generalization of the PCM yields the generalized partial credit model (GPCM) (Muraki 1992). The generalization implies that a different discrimination per item is added to the PCM. The weight or score parameters (the coefficient of θ) for category j in the two models is:

PCM: $j,$

GPCM: $j \times \alpha_i.$

The parameter α_i is a discrimination parameter for item i. The GPCM relates to the PCM as the 2PLM relates to the Rasch model.

5.3 The graded response model (GRM)

This model (Samejima 1969, 1972, 1973) allows for collapsing of adjacent categories in a double sense: the parameters are invariant, and if the model is valid before collapsing, it remains valid after collapsing.

An easy way to see the structure of the model is to use *cumulative* logits (Agresti 1990: 321), which are logits defined on cumulative probabilities: the probability of obtaining category j or higher is compared to its complement, the probability of obtaining a category lower than j. The GRM assumes that these cumulative logits are linear in θ:

$$\ln \frac{P(X_i \geq j \mid \theta)}{P(X_i < j \mid \theta)} = \theta - \beta_{ij}, \ (j = 1,\ldots,m_i). \tag{24}$$

Notice that the right-hand sides of equations (22) – the PCM – and (24) – the GRM – have an identical structure, but the interpretation is quite different. Equation (24) is equivalent with

$$P(X_i \geq j \mid \theta) = \frac{\exp(\theta - \beta_{ij})}{1 + \exp(\theta - \beta_{ij})}, \ (j = 1,\ldots,m_i), \tag{25}$$

where one sees again the same structure as in the Rasch model. However, (25) is not an expression for the category response functions, because it expresses the probability that the response is observed in category j or higher. The category response functions then are given by

$$P(X_i = 0|\theta) = 1 - P(X_i \geq 1|\theta), \tag{26a}$$

$$P(X_i = j|\theta) = P(X_i \geq j|\theta) - P(X_i \geq j + 1|\theta), \; (j = 1, \ldots, m_i - 1), \tag{26b}$$

$$P(X_i = m_i|\theta) = P(X_i \geq m_i|\theta). \tag{26c}$$

If the items are binary, that is, for all items it holds that $m_i = 1$, then only (26a) and (26c) apply, and the model is identical to the Rasch model. If $m_i > 1$ for one or more items, then (26b) applies for the middle categories, and the category response function contains a difference of two logistic functions, and this means that the model is not an exponential family model.

Figure 8.2 is a graph of the functions (25) for a four-category item – that is, $m_i = 3$. However, where in this figure – which was meant as an illustration of the Rasch model – each curve represented a separate item, now the three curves have to be interpreted as belonging to the same four-category item. The labels for the parameters in the figure (β_i, β_j and β_m) have to be replaced by β_{i1}, β_{i2} and β_{i3} respectively, where i is the index for the item. In the GRM the category parameters are necessarily ordered in increasing order of the category numbers, otherwise equation (26b) would yield a negative probability.

In Figure 8.9, the category response curves, corresponding to the three cumulative curves given in Figure 8.1 are displayed. Notice that, similar to the PCM, the curve corresponding to the zero category is decreasing, the curve corresponding to the highest category is increasing and curves corresponding to all other categories are single-peaked. In this figure, the location of the category parameters do not have an elegant interpretation, unlike in the PCM; the obvious interpretation is associated with Figure 8.1.

The collapsibility of adjacent categories is immediately clear from equation (25): the parameter β_{ij} is the location where the probability of obtaining category

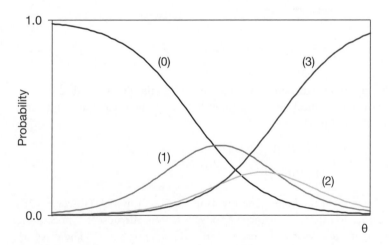

Figure 8.9 Category response functions in the GRM

j or higher is 50 per cent, and this not dependent on how lower or higher categories are defined. In this sense, the GRM has a nice interpretation in terms of Thurstonian thresholds, which the PCM has not.

6 Multidimensional models

All models discussed thus far have one very important feature in common that has not been discussed explicitly thus far: they all assume that the items in the test are indicators of one latent variable. The assumption of conditional independence amounts to claiming that any pair of items do not share any variance beyond the variance that can be attributed to that latent variable. However, this is precisely what is assumed in the one-factor model. In that sense, unidimensional IRT models are just variations of the factor analytical model for a single factor. This relation has been discussed in detail by Takane and De Leeuw (1987), and a formal proof is given that the two parameter normal ogive model as discussed above is exactly equivalent with the one-factor model.

The generalization to multidimensional models is then straightforward and can be conceptualized as consisting of three components:

- For each item the performance is dependent on a linear combination of abilities:

$$\alpha_i'\theta = \alpha_{i1}\theta_1 + \alpha_{i2}\theta_2 + \ldots + \alpha_{ip}\theta_p, \tag{27}$$

where the coefficients $\alpha_{i1}, \ldots, \alpha_{ip}$ have exactly the same meaning as in factor analysis and are commonly referred to as factor loadings.
- The assumption of a latent response z_i, which is a random draw from some hypothesized distribution, as exemplified in Figure 8.5. The mean of this distribution is the linear combination given by (25). In the tradition of factor analysis, the standard deviation of this distribution can vary across items, and the distribution itself is assumed to be normal, but there is no objection in principle to assuming that this distribution is logistic, or might have yet another form. In most applications, it is assumed that the latent responses are conditionally independent. The possibility provided in SEM for 'correlated errors' is not to be conceived as a new feature of these models. It fits in the general model described here, but in a concrete application a specification error might occur, because 'in reality' there are p factors and the model assumes that there are less. The unexplained covariance caused by this underspecification may then show up as correlated residuals.
- If the latent response variables z_i were observable, the preceding model assumptions would be nothing else than the theory on factor analysis. However, the variables z_i are continuous, and the data delivered from a test administration are highly discrete. So, one needs a mechanism to convert the continuous latent responses to discrete overt responses. This mechanism

is the model of a Thurstonian threshold, exemplified in Figure 8.5. Generalizations to polytomous observations are obvious: the number of thresholds equals the number of observable categories minus one (Bock and Lieberman 1970; Christofferson 1975: Muthén 1978). It is even possible to conceive of these thresholds as linear combinations of dimension-wise thresholds (Glas and Verhelst 1995, Kelderman and Rijkes 1994).

A model where the performance depends on a linear combination of latent abilities is a *compensatory* model: a low ability on one dimension or factor may be compensated by a high value on one or more other dimensions; the probability of a correct answer only depends on the result of the linear combination, and not on its components.

There may be situations in educational assessment where such a compensatory rule is not realistic. To find the solution to a mathematics problem that is embedded in a more or less complicated description of a real-life situation, one might hypothesize that a successful performance will depend on a sufficient reading ability *and* a sufficient mathematics ability, but that deficiency in either of these abilities cannot be compensated by an excess in the other. Models that require such a multiple requirement are known as 'conjunctive' models (Hendrickson and Mislevy 2005; Maris 1995; van Leeuwe and Roskam 1991).

A model that is logically tightly related to the conjunctive model is the disjunctive model, where it is assumed that an item or a task can be successfully solved by appealing to one of several abilities. In fact, both models are logically equivalent: requiring sufficient reading *and* mathematics ability to *solve* an item, is logically equivalent to requiring *in*sufficient reading *or* mathematics ability to *fail* the item. This means that using the complement of the observed data (exchanging ones and zeros) and reversing the direction of the latent dimensions turns a conjunctive model into a disjunctive one and vice versa. An example is a test where the use of different strategies may lead to the correct solution. The multidimensional ability then refers to the ability to successfully handle these strategies. This might be reflected, for example, in mathematics problems where different strategies may be used to find the solution to a task, for example, by using mainly algebraic arguments or mainly geometric ones.

7 Concluding remarks

The overview of IRT models presented in the preceding sections may leave an impression of abundance and therefore of confusion: what to choose in a concrete situation and how to decide if the choice made is the best possible one. It may look as if the choice of the most complicated model is the best – it avoids as many pitfalls and shortcomings as possible – and after the analysis it will show 'automatically' whether a simpler model is applicable.

Such a conception, however, is mistaken for two reasons. First, working with complicated models usually causes problems in the parameter estimation, which may be of a technical nature (the software 'does not find' the estimates) but also of a statistical nature: the estimates will tend to have large standard errors and in many cases be highly correlated. In practice this means that a small change in the data may lead to quite large shifts in the estimated values, which in turn may require a substantial change in the interpretation of the obtained results.

The second misconception has to do with a more general approach to scientific problems, where it is sometimes thought that complicated mathematical models will reveal the true structure of the world. However, the real key to understanding the determinants of educational performance is the setting up of clever and well-considered research programmes, with directed and specific hypotheses that can be tested empirically. The use of IRT models in testing these hypotheses is certainly recommended, but the decision as to which kind of data to collect under which conditions is a prerequisite for good research.

In the national assessment programme for basic education in the Netherlands, started in 1987 for arithmetic, it was decided from the onset that the analyses would be carried out at the level of minimal curricular units, that is, units described in the curriculum that were thought to be homogeneous enough in content, didactic approach and thinking processes, such that the responses to items belonging to the same unit could be described by a simple unidimensional IRT model. Such an approach, which required a careful design and a rather elaborate construction process of the item material, has proven to be useful. A trend analysis of the results of four waves of the assessment showed a rather dramatic decrease in the performance of the operations of multiplication and division. It is very unlikely that such a trend would have been found if the test had consisted of a 'well-balanced' mixture of material, covering the whole curriculum but not fine grained enough to draw conclusions in any specific domain. This implies that researchers in the area of educational effectiveness should make use of IRT models to develop psychometrically appropriate scales, but in order to do so they should seriously take into account the theoretical background upon which a test or an instrument measuring a specific factor has been developed. For example, the partial credit model may be found useful in analysing data emerging from a high-inference observation instrument, and thereby a valid measure of quality of teaching may emerge (Kyriakides *et al.* 2009). Another issue that researchers in the area of EER should take into account has to do with the fact that IRT can be applied in incomplete designs that are very likely to be used for measuring student achievement in longitudinal studies. In this context, issues concerned with the use of different designs in applying IRT and parameter estimation are discussed in the next chapter.

References

Agresti, A. (1990) *Categorical data analysis,* New York, NY: Wiley.
Andersen, E.B. (1977) 'Sufficient statistics and latent trait models', *Psychometrika*, 42(1): 69–81.

Bock, R.D. (1972) 'Estimating item parameters and latent ability when responses are scored in two or more nominal categories', *Psychometrika*, 37: 29–51.

Bock, R.D. and Lieberman, M. (1970) 'Fitting a response model for *n* dichotomously scored items', *Psychometrika*, 35: 179–97.

Christoffersson, A. (1975) 'Factor analysis of dichotomized variables', *Psychometrika*, 40: 5–22.

Fischer, G.H. (1974) *Einführung in die Theorie Psychologischer Tests* [*Introduction into the theory of psychological tests*], Bern: Huber.

Fischer, G.H. (1995) 'Derivations of the Rasch model', in G.H. Fischer and I.W. Molenaar (eds) *Rasch models: Foundations, recent developments and applications*, New York: Springer, pp. 39–52.

Glas, C.A.W. and Verhelst, N.D. (1995) 'Tests of fit for polytomous Rasch models', in G.H. Fischer and I.W. Molenaar (eds) *Rasch models: Foundations, recent developments and applications*, New York: Springer, pp. 325–52.

Guttman, L.A. (1950) 'The basis of scalogram analysis', in S.A. Stouffer, L.A. Guttman, E.A. Sachman, P.F. Lazarsfeld, S.A. Star and J.A. Clausen (eds) *Measurement and prediction: Studies in social psychology in World War II, Vol 4*, Princeton, NJ: Princeton University Press.

Hendrickson, A.B. and Mislevy, R.J. (2005) 'Item response theory (IRT): Cognitive models', in B.S. Everitt and D.C. Howell (eds) *Encyclopedia of statistics in behavioral science, Volume 2*, Chichester: Wiley, pp. 978–82.

Kelderman, H. and Rijkes, C.P.M. (1994) 'Computing maximum likelihood estimates of loglinear IRT models from marginal sums', *Psychometrika*, 57: 437–50.

Kyriakides, L., Creemers, B.P.M. and Antoniou, P. (2009) 'Teacher behaviour and student outcomes: Suggestions for research on teacher training and professional development', *Teaching and Teacher Education*, 25(1): 12–23.

Lord, F.M. and Novick, M.R. (1968) *Statistical theories of mental test scores*, Reading: Addison-Wesley.

Maris, E. (1995) 'Psychometric latent response models', *Psychometrika*, 60: 523–48.

Masters, G.N. (1982) 'A Rasch model for partial credit scoring', *Psychometrika*, 47: 149–74.

Muraki, E. (1992) 'A generalized partial credit model: Application of an EM algorithm', *Applied Psychological Measurement*, 16: 159–76.

Muthén, B.O. (1978) 'Contributions to factor analysis of dichotomous variables', *Psychometrika*, 43: 551–60.

Rasch, G. (1960) *Probabilistic models for some intelligence and attainment tests*, Copenhagen: Danish Institute for Educational Research.

Samejima, F. (1969) 'Estimation of latent ability using a pattern of graded scores', *Psychometrika, Monograph Supplement*, No. 17.

Samejima, F. (1972) 'A general model for free response data', *Psychometrika, Monograph Supplement*, No. 18.

Samejima, F. (1973) 'Homogeneous case of the continuous response model', *Psychometrika*, 38: 203–19.

Takane, Y. and De Leeuw, J. (1987) 'On the relationship between item response theory and factor analysis of discretized variables', *Psychometrika*, 52: 393–408.

van Leeuwe, J.F.J. and Roskam, E.E. (1991) 'The conjunctive item response model: A probabilistic extension of the Coombs and Kao model', *Methodika*, 5: 14–32.

Chapter 9

IRT models

Parameter estimation, statistical testing and application in EER

Norman Verhelst
CITO, The Netherlands

As was indicated in Chapter 8, the most important advantage of using IRT is the possibility of applying it in incomplete designs. This does not mean, however, that there are no restrictions on the test designs that can be used in connection with IRT. For this reason, the first section of this chapter is concerned with important features of designs that can be used with IRT models. The next section refers to the problem of parameter estimation. In statistical modelling, the problem of parameter estimation is in many cases technically quite involved, because it amounts generally to solving a complicated set of equations. In this section, technicalities will be skipped almost entirely, because of space limits and, more important, because estimation procedures are usually made available in computer programs that do not require the user to understand all technical considerations. In Section 3, statistical tests are discussed and special attention is given to the problem of power. An IRT model, considered as a complex hypothesis, may be defective in many ways, and some tests are not sensitive to specific defects. It is argued that the most important aspect of testing is the creativity to find ways in which defects may be reflected in some aspects of the data. Careful statistical testing is the key procedure needed to make a considered decision of accepting or rejecting an IRT model and can also be found useful in choosing the most appropriate IRT model and generating relevant person estimates. Finally, in the last section of this chapter, we discuss the problem of how to use the results of an IRT analysis in estimating student achievement and searching for the impact of effectiveness factors operating at different levels.

I Incomplete designs

The basic idea of using IRT models where not all students take the same test is that two students will only be comparable if the tests they took have something in common or, exchanging the roles of students and items, that two items are comparable if there are at least some students having taken both items. Graphically, this amounts to a very simple design requirement, which is exemplified in Figure 9.1, for two groups of students. The shaded cells represent the sets of items administered to each group. In the left-hand panel, there are

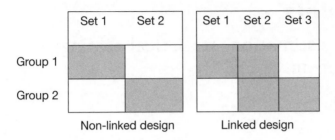

Figure 9.1 Simple two-group designs

two tests, coinciding with two disjointed sets of items. In this design it seems to be impossible to compare the two groups of students, since they have no items in common, nor to compare items from set 1 and set 2, because they have no students in common. It is said that this design is not linked. In the right-hand panel, the items are partitioned into three sets, and the first test contains sets 1 and 2 and the second sets 2 and 3, so that set 2 is common to both tests and comparisons are possible. Notice that in this design, items of set 1 can be compared to items of set 3, although indirectly, because items in these two set are comparable to the items of the common set 2.

This kind of indirect comparability is used to define linked designs for an arbitrary number of sets of items and an arbitrary number of groups of students. Formally, any two items, i and m, say, are linked if there exists a chain of items $(i, j, g, \ldots, h, m)$ such that each adjacent pair (i, j), (j, g), $\ldots$, (h, m) of items in the chain has been administered to at least one student. The design is said to be linked if all pairs of items are linked in this way.

There exist a number of frequently used designs, which will be discussed briefly. Figure 9.2 contains an anchor test design and Figure 9.3 displays two block-interlaced anchoring designs. The sets of items referred to in Figure 9.1 are usually called 'blocks'. In the anchor test design one block of items is common for all groups of students. This block is the anchor test. In the interlaced design, a kind of chain with overlapping blocks is constructed. Notice that the resulting figure looks a bit similar to a staircase, but an important feature is given by the shaded blocks in the bottom left of the figure.

In the anchor test design with m groups of students, there are $m + 1$ blocks; one block is common to all groups and all other blocks are unique. So there are m mutually disjointed groups of students. In the interlaced case, all blocks are administered to an equal number of groups, and, if there are m blocks, the total number of groups required is m. In these designs, it is not required that blocks contain the same number of items.

Using linked designs is by far the most important feature in choosing test designs, as parameter estimation is hard or even impossible in non-linked designs. However, there are more things worth considering about test designs:

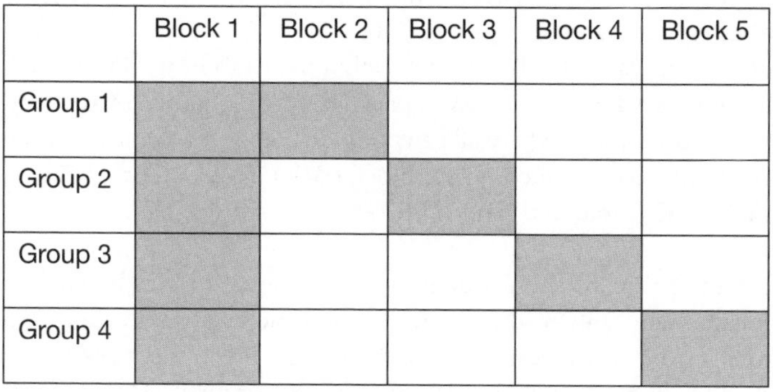

	Block 1	Block 2	Block 3	Block 4	Block 5
Group 1	▓	▓			
Group 2	▓		▓		
Group 3	▓			▓	
Group 4	▓				▓

Figure 9.2 Anchor test design

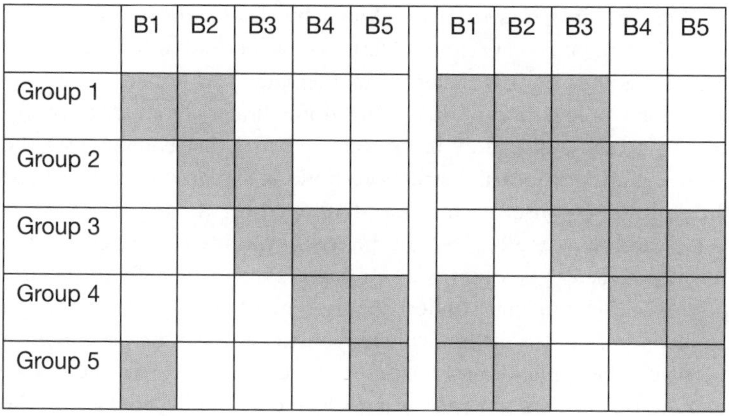

	B1	B2	B3	B4	B5		B1	B2	B3	B4	B5
Group 1	▓	▓					▓	▓			
Group 2		▓	▓					▓	▓		
Group 3			▓	▓					▓	▓	
Group 4				▓	▓		▓				▓
Group 5	▓				▓			▓			▓

Figure 9.3 Two block-interlaced anchoring designs

- How are individual students assigned to one of the five groups (see Figure 9.3)? By far the safest procedure is to use random assignment, although this is not always possible because of practical constraints – for example, if a whole class has to take the same test because the items are read aloud by the teacher.
- An implicit assumption in the application of IRT models is that the latent ability of individual students remains constant during the test administration, but in practice, effects such as fatigue and boredom may lead to violations of this assumption. Therefore, it is recommended to control for sequential effects by making sure that the same block of items does not always appear at the beginning or at the end of the tests in which it appears.
- Linking is not merely an all-or-none feature. Links can be strong or weak. In the left-hand panel of Figure 9.3, each of the five blocks is linked to two other blocks and not linked (directly) to two other blocks, while in the

right-hand panel all pairs of blocks are linked directly, although not an equal number of times. For example, the pair (B1, B2) occurs twice (in Groups 1 and 5), while the pair (B1, B3) occurs only once (in Group 1).

• Incomplete designs where all blocks appear an equal number of times in each sequential position and where all pairs of blocks appear an equal number of times are called balanced incomplete block (BIB) designs. For details on such designs, see Cochran and Cox (1957).

To have the full advantage of the features of BIB designs, it is assumed that students are allocated randomly to the test forms, and such a random allocation is usually assumed in the other designs as well. In experimental studies where such a random allocation is feasible, BIB designs are optimal. However, in developmental studies they are typically not suited, as are neither of the other designs discussed so far.

In the student monitoring system developed by the National Institute for Educational Measurement (CITO) in the Netherlands, performances in a certain domain (such as reading comprehension or mathematics) are scaled so as to be comparable for the whole period of basic education (running from six to twelve years of age). In a calibration study using item material that encompasses the curriculum of six grades of formal instruction, none of the designs discussed so far would be realistic, because the material developed for the higher grades is inaccessible for the lower grades, and the material typically developed for the lower grades will in many cases be trivial for the higher grades. Or to put it a bit differently, in developmental studies the content of the test forms has to correspond quite accurately to the implemented curriculum. So the general form of a design that can be applied in such cases is something similar to the design presented in Figure 9.4. This approach was also used by studies measuring the effect of schooling by collecting data from different age groups of students (Kyriakides and Luyten 2009).

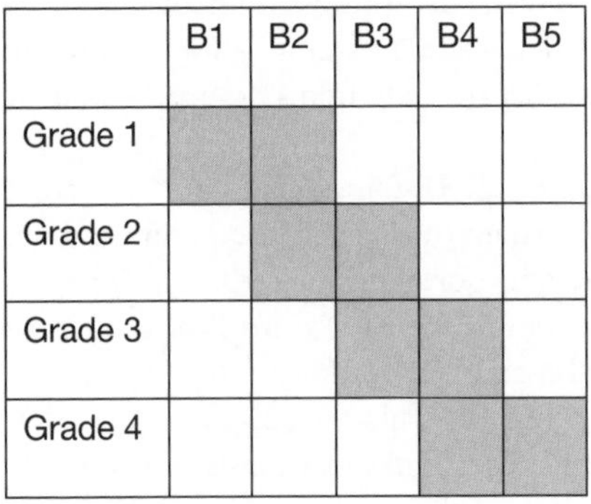

	B1	B2	B3	B4	B5
Grade 1	▓	▓			
Grade 2		▓	▓		
Grade 3			▓	▓	
Grade 4				▓	▓

Figure 9.4 Test design for developmental studies

Although the design displayed in Figure 9.4 looks similar to the block-interlaced anchoring design of Figure 9.3 (left-hand panel), there are three important differences:

- The groups of students in the present design are statistically not equivalent; to the contrary they are selected to be homogeneous with respect to the concept to be measured. The label 'grade' is just a reminder that such a selection is in operation.
- The construction of the blocks of items is restricted: for example, it is assumed that blocks 1 and 2 are suitable for grade 1 students. In general, the blocks will be ordered roughly in terms of the difficulty of the items they contain.
- As a natural consequence of the two preceding features, there will be no shaded cell in the bottom left corner of the design table. In a statistical sense this makes the design less stable than the interlaced design, but this is a restriction one cannot escape when applying IRT in developmental studies.

A further complication arises when the study is a longitudinal study, where the same cohort of students is followed for a number of years. Applying the design of Figure 9.4 as it is presented here may cause unwanted effects. If the sample of students consists of the same people in all four grades, one block of items will be administered twice to the same students in two consecutive years, and the difference between performances may be attributed to growth in the ability or to memory effects, and these two causes are confounded. To avoid such a situation, a more complicated design is needed. The blocks B1 to B5 referred to in Figure 9.4 are to be conceived of as composed of different blocks, and the design has to take care that no student will get the same block in two consecutive years. A small example is given in Figure 9.5. Here it is assumed that students belonging to group 'grade 1(a)' belong to the group 'grade 2(a)' the next year, and similarly for the (b) students. The design in Figure 9.5 is linked, and no student sees the same items twice.

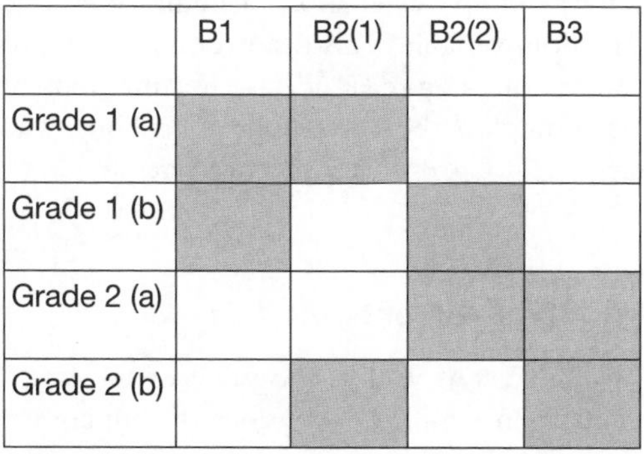

	B1	B2(1)	B2(2)	B3
Grade 1 (a)				
Grade 1 (b)				
Grade 2 (a)				
Grade 2 (b)				

Figure 9.5 A design suited to longitudinal studies

This design is used in longitudinal studies measuring the short- and long-term effect of schools (Kyriakides and Creemers 2008).

Incomplete designs and missing observations

The theory of parameter estimation, to be discussed in the next section, is in general easily adapted to incomplete designs, making the comparison of test performances possible, even in longitudinal studies, where at each measurement occasion the test form administered to any student does not contain any items answered before. This high degree of flexibility might suggest the idea that the use of incomplete designs is also the ultimate elegant solution to treat missing observations in a data matrix: one just treats an incomplete data matrix as the realization of an incomplete design. The implication of such an approach – which is flawed in general – is that every skipped item (by the student) is treated as if this item has not been administered, but a clever student, being aware of this approach, can develop a strategy of skipping all items where he is not very sure about the correct answer. This will increase his test score on the answered items and in general will lead to a biased estimate of his ability.

In general, there is no unique methodology on how to treat missing observations, and all approaches usually rest on assumptions that should be carefully checked. More information on treating missing observations can be found in the seminal paper by Rubin (1976) and in Little and Rubin (1987).

2 Parameter estimation

In the overview of IRT models in Chapter 8, a distinction was made between parameters of the model – which in IRT are always parameters associated with items – and the latent variable θ. In specifying the model, the item parameters as well as the θ-value of individual students are unknown, and will have to be estimated from the data in some way. However, until now, nothing has been said about the status of θ. There are two possibilities: either one can treat the individual θ-values of the students in the sample as unknown parameters or one can treat them as realizations of a random variable. This distinction amounts to considering the θ-values as *fixed* effects or as *random* effects, and methods of parameter estimation will differ according to the choice one is making. The present section discusses maximum likelihood estimation procedures for both possibilities.

2.1 Parameter estimation in fixed-effects models

In fixed-effects models, the item parameters as well as the value of the latent ability for each student v in the calibration sample are considered as unknown parameters that have to be estimated from the observed item responses in the calibration sample. Suppose one applies an incomplete design, where each student from a sample of, in total, n students answers a subset of, in total, k items. The measurement model is the Rasch model. In a fixed-effects model the latent ability of each student is treated as a model parameter that has to be estimated from the data; so there are $n + k - 1$ free parameters, because one parameter can be freely fixed for normalization purposes.

Maximum likelihood estimates are those values of the model parameters that jointly make the likelihood function attain its maximal value. However, these values are the same as those that make the log-likelihood function maximal, because the logarithm is an increasing function of its argument. To find this maximum, the partial derivatives of the log-likelihood function are equated to zero. These equations are called the 'likelihood equations', and their solution yields the maximum likelihood estimates. The log-likelihood function in the Rasch model when applied to incomplete designs is given in equation (1), which is given here explicitly as a function of the unknown parameters.

$$\ln L(\beta_2,\ldots,\beta_k,\theta_1,\ldots,\theta_n;\mathbf{x},\mathbf{d})$$
$$= \sum_{v=1}^{n} s_v \theta_v + \sum_{i=1}^{k} t_i(-\beta_i) - \sum_{v=1}^{n}\sum_{i=1}^{k} d_{vi}\ln\left[1 + \exp(\theta_v - \beta_i)\right]. \tag{1}$$

In the right-hand side of (1), the variable d_{vi} is an indicator variable for the design, taking the value one if item i has been administered to student v, and zero otherwise. The symbol d in the left-hand side represents the matrix of indicator variables. The sufficient statistic s_v and t_i also have a slightly different meaning in incomplete designs:

$$s_v = \sum_{i=1}^{k} d_{vi}x_{vi} \text{ and } t_i = \sum_{v=1}^{n} d_{vi}x_{vi}.$$

This implies that the test score of a student is the number of correctly answered items that have been administered. If $d_{vi} = 0$, then x_{vi} can have an arbitrary numeric value; it will never influence the outcome of an analysis since it is always multiplied by zero. Notice that the parameter β_1 does not appear in the left-hand side of (1), because it is fixed at some constant to normalize the solution – but it does appear in the right-hand side.

The derivation of the likelihood equations is beyond the scope of this chapter. Details can be found in Fischer (1974) and Molenaar (1995). It is, however, important to note that there are no explicit solutions for these equations but that they have to be approximated iteratively. This is true for the Rasch model, the simplest of all IRT models, and it holds *a fortiori* for all IRT models.

Solutions do not exist for θ_v if student v has administered all items correctly or all incorrectly. Similarly, there is not a solution for β_i if the answers given to item i are all correct or all incorrect.

As the preceding restriction might be seen as a disadvantage of the Rasch model, it can be repaired relatively easily by increasing the sample size in such a way that at least one correct and one incorrect answer is given to each item. However, students with all items correct (getting a perfect score) or all incorrect (getting a zero score) have to be left out of the analysis.

The bad news about this fixed-effects Rasch model is that the parameter estimators are not consistent. If the sample size keeps growing, the item parameter estimates do not converge to their true value. Loosely speaking, the reason is that to collect more information about the item parameters, the sample size has to increase, but with every added student, a new parameter (his or her θ-value) is added to the problem, such that the number of parameters grows at the same rate as the sample size.

Correction formulae exist to correct for this inconsistency, but they apply only to complete designs. In incomplete designs there is no general correction formula. And there is even more bad news: when using likelihood maximization, a number of theoretical results are available to deduce good estimates of the standard errors of the estimates and to construct valid statistical tests of goodness-of-fit, but these results do not apply in the fixed-effects Rasch model. In general, therefore, it is not known to what extent reported standard errors or results of statistical tests are to be trusted if they are based on this method of estimation. Nevertheless, this method of estimation is still quite popular and is used, for example, in the programs WINSTEPS and FACETS.

Although there are few results from this method of estimation for other models than the Rasch model, it is to be expected that this kind of inconsistency will occur in other models as well. Therefore, it is advisable to avoid this method. The method of estimation described here is known in the literature as the unconditional maximum likelihood (UML) or joint maximum likelihood (JML) method of estimation. The latter name is the most used nowadays.

2.2 Parameter estimation in mixed-effects models

In the mixed model approach, the item effects are considered as fixed effects, but the values of the latent variable are treated as random effects. This means that the sample of students is considered as a sample from some population, and that in this population the latent variable follows some distribution. If one can assume that this distribution can be described with a probability density function of, say, $g(\theta)$, then the *marginal likelihood* of a data vector $\underline{x}_v$ and the corresponding design vector $\underline{d}_v$ is given by

$$L(\beta_1,\ldots,\beta_k,\eta_1,\ldots,\eta_p;\underline{x}_v,\underline{d}_v) = \int \prod_{i=1}^{k} [f_i(\theta)]^{d_{vi}x_{vi}} [1 - f_i(\theta)]^{d_{vi}(1-x_{vi})} \times g(\theta)d\theta, \quad (2)$$

where $f_i(\theta)$ is the IRF of item i and depends on the item parameter β_i, and $g(\theta)$ depends on the p 'population' parameters $\eta_1, \ldots, \eta_p$. For example, if it is assumed that the latent variable is normally distributed, the two population parameters are the mean and the variance of this distribution and $p = 2$.

It is important to read the right-hand side of equation (2) correctly. The ability of student v, θ_v, does not appear in this expression; the only reference to student v is through the design variables d_{vi} and the observed responses x_{vi}. The latent variable θ is the integration variable, and it is integrated out. So the right-hand side of (2) must be read as 'the probability of observing $\underline{x}_v$, given $\underline{d}_v$ from a student randomly drawn from the population where the probability density function of the latent variable is given by $g(\theta)$'. This likelihood is called the marginal likelihood. The likelihood for a matrix of observed responses x is just the product (over v) of the expression in (2):

$$L(\beta_1,\ldots,\beta_k,\eta_1,\ldots,\eta_p;x,d) = \prod_{v=1}^{n} \int \prod_{i=1}^{k} [f_i(\theta)]^{d_{vi}x_{vi}} [1 - f_i(\theta)]^{d_{vi}(1-x_{vi})} \times g(\theta)d\theta. \quad (3)$$

Maximizing the right-hand side of (3), or its logarithm with respect to all model parameters (that is, item parameters and population parameters), jointly yields the marginal maximum likelihood (MML) estimates of the parameters. This procedure leads to consistent estimates of all model parameters and is a good basis on which to make estimates of the standard errors and to build statistical goodness-of-fit tests.

Notice that the right-hand side of (3) is a generic expression for all unidimensional IRT-models and all population models where the distribution can be described with a probability density function. The technical procedures actually to compute the parameter estimates, of course, will differ from model to model. For a detailed explanation of the Rasch model, see Glas (1989) or Molenaar (1995).

Identifiability

Fixed-effects models are not identified if the design is not linked. This is easy to understand because the unit and the origin of the scale can be freely chosen for each set of test forms that are not linked to any of the other test forms. In the left-hand panel of Figure 9.1, this means that for each of the sets an arbitrary unit and origin can be chosen for each of the two sets of items, and there is no means to bring the two sets onto a common scale.

When using MML, the design restrictions can be relaxed. Referring again to the left-hand panel of Figure 9.1, the model is identified if the two groups of students are considered as equivalent samples from the same population. Although the groups do not share any item, they are tied together by the equivalence of their ability distribution, so that it is possible to choose a common unit and origin, for example, the standard deviation and the mean of the common distribution. Although this situation is comfortable, one should be careful with the assumption of statistical equivalence of the two samples. If this assumption is not fulfilled, all parameter estimates will be biased. In practice, using this assumption will in general be satisfied only in an experimental set-up where students are allocated randomly to one of the two groups.

About $g(\theta)$

In principle, any $g(\theta)$ can be used in equation (3). The most widely used one is the normal distribution. Sometimes, however, a discrete distribution is used as well, where it is assumed that the latent variable can assume only m different values, called support points. In such a case, again, two different approaches are possible. In the first approach the support points are considered as known, for example, m Gauss-Hermite quadrature points, and for each quadrature point the probability mass has to be estimated, leaving $m - 1$ free parameters, since the sum of the probability masses equals one. Details of such an approach are given by Bock and Aitken (1981). In the other approach, support points and their associated masses have to be estimated jointly. For the Rasch model, this has been investigated by De Leeuw and Verhelst (1986); but see also Forman (1995) and Laird (1978). In this latter approach there are also theoretical results for the value of m. Although, such an approach looks attractive, there are two drawbacks: the number of parameters to be estimated is generally larger than when using a parametric distribution, and the estimated distribution is in general not unique.

But there is a more serious practical drawback to the use of the MML procedure. The use of the first multiplication sign in (3) – the multiplication over students – implies that one assumes the latent value is identically distributed for all students in the sample. This is equivalent to assuming that the students represent a simple random sample from a distribution $g(\theta)$, and this in practical applications in EER is seldom the case. Suppose a sample of students is drawn using a two-stage cluster sampling procedure (first schools, then students within schools), and one applies (3) as it stands, then the estimates of all parameters, inclusive of the item parameters, may be systematically affected, even if it is true that $g(\theta)$ is the correct distribution for the whole student population.

Assume, as an example, that one wants to apply a two-level model, where the school effects, u_j, are assumed to be normally distributed with mean μ_0 and variance τ^2, and the student-within-school effects θ_{vj} are normally distributed with mean zero and common variance σ^2. If so, then the likelihood (3) has to be replaced with

$$L(\beta_1,\ldots,\beta_k,\eta_1,\ldots,\eta_p;\boldsymbol{x},\boldsymbol{d}) = \prod_j \int \prod_{v=1}^{n_j} \int \prod_{i=1}^{k} [f_i(\theta)]^{d_{vi}x_{vi}}[1 - f_i(\theta)]^{d_{vi}(1-x_{vi})} \qquad (4)$$

$$\times g_1(\theta)g_2(u)d\theta du,$$

where $g_1(\theta)$ is the probability density function for the normal distribution $N(0, \sigma^2)$ and $g_2(\theta)$ is the probability density function for $N(\mu_0, \tau^2)$. The first product sign in (4) runs over schools, the second over students within schools, and the right-most one runs over items.

The previous example makes clear what the general problem is: the measurement model, be it the Rasch model or any other model, is, for the sake of its item parameter estimation, embedded in a structural model – via the likelihood function, which causes two kinds of problems:

- The first one is of a technical nature: both models can be quite complicated, and finding the maximum of the likelihood function is not a trivial task, as can be seen from the sandwich structure of multiplication signs and integral signs in (4).
- The second problem is a more principled one: it is true that if the models are known to be the correct ones, maximizing the likelihood estimation will yield estimates that are optimal in a number of respects, but the problem is usually that in any application one cannot be sure that the models are correct. It may be the case, for example, that in the structural model (as in (4)) there is a large gender effect, which has been ignored. In such a case, and dependent on the design, such a specification error may lead to biases in the estimates of the parameters of the measurement model, and it is very difficult to find out in general terms how severe these biases will be. Or to put it a bit differently, using some distributional assumption about the latent variable will affect the estimates of the measurement model. Conversely, a defect in the measurement model will affect the inferences about the structural model, also to an unknown extent. For example, it may happen that one finds a seemingly large difference between the mean ability of boys and girls, but that this difference is caused by the presence of a few items that do not fit the assumptions of the measurement model.

These problems make it clear that it would be worthwhile to have a method to estimate the parameters of the measurement model, and to check the validity of the model, in a way that is not affected by any assumption about the distribution of the latent variable. Such a method is discussed in the next section.

2.3 Conditional maximum likelihood (CML) estimation

When one is interested primarily in the measurement model, the abilities of the students in the sample are a kind of nuisance, and therefore they are sometimes called 'nuisance parameters'.

Assuming a certain distribution in the population and using MML estimation is one way of getting rid of these nuisance parameters. Another way, which can only be applied with exponential family models, is conditional maximum likelihood estimation. The principle is that one maximizes the probability of the observed data (the likelihood), conditional on sufficient statistics for the nuisance parameters.

To gain an impression of how this works, an example is given for the Rasch model with $k = 3$ and the score $s = 2$. It is easy to see that for a student with ability θ, the conditional probability of obtaining the response pattern $(0, 1, 1)$ is given by

$$P[(0,1,1)\,|\,\theta, s = 2] = \frac{P[(0,1,1)\,|\,\theta]}{P[(0,1,1)\,|\,\theta] + P[(1,0,1)\,|\,\theta] + P(1,1,0)\,|\,\theta]}, \qquad (5)$$

where the denominator is the sum over all response patterns yielding a score of 2. To obtain a less complicated expression, a simple reparameterization of the model is introduced. We define

$$\varepsilon_i = \exp(-\beta_i).$$

Using this, one can write

$$P[(0,1,1)\,|\,\theta] = \frac{\exp(2\theta)}{\prod_i [1 + \varepsilon_i \exp(\theta)]} \times \varepsilon_2 \varepsilon_3,$$

where the right-hand side consists of a fraction multiplied by a product of item parameters. It is easy to check that the same fraction will appear in all probabilities in the denominator of (5), from which one obtains immediately the very important result:

$$P[(0,1,1)\,|\,\theta, s = 2] = \frac{\varepsilon_2 \varepsilon_3}{\varepsilon_2 \varepsilon_3 + \varepsilon_1 \varepsilon_3 + \varepsilon_1 \varepsilon_2} \tag{6}$$

where the right-hand side is independent of θ and is only a function of the item parameters. Equation (6), considered as a function of the item parameters, is called the conditional likelihood of the response pattern $(0, 1, 1)$. The conditional likelihood of a data set is just the product of the conditional likelihood of all response patterns. The conditional maximum likelihood (CML) estimates are the values of the parameters that maximize this product (or its logarithm).

This method was proposed by Rasch (1960) and is to be considered as a great discovery. Note that the condition in (6) is the test score, and it is only by conditioning on the test score that the conditional likelihood is independent of θ. This result can be generalized, however, to other models: in the Rasch model, this independence is obtained because the test score is the sufficient statistic for θ. The generalization then amounts to the statement that by CML one can get rid of the nuisance parameters if they have a sufficient statistic and if one conditions on these statistics.

Andersen (1973) has shown that CML yields consistent estimates under very broad conditions. Software that allows one to implement this method for the Rasch model includes OPLM (Verhelst, Glas and Verstralen 1994) and the eRm package in R (Mair and Hatzinger 2007). The method is easily applicable in incomplete designs (Molenaar 1995). For the model to be identified, the design must be linked.

The important theoretical advantage of using CML is that the estimates are consistent independently of the way the sample has been drawn. There is no requirement whatsoever to draw representative samples, and the method is applicable under multiple stage sampling. Application in longitudinal studies is also perfectly possible, as the only assumption that is made is that the ability of the student is constant for all the item responses he or she has given. This means that in longitudinal studies, students having taken part in the study at two or more occasions are formally treated as different students at every testing occasion. This so-called sampling independence is an important theoretical advantage that is sometimes incorrectly used. Here are two comments on this:

- It should be clear that the advantages of the CML method only apply if the model is valid; they do not follow from the mechanical application of a computational routine. The validity of the model has to be tested carefully, and one has to be careful with generalizations. Suppose an achievement test has been validated using the Rasch model in some stable setting of the educational conditions (for example, in schools of a specific local educational authority, or schools that use a specific curriculum). This implies that if the curriculum changes drastically at some point, it does not follow that the test remains valid in the same way as before the reorganization. It is an (important) empirical question if it does or does not, and a justification based on the result of sampling independence is not justified.
- The principle of sampling independence does not imply – even if the model is valid – that all samples are equally well suited for estimation purposes. The accuracy of the estimates depends on the amount of statistical information that is collected, and this in turn depends on the sample size and on the match between student ability and item difficulty. Loosely speaking, this means that one collects the maximal information on an item parameter from a student's response if the probability of a correct response is 50 per cent. Conversely, if an item is too difficult or too easy relative to the ability of the tested student, one collects little information, and the estimates will be less accurate than with a good match between difficulty and ability.

Of all the models introduced in Chapter 8, the Rasch model and the partial credit model are the only two models where CML estimation of the item parameters is possible. The Rasch model, however, is quite strict in its assumptions, and in empirical applications the requirement of equal item discriminations is often not attained, unless the development of the test is based on the assumption that each item should be able to discriminate between students. In the 2PLM, the weighted score, with the discrimination parameters as weights, is a sufficient statistic, but to condition on it, the weighted score must be known. If we treat the discrimination parameters as if they were known then we fix their values *by hypothesis*. Thus, in the 2PLM specialized to this particular case, CML is possible in principle. Since of the two parameters per item, one has been fixed, there remains only one parameter to be estimated for each item; hence the name One Parameter Logistic Model (OPLM; Verhelst and Eggen 1989; Verhelst and Glas 1995). Applying the same rationale to the generalized partial credit model (GPCM) also makes CML possible.

The existence of sufficient statistical is necessary for CML to be possible, but it is not the only condition that must be satisfied, as the following example shows. Assume $k = 3$, and the discrimination parameters are fixed at 1, π and ε, respectively. For all students having two of the three items correct, their weighted score is $(1 + \pi)$, $(1 + \varepsilon)$ or $(\pi + \varepsilon)$, and these three numbers are different from each other. An analogous result holds for students having zero, one or all three items correct. So, there is a one-to-one relation between response patterns and weighted score, meaning that from the weighted score one can deduce with certainty the response pattern, or that it holds that $P(\underline{x}|s) = 1$, independently of the item parameters. More generally said, the sufficient statistics do not lead to a reduction of the data: they can assume as many different values as there are response patterns, and therefore the conditional likelihood function is constant and has no maximum.

To ensure that there is sufficient reduction, in the software package OPLM the discrimination parameters must be fixed at integer values in the range [1, 15]. Years of experience with the program have shown that in most cases, unique estimates of the item parameters are obtained. A general theoretical result that describes when the estimates exist or do not, however, is not available.

2.4 Bayesian estimation

In procedures using maximum likelihood, the parameters are considered as unknown but fixed constants. In a Bayesian approach the parameters are considered as random variables having some distribution. The distribution can be thought of as representing a summary of one's knowledge about the parameters. If it is very peaked with a small variance, this represents a state of knowledge where one is quite certain about the parameter: a small range around a central value has a large probability, indicating that one is quite certain that the parameter falls in that range. If the variance is large, the uncertainty is great.

In Bayesian estimation procedures, one has to specify the distribution of the parameters before the data are collected. This distribution is known as the prior distribution. The data themselves provide information about the parameters, that is, they add to our knowledge about them, so that after the data are collected (and properly analysed) the distribution of the parameters will have changed. This changed distribution is called the 'posterior distribution' and represents one's knowledge after having collected the data. In general, it is determined by the product of the prior probability density function and the likelihood. If one wants a point estimator, usually the mean of the posterior distribution is taken and, as a measure of uncertainty, one can take its standard deviation.

This very concise description hides one of the significant problems of Bayesian estimation: the equation of the posterior probability density function is very complicated and, mathematically, hardly tractable (except in very special cases, which are not of much interest in the framework of IRT modelling). In the 1990s a sampling approach to Bayesian estimation in complex statistical models became rather popular, due to the rapidly increasing computational power of modern computers. This approach has been embedded in the general theory of Markov chains and is known as Markov Chain Monte Carlo (MCMC). A concrete application in IRT can be found in Albert (1992), using the two-parameter normal ogive model in conjunction with a normally distributed latent variable. A more general introduction to Bayesian data analysis can be found in Gelman *et al.* (2003), and an application to the Rasch model is discussed in Maris and Maris (2002).

Free software is provided by the BUGS project (Lunn *et al.* 2000) and can be applied to – in principle – arbitrary complex models.

3 Testing IRT models

All statistical models have, in principle, the status of a hypothesis, and an important aspect of their use is testing whether this hypothesis is tenable. Such testing can be done in a formal way or an informal way. Formal procedures commonly take the form of statistical hypothesis testing, while informal procedures are those that indicate the ways one can make the model look acceptable, or not.

Proponents of a certain measurement model usually want the model to be the 'correct' one, and an easy way not to have to reject the model is not to look too critically to the correspondence between observed data and the model predictions of it. More formally, this means that in a statistical sense, the model is the null hypothesis, and in contrast to experimental set-ups, the researcher does not hope to reject the null hypothesis in favour of an alternative hypothesis (corresponding to the research hypothesis), but hopes *not* to be forced to reject it. Statistical tests used for this purpose are summarized under the name goodness-of-fit tests, and in general they look at the correspondence between some features of the observed data and the prediction of these same features from the model.

In this section some broad categories of statistical tests will be reviewed. The main distinction that will be considered is the one between exact tests (Section 3.1) and asymptotic tests (Section 3.2): the former category yields exact results whatever the sample size, while asymptotic tests are only exact as the sample size tends to infinity and are useful in practice only when the sample size is large – where it is often not too clear what is meant by large.

3.1 Non-parametric tests of the Rasch model

In exponential family models, the likelihood of the observed data depends on the observed data only through the sufficient statistics (see section 2.1). This has an important implication: if the model is valid, all data sets with the same sufficient statistics are equiprobable. Take a coin-tossing experiment as an example. Suppose a coin is tossed n times and lands heads (= success) m times. The model for the outcomes is relatively simple: it states that the probability of landing heads is π for all trials and that all outcomes are mutually independent. The likelihood of the outcomes under this model is $\pi^m(1 - \pi)^{n-m}$, that is, the number of successes is the sufficient statistic for the parameter π. To estimate the parameter π, only the proportion of successes is used, but one can look at the internal structure of the data to judge the trustworthiness of the model. Suppose, for example, that $n = 500$ and $m = 250$. The ML estimate of π is $250/500 = 0.5$, but on closer inspection of the outcome sequences, it appears that the first 250 trials were a success and the last 250 a failure. Although such a sequence is as probable as any other sequence with 250 successes, it is very likely that one will not accept the model because it has too few runs. (A run is a sequence of equal outcomes. In the example there are two runs). One might question, therefore, the assumption of independence of the trial outcomes. To have a rational judgement on the number of runs, one needs to know the distribution of the number of runs under the null hypothesis and conditional on the value of the sufficient statistic (that is, 250 of the 500 trials were a success). For this example, this distribution can be derived mathematically – see the discussion of the runs test in Siegel and Castellan (1988) – but the distribution can also be approximated to an arbitrary degree of accuracy by sampling a large number of sequences of 500 trials with exactly 250 successes and the number of runs determined for each sequence; the percentile rank of the empirical outcome can be determined in this distribution. If it is smaller than 2.5 or larger than 97.5, the null hypothesis (the model) is rejected – that is, the test rejects at a significance level of 5 per cent.

The versatility of this approach is clear from the fact that we may apply it to other statistics than the number of runs. In fact, it can be applied to any statistic, and it depends on the imagination of the researcher to find a statistic that may be indicative for some special defect in the hypothesis. Suppose, for example, that one has a suspicion that the value of π has decreased systematically during the experiment. If this were true one would expect fewer successes in the second half of the experiment than in the first half, and so a suitable statistic to test this hypothesis would be the difference in number of successes between the first and second half of the experiment.

Exactly the same reasoning as in the coin tossing example may be applied to the Rasch model: the sufficient statistics for the item parameters and the latent values of the tested students are the marginal totals of the data matrix. This means that, if the Rasch model is valid, all $n \times k$ binary tables with the same marginal totals as the observed one are equiprobable, and for any statistic one can approximate the sampling distribution by drawing at random a large number of these tables and by computing the statistic on each of these. The value of the statistic in the empirical table can then be compared to the simulated distribution, that is, its p-value can be computed.

The important difference between an application with the coin tossing example and the Rasch model is that in the former it is easy to draw a random sequence of 500 outcomes with 250 successes, while drawing at random a binary table with given marginal totals is extremely difficult; in fact, no procedure for how to accomplish this has thus far been found. Methods exist, however, for sampling in a way that gives a simulated sampling distribution that approximates the true distribution. Two classes are studied in the literature, one based on importance sampling and one based on MCMC techniques. A detailed account with references to earlier work can be found in Verhelst (2008). Applications for any statistic can be run in R (Verhelst, Hatzinger and Mair 2007). The user has to program a function in R where the statistic(s) of interest is computed. Unfortunately, the sampling procedure only applies to the Rasch model in a complete design. Generalizations to incomplete designs and to exponential family models for polytomous data, such as the PCM, are still needed.

3.2 Pearson-like tests

Pearson's chi-squared test, applied to contingency tables, is often used in IRT modelling, and it is taken for granted that the test statistic is asymptotically chi-squared distributed. The applicability of this test to complicated models, however, is not trivial, and inconsiderate use may lead to serious errors. A theoretically satisfactory solution was presented by Glas and Verhelst (1989, 1995) who defined a broad class of Pearson-like tests that are asymptotically chi-squared distributed. Unfortunately, the computation of the test statistics is rather complicated; see Verhelst and Glas (1995) for a detailed account. In this chapter, only a brief account will be given on an item-orientated test statistic in the Rasch model, labelled S_i.

To remain in the general framework of Pearson-like tests, a $k - 1 \times 2$ table is considered, the rows indicating the scores on the test and the columns indicating the quality of the answer, 1 for a correct answer and 0 for a wrong answer for some item i. Zero scores and perfect scores are omitted. See Table 9.1, where O indicates observed frequencies and E expected frequencies. Define $p_{i|s}$ as the proportion of correct answers to item i in the score group of students with score s. And similarly, define $\pi_{i|s}$ as the theoretical conditional probability (under the model) of a correct response, given that the score equals s. Clearly then, one can write

$$O_{s1} = n_s p_{i|s} \text{ and } E_{s1} = n_s \pi_{i|s}$$

where n_s is the number of students with score s. Using these definitions, the well-known expression for Pearson's chi-squared statistic can be written as

$$
\begin{aligned}
S_i^{\star} &= \sum_s \frac{(O_{s1} - E_{s1})^2}{E_{s1}} + \sum_s \frac{(O_{s0} - E_{s0})^2}{E_{s0}} \\
&= \sum_s \frac{n_s^2 (p_{i|s} - \pi_{i|s})^2}{n_s \pi_{i|s}} + \sum_s \frac{n_s^2 (p_{i|s} - \pi_{i|s})^2}{n_s (1 - \pi_{i|s})} \\
&= \sum_s \frac{n_s^2 (p_{i|s} - \pi_{i|s})^2}{n_s \pi_{i|s} (1 - \pi_{i|s})}.
\end{aligned}
\tag{7}
$$

Table 9.1 Bivariate frequency table for item *i*

	Item response		
Score	1	0	total
1	O_{11} (E_{11})	O_{10} (E_{10})	n_1
...	...	...	
s	O_{s1} (E_{s1})	O_{s0} (E_{s0})	n_s
...	...	...	
k − 1	$O_{k-1,1}$ ($E_{k-1,1}$)	$O_{k-1,0}$ ($E_{k-1,0}$)	n_{k-1}

If the theoretical probabilities $\pi_{i|s}$ were known exactly, then the test statistic would be asymptotically chi-squared, distributed with $k - 1$ degrees of freedom; but we only have estimates, and the problem arises because the estimate of $\pi_{i|s}$ depends on all item parameters, and if we subtract a degree of freedom for each estimated parameter, we would end up with zero degrees of freedom. This shows that the problem is not simple; indeed, it is technically quite involved. Generally speaking, the solution consists in applying a certain correction to the test statistic, which takes into account that the parameters have been estimated from the data. Details can be found in Verhelst and Glas (1995). The corrected statistics (indicated as S_i) are computed for the Rasch model and OPLM in the OPLM software package.

Apart from the theoretical burden to show the correctness of the chi-squared distribution, there is also a practical problem. The theoretical chi-squared distribution is only an approximation to the true distribution of S_i, and it is known that the approximation improves as the sample size increases. The practical problem is to know when the approximation is good enough to be useful with finite sample sizes. From research in statistics, it is known that Pearson's statistic gives odd results if expected frequencies in the table become very small. To avoid such a situation, Table 9.1 may be condensed by taking some adjacent score groups together (such that observed and expected frequencies in a number of adjacent rows are just summed together). In such a case the scores are grouped into Q groups, $G_1, \ldots, G_q, \ldots, G_Q$. For example, the lowest score group $G_1 = \{1, 2, 3, 4\}$ means that the scores 1 to 4 are taken together to form one single score group. The expression for the approximate statistic S_i^* is then given by

$$S_i^* = \sum_{q=1}^{Q} \frac{\left[\sum_{s \in G_q} n_s \left(p_{i|s} - \pi_{i|s}\right)\right]^2}{\sum_{s \in G_q} n_s \pi_{i|s}\left(1 - \pi_{i|s}\right)} \ . \tag{8}$$

If the necessary correction for the estimation of the item parameters is applied, the resulting statistic is (asymptotically) chi-squared distributed with $Q - 1$ degrees of freedom.

In the program package OPLM, groups of scores are formed such that the expected number of correct and incorrect answers is at least five in each group. Extended simulation studies have shown that the distribution of the S_i statistics is very well approximated by the chi-squared distribution.

An application: differential item functioning (DIF)

Applying an IRT model in an empirical population assumes that the model is valid in every sub-population in the same way. It may happen, however, that some items function differently in different sub-populations (see Holland and Wainer 1993, for an extensive discussion). Formally, an item is said to show differential functioning of item i with respect to two populations, P_1 and P_2, say, if for some ability value θ it holds that

$$P(X_i = 1|\theta, P_1) \neq P(X_i = 1|\theta, P_2). \tag{9}$$

For applications in EER it is important to look for items that show DIF with respect to important variables, such as gender, SES or method of instruction (Kyriakides and Antoniou 2009). When longitudinal studies are conducted in order to measure the long-term effect of teachers and schools, it is important to look for DIF at different moments of time. If part of the test material has become known between the first and second measurement moment, these items might show DIF in favour of the second measurement moment. If this is not recognized, and the analyses are carried out as if the measurement is valid, this will result in a biased estimate of the trend and may result in an underestimation of the long-term effect of school.

The way DIF is detected in the OPLM package is fairly simple. Suppose item i has been applied in two cycles of a survey, then (implicitly) two tables such as Table 9.1 are built, and the sum of squares given in (8) is simply added for the two cycles. If the correction due to the estimation of the parameters is applied properly, then the resulting statistic is asymptotically chi-squared distributed with degrees of freedom equal to the total number of score groups (in the two cycles jointly) minus 1. In Figure 9.6 a graphical display is given of the results of such an analysis in the PISA project. The item is a mathematics item administered in the cycles of 2000 and 2003. The results apply to one of the participating countries. The S_i statistic for this item is 42.92 with 14 degrees of freedom, and is highly significant.

The horizontal axes in both figures are to be read as ordinal axes. The symbols in the figures (crosses or bullets) indicate the proportion of correct responses in each of the score groups. The middle smooth line represents the predicted proportion (the points are connected by a smoothed line), and the two outer smoothed lines represent an approximate 95 per cent confidence envelope. If the model is true, then the observed proportions should fall (in 95 per cent of the cases) within this envelope. In the two figures, one can see that this is the

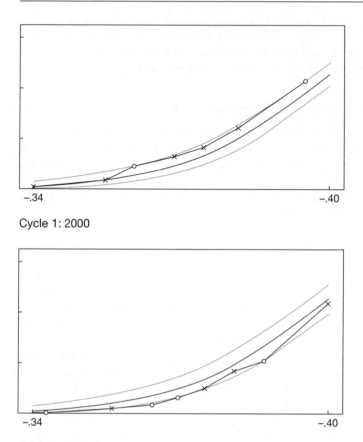

Cycle 1: 2000

Cycle 2: 2003

Figure 9.6 DIF of a PISA mathematics item (DIF is with respect to cycle)

case, but on the other hand, there is a systematic difference between the two figures: in the 2000 cycle students perform better than predicted by the model, while in the 2003 cycle the performance is worse than predicted, and this systematic difference is detected by the formal statistical test, which gives a very significant result.

3.3 Three classes of statistical tests

To exemplify the three classes of model tests, we take the preceding example of DIF as a starting point. Suppose the item displayed in Figure 9.6, henceforth called the target item, is the only item for which there is DIF and that for the other items the model as specified is valid. As the data have been analysed with OPLM, we assume also that the discrimination parameters for all items are well specified, and that for the Figure 9.6 target item, the discrimination parameter is valid for the two cycles. This means that in the specification of the model, there was only one error: the difficulty of the target item is different in the two cycles. One could in principle cope with this situation by considering the target item conceptually as different items in the two cycles (with possibly two different difficulty parameters), and then the model would be a correct description of the reality. The model that has been applied, however, represents a restriction on the parameters of the general model in that it requires that the difficulty parameter of these two conceptual items be equal in the two cycles. So the model as applied imposes a restriction on the parameter space of the general or encompassing model.

In statistical terms, the null hypothesis of the statistical test is the restricted model, while the encompassing model is the alternative hypothesis. There are three ways of testing such hypotheses, which are asymptotically equivalent but which imply different procedures. These tests are likelihood ratio tests, Wald-type tests and Lagrange multiplier tests. These tests are discussed below and are also discussed in relation to Structural Equation Modelling in Chapter 12.

Likelihood ratio tests

In this class of tests, the parameters are estimated (by maximum likelihood) under both the general model and the restricted model, and their maximal values under both models are compared. The test statistic is

$$LR = -2\ln\frac{L_r^*}{L_g^*},\tag{10}$$

where the '*' indicates that the value of the likelihood function has to be taken at its maximum. The subscript g stands for the general model and the subscript r for the restricted model. LR is asymptotically chi-squared distributed and the number of degrees of freedom equals the number of restrictions that were imposed to specify the restricted model.

In the example of the DIF item, this would mean that we would have to estimate the parameters twice: once in a model where the target item is treated as identical in the two cycles and once where it is treated as two different items. The LR-test would give a test statistic with one degree of freedom. However, if this procedure has to be applied for each item, then the number of estimation procedures would be one plus the number of common items in both cycles.

Wald-type tests

To apply this class of statistical tests, the parameters of the model have to be estimated under the general model. In the DIF example this means that the difficulty parameter for the target item has to be estimated as a different parameter in both cycles. Denote these parameters as β_{i1} and β_{i2} respectively. Then the restricted model, which is the null hypothesis, states that

$$H_0 : \beta_{i1} - \beta_{i2} = 0, \tag{11}$$

and if this hypothesis is true, then it may be expected that the estimates of both parameters are reasonably close to each other. The test statistic is just the squared difference between the two estimates divided by the (estimated) variance of the difference, that is:

$$W_i = \frac{(\hat{\beta}_{i1} - \hat{\beta}_{i2})^2}{Var(\hat{\beta}_{i1} - \hat{\beta}_{i2})} = \frac{(\hat{\beta}_{i1} - \hat{\beta}_{i2})^2}{SE^2(\hat{\beta}_{i1}) + SE^2(\hat{\beta}_{i2}) - 2Cov(\hat{\beta}_{i1}, \hat{\beta}_{i2})}. \tag{12}$$

The right-hand side of the preceding equation makes clear that the estimates of both parameters are correlated in general, and that one has to take the covariance of the estimates into account when computing the test statistic. W_i is asymptotically chi-squared distributed with one degree of freedom.

This example is a bit artificial because it reflects a procedure where one wants to test DIF only for a single item, while in the construction of a measurement model one would usually want to investigate DIF for all items. In such a case the general model states that in the two cycles all item parameters could possibly have different values, and estimating the difficulty parameters under this model amounts to estimating the parameters separately from the data of the two cycles. One can then test the null hypothesis (11) for each item in turn, and the test statistic is still given by (12) but in this case the covariance term vanishes because item parameters have been estimated from independent samples. It is also possible to estimate all these hypotheses jointly. The test statistic in this case is

$$W = (\hat{\beta}_1 - \hat{\beta}_2)'(\Sigma_1 + \Sigma_2)^{-1}(\hat{\beta}_1 - \hat{\beta}_2), \tag{13}$$

where $\beta_j (j = 1, 2)$ denotes the vector of parameter estimates and Σ denotes the (estimated) variance-covariance matrix of the estimates. The test statistic is asymptotically chi-squared distributed and the degrees of freedom are equal to the number of restrictions implied by the null hypothesis.

To make results of surveys comparable across cycles, the tests administered in both cycles must have some items in common, but usually they also contain unique material. Of course, the W-statistic to detect DIF can only be applied to the common items; suppose there are m of them. Furthermore, assume parameters have been estimated separately for the two cycles. However, this means that in the two estimation procedures the normalization is free, and one can always choose two normalizations such that the W-statistic takes an arbitrary, large value, for example, by setting the average of the common parameters in the first cycle equal to zero and in the second cycle to an arbitrary non-zero value. Therefore one must choose a normalization such that the estimates are meaningfully comparable across the two cycles. A good way of accomplishing this is to make the sum of the parameters of the common items in both cycles equal to each other. The number of degrees of freedom for the test is then $m - 1$.

Lagrange multiplier tests

In this class of tests, parameters are estimated only in the restricted model (that is, assuming that the null hypothesis is true). In the DIF example, this means that item parameters are estimated jointly from the data of the two cycles. The idea behind the test procedure is that at the maximum of the likelihood function, the change of the function with respect to the unrestricted parameters will be small and hence that the partial derivative of the (log-)likelihood function with respect to the unrestricted parameters will be close to zero. It has been shown that the Pearson-like tests (with proper correction for the fact that the parameters are estimated from the data) are test procedures of this class. The advantage of the Pearson-like approach, however, is that one does not need to write down explicitly the likelihood function for the general model but that one can suffice with the specification of one or more contrast vectors. In the case of the DIF example, this amounts to specifying the target item and indicating for each observed response pattern in which cycle it has been observed. A more complicated example to test the unidimensionality assumption in the Rasch model is discussed in detail in Verhelst (2001).

3.4 Informal procedures

Every statistical model, no matter how complicated it may be, is a simplification of reality, and therefore it cannot be the 'true' model. This implies that if one uses tests with enough power, for example by using huge samples, these tests will eventually all lead to significant results, and reasoning in a pure formal way, one cannot but reject the model. The search for the true model is vain, and a much more comfortable approach is to search for a useful model – that is, a model that represents (and can reproduce) important characteristics of the real world, where 'important' is always to be understood as important to one's purposes. The model of the sea level as a flat surface is useful for geography, but it will not be of any use for a shipwrecked person fighting to survive in a storm.

Therefore, a far more constructive attitude towards statistical models than the pure formal binary-decision directed attitude of statistical testing (accept or reject) is to try to come to a judgment if the model is a reasonably good approximation to reality or not. There is a lot one can do to judge on this reasonableness, and the actions one can take could be summarized under the name 'give your model a chance'. We discuss some examples below.

Suppose that for some research purposes one has administered a test of 40 arithmetic items to a sample of young students. The general assumption is that the scores obtained on this test will reflect the mathematics ability of the students, and a more fine-grained assumption is, for example, that the Rasch model (or any other model, for that sake) might be well suited to describe the empirical data. There are a number of things that one could (and should) do before starting the IRT analysis. Three suggestions follow.

Inspect the histogram of the score distribution. An unexpectedly high frequency of zero (or very low scores) may point to students who were not really taking the test.

Be sure to have a reasonable prior estimate of the difficulty of the items. If an item judged to be relatively easy by the test constructor turns out to be very difficult empirically, this may point to very practical problems such as an error in the key for multiple choice items or the effect of time pressure.

If data are collected through a two-stage sampling (first school, then students within schools), something might have gone wrong in a particular school (testing time too short, misunderstanding of the instructions, and so on). An efficient way to find out if such systematic errors have occurred is to run an analysis with an overparameterized model that makes very weak assumptions about the data. A good candidate is homogeneity analysis (Gifi 1990; Michailidis and De Leeuw 1998). In this analysis, the data are considered as nominal variables. The outcome of the analysis represents students as well as item categories as points in a Euclidean space of low dimensionality. The point representing the student is the midpoint (centre of gravity) of all the category points that represent his response pattern. Schools can be represented as the midpoint of all the student points of the students belonging to the same school. If the analysis is done in two or three dimensions, a graphical representation can be constructed where all schools are represented as a single point, and outlying schools are easily detected.

An important assumption of the IRT models discussed in this chapter is unidimensionality. One can apply a formal test of this assumption, as was mentioned in Section 3.3, but a simple Exploratory Factor Analysis (EFA) may be of equal use. In Figure 9.7, the factor pattern resulting from a factor analysis with two factors is displayed graphically. The data are the responses of 1,332 Hungarian students on a reading and listening test for English (the author is indebted to Euro Examinations in Budapest and, especially, to Zoltán Lukacsi for the permission to use the language test data for illustrative purposes). The reading part and the listening part both consist of 25 binary items. In the graph, the items are not identified, only the skill they belong to is indicated: R for reading and L for listening. It can be clearly seen that the vertical axis (the second factor) distinguishes between these two skills, and therefore it might be wiser to consider the two skills as representing two different abilities, rather than to treat them as representing the same ability.

Some comments are in order when using factor analysis on binary data:

• It is highly advisable to use tetrachoric correlations instead of Pearson product-moment correlations, as the latter tend to produce more factors

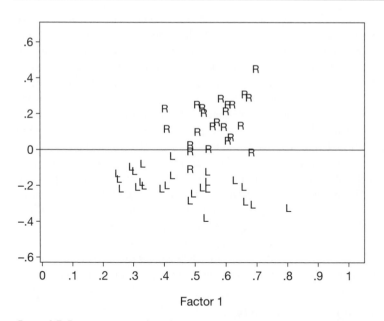

Figure 9.7 Factor pattern of reading and listening items

that are barely interpretable. For partial credit items, polychoric correlations are the preferred ones.

- The matrix of tetrachoric (or polychoric) correlations computed from finite data sets is often not positive semi definite (psd) and therefore cannot be used as input for factor analytic procedures that presuppose a psd correlation matrix, such as maximum likelihood factor analysis. To cope with such a situation one can follow two different strategies; either the computed correlation matrix is replaced by a similar one that is psd (Knol and Ten Berge 1989), or a factor analytic procedure is chosen that does not require a psd matrix as input. Good and easily available techniques include principal factor analysis (Harman 1960) or the minimizing residuals (MINRES) method (Harman and Jones 1966). If only exploratory analyses are done, using techniques that do not require a psd input matrix is the easiest way. For confirmatory analyses, the requirement of a psd matrix is unavoidable.

4 Applying IRT models in EER

The theory described in the preceding sections is aimed at preparing one for an important decision: accepting or rejecting a specific measurement model. It has been argued that acceptance of an IRT model does not mean that the model is perfect, but that it is good enough to be used in practical applications. For example, such a decision can help researchers in the area of EER to find out whether a specific IRT model can be used in order to estimate the latent ability of individual students in specific outcomes of schooling and then search for factors that may explain variation in student achievement. Thus, the present section of this chapter is meant to treat some approaches to this kind of problem and to present how researchers in the area of EER can make use of different IRT models to develop appropriate psychometric scales and search for the impact of specific factors on student achievement. More specifically, in Section 4.1 the estimation problem of individual latent abilities is treated. The next two sections treat the general problem of latent regression and explain how EER researchers can apply a multiple regression analysis where the dependent variable is an unobserved quantity, the latent ability of individual students. In Section 4.3, latent regression is treated but in this case the dependent variable is replaced by a proxy (that is, an estimate of the latent ability). The results of a simulation study that provides support for this approach are also presented. Finally, we draw some more general implications for the development of EER that are concerned with the use of different IRT models to generate valid and reliable measures of student achievement and to identify the impact of effectiveness factors on student achievement.

4.1 Estimating latent abilities

Maximum likelihood (ML) estimates

Acceptance of a measurement model on the basis of a well designed and thoroughly investigated measurement model means in practice that the item parameters of the model are replaced by their estimates and subsequently treated as known quantities. The likelihood of an observed response pattern $\underline{x}$ on k binary items is then

$$L(\theta;\underline{x}) = \prod_{i=1}^{k} f_i(\theta)^{x_i} \times [1 - f_i(\theta)]^{1-x_i}, \tag{14}$$

which now only depends on a single unknown quantity, θ, and the value of θ that maximizes the right-hand side of (14) is the maximum likelihood estimate of θ. Once the item parameters are fixed, the 2PLM is also an exponential family model, and the sufficient statistic for θ is the weighted score (with the discrimination parameters as weights). Denoting the sufficient statistic for θ generically as s, the ML estimate of θ in the 2PLM is the solution of the likelihood equation

$$s = \sum_{i=1}^{k} \alpha_i f_i(\theta). \tag{15}$$

For the Rasch model it suffices to replace the α-parameters by one. Some of the models discussed in previous sections, however, do not belong to the exponential family, even when the item parameters are fixed. The 3PLM is such a case, as well as the graded response model and all normal ogive models. For these models there is no sufficient statistic for θ, and to find the ML estimate, the right-hand side of (14) must be maximized.

A disadvantage of ML estimates is that (15) has no solution if s is zero or s equals the maximal score because the right-hand side of (15) is always a positive number (all response probabilities are positive), and it is always smaller than the maximal score, because all response probabilities are strictly smaller than one.

One of the attractive features of maximum likelihood estimation is the availability of the standard errors of the estimates, which are derived from a quantity known as Fisher information. The information function is defined as the negative of the expected value of the second derivative of the log-likelihood function:

$$I(\theta) = -E\left[\frac{d^2 \ln L(\theta; \underline{x})}{d\theta^2}\right] \tag{16}$$

The expected value is to be taken over all possible response patterns. The relationship with the standard error of the ML estimate $\hat{\theta}$ is this:

$$SE(\hat{\theta}) \approx \frac{1}{\sqrt{I(\theta)}} \approx \frac{1}{\sqrt{I(\hat{\theta})}}. \tag{17}$$

Notice that in (17) two approximations are used. The first one is there because the result is only valid asymptotically – that is, when the number of items tends to infinity. The second one is needed because the information function is a function of θ, and since θ is not known, its value is replaced by a proxy, the estimate.

In the 2PLM the information function is given by

$$I(\theta) = \sum_{i=1}^{k} \alpha_i^2 f_i(\theta)[1 - f_i(\theta)]. \tag{18}$$

Conditional unbiasedness

It seems a reasonable requirement that upon (independent) replicated administrations of the same test, the average estimate of the ability equals the true ability. Formally the requirement is that

$$E(\hat{\theta}|\theta) - \theta = 0. \tag{19}$$

The estimator $\hat{\theta}$ is said to be *conditionally unbiased* if (19) holds for all values of θ.

The maximum likelihood estimator of θ is conditionally biased (Lord 1983). In Figure 9.8, the bias of the ML estimator (dashed curve) – that is, the value of the left-hand side of (19), is displayed graphically for a test of 40 items complying with the Rasch model. The item parameters range from −1.05 to +1.7 with an average value of 0.5. For zero and perfect scores, values of −5 and +5 have been used respectively as estimates of the latent ability.

In the figure (dashed curve) it is clearly seen that the bias is zero only for one value of θ, θ_0 say. For values larger than θ_0, the bias is positive, meaning that on the average, the real value of θ will tend to be overestimated by the ML estimate, while for values smaller than θ_0, they will be underestimated. In general, this means that the ML estimates are stretching out the real values of θ. The relation between the item parameters and the value of θ_0 has not yet been determined mathematically but in a number of simulations it has appeared that θ_0 coincides with the point of maximal information. However, independently of the correctness of the previous statement, it should be kept in mind that the value of θ_0, the bias function as displayed in the figure and the information function are completely determined by the item parameters and are not in any way related to the distribution of the latent variable θ in whatever population.

Suppose that one wants to compare the ability of girls and boys, for example by a t-test, and one uses the ML estimates as proxies for θ. If the average estimate of the girls is larger than θ_0 and the average of the boys is smaller, then the difference of the averages will be an overestimation of the true difference between the two groups.

The conditional bias and the fact that the estimate does not exist for zero nor for perfect scores makes the ML estimates unsuitable for statistical applications. The results discussed here apply to models of the logistic family

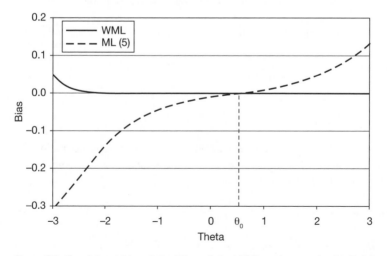

Figure 9.8 Conditional bias of the ML and the WML estimators in the Rasch model

(the Rasch model, OPLM, (G)PCM, 2PLM and 3PLM). Similar theoretical results for the GRM and the normal ogive models are not known.

Weighted maximum likelihood (WML) estimates

Although it is not possible to find an estimator of θ that is conditionally unbiased, Warm (1989) developed an estimator that is almost unbiased. The estimate is the value of θ that maximizes the weighted likelihood – that is, the product of the likelihood function multiplied by a weight function that depends on θ but not on the response pattern $\underline{x}$:

$$w(\theta) \times L(\theta; \underline{x}) \tag{20}$$

Warm's purpose was to find the weight function such that the bias disappeared as much as possible. It turned out that in the Rasch model and in the 2PLM the weight function is given by

$$w(\theta) = \sqrt{I(\theta)},$$

the square root of the information function. He also found the weight function for the 3PLM, but in that case it is more complicated.

This estimator, referred to as the weighted maximum likelihood or Warm estimator, is almost unbiased for a wide range of θ-values. Moreover, the estimator exists for all possible values of the score, including zero and perfect scores. For extreme values of θ, the bias remains, but it is in the opposite direction from the bias of the ML estimator: for values much higher than the point of maximal information the bias is negative and for small values it is positive – the estimates tend to shrink compared to the true values. In Figure 9.8 (solid line) the bias is displayed graphically and can be compared directly to the bias of the ML estimator. Notice that the bias is very small (less than 0.01 in absolute value) in the range (–2.5, 3), which is much wider than the range of the difficulty parameters.

The availability of an (almost) unbiased estimator is a great advantage for statistical applications, as will be discussed in the next sections.

4.2 Regression with measurement error

Multiple regression analysis is probably the most widely used analysis tool to investigate the relation between educational performances and one or more background variables, such as gender or socio-economic status. In EER, the most interesting variables are usually constant within schools but vary across schools, while the basic measurements – the performances of the students – are collected at the student level, necessitating a two-level (or more generally, a multilevel) approach to the analysis of the data (see Chapter 11). In this chapter, the discussion will be restricted to a simple linear two-level model with a random intercept, which may be represented as follows:

$$Y_{ij} = \sum_{g=1}^{p} \beta_g z_{ij}^{(g)} + u_j + \varepsilon_{ij}. \tag{21}$$

The dependent variable Y_{ij} is some observed measure on student i in school j. The p regressors $z^{(1)}, \ldots, z^{(p)}$ are fixed constants that do or do not vary across students of the same school. Notice that the characterization of the model as a two-level model does not depend on this variation, but on the presence of the latter two terms, u_j and ε_{ij} in the right-hand side of (21). Both are to be considered as realizations of two random variables: the random intercept at the school level (u_j) and the residual at the student level (ε_{ij}). In most applications of multilevel modelling these two random variables are considered as statistically independent, and as being normally distributed. In the simplest case, these are the two assumptions:

$$\varepsilon_{ij} \sim N(0, \sigma^2) \text{ and } u_j \sim N(0, \tau^2). \tag{22}$$

The estimation problem in multilevel analysis is then to obtain estimates of the regression coefficients $\beta_1, \ldots, \beta_p$ and of the two variance components σ^2 and τ^2.

A conceptual problem is associated with the fact that the observed dependent variable Y is never a pure operationalization of the concept in which one is interested, but is in a sense polluted by measurement error, implying that at the lowest level, true variance and error variance are subsumed in σ^2, or equivalently, that the residual variance will increase as the reliability of the measurement decreases. Variation in the reliability has the following effects on the results of the multilevel regression analysis:

- There is no bias in the estimates of the regression coefficients (Cook and Campbell 1979, Chapter 4).
- The standard errors of the regression coefficients increase with decreasing reliability.
- The residual variance σ^2 increases if the reliability decreases.
- The higher level variance τ^2 is not affected in a systematic way. Although no proof seems to be available for this, it appears to be the case in a significant number of simulation studies.

The latter two bullet points have consequences when the intra-class correlation ρ is considered:

$$\rho = \frac{\tau^2}{\sigma^2 + \tau^2} \tag{23}$$

Using the estimates of both variance components to estimate ρ will not affect the numerator of (23) but will systematically inflate the denominator as the reliability decreases, and this will affect a clear interpretation of the intra-class correlation, a variable of considerable importance in EER.

Latent regression

As in IRT, where the concept to be measured is at the centre of the model, it would be nice if one could carry out a regression analysis where the dependent variable is the latent variable. So the basic regression model given by (21) is changed to

$$\theta_{ij} = \sum_{g=1}^{p} \beta_g z_{ij}^{(g)} + u_j + \varepsilon_{ij}. \tag{24}$$

The term latent regression is shorthand for 'regression model where the dependent variable is not directly observed'. Basically, two approaches can be used to analyse model (24): either one substitutes the latent observation θ_{ij} by a proxy – an estimate of it – or one tries to carry out the analysis without using proxies. In the first approach, an estimation error is re-introduced, but not in the second approach. The use of the first approach is recommended here and is presented in the final section of this chapter. For the second approach, see Verhelst and Verstralen (2002).

4.3 Latent regression using a proxy for θ

The fact that in ordinary regression the estimates of the regression parameters are unbiased when noise is added is due to the conditional unbiasedness of the observed score in Classical Test Theory: the expectation of the observed score (under equivalent replications) is by definition the true score. If we want the same unbiasedness when using proxies in latent regression, it is clear that the proxies will have to be conditionally unbiased. Although such proxies do not exist in the strict sense, there is a reasonable approximation with the Warm estimates in the logistic family of IRT models.

The present section is mainly meant as an illustration of a simple multilevel analysis using the Warm estimates as the dependent variable. In the first part of the section, a simulation study is reported. Data are generated following the Rasch model on a test consisting of 40 items in total; the 20 positive item parameters are 8*0.5, 5*1, 4*1.5, 2*2 and 1*2.5. The 20 negative ones are just the opposite of the positive parameters. In both studies two background variables are used, which we will refer to as gender (with two values) and region (with three values). The regressors are the constant and three dummy variables (one for gender and two for regions); 'boys' and 'region 1' are used as reference categories respectively. The true regression parameters are 0.9 for girls, 0.3 for region 2 and 0.7 for region 3. The average ability in the combined reference categories (boys in region 1) is –1.1, which is the true parameter of the intercept.

One thousand response patterns per region are generated. It is assumed that per region 40 schools are sampled and within each school ten students are sampled. The between school variance, τ^2 is set at 0.15 and the within school variance, σ^2 at 0.85. In each school the 'gender' of the simulated student is chosen at random, such that the number of boys across schools is not constant but follows a binomial distribution.

The generation of the data proceeds as follows:

1   For each region, the regional component is determined. For region 1, this is just the intercept (– 1.1); for region 2, this is the intercept plus the effect of region 2: –1.1 + 0.3 = –0.8.
2   For each school within the region, a school effect is generated at random from $N(0, \tau^2)$ and added to the regional component.
3   For each student within the school the gender is determined at random. If the result is 'girl', the gender effect is added to the regional component, otherwise no change occurs. Next, a random variate generated form $N(0, \sigma^2)$ is added to the systematic effects of region and gender. The resulting sum is the latent value associated with the sampled student. This value is kept constant in step 4.
4   A response pattern is generated using the 40 item parameters and the θ-value from step 3.

If steps 1 to 4 are completed for all regions and schools, the result is a data set with item responses and a set of generated θ-values that are subsequently analysed in three different ways. For each analysis a multilevel model is used as given by the right-hand side of equation (21), but the dependent variable differs across the analyses. In the first analysis, the dependent variable is the true θ-value generated for each student; in the other two analyses the Warm estimate of the θ-value is used. As this estimate is completely determined by the score and by the item parameters, two different estimates could be used. In analysis 2, the dependent variable is the Warm estimate computed for each obtained score and using the true item parameter values. In the third analysis, CML estimates of the item parameters were obtained, and these estimates were used to compute the Warm estimate for each student.

Generating a data set according to the above described procedure and carrying out the three analyses constitutes one replication. One thousand replications were carried out. In Table 9.2 the results are displayed. Averages and standard deviations are computed across replications.

The following observations arise from Table 9.2:

1   The standard deviations across replications are good estimates of the standard errors, as they are affected by sampling error: the school effects (u_j), as well as the latent values, are sampled anew in each replication.

Table 9.2 Results of the simulation study

Dependent variable	True parameters	Constant −1.1	Region 2 0.3	Region 3 0.7	Girl 0.9	τ^2 0.15	σ^2 0.85
θ	average	−1.100	0.299	0.700	0.902	0.148	0.850
	SD	0.052	0.067	0.068	0.035	0.020	0.023
$\tilde{\theta}$	average	−1.100	0.299	0.700	0.901	0.148	1.011
	SD	0.054	0.069	0.071	0.038	0.021	0.030
$\hat{\theta}$	average	−1.100	0.299	0.700	0.901	0.148	1.012
	SD	0.054	0.069	0.071	0.038	0.021	0.030

$\tilde{\theta}$ = Warm estimates based on true item parameters
$\hat{\theta}$ = Warm estimates based on estimated item parameters (CML)

2   The most important result is that all average parameter estimates, except the within-school variance (σ^2), are very close to their true value.
3   The within-school variance (σ^2) is much affected by the kind of analysis, and the results are in line with those discussed above: the Warm estimates contain an estimation error, and this error is reflected in a larger estimate of the residual variance. If we take the average estimated variances as our best guess, then the estimated intraclass correlation, using estimates of θ is $0.148/(0.148 + 1.012) = 0.128$, while the true value is 0.15. This may not look very dramatic, but the test used has a reliability of around 0.9, which is quite high, and may not always be reached in educational research.
4   The table does not show any but trivial differences between the analyses using Warm estimates: whether the true item parameters are used or whether the estimated ones are used, it does not make any difference, although the standard errors of the item parameter estimates have values between 0.042 and 0.065. One should, however, be careful in generalizing this result. For example, using very small calibration samples might have an influence on the results of the regression analysis. In large studies such as international surveys or national assessment programmes, the sample size used is usually well comparable to the one used in the simulation study.

Although the simulation study reported here is restricted in scope, it nevertheless seems justified to draw the following conclusions:

• Using (almost) unbiased estimates of the latent ability as the dependent variable in multilevel regression does not lead to systematic distortions of the regression parameters, with the exception of the level one variance, which is inflated by the estimation errors. This makes the situation fully comparable with the use of multiple regression analysis in the framework of Classical Test Theory.

- The practical advantage of this approach is that multilevel analyses can be carried out using standard software. In fact, the estimates of the latent ability can be treated as observed variables, and they are comparable even in cases where the test forms used are not equivalent (incomplete designs).
- The key concept in producing these advantages is of course the conditional unbiasedness of the estimates. In the logistic family, the Warm estimator seems to do a good job, although one has to be careful to watch for remaining bias in ranges of the latent variable where the information function is too low. For other IRT models, these kinds of unbiased estimators are not available, and developing them might be a useful research topic, especially for researchers in the area of educational effectiveness who make use of IRT models to identify the impact on student achievement of effectiveness factors at different levels.

Finally, we would like to argue that this chapter has shown that researchers within EER can make use of IRT models to generate reliable and valid estimates of student achievement and use them to identify the impact of specific factors on achievement. This is especially true when different types of test are used to collect data on achievement at different time points, and researchers should consider the IRT models when analysing data from different incomplete designs of administering tests to different age groups of students and at different time points. Thus, by making use of different IRT models and selecting the most appropriate to be used in each case, EER researchers will not only be able to develop the methodology of their studies further but also to improve the theoretical framework of the field by raising issues such as the measurement of the long- and short-term effect of schools, which will help us better understand the complex process of change.

References

Albert, J.H. (1992) 'Bayesian estimation of normal ogive item response functions using Gibbs sampling', *Journal of Educational Statistics*, 17: 251–69.

Andersen, E.B. (1973) 'Conditional inference and models for measuring', unpublished dissertation, Mentalhygienisk Forskningsinstitut, Copenhagen.

Bock, R.D. and Aitkin, M. (1981) 'Marginal maximum likelihood estimation of item parameters: An application of an EM-algorithm', *Psychometrika*, 46: 443–59.

Cochran, W.G. and Cox, G.M. (1957) *Experimental designs*, New York: Wiley.

Cook, T.D. and Campbell, D.T. (1979) *Quasi-experimentation, design, & analysis issues for field settings*, Chicago: Rand McNally College Publishing Company.

De Leeuw, J. and Verhelst, N.D. (1986) 'Maximum likelihood estimation in generalized Rasch models', *Journal of Educational Statistics*, 11: 183–96.

Fischer, G.H. (1974) *Einführung in die Theorie Psychologischer Tests* [*Introduction to the theory of psychological tests*], Bern: Huber.

Formann, A.K. (1995) 'Linear logistic latent class analysis and the Rasch model', in G.H. Fischer and I.W. Molenaar (eds) *Rasch models: Foundations, recent developments and applications*, New York: Springer, pp. 239–55.

Gelman, A., Carlin, J.B., Stern, H.S. and Rubin, D.B. (2003) *Bayesian data analysis*, 2nd edn, London: Chapman and Hall.

Gifi, A. (1990) *Nonlinear multivariate analysis*, New York: Wiley.

Glas, C.A.W. (1989) *Contributions to estimating and testing Rasch models*, Arnhem: CITO.

Glas, C.A.W. and Verhelst, N.D. (1989) 'Extensions of the partial credit model', *Psychometrika*, 54: 635–59.

Glas, C.A.W. and Verhelst, N.D. (1995) 'Testing the Rasch model', in G.H. Fischer and I.W. Molenaar (eds) *Rasch models: Foundations, recent developments and applications* 69–96, New York: Springer.

Harman, H.H. (1960) *Modern factor analysis*, Chicago: University of Chicago Press.

Harman, H.H. and Jones, W.H. (1966) 'Factor analysis by minimizing residuals (MINRES)', *Psychometrika*, 31: 351–68.

Holland, P.W. and Wainer, H. (eds) (1993) *Differential item functioning*, Hillsdale, NJ: Lawrence Erlbaum Associates.

Knol, D.L. and Ten Berge, J.M.F. (1989) 'Least-squares approximation of an improper by a proper correlation matrix', *Psychometrika*, 54: 53–61.

Kyriakides, L. and Antoniou, P. (2009) 'Gender differences in mathematics achievement: An investigation of gender differences by item difficulty interactions', Educational Research & Evaluation, 15(3): 223–42.

Kyriakides, L. and Creemers, B.P.M. (2008) 'A longitudinal study on the stability over time of school and teacher effects on student learning outcomes', *Oxford Review of Education*, 34(5): 521–45.

Kyriakides, L. and Luyten, H. (2009) 'The contribution of schooling to the cognitive development of secondary education students in Cyprus: An application of regression discontinuity with multiple cut-off points', *School Effectiveness and School Improvement*, 20(2): 167–86.

Laird, N. (1978) 'Nonparametric maximum likelihood estimation of a mixing distribution', *Journal of the American Statistical Association*, 73: 805–11.

Little, R.J.A. and Rubin, D.B. (1987) *Statistical analysis with missing data*, New York: Wiley.

Lord, F.M. (1983) 'Unbiased estimators of ability parameters, of their variance and of their parallel-forms reliability', *Psychometrika* 48: 233–45.

Lunn, D.J., Thomas, A., Best, N. and Spiegelhalter, D. (2000) 'WinBUGS – a Bayesian modelling framework: concepts, structure, and extensibility', *Statistics and Computing*, 10: 325–37.

Mair, P. and Hatzinger, R. (2007) 'Extended Rasch modeling: The eRm package for the application of IRT models', *Journal of Statistical Software*, 20(8). Online. Available at: www.jstatsoft.org/ [accessed 17 January 2010].

Maris, G. and Maris, E. (2002) 'A MCMC-method for models with continuous latent responses', *Psychometrika*, 67: 335–50.

Michailidis, G. and De Leeuw, J. (1998) 'The Gifi system of descriptive multivariate analysis', *Statistical Science*, 13: 307–36.

Molenaar, I.W. (1995) 'Estimation of item parameters', in G.H. Fischer and I.W. Molenaar (eds) *Rasch models: Foundations, recent developments and applications*, New York: Springer.

Rasch, G. (1960) *Probabilistic models for some intelligence and attainment tests*, Copenhagen: Danish Institute for Educational Research.

Rubin, D.B. (1976) 'Inference and missing data', *Biometrika*, 63: 581–92.

Siegel, S. and Castellan, N.J. (1988) *Non-parametric statistics for the behavioral sciences*, 2nd edn, New York: McGraw-Hill.

Verhelst, N.D. (2001) 'Testing the unidimensionality assumption in the Rasch model', *Methods of Psychological Research – online*, 6: 231–71.

Verhelst, N.D. (2008) 'An efficient MCMC algorithm to sample binary matrices with fixed marginals', *Psychometrika*, 73: 705–28.

Verhelst, N.D. and Eggen, T.J.H.M. (1989) 'Psychometrische en statistische aspecten van peilingsonderzoek [Psychometric and statistical aspects of assessment research]', *PPON-rapport*, 4, Arnhem: CITO.

Verhelst, N.D. and Glas, C.A.W. (1995) 'The generalized one parameter model: OPLM', in G.H. Fischer and I.W. Molenaar (eds) *Rasch models: Their foundations, recent developments and applications*, New York: Springer.

Verhelst, N.D., Glas, C.A.W. and Verstralen, H.H.F.M. (1994) *OPLM: computer program and manual*, Arnhem: Cito.

Verhelst, N.D., Hatzinger, R. and Mair, P. (2007) 'The Rasch sampler', *Journal of Statistical Software*, 20(4). Online. Available at: www.jstatsoft.org/v20/i04/paper [accessed 17 January 2010].

Verhelst, N.D. and Verstralen, H.H.F.M. (2002) *Structural Analysis of a Univariate Latent Variable (SAUL). Theory and a computer program*, Arnhem: CITO.

Warm, T.A. (1989) 'Weighted likelihood estimation of ability in item response theory', *Psychometrika*, 54: 427–50.

Chapter 10

Using Generalizability Theory

George A. Marcoulides and Leonidas Kyriakides
University of California, Riverside and University of Cyprus
(respectively)

Introduction

It is well known that most measurement devices are not perfect. Physical scientists have recognized this fact for many years and have learned to repeat their measurements many times to obtain results in which they can be confident. Repeated measures can provide the average of a set of recurring results, which is expected to provide a more precise estimate of what is being appraised than just a single measurement. Unfortunately, within the educational arena commonly obtained measurements cannot be repeated as straightforwardly as in the physical sciences. Because the results of measurements in education can have a profound influence on an individual's life, the derivation and accuracy of the scores have been the subject of extensive research in the so-called psychometric literature. There are currently two major psychometric theories for the study of measurement procedures: random sampling theory and latent trait theory, which is also known as Item Response Theory (Suen 1990). Within random sampling theory there are two approaches, the Classical Test Theory approach and the Generalizability Theory approach (Cronbach *et al.* 1963; Cronbach *et al.* 1972; Gleser *et al.* 1965), whereas within IRT there are more than two dozen approaches (Bond and Fox 2001, Chapter 9; Embretson and Reise 2000).

This chapter provides an overview of Generalizability Theory and shows how it can be used to design, assess and improve the dependability of measurement procedures. In this way researchers within EER can make use of Generalizability Theory in testing the quality of their data. To gain a perspective from which to view the application of this approach and to provide a frame of reference, Generalizability Theory is initially compared with the traditionally used classical reliability theory approach. The first section of this chapter gives an overview of the fundamentals of Generalizability Theory. Although Generalizability Theory can be applied in a variety of scenarios, this section spotlights the simple one-facet model, which is the most common measurement procedure used and readily provides a mechanism for a comparison of results obtained with Classical Test Theory. Different types of error variance and generalizability coefficient estimates are then introduced to illustrate the distinct advantages of

Generalizability Theory over Classical Test Theory. The next sections give an overview of the basic concepts extended to multifaceted and multivariate measurement designs. A brief summary of computer programs that can be used to conduct generalizability analyses are presented in the fourth section. The final section introduces some recent advances and extensions to Generalizability Theory modelling that can address significant methodological issues of effectiveness studies.

Overview of fundamentals

Generalizability Theory is a random sampling theory concerning the dependability of behavioural measurements (Shavelson and Webb 1991). Because of its ability to model a wide array of measurement conditions through which a wealth of psychometric information can be obtained (Marcoulides 1989), Generalizability Theory has even been proclaimed as 'the most broadly defined psychometric model currently in existence' (Brennan 1983: xiii). Although many researchers were instrumental in its original development (Burt 1936, 1947; Hoyt 1941), it was formally introduced by Cronbach and his associates (Cronbach *et al.* 1963; Cronbach *et al.* 1972; Gleser *et al.* 1965). Since the major publication by Cronbach *et al.* (1972), Generalizability Theory has received much attention in the literature as a more liberalized approach to measurement than Classical Test Theory.

The fundamental tenet of the Classical Test Theory approach is that any observed score (X) for an individual obtained through some measurement device can be decomposed into the true score (for example, with a measure of ability this would represent the true ability of an individual) and an unsystematic random error (E) component. This can be symbolized as: $X = T + E$. The better a measurement device is at providing an accurate value for T, the smaller the magnitude of the E component will be. Estimation of the degree of accuracy with which the T component is determined can be assessed using a so-called reliability coefficient. The reliability coefficient is typically defined as the ratio of the true score variance (σ^2_T) to the observed score variance (σ^2_X or equivalently $\sigma^2_T + \sigma^2_E$). Thus, the notion of the reliability coefficient corresponds to the proportion of observed score variability that is attributable to true score variability across individuals, which essentially increases as the occurrence of error decreases.

A number of different strategies can be used to obtain estimates of the reliability coefficient in Classical Test Theory. For example, a test-retest reliability estimate can be used to provide an indication of how consistently a measurement device rank-orders individuals over time. This type of reliability requires administration on two different occasions and examining the correlation between observed scores on the two occasions to determine stability over time. Internal consistency is another method to obtain reliability and considers the degree to which test items provide similar and consistent results about individuals. Another method to estimate reliability involves administering two so-called 'parallel' forms of the same test at different times and examining the correlation between the forms.

Unfortunately, many of the assumptions of Classical Test Theory are often problematic, particularly the existence of an undifferentiated error in measurement. For example, in the above-mentioned strategies for estimating reliability, it is quite unclear which interpretation of error is most suitable. To make things worse, one may be faced with the uncomfortable fact that scores obtained from measurement devices used on the same individuals often yield different values on these reliability coefficients. In contrast, Generalizability Theory acknowledges that multiple sources of error may simultaneously occur in measurement (for example, errors attributable to different testing occasions and/or different test items) and enables the estimation of the multifaceted error effects.

In their original formulation of Generalizability Theory, Cronbach *et al.* (1972) advocated that observed scores obtained through a measurement procedure be gathered as a basis for making decisions or drawing conclusions. Cronbach *et al.* (1972) provided the following argument for their perspective:

> The score on which the decision is to be based is only one of many scores that might serve the same purpose. The decision maker is almost never interested in the response given to the particular stimulus objects or questions, to the particular tester, at the particular moment of testing. Some, at least, of these conditions of measurement could be altered without making the score any less acceptable to the decision maker. That is to say, there is a universe of observations, any of which would have yielded a usable basis for the decision. The ideal datum on which to base the decision would be something such as the person's mean score over all acceptable observations, which we shall call his 'universe score.' The investigator uses the observed score or some function of it as if it were the universe score. That is, he generalizes from sample to universe.
>
> (Cronbach *et al.* 1972: 15)

Based upon the above contention, Cronbach *et al.* (1972) placed the notion of a 'universe' at the heart of Generalizability Theory. All measurements are deemed to be samples from a universe of admissible observations. A universe is defined in terms of those aspects (called 'facets') of the observations that determine the conditions under which an acceptable score can be obtained. For example, the facets that define one universe could be personality tests administered to new employees during their first week of employment. Since it is possible to conceive of many different universes to which any particular measurement might generalize, it is essential that investigators define explicitly the facets that can change without making the observation unacceptable or unreliable. For example, if test scores might be expected to vary from one occasion to another, then the 'occasions' facet is one defining characteristic of the universe and multiple testing times must be included in the measurement procedure. The same would hold true for the choice of test items and other aspects of the measurement procedure. Ideally, the measurement procedure should yield information about an individual's universe score over all combinations of facets, but in reality, investigators are limited in their choice of particular occasions, items or other facets. The need to sample facets introduces error into the measurement procedure and limits investigators to estimating rather than actually measuring the universe score. Thus, the Classical Test Theory concept of reliability is replaced by the broader notion of generalizability (Shavelson *et al.* 1989). Instead of asking 'how accurately observed scores reflect corresponding true scores', Generalizability Theory asks 'how accurately observed scores permit us to generalize about persons' behaviour in a defined universe' (Shavelson *et al.* 1989). Although in most instances some attribute of persons will usually be the object of measurement, it is possible to consider other facets as the object of measurement. In such a case, the facet for persons is then treated as an error component. This feature has been termed the 'principle of symmetry' (Cardinet *et al.* 1976).

A one-facet crossed design

A common educational measurement procedure is to administer a multiple-choice test consisting of a random sample if n_i items from a universe of items to a random sample of n_p persons from a population of persons. Such a design is called a one-facet person-crossed-with-items ($p \times i$) design because the items facet is the only potential source of error included in the measurement procedure. A one-facet design can be viewed as an analysis of variance (ANOVA) design with a single random or fixed factor. Denoting the observed score of person p on item i as X_{pi}, one can decompose the score as (provided below in both equation and verbal statement form in terms of effect decomposition):

$$X_{pi} = \mu + (\mu_p - \mu) + (\mu_i - \mu) + (X_{pi} - \mu_p - \mu_i + \mu)$$

$$= \text{grand mean} + \text{person effect} + \text{item effect} + \text{residual effect,}$$

where $\mu_p = E_i X_{pi}$ is the person's universe score (that is, the expected value of the random variable X_{pi} across items), $\mu_i = E_p X_{pi}$ is the person population mean for item i, and $\mu = E_p E_i X_{pi}$ is the mean over both the person population and universe of possible scores (the entire item universe). Because there is only one observation for each person–item combination, the residual effect corresponds to a score effect attributable to the interaction of person p with item i confounded with experimental error. Cronbach *et al.* (1972) represented this confounding with the notation pi,e. The associated observed variance decomposition of these effects is as follows:

$$\sigma^2(X_{pi}) = \sigma^2_p + \sigma^2_i + \sigma^2_{pi,e},$$

where the symbols on the right-hand side correspond respectively to the variance due to persons, items and the residual effect.

Generalizability Theory places considerable importance on the variance components of the effects in the model because their magnitude provides information about the potential sources of error influencing a measurement. The estimated variance components are the basis for determining the relative contribution of each potential source of error and for determining the dependability of a measurement. In actual practice the estimation of the variance components is achieved by calculating observed mean squares from an ANOVA, equating these values to their expected values and solving a set of linear equations. Table 10.1 provides the ANOVA results from a hypothetical one-facet study in which a sample of 20 students were administered a five-item test. It is important to note that for purposes of illustration we have intentionally kept the number of persons and items small. In most pragmatic studies these numbers would likely be much larger. Table 10.1 also provides the computational formulae for determining the variance components associated with the score effects in the model. Estimation of the variance components is basically achieved by equating the observed mean squares from the ANOVA to their expected values and solving the set of linear equations; the resulting solution for the components comprises the estimates (Cornfield and Tukey 1956).

It is important to note that other procedures can also be used to estimate variance components. Numerous methods of estimation that can be used to provide the same information as ANOVA have been developed, including Bayesian, minimum variance, restricted maximum likelihood and covariance structure methods (Marcoulides 1987, 1989, 1990, 1996; Shavelson and Webb 1981). These methods often provide more accurate estimates of variance components than ANOVA in cases involving small sample sizes, dichotomous data, unbalanced designs or data with missing observations (Marcoulides, 1987, 1996; Muthén 1983). ANOVA is much easier to implement, however, and it continues to be the most commonly used estimation method in Generalizability Theory. Because

Table 10.1 ANOVA estimates of variance components for a hypothetical one-facet crossed design

Source of variation	df	SS	MS	Variance components	Expected mean squares
Persons (p)	19	180.22	9.48	1.73	$\sigma^2_{pi,e} + n_i\sigma^2_p$
Items (i)	4	25.36	6.34	0.27	$\sigma^2_{pi,e} + n_p\sigma^2_i$
Residual (pi,e)	76	63.84	0.84	0.84	$\sigma^2_{pi,e}$

Note: The estimated variance components for the above one-facet design are calculated as follows:

$$\sigma^2_p = \frac{MS_p - MS_{pi,e}}{n_i} = \frac{9.48 - 0.84}{5} = 1.73 \qquad \sigma^2_i = \frac{MS_i - MS_{pi,e}}{n_p} = \frac{6.34 - 0.84}{20} = 0.275$$

$$\sigma^2_{pi} = MS_{pi,e} = 0.84$$

estimated variance components are the basis for indexing the relative contribution of each source of error and determining the dependability of a measurement, the estimation of variance components has been referred to as the 'Achilles heel of G theory' (Shavelson and Webb 1981).

Types of error variances

Relative and absolute decisions. Generalizability Theory distinguishes between two types of error variance, which correspond to relative decisions (that is, decisions about individual differences between persons) and absolute decisions (that is, decisions about the level of performance). Relative error variance (also called δ-type error) relates to decisions that involve the rank ordering of individuals. In such instances, all sources of variation that include persons are considered measurement error. For example, in a one-facet design the relative error variance (symbolized by σ^2_δ) includes the variance components due to the residual averaged over the number of items used in the measurement. Using the results in Table 10.1, this value is 0.17.

The square root of this index ($\sigma_\delta = 0.41$) is considered the δ-type (relative) standard error of measurement. Using the value of σ_δ, a confidence interval that contains the universe score (with some degree of certainty) can also be determined. For example, a 68 per cent confidence interval for a person with an overall score of 8 would extend from 7.59 to 8.41 (that is, $8 \pm Z_{\alpha/2}\sigma_\delta$). It is important to note that it is traditional to assume a normal distribution in order to attach a probability statement to the confidence interval. Generalizability Theory makes no distributional assumption about the form of the observed scores or the scores' effects, but such an assumption is required to establish appropriate confidence intervals.

When dealing with issues about whether an examinee can perform at a pre-specified competence level, it is the absolute error variance (called a Δ-type error) that is of concern. The absolute error variance reflects both information about the rank ordering of persons and any differences in average scores. For example, in the one-facet design the absolute error (denoted as σ^2_δ) includes the variance components due to both the item effect and the residual effect averaged over the number of items used in the measurement. Using the results in Table 10.1, this value is 0.22. The square root of this index ($\sigma_\Delta = 0.47$) can also be used to determine a confidence interval that contains the universe score. For example, a 68 per cent confidence interval for a person with a score of 8 would extend from 7.53 to 8.47 (that is, $8 \pm Z_{\alpha/2}\sigma_\Delta$).

Generalizability coefficients

Although Generalizability Theory underscores the importance of variance components, it also provides generalizability coefficients that can be used to index the dependability of a measurement procedure (the value ranges from 0 to 1.0, with higher values reflecting more dependable procedures). Generalizability coefficients are available for both relative (symbolized by $E\rho_\delta^2$) and absolute error (symbolized by ρ_Δ^2 or Φ – the notation is often used interchangeably). For the one-facet example design these values are as follows:

$$E\rho_\delta^2 = \frac{\sigma_p^2}{\sigma_p^2 + \sigma_\delta^2} = \frac{1.73}{1.73 + 0.17} = 0.91$$

and

$$\rho_\Delta^2 = \Phi = \frac{\sigma_p^2}{\sigma_p^2 + \sigma_\Delta^2} = \frac{1.73}{1.73 + 0.22} = 0.89.$$

We note that the value of $E\rho_\delta^2$ in the one-facet design is equal to the Classical Test Theory internal consistency estimate, Cronbach's coefficient α for items scored on a metric and equal to Kuder-Richardson Formula 20 (KR-20) and Cronbach's coefficient α-20 when items are scored dichotomously.

Brennan (1983) indicated that the ρ_Δ^2 (or Φ) generalizability coefficient may be viewed as a general purpose index of dependability for domain-referenced (criterion-referenced or content-referenced) interpretations of examinee scores. The observed examinee score is interpreted as being representative of the universe of the domain from which it was sampled and interest is placed on the dependability of an examinee's score that is independent of the performance of others (that is, independent of the universe scores of other examinees). However, if emphasis is placed on the dependability of an individual's performance in relation to a particular cut-off score (for example, a domain-referenced test that has a fixed cut-off score and classifies examinees who match or exceed this score as having mastered the content represented by the domain), a different generalizability index must be computed (Brennan and Kane 1977). The index is denoted by $\Phi(\lambda)$ and represents domain-referenced interpretations involving a fixed cut-off score. The value of (λ) is determined by:

$$\Phi(\lambda) = \frac{\sigma_p^2 + (\mu - \lambda)^2}{\sigma_p^2 + (\mu - \lambda)^2 + \sigma_\Delta^2}.$$

For computational ease, an unbiased estimator of $(\mu - \lambda)^2$ is determined by using $(\bar{X} - \lambda)^2 - \sigma_{\bar{X}}^2$. Where $\sigma_{\bar{X}}^2$ represents the mean error variance and represents the error variance involved in using the mean $(\bar{X})$ over the sample of both persons and items as an estimate of the overall mean (μ) in the population of persons and the universe of items; the smaller the mean error variance the more stable the population estimate (Marcoulides 1993). Using the estimates obtained above, the mean error variance is equal to:

$$\sigma_{\bar{X}}^2 = \frac{\sigma_p^2}{n_p} + \frac{\sigma_i^2}{n_i} + \frac{\sigma_{pi,e}^2}{n_p n_i} = \frac{1.73}{20} + \frac{0.27}{5} + \frac{0.84}{100} = 0.15.$$

With the cut-off score in the hypothetical study set at $\lambda = 8$ and $\bar{X} = 6.36$, the value of $\Phi(\lambda)$ is equal to 0.95.

As demonstrated above, a generalizability analysis enables the pinpointing of the sources of measurement error and the determination of exactly how many conditions of each facet are needed in order to achieve optimal generalizability for making different types of future decisions (for example, relative or absolute – Marcoulides and Goldstein 1990, 1991, 1992). Indeed, generalizability co-efficients for an assortment of studies with alternate numbers of items can be computed in much the same way as the Spearman-Brown Prophecy Formula is used in Classical Test Theory to determine the appropriate length of a test. For example, with $n_i = 1$ the generalizability coefficients for relative and absolute decisions are $E\rho_\delta^2 = 0.67$ and $\rho_\Delta^2 = 0.61$, whereas with $n_i = 10$ the coefficients are $E\rho_\delta^2 = 0.95$ and $\rho_\Delta^2 = 0.94$. We note that because the items are a source of measurement error in the example design, increasing the number of items in the measurement procedure increases the generalizability coefficients.

Generalizability Theory refers to the initial study of a measurement procedure as a generalizability (G) study (Shavelson and Webb 1981). However, it is quite possible that, after conducting a generalizability analysis, one may want to design a measurement procedure that differs from the G study. For example, if the results of a G study show that some sources of error are small, then one may select a measurement procedure that reduces the number of levels of that facet (for example, number of items) or even ignore that facet (which can be critically important in multifaceted designs – see next section). Alternatively, if the results of a G study show that some sources of error in the design are very large, one may increase the levels of that facet in order to maximize generalizability. Generalizability Theory refers to the process by which facets are modified on the basis of information obtained in a G study as decision (D) studies.

However, there appears to be much confusion in the literature concerning the differences between a G study and a D study. Cronbach *et al.* (1972) indicate that the distinction between a G study and a D study is just an affirmation that certain studies are carried out while developing a measurement procedure and then the procedure is put into use or action. In general, a D study can be conceptualized as the point at which one looks back at the G study and examines the measurement procedure in order to make recommendations for change. A D study can be thought of as tackling the question, 'What should be done differently if you are going to rely on this measurement procedure for making future decisions or drawing conclusions?' In the case where no changes should be made, the G study acts as the D study (that is, one uses the same sample of items used in the initial study).

Although Generalizability Theory will generally get better as the number of conditions in a facet is increased, this number can potentially become somewhat unrealistic. More important is the question of the 'exchange rate' or 'trade off' between conditions of a facet within some cost considerations (Cronbach *et al.* 1972). Typically, in multifaceted studies there can be several D study designs that yield the same level of generalizability. For example, if one desires to develop a measurement procedure with a relative generalizability coefficient of 0.90, there might be two distinct D study designs from which to choose. Clearly, in such cases one must consider resource constraints in order to choose the appropriate D study design. The question then becomes how to maximize generalizability within a prespecified set of limited resources. Of course, in a one-faceted person by item ($p \times i$) design, the question of satisfying resource constraints while maximizing generalizability is simple. One chooses the greatest number of items without violating the budget. When other facets are added to the design, obtaining a solution is much more complicated. Goldstein and Marcoulides (1991), Marcoulides and Goldstein (1990, 1991) and Marcoulides (1993, 1995) developed various procedures that can be used to determine the optimal number of conditions that maximize generalizability under various constraints (see also the next section).

A two-facet crossed design

Generalizability Theory can also be used to examine the dependability of measurements in a variety of multifaceted designs. For example, effectiveness studies measuring quality of teaching by using external observers can make use of Generalizability Theory in order to evaluate the quality of the data collected. In such a case, a study might be conducted to determine the dependability of measures of teacher ratings of performance by external observers. Such a design might involve teachers (p) being observed by raters or judges (j) on their teaching performance in different subjects areas (s). Such a design can be considered a completely crossed $p \times j \times s$ design in which each judge rates each teacher on each subject (we note that in this study, subject area is considered a random facet selected from a universe of possible subjects areas – Shavelson and Webb 1991). A similar approach is used in studies where questionnaires are administered to teachers in order to evaluate the quality of teaching in different subjects (Kyriakides and Creemers 2008).

Several sources of variability can contribute to error in this two-faceted study of the dependability of the performance measures in which teachers (persons) are the object of measurement. Using the ANOVA approach, variance components for the three main effects in the design (persons, judges, subjects), the three two-way interactions between these main effects and the three-way interaction (confounded again with random error) are estimated. The total variance of the observed score is equal to the sum of these variance components:

$$\sigma^2 X_{pjs} = \sigma_p^2 + \sigma_j^2 + \sigma_s^2 + \sigma_{pj}^2 + \sigma_{ps}^2 + \sigma_{js}^2 + \sigma_{pjs,e}^2.$$

Table 10.2 provides the ANOVA source table and the estimated variance components for the above example two-facet design. As can be seen in Table 10.2, the variance component for teachers indicates that there are differences among the teachers' performances (22.95 per cent variance). The magnitude of

Table 10.2 Generalizability study results for teacher performance data

Source of variation	df	Sum of squares	Mean square	Variance component	% variance explained
Teachers (p)	7	111.65	15.95	1.17	22.95
Judges (j)	2	4.88	2.44	0.02	0.29
Subject (s)	1	12.00	12.00	0.16	3.09
p × j	14	26.46	1.89	0.51	9.90
p × s	7	55.30	7.90	2.34	45.82
j × s	2	2.38	1.19	0.04	0.76
pjs,e	14	12.32	0.88	0.88	17.18
Total					100.00

Note: The estimated variance components for the above two-facet design are determined as follows:

$$\sigma^2_{pjs,e} = MS_{pjs,e} = .88$$

$$\sigma^2_{js} = \frac{MS_{pjs,e} - MS_{pjs,e}}{n_p} = \frac{1.19 - 0.88}{8} = 0.4$$

$$\sigma^2_{ps} = \frac{MS_{ps} - MS_{pjs,e}}{n_j} = \frac{7.90 - 0.88}{3} = 2.34$$

$$\sigma^2_{pj} = \frac{MS_{pj} - MS_{pjs,e}}{n_s} = \frac{1.89 - 0.88}{2} = 0.51$$

$$\sigma^2_p = \frac{MS_p - MS_{pjs,e} - n_j \sigma^2_{ps} + n_s \sigma^2_{pj}}{n_j n_s} = \frac{15.95 - 0.88 - (3)(2.34) + (2)(0.51)}{(3)(2)} = 1.17$$

$$\sigma^2_j = \frac{MS_j - MS_{pjs,e} - n_p \sigma^2_{js} + n_s \sigma^2_{pj}}{n_p n_s} = \frac{2.44 - 0.88 - (8)(.04) + (2)(0.51)}{(8)(2)} = 0.02$$

$$\sigma^2_s = \frac{MS_s - MS_{pjs,e} - n_j \sigma^2_{ps} + n_p \sigma^2_{js}}{n_p n_j} = \frac{12 - 0.88 - (3)(2.34) + (8)(0.04)}{(3)(8)} = 0.16,$$

the variance component for the teacher by judge interaction (9.9 per cent) suggests that judges differed in their grading of the teachers' performance. The teacher by subject interaction (45.8 per cent) indicates that the relative ranking of each teacher differed substantially across the two subject areas. The relative error variance associated with this measurement procedure is:

$$\sigma^2_\delta = \frac{\sigma^2_{pj}}{n_j} + \frac{\sigma^2_{ps}}{ns} + \frac{\sigma^2_{pjs,e}}{n_j n_s} = \frac{0.51}{3} + \frac{2.34}{2} + \frac{0.88}{6} = 1.49$$

and the generalizability coefficient for a relative decision is:

$$E\rho^2_\delta = \frac{1.17}{1.17 + .1.49} = 0.44.$$

The absolute error variance associated with this measurement procedure is:

$$\sigma^2_\Delta = \frac{\sigma^2_j}{n_j} + \frac{\sigma^2_s}{n_s} + \frac{\sigma^2_{pj}}{n_j} + \frac{\sigma^2_{ps}}{n_s} + \frac{\sigma^2_{js}}{n_j n_s} + \frac{\sigma^2_{pjs,e}}{n_j n_s}$$

or simply:

$$\sigma_\Delta^2 = \frac{0.02}{3} + \frac{0.16}{2} + \frac{0.51}{3} + \frac{2.34}{2} + \frac{0.04}{6} + \frac{0.88}{6} = 1.58.$$

With a generalizability coefficient for an absolute decision equal to:

$$\rho_\Delta^2 = \Phi = \frac{1.17}{1.17 + 1.58} = 0.42.$$

As previously illustrated, a variety of D studies with different combinations of judges and subject areas can be examined. For example, with $n_j = 3$ and $n_s = 4$ the generalizability coefficients for relative and absolute decisions are $E\rho_\delta^2 = 0.59$ and $\rho_\Delta^2 = 0.57$. Whereas with $n_j = 3$ and $n_s = 8$, the generalizability coefficients become to $E\rho_\delta^2 = 0.70$ and $\rho_\Delta^2 = 0.69$. Since it is evident that the subject areas facet is a major source of measurement error, increasing the number of subject areas in the measurement procedure considerably increases the generalizability coefficients. We note again that when selecting between various D studies, one should always consider possible resource or other imposed constraints on the measurement procedures before making final decisions about a D study design (Marcoulides and Goldstein 1990). For example, if the total available budget (B) for the two-faceted design is \$5,000 and if the cost (c) for each judge to observe a teacher in a subject area is \$120, then the optimal number of judges can be determined using the following equation:

$$n_j = \sqrt{\frac{\sigma_{pj}^2}{\sigma_{ps}^2} \left(\frac{B}{c}\right)} = \sqrt{\frac{.51}{2.34}\left(\frac{5,000}{120}\right)} = 3,$$

Thus, D studies are very important when attempting to improve the dependability of measurement procedures because they can provide values for both realistic and optimum numbers of measurement conditions. For example, they can help researchers within EER to identify the optimal number of external observations for measuring quality of teaching (Campbell *et al.* 2004).

Extensions to multivariate measurement designs

Behavioral measurements may also involve multiple scores in order to describe an individual's aptitude or skills. For example, the Revised Stanford-Binet Intelligence Scale (Terman and Merrill 1973) uses 15 subtests to measure four dimensions: short-term memory, verbal reasoning, quantitative reasoning and abstract/visual reasoning. The most commonly used procedure to examine measurements with multiple scores is to assess the dependability of the scores separately (that is, using a univariate generalizability analysis – Marcoulides 1994). In contrast, an analysis of such measurement procedures via a multivariate analysis provides information about facets that contribute to covariance among the multiple scores that cannot be obtained in a univariate analysis. This information is essential for designing optimal decision studies that maximize the dependability of measurement procedures.

The two-facet design examined in the previous section attempted to determine the dependability of the measurement procedure using a univariate approach (that is, one in which judges and subject matter were treated as separate sources of error variance – as facets). However, by treating the subject matter as a separate source of error variance, no information was obtained on the sources of co-variation (correlation) that might exist among the two examined conditions. Such information may be important for correctly determining the magnitude of sources of error influencing the measurement procedure. In other words, when obtaining behavioural measurements, the covariance for the sampled conditions and the unsystematic error might be a non-zero value. As it turns out, this correlated error can influence the estimated variance components in a general-izability analysis (Marcoulides 1987). One way to overcome the above-mentioned problem is to conduct a multivariate G study and compare the results with those obtained from the univariate results. If there are no differences, one can just proceed with the information obtained from the univariate analysis.

The easiest way to explain the multivariate case is by analogy to the univariate case. As illustrated in the previous section, the observed score for a person in the $p \times j \times s$ design was decomposed into the error sources corresponding to judges, subject matter, and their interactions with each other and persons. In extending the notion of multifaceted error variance from the univariate case to the multi-variate, one must not treat subject matter as a facet contributing variation to the design but as a vector of outcome scores (that is, as a vector with two dependent variables). Thus, using v to symbolize the subject matter vector in the measurement design provides:

$$vX_{pj} = v\mu \qquad \text{(mean for } v\text{)}$$
$$+ (v\mu_p - v\mu) \qquad \text{(person effect)}$$
$$+ (v\mu_j - v\mu) \qquad \text{(judge effect)}$$
$$+ (vX_{pj} - v\mu_p - v\mu_j - v\mu) \quad \text{(residual effect).}$$

The total variance of the observed score $\sigma_v^2 X_{pj}$ (which is analogous to $\sigma^2 X_{pjs}$ in the univariate case) is:

$$\sigma_v^2 X_{pj} = \sigma_{vp}^2 + \sigma_{vj}^2 + \sigma_{vpj,e}^2 .$$

As discussed in the previous section, univariate G theory focuses on the estimation of variance components because their magnitude provides information about the sources of error influencing a measurement design. In a multivariate analysis the focus is on variance and covariance components. As such, a matrix of both variances and covariances among observed scores is decomposed into matrices of components of variance and covariance. And, just as the ANOVA can be used to obtain estimates of variance components, multivariate analysis of variance (MANOVA) provides estimates of variance and covariance components. It is important to note that if the symmetric covariance values for $\sigma_1 X_{pj} - \sigma_2 X_{pj} = 0$ (that is, the covariance between the two subject areas is zero), the diagonal variance estimates for $\sigma_1^2 X_{pj}$, $\sigma_2^2 X_{pj}$ would be equivalent to the observed score variance in which subject matter is examined separately.

It is also easy to extend the notion of a generalizability coefficient to the multivariate case (Joe and Woodward 1976; Marcoulides 1995; Woodward and Joe 1973). For example, a generalizability coefficient for the above study could be computed as:

$$\rho^2 = \frac{a'\Sigma_p a}{a'\Sigma_p a + \dfrac{a'\Sigma_{pj,e} a}{n_j}},$$

where a = a weighting scheme for the dependent variables used in the multivariate measurement design (that is, in the example design this would correspond to a weight vector for the subject areas considered).

Unfortunately, the determination of appropriate weights to use for the computation of a multivariate generalizability coefficient is not without controversy. To date, a considerable amount of research has been conducted in an attempt to settle the weighting issue, and various approaches have been proposed in the literature. A detailed discussion of different approaches to the estimation of weights is provided by Marcoulides (1994), Shavelson et al. (1989), Srinivasan and Shocker (1973) and Weichang (1990). The different approaches presented are based on either empirical or theoretical criteria and include: (a) weightings based on expert ratings, (b) weightings based on models examined through a CFA (see Chapter 12), (c) equal or unit weights, (d) weightings proportional to observed reliability estimates, (e) weightings proportional to an average correlation with another sub-criteria, and (f) weightings based on an eigenvalue decomposition criteria. In general, criticisms of the various approaches can be based on three criteria (relevance, multidimensionality and measurability) and discussion concerning which approach to use continues in the literature. Marcoulides (1994) examined the effects of different weighting schemes on selecting the optimal number of observations in multivariate-multifaceted generelizability designs when cost constraints are imposed and found that all weighting schemes produce similar optimal values (see also Marcoulides and Goldstein 1991, 1992 for further discussion concerning procedures to determine the optimal number of conditions that maximize multivariate generalizability). Based on these results, Marcoulides (1994) suggested that in practice, selecting a weighting scheme for conducting a multivariate analysis should be guided more by underlying theory than by empirical criteria.

Computer programs for generalizability analyses

The computational requirements involved in estimating variance components for use in a Generalizability Theory analysis can be demanding, especially in multifaceted designs. As a consequence, computer programs are generally used to obtain the necessary estimates. Several tailored computer programs have been developed for conducting univariate and multivariate generalizability analyses including GENOVA, urGENOVA, mGENOVA (Brennan 1983, 2001), EduG (Cardinet *et al.* 2009; the program is also available with manuals from www.irdp. ch/edumetrie/englishprogram.htm). These programs are relatively easy to use, and they provide excellent procedures for handling most of the computational complexities of Generalizability Theory. Other general purpose programs that can be used to estimate variance components for a generalizability analysis include the REML program (Robinson 1987), the SAS-PROC VARCOMP and SAS-PROC MIXED procedures (SAS Institute 1994), the SPSS variance components procedure, and even general-purpose SEM programs such as Amos, LISREL, EQS and Mplus (Marcoulides 1996).

As an illustration, Appendix A contains examples of GENOVA program setups for the above considered one-facet crossed design using raw data, mean squares and variance components as input. One nice feature of the GENOVA program is that any number of D study designs can also be specified for estimation. For example, lines 21–27 specify four crossed D studies with different choices (1, 5, 10 and 20) for the number of conditions of the item facet. Appendix B contains an example SAS-PROC VARCOMP program setup and sample output for the same one-facet crossed design. As can be seen in Appendix B, the program provides the estimated variance components, but the user must compute the relative and absolute error variances and generalizability coefficients separately. Appendix C contains an example LISREL program code for examining the two-facet model illustrated in Figure 10.1, which is presented in the next section.

Recent extensions to Generalizability Theory

SEM applications

Reliability estimation using SEM has received considerable attention in the literature. Work by Bollen (1989), Gessaroli and Folske (2002), Hagtvet (1997, 1998), Hancock and Mueller (2001), Höft (1996), Marcoulides (1996, 2000), Miller (1995), Komaroff (1997), Raykov (1997, 2001) and Raykov and Marcoulides (2006a,b) has contributed to popularizing the SEM approach for point and interval reliability estimation within both the Classical Test Theory and Generalizability Theory frameworks. Additionally, the relationship between covariance structure analysis and the random effects ANOVA approach for estimating variance components was also pointed out much earlier by a number of authors (Bock 1966; Bock and Bargmann 1966; Joreskog 1971; Linn and Werts 1977; Wiley *et al.* 1973), although the original idea for analysing measurement designs in this manner is probably due to Burt (1947).

The SEM approach to reliability estimation within Classical Test Theory primarily utilizes the model of congeneric measures (items). If $\Upsilon_1, \Upsilon_2, \ldots, \Upsilon_k$ ($k > 1$) are congeneric measures, the following model can be used: $\Upsilon_i = \lambda_i \eta + e_i$, where λ_i is a scale parameter for the ith test, η is the common true score (that is, $\eta = T_1$, the true score of Υ_1), and e_i are measurement errors that are assumed to be uncorrelated. Setting the variance of the factor as $Var(\eta) = 1$, the reliability coefficient of the scale score $\Upsilon = \Upsilon_1 + \Upsilon_2 + \ldots + \Upsilon_k$, can be determined as follows (which is equal to the ratio of true to observed variance in Υ):

$$\rho_\Upsilon = \frac{(\sum\limits_{i=1}^{k}\lambda_i)^2}{(\sum\limits_{i=1}^{k}\lambda_i)^2 + \sum\limits_{i=1}^{k}\theta_i},$$

where $\theta_i = Var(e_i)$ ($i = 1, \ldots, k$). Raykov and Shrout (2002) subsequently extended the above approach to the case of non-homogeneous scales (that is, when the set of considered components exhibits variability that cannot be explained by a single underlying latent dimension), thereby enabling interval estimation of their reliability as a byproduct (see also Gessaroli and Folske 2002). Specifically, if $\Upsilon_1, \Upsilon_2, \ldots, \Upsilon_k$ measure the factors $\eta_1, \eta_2, \ldots, \eta_m$, then reliability equals:

$$\rho_\Upsilon = \frac{(\sum\limits_{i=1}^{k}\sum\limits_{j=1}^{m}\lambda_{ij})^2}{(\sum\limits_{i=1}^{k}\sum\limits_{j=1}^{m}\lambda_{ij})^2 + \sum\limits_{i=1}^{k}\theta_i},$$

where λ_{ij} is the loading of the ith component on the jth factor ($i = 1, \ldots, k$; $j = 1, \ldots, m$).

The applicability of the above SEM approach for purposes of Generalizability Theory analyses was originally considered in earlier discussions by Marcoulides (1996 and references therein) and extended more recently by Raykov and Marcoulides (2006b). For example, in the context of the two-facet design illustrated previously, a CFA model can be used to estimate all the variance components that involve persons (that is, σ_p^2, σ_{pr}^2, σ_{ps}^2 and $\sigma_{prs,e}^2$). Marcoulides (2000) also illustrated that instead of analysing the relations among variables, for which only variance components for persons and any interactions with persons can be estimated, analysing the matrix of correlations among persons leads to the variance components for the other facets. As such, all potential sources of measurement error in a design can be estimated.

Using the approach proposed by Raykov and Marcoulides (2006b), this application is graphically represented in Figure 10.1 for the case of $n_r = 4$ raters assessing teachers on two occasions on two subject areas ($n_o = 2$). The figure follows widely adopted notation for displaying structural equation models (see Chapter 12).

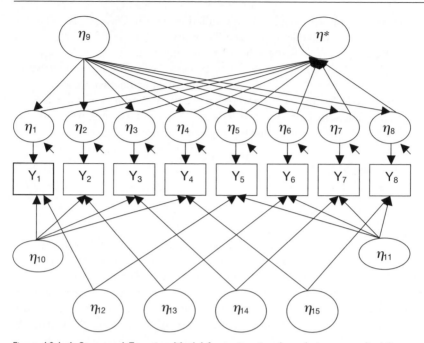

Figure 10.1 A Structural Equation Model for estimating the relative generalizability coefficient in a two-facet crossed design

Note: All one-way paths fixed at I, and all residual variances set equal (for simplicity of graphical notation, symbols of residual terms are omitted); $Var(\eta_9) = \sigma_p^2$, $Var(\eta_{10}) = Var(\eta_{11}) = \sigma_o^2$, and $Var(\eta_{12})$ $= Var(\eta_{13}) = Var(\eta_{14}) = Var(\eta_{15}) = \sigma_r^2$ (Marcoulides 1996); $\eta_i = Y_i$ ($i = 1, \ldots, 8$), $\eta^* = Y$ (with the described vector η corresponding to ($\eta_9, \eta_{10}, \ldots, \eta_{15}, \eta_{16} = \eta^*$).

The essential part of the approach involves an evaluation of the observed score variance, $Var(Y)$. As illustrated in Figure 10.1, this is accomplished through the introduction of a dummy variable $\eta^* = Y$ (that is, the sum of all $k = n_r n_o$ observed variables $Y_1, Y_2, \ldots, Y_k$) in the following manner:

$$\eta^* = \sum_{i=1}^{n_r n_o} Y_i = Y = \sum_{i=1}^{n_r} Y_i + \sum_{i=1}^{n_r} Y_i + \ldots + \sum_{i=1}^{n_r} Y_i \ (n_o \text{ times, once for each occasion})$$

$$= n_r \eta_1 + n_r \eta_{ne+3} + \sum_{i=1}^{n_r} \eta_{i+1} + \sum_{i=1}^{n_r} \varepsilon_i$$

$$+ n_r \eta_1 + n_r \eta_{nr+3} + \sum_{i=1}^{n_r} \eta_{i+1} + \sum_{i=1}^{n_r} \varepsilon_{n_r+i}$$

$$+ \ldots + n_r \eta_1 + n_r \eta_{n_r+n_o+1} + \sum_{i=1}^{n_r} \eta_{i+1} + \sum_{i=1}^{n_r} \varepsilon_{(n_o-1)n_r+i},$$

whereby each of the last n_o rows represents the sum of observed variables pertaining to the two assessment occasions. Thus, with the assumption of equal variances for the unrelated latent variables (Marcoulides 1996, 2000), the observed score variance is obtained by taking variance from both sides in the above equation and leads to:

$$\mathrm{Var}(\Upsilon) = \mathrm{Var}(\eta^*) = n^2_r n^2_o \sigma^2_p + n^2_r n_o \sigma^2_{pr} + n^2_o n_r \sigma^2_{po} + n_r n_o \sigma^2_{pro,e}.$$

Because in Generalizability Theory variability of the two facets constitutes error variance when making generalizations over the object of measurement, it follows that T_Υ is that part of the sum score Υ that has only to do with persons:

$$T_\Upsilon = n_r \eta_1 + n_r \eta_1 + \ldots + n_r \eta_1 \quad (n_o \text{ times, once for each assessment}$$
$$= n_r n_o \eta_1. \qquad\qquad\qquad\qquad \text{occasion})$$

Hence the variance of the score is determined to be:

$$\mathrm{Var}(T_\Upsilon) = n^2_r n^2_o \sigma^2_p.$$

Thus, the reliability of the observed score Υ is:

$$\rho_\Upsilon = \frac{\mathrm{Var}(T_\Upsilon)}{\mathrm{Var}(\Upsilon)} = Corr^2(T_\Upsilon, \Upsilon) = Corr^2(\eta_1, \eta^*)$$

$$= \frac{n_r^2 n_o^2 \sigma_p^2}{n_r^2 n_o^2 \sigma_p^2 + n_r^2 n_o \sigma_{pr}^2 + n_o^2 n_r \sigma_{po}^2 + n_r n_o \sigma_{pro,e}^2}$$

$$= \frac{\sigma_p^2}{\sigma_p^2 + \dfrac{\sigma_{pr}^2}{n_r} + \dfrac{\sigma_{po}^2}{n_o} + \dfrac{\sigma_{pro,e}^2}{n_r n_o}} = E\rho_\delta^2.$$

Applying the above equations to data from a two-facet crossed design, one can obtain an estimate of the relative generalizability coefficient. This estimate simply equals the squared correlation between (a) the used dummy variable that is set equal to the sum of all evaluations of the object of measurement under all combinations of the levels of the two facets, and (b) the corresponding latent variable that is loading on all the manifest variables. We note that since an application of the SEM approach yields the same estimates as would be obtained with ANOVA (or even alternative estimation approaches), the results already displayed in Table 10.2 are not repeated.

Generalizability Theory as a latent trait theory

A number of researchers have provided comparisons between Generalizability Theory and IRT approaches (particularly the Rasch model) and illustrated how both approaches can be used to provide information with respect to measurement designs, especially those that involve judges using defined rating scales (Bachman et al. 1993; Bachman et al. 1995; Harris et al. 2000; Lynch and McNamara 1998; Macmillan 2000; Marcoulides 1999; Marcoulides and Kyriakides 2002; Stahl and Lunz 1993; Stahl 1994). Although estimating a person's ability level is considered by many researchers to be fundamentally different in the two comparison theories (Embretson and Hershberger 1999), Marcoulides (1997, 1999, 2000) has argued that the theories can be conceptualized as merely alternative representations of similar information. Marcoulides (1999) also introduced an extension to the traditional Generalizability Theory model (called the MD model – see Marcoulides and Drezner 1993, 1995, 1997, 2000) that can be used to estimate latent traits such as examinee ability estimates, rater severity and item difficulties, to name a few. The above extension to Generalizability Theory can be considered a special type of IRT model capable of estimating all latent traits of interest. Somewhat similar to IRT, where detecting a person's trait level is considered to be analogous to the clinical inference process, the Marcoulides and Drezner (MD) model infers trait levels on the basis of the presented behaviours and places each individual on a trait continuum.

The MD model is based on the assumption that observed points (that is, examinees, judges, items or any other set of observations that define a facet of interest) are located in an n-dimensional space and that weights (w_{ij}) can be calculated that indicate the relation between any pair of points in this n-dimensional space. These weights constitute a measure of the similarity of any pair of examinees in terms of ability level, any pair of judges in terms of severity estimates or any pair of items in terms of difficulty (Marcoulides and Drezner 1993). For example, in the previously considered two-faceted measurement design with teachers, the MD model provides information concerning teacher ability and rater severity estimates. We note that the MD model can also be extended to include other latent traits of interest depending on the facets included in the original measurement study. For example, item difficulty estimates could be calculated if teachers had been rated using some set of items. An effectiveness study that made use of this approach and demonstrated its strengths, especially for measuring teachers' skills, is Kyriakides et al. (2009). Marcoulides and Drezner (1997) referred to the ability measure for each examinee (Se) as the Examinee Index (the ability estimate is similar to the ability estimate used in IRT models, which is generally represented as θ), and the severity estimate for each judge (Sj) as the Judges Index. Because the MD model independently calibrates the examinees and judges so that all observations are positioned on the same scale, the scales range from +1 to –1. Thus, negative values of the Examinee Index indicate relatively less-able examinees and positive values relatively more-able examinees. Similarly, negative values of the Judges Index indicate relatively lenient judges and positive values indicate relatively severe judges.

Mathematically the MD model posits that in any measurement design with a distribution of random observations $X = (x_{ijk\ldots n})$ ($i = 1, \ldots, m; j = 1, \ldots, p; k = 1, \ldots, q; n = 1, \ldots, r$) (for example, representing m people taking a test with p items), n points (for example, an examinee's score) are located in a dimensional space and weights (w_{ij}) between points that need to be determined for $i, j = 1, \ldots, n$. The weights express the importance of the proximity between points in space (for example, the similarity in examinee ability level estimates or item difficulty). One can find the points by minimizing the objective function:

$$f(X)\frac{\sum\limits_{i,j=1}^{n} w_{ij}d_{ij}^2}{\sum\limits_{i,j=1}^{n} d_{ij}^2},$$

where X is a vector of values for the points (defined according to the latent trait of interest – either examinee ability, item difficulty, and so on), d_{ij} is the Euclidean distance between points i and j, and weights (with $w_{ii} = 0$ for $i = 1, \ldots, n$ and $w_{ij} = w_{ji}$) are determined by using:

$$w_{ij} = \frac{1}{D_{ij}^p},$$

where D is the n-dimensional distance between points i and j, and the power p is a parameter that maximizes the correlation coefficient r between the vectors d_{ij} and D_{ij} for $i > j$ (for further details, see Marcoulides and Drezner 1993, 1995, 1997). The actual values of X (that is, the observed values of the latent trait of interest) are determined by calculating the eigenvectors of the second smallest eigenvalues of a matrix S (whose elements are defined as $s_{ij} = \Sigma_j\, w_{ij}$ and $s_{ij} = -w_{ij}$). The eigenvectors associated with the eigenvalues of S also provide coordinates of a diagnostic scatter plot (either one-dimensional or two-dimensional) for examining the various observations and conditions within a facet in any measurement design. Examination of the diagnostic scatter plot can assist with detecting unusual examinee performances and/or unusual patterns of judges' ratings. All the eigenvalues are non-negative (for non-negative weights) with the smallest one being zero, with an associated eigenvector consisting of ones. It is important to note that the problem is invariant under the transformation $w_{ij} = w_{ij} + c$ for any given constant c. As such, even if there are any negative points, the problem can be solved by adding a positive constant c so that all points are non-negative.

As example illustrations that highlight the diagnostic capabilities of the MD method and exemplify the discrepancies between the MD and Rasch approaches, we consider three different measurement situations (Marcoulides and Kyriakides 2002). The first two examples are used to illustrate the difficulties that the Rasch model has with ordering persons having the same raw score but who perform/answer different items correctly. The third example illustrates the difficulty of the Rasch model with providing estimates of perfect performance scores or completely failing performances. The last example also illustrates the model's difficulty distinguishing a group of individuals when each one receives a different score from any other member of the group and thereby there is a perfect discrimination in the raw scores of the examinees.

For the first example, let us assume that the data presented in Table 10.3 are observed. Such data will serve to illustrate the difficulty the Rasch model has with ordering persons that have the same raw score (Wright 1998). A fictitious

Table 10.3 Data for first hypothetical high jumping example

HEIGHT	1	2	3	4	5	6
Person						
1	0	0	0	0	1	1
2	0	0	0	1	0	1
3	1	0	1	0	0	0
4	0	1	1	0	0	0

high jumping event in which four athletes participated would exemplify such a situation – a value of zero (0) implies the high jumper skipped the height and a value of one (1) implies the height was cleared. Such a situation would also be similar to examining data in which a group of students performed tasks exhibiting increasing levels of difficulty. In the fictitious example, all athletes have jumped two heights (performed two tasks) and, according to the Rasch model, have the same estimated ability trait level score of –0.96 with a relatively high standard error value (that is, 0.64). The data were analysed by using the computer program MULTILOG (Thissen 1991). Thus, regardless of how an individual gets a particular score, any other similar individual score will always yield the same trait level estimate (Embretson and Reise 2000). Nevertheless, it is obvious that Person 1 and Person 2 have jumped the highest and the MD model provides the following ability estimates: person 1 = 0.5; person 2 = 0.5; person 3 = –0.5; person 4 = –0.5. The MD model also provides the following task estimates – indicating that height 6 is the hardest: height 1 = –0.5658; height 2 = –0.2999; height 3 = –0.2999; height 4 = 0.2999; height 5 = 0.2999; height 6 = 0.5658. In this example, it is clear that the MD model is able to differentiate the fact that Person 1 and Person 2 were able to jump higher, and therefore gives them a higher ability estimate in comparison to the other persons.

Table 10.4 Data for second hypothetical high jumping example

ITEM	1	2	3	4	5	6	7	8	9	10
Person										
1	1	1	1	0	0	0	0	0	0	0
2	0	1	1	1	0	0	0	0	0	0
3	0	0	1	1	1	0	0	0	0	0
4	0	0	0	1	1	1	0	0	0	0
5	0	0	0	0	1	1	1	0	0	0
6	0	0	0	0	0	1	1	1	0	0
7	0	0	0	0	0	0	1	1	1	0
8	0	0	0	0	0	0	0	1	1	1

The data presented in Table 10.4 provide another example in which a group of athletes all jump exactly three heights (that is, obtain the same raw score). In this example, however, the score patterns are ordered according to their Guttman scalability. As such, the first athlete is able to jump the three lowest heights, whereas the last athlete is able to jump the three highest heights. Once again, because all athletes have jumped the same number of heights, when the data are analysed using MULTILOG, the Rasch model provides the same estimated ability trait level score of –0.92 (Se = 0.55) for each athlete. However, it is obvious that Person 8 has jumped the highest and should not receive the same ability estimate as the other athletes. In contrast, the MD model is again able to differentiate between the different abilities and provides the following ability estimates: Person 1 = –0.6156; Person 2 = –0.3026; Person 3 = –0.1629; Person 4 = –0.0536; Person 5 = 0.0536; Person 6 = 0.1629; Person 7 = 0.3026; Person 8 = 0.6156.

The data presented in Table 10.5 provide another example in which a group of athletes are asked to jump ten heights. As can be seen in Table 10.5, Person 1 is unable to jump a single height, whereas Person 11 manages to jump all ten heights. An analysis of the data based upon the Rasch model provides the following results: Person 1 = cannot be computed; Person 2 = –2.20; Person 3 = –1.47; Person 4 = –0.92; Person 5 = –0.45; Person 6 = 0.0000; Person 7 = 0.45; Person 8 = 0.92; Person 9 = 1.47; Person 10 = 2.20; and Person 11 = cannot be computed. In contrast, the MD model provides the following results: Person 1 = –0.6387; Person 2 = –0.2513; Person 3 = –0.1432; Person 4 = –0.0830; Person 5 = –0.0387; Person 6 = 0.0000; Person 7 = 0.0387; Person 8 = 0.0830; Person 9 = 0.1432; Person 10 = 0.2513; Person 11 = 0.6387. Such a data set serves to illustrate the difficulty of the Rasch model in comparison to the MD model for providing estimates of perfect performance scores or completely failing performances (or scores). Indeed, as indicated by Bond and

Table 10.5 Data for third hypothetical high jumping example

ITEM	1	2	3	4	5	6	7	8	9	10
Person										
1	0	0	0	0	0	0	0	0	0	0
2	1	0	0	0	0	0	0	0	0	0
3	1	1	0	0	0	0	0	0	0	0
4	1	1	1	0	0	0	0	0	0	0
5	1	1	1	1	0	0	0	0	0	0
6	1	1	1	1	1	0	0	0	0	0
7	1	1	1	1	1	1	0	0	0	0
8	1	1	1	1	1	1	1	0	0	0
9	1	1	1	1	1	1	1	1	0	0
10	1	1	1	1	1	1	1	1	1	0
11	1	1	1	1	1	1	1	1	1	1

Fox (2001), the Rasch model cannot provide estimates of perfectly good or completely failing scores. Although some researchers (Endler 1998; Wright 1998) have provided guidelines for the approximation of ability measures under such circumstances, others have suggested that such scores should be removed from the data set (Masters and Keeves 1999). As such, there does not appear to be complete agreement as to how to handle these types of situations. For example, Wright (1998) has provided some guidelines for the extrapolation of approximate measures of perfect scores, with a preference toward 'extreme score adjustment' – because it has proved robust and flexible for small samples with missing data. Endler (1998) also proposed the addition of 1 logit score to the highest/lowest ability estimate in order to deal with the matter. Based upon the above examples, it should be clear that the diagnostic capabilities of the MD method can be used alongside the traditional Generalizability Theory approach to obtain a wealth of information about the psychometric properties of measurement procedures.

Concluding comments: application of Generalizability Theory to EER

In this chapter, an overview of Generalizability Theory has been provided and we have shown how this theory can be used to design, assess and improve the dependability of measurement procedures. Obviously, the issues raised in this chapter can help researchers in any field to improve the quality of their studies. However, within EER, there are specific reasons to make use of Generalizability Theory. First, the measurement of the functioning of factors operating at teacher and school level is based on using different sources of data provided by different groups of participants in education. For example, student questionnaires or external observations are used to collect data on quality of teaching. Similarly, the functioning of school factors is usually measured by looking at the perceptions of teachers. In any of these cases, the object of measurement has to be identified. By conducting a generalizability study, researchers can identify the extent to which the data are generalizable to the level of teacher or school respectively. To address this need, sometimes more complicated models involving additional facets have to be developed, especially in using ratings of secondary students (or even university students) to measure the skills of teachers who offer lessons to different age groups of students. Second, a D study can help researchers to take decisions about the optimal design of their studies in relation to its purpose. For example, it is a common practice to use external observers in order to evaluate the skills of teachers. Given the practical difficulties (including the cost) of conducting external observations, a D study can be conducted in order to help researchers within EER to identify the optimal number of observations that have to be conducted in order to measure the skills of teachers and/or the number of external observers that could be involved in collecting data. Furthermore, Generalizability Theory can be found useful for conducting mixed methods studies. In one of the examples given in Chapter 7 where both qualitative and quantitative methods were used to develop an instrument measuring teacher effectiveness across countries, the use of Generalizability Theory was essential. Specifically, at each stage of the ISTOF study, a generalizability analysis was conducted to identify the extent to which data generated by different participants (who were coming from different countries and had different professional responsibilities) could be used for establishing consensus between and within countries about the importance of specific components of effective teaching and specific items of an observation instrument (Teddlie *et al.* 2006). Finally, within EER there are contrasting views on the possibilities of developing generic or differential models to explain educational effectiveness (Kyriakides and Creemers 2009; Campbell *et al.* 2003; and see Chapters 3 and 7). Generalizability Theory can be found useful in identifying whether the effects of specific factors operating at teacher and school levels indicate that the factors can be treated as generic. Answers to this type of question can also be given by conducting quantitative synthesis of effectiveness studies (see Chapter 13). Therefore, by making use of Generalizability Theory, a much broader spectrum of research questions within the field of EER can be investigated.

References

Bachman, L.F., Boodoo, G., Linancre, J.M., Lunz, M.E., Marcoulides, G.A. and Myford, C. 'Generalizability theory and many-faceted Rasch modelling', invited presentation at the joint annual meeting of the American Educational Research Association and the National Council on Measurement in Education, Atlanta, GA, April 1993.

Bachman, L.F., Lynch, B.K. and Mason, M. (1995) 'Investigating variability in tasks and rater judgments in a performance test of foreign language speaking', *Language Testing,* 12: 238–57.

Bock, R.D. (1966) 'Components of variance analysis as a structural and discriminant analysis of psychological tests', *British Journal of Statistical Psychology,* 13: 507–34.

Bock, R.D. and Borgmann, R.E. (1966) 'Analysis of covariance structures', *Psychometrika,* 1: 507–34.

Bollen, K.A. (1989) *Structural equations with latent variables,* New York: Wiley.

Bond, T.G. and Fox, C.M. (2001) *Applying the Rasch model: Fundamental measurement in the human sciences,* Mahwah, NJ: Lawrence Erlbaum Associates.

Brennan, R.L. (1983) *Elements of Generalizability Theory,* Iowa City, IA: American College Testing.

Brennan, R.L. (2001) *Generalizability Theory,* New York: Springer.

Brennan, R.L. and Kane, M.T. (1977) 'An index of dependability for mastery of tests', *Journal of Educational Measurement,* 14: 277–89.

Burt, C. (1936) 'The analysis of examination marks', in P. Hartog and E.C. Rhodes (eds) *The marks of examiners,* London: Macmillan.

Burt, C. (1947) 'Factor analysis and analysis of variance', *British Journal of Psychology,* 1: 3–26.

Campbell, R.J., Kyriakides, L., Muijs, R.D. and Robinson, W. (2004) *Assessing teacher effectiveness: A differentiated model,* London: RoutledgeFalmer.

Campbell, R.J., Muijs, R.D., Robinson, W. and Kyriakides, L. (2003) 'Measuring teachers' performance: A case for differentiation', *Education 3–13*, 31(2): 9–18.

Cardinet, J., Johnson, S. and Pini, G. (2009) *Applying Generalizability Theory using EduG*, New York: Routledge.

Cardinet, J., Tourneur, Y. and Allal, L. (1976) 'The symmetry of Generalizability Theory: Application to educational measurement', *Journal of Educational Measurement*, 13: 119–35.

Cornfield, J. and Tukey, J.W. (1956) 'Average values of mean squares in factorials', *Annals of Mathematical Statistics*, 27: 907–49.

Cronbach, L.J., Gleser, G.C., Nanda, H. and Rajaratnam, N. (1972) *The dependability of behavioral measurements: Theory of generalizability scores and profiles*, New York: Wiley.

Cronbach, L.J., Rajaratnam, N. and Gleser, G.C. (1963) 'Theory of generalizability: A liberization of reliability theory', *British Journal of Statistical Psychology*, 16: 137–63.

Embretson, S.E. and Hershberger, S.L. (1999) *The new rules of measurement: What every psychologist and educator should know*, Mahwah, NJ: Lawrence Erlbaum Associates.

Embretson, S.E. and Reise, S.P. (2000) *Item Response Theory for psychologists*, Mahwah, NJ: Lawrence Erlbaum Associates.

Endler, L.C. (1998) 'Cognitive development in a secondary science setting', unpublished thesis, James Cook University, Townsville, Queensland, Australia.

Gessaroli, M.E. and Folske, J.C. (2002) 'Generalizing the reliability of tests comprised of testlets', *International Journal on Testing*, 2: 277–95.

Gleser, G.C., Cronbach, L.J. and Rajaratnam, N. (1965) 'Generalizability of scores influenced by multiple sources of variance', *Psychometrika*, 30(4): 395–418.

Goldstein, Z. and Marcoulides, G.A. (1991) 'Maximizing the coefficient of generalizability in decision studies', *Educational and Psychological Measurement*, 51(1): 55–65.

Hagtvet, K.A. 'The error structure of constructs: A joint application of generalizability analysis and covariance structure modelling', paper presented at the annual meeting of the National Council on Measurement in Education, Chicago, March 1997.

Hagtvet, K.A. (1998) 'Assessment of latent constructs: A joint application of Generalizability Theory and covariance structure modelling with an emphasis on inference and structure', *Scandinavian Journal of Educational Research*, 42: 41–63.

Hancock, G.R. and Mueller, R.O. (2001) 'Rethinking construct reliability within latent variable systems', in R. Cudeck, S. du Toit and D. Sörbom (eds), *Structural equation modelling: Present and future – A Festschrift in honor of Karl G. Jöreskog*, Lincolnwood, IL: Scientific Software International.

Harris, D.J., Hanson, B.A. and Gao, X. (2000) 'A comparison of Generalizability Theory and IRT methodology in estimating domain scores', paper presented at the annual meeting of the American Educational Research Association, New Orleans, April 2000.

Höft, S. (1996) *Generalisierbarkeitstheorie über strukturgleichungsmodelle: Eine darstellung und anwendung auf die konstruktvalidität von assessment centern (Generalizability theory using structural equation modelling)*, University of Hohenheim, Stuttgart, Germany.

Hoyt, C.J. (1941) 'Test reliability estimated by analysis of variance', *Psychometrika*, 6: 153–60.

Joe, G.W. and Woodward, J.A. (1976) 'Some developments in multivariate generalizability', *Psychometrika*, 41: 205–17.

Jöreskog, K.G. (1971) 'Statistical analysis of sets of congeneric tests', *Psychometrika*, 36: 109–33.

Komaroff, E. (1997) 'Effect of simultaneous violations of essential tau-equivalence and correlated errors on coefficient alpha', *Applied Psychological Measurement*, 21: 337–48.

Kyriakides, L. and Creemers, B.P.M. (2008) 'Using a multidimensional approach to measure the impact of classroom level factors upon student achievement: A study testing the validity of the dynamic model', *School Effectiveness and School Improvement*, 19(2): 183–205.

Kyriakides, L. and Creemers, B.P.M. (2009) 'The effects of teacher factors on different outcomes: Two studies testing the validity of the dynamic model', *Effective Education*, 1: 61–86.

Kyriakides, L., Creemers, B.P.M. and Antoniou, P. (2009) 'Teacher behaviour and student outcomes: Suggestions for research on teacher training and professional development', *Teaching and Teacher Education*, 25(1): 12–23.

Linn, R.L. and Werts, C.E. (1977) 'Covariance structure and their analysis', in R.E. Straub (ed.) *New directions for testing and measurement: Methodological developments*, 4: 53–73, San Francisco, CA: Jossey-Bass.

Lynch, B.K. and McNamara, T.F. (1998) 'Using g-theory and many-facet Rasch measurement in the development of performance assessments of the ESL speaking skills of immigrants', *Language Testing*, 15: 158–89.

MacMillan, P.D. (2000) 'Classical, generalizability and multifaceted Rasch detection of interrater variability in large, sparse data sets', *Journal of Experimental Education*, 68(2): 167–90.

Marcoulides, G.A. (1987) 'An alternative method for variance component estimation: Applications to Generalizability Theory', unpublished doctoral dissertation, University of California, Los Angeles.

Marcoulides, G.A. (1989) 'The application of Generalizability Theory to observational studies', *Quality & Quantity*, 23(2): 115–27.

Marcoulides, G.A. (1990) 'An alternative method for estimating variance components in Generalizability Theory', *Psychological Reports*, 66(2): 102–09.

Marcoulides, G.A. (1993) 'Maximizing power in generalizability studies under budget Constraints', *Journal of Educational Statistics*, 18(2): 197–206.

Marcoulides, G.A (1994) 'Selecting weighting schemes in multivariate generalizability studies', *Educational and Psychological Measurement*, 54(1): 3–7.

Marcoulides, G.A. (1995) 'Designing measurement studies under budget constraints: Controlling error of measurement and power', *Educational and Psychological Measurement*, 55(3): 423–28.

Marcoulides, G.A. (1996) 'Estimating variance components in Generalizability Theory: The covariance structure analysis approach', *Structural Equation Modeling*, 3(3): 290–9.

Marcoulides, G.A. (1997) 'Generalizability theory: Models and applications', invited presentation at the annual meeting of the American Educational Research Association, Chicago, March 1997.

Marcoulides, G.A. (1999) 'Generalizability theory: Picking up where the Rasch IRT leaves off?', in S. Embretson and S. L. Hershberger (eds) *The new rules of measurement: What every psychologist and educator should know*, Mahwah, NJ: Lawrence Erlbaum Associates.

Marcoulides, G.A. (2000) 'Generalizability theory', in H.E.A. Tinsley and S. Brown (eds) *Handbook of applied multivariate statistics and mathematical modelling*, San Diego, CA: Academic Press.

Marcoulides, G.A. and Drezner, Z. (1993) 'A procedure for transforming points in multidimensional space to a two-dimensional representation', *Educational and Psychological Measurement*, 53(4): 933–40.

Marcoulides, G.A. and Drezner, Z. (1995) 'A new method for analyzing performance assessments', paper presented at the Eighth International Objective Measurement Workshop, Berkley, CA, April 1995.

Marcoulides, G.A. and Drezner, Z. (1997) 'A method for analyzing performance assessments', in M. Wilson, K. Draney and G. Engelhard, Jr (eds) *Objective measurement: Theory into practice*, Stamford, CT: Ablex Publishing Corporation.

Marcoulides, G.A. and Drezner, Z. (2000) 'A procedure for detecting pattern clustering in measurement designs', in M. Wilson and G. Engelhard, Jr (eds) *Objective measurement: Theory into practice*, Ablex Publishing Corporation.

Marcoulides, G.A. and Goldstein, Z. (1990) 'The optimization of generalizability studies with resource constraints', *Educational and Psychological Measurement*, 50(4): 782–9.

Marcoulides, G.A. and Goldstein, Z. (1991) 'Selecting the number of observations in multivariate measurement designs under budget constraints', *Educational and Psychological Measurement*, 51(4): 573–84.

Marcoulides, G.A. and Goldstein, Z. (1992) 'The optimization of multivariate generalizability studies under budget constraints', *Educational and Psychological Measurement*, 52(3): 301–08.

Marcoulides, G.A. and Kyriakides, L. 'Applying the Rasch and extended Generalizability Theory models: Discrepancies between approaches', paper presented at the 11th International Objective Measurement Workshop, New Orleans, April 2002.

Masters, G.N. and Keeves, J.P. (1999) *Advances in measurement in educational research assessment*, The Netherlands: Pergamon.

Miller, M.B. (1995) 'Coefficient alpha: A basic introduction from the perspectives of Classical Test Theory and Structural Equation Modeling', *Structural Equation Modeling*, 2: 255–73.

Muthén, L.K. (1983) 'The estimation of variance components for dichotomous dependent variables: Applications to test theory', unpublished doctoral dissertation, University of California, Los Angeles.

Rasch, G. (1960/1980) *Probabilistic models for some intelligence and attainment tests*, Chicago: University of Chicago Press.

Raykov, T. (1997) 'Estimation of composite reliability for congeneric measures', *Applied Psychological Measurement*, 22: 175–83.

Raykov, T. (2001) 'Estimation of congeneric scale reliability via covariance structure models with nonlinear constraints', *British Journal of Mathematical and Statistical Psychology*, 54: 315–23.

Raykov, T. and Marcoulides, G.A. (2006a) 'On multilevel model reliability estimation from the perspective of Structural Equation Modeling', *Structural Equation Modeling*, 13: 130–44.

Raykov, T. and Marcoulides, G.A. (2006b) 'Estimation of generalizability coefficients via a Structural Equation Modeling approach to scale reliability evaluation', *International Journal of Testing*, 6: 81–95.

Raykov, T. and Shrout, P.E. (2002) 'Reliability of scales with general structure: Point and interval estimation using a Structural Equation Modeling approach', *Structural Equation Modeling*, 9: 195–212.

Robinson, D.L. (1987) 'Estimation and use of variance components', *The Statistician*, 36: 3–14.

SAS Institute (1994) *SAS user's guide, version 6*, Cary, NC: SAS Institute.

Shavelson, R.J. and Webb, N.M. (1981) 'Generalizability Theory: 1973–1980', *British Journal of Mathematical and Statistical Psychology*, 34: 133–66.

Shavelson, R.J. and Webb, N.M. (1991) *Generalizability Theory: A primer*, Newbury Park, CA: Sage Publications.

Shavelson, R.J., Webb, N.M. and Rowley, G.L. (1989) 'Generalizability Theory', *American Psychologist*, 44(6): 922–32.

Srinivasan, V. and Shocker, A.D. (1973) 'Estimating weights for multiple attributes in a composite criterions using pairwise judgments', *Psychometrika*, 38(4): 473–93.

Stahl, J.A. (1994) 'What does Generalizability Theory offer that many-facet Rasch measurement cannot duplicate?', *Rasch Measurement Transactions*, 8(1): 342–3.

Stahl, J.A. and Lunz, M.E. 'A comparison of Generalizability Theory and multi-faceted Rasch measurement', paper presented at the annual meeting of the American Educational Research Association, Atlanta, Georgia, March 1993.

Suen, H.K. (1990) *Principles of test theories*, Hillsdale, NJ: Lawrence Erlbaum Associates.

Teddlie, C., Creemers, B., Kyriakides, L., Muijs, D. and Yu, F. (2006) 'The International System for Teacher Observation and Feedback: Evolution of an international study of teacher effectiveness constructs', *Educational Research and Evaluation*, 12: 561–82.

Terman, L.M. and Merrill, M.A. (1973) *Stanford-Biner intelligence scale*, Chicago: Riverside Publishing.

Thissen, D. (1991) *MULTILOG User's Guide: Multiple, Categorical Item Analysis and Test Scoring Using Item Response Theory*, Lincolnwood, IL: Scientific Software International.

Weichang, L. (1990) 'Multivariate generalizability of hierarchical measurements', unpublished doctoral dissertation, University of California, Los Angeles.

Wiley, D.E., Schmidt, W.H. and Bramble, W.J. (1973) 'Studies of a class of covariance structure models', *Journal of the American Statistical Association*, 68: 317–23.

Woodward, J.A. and Joe, G.W. (1973) 'Maximizing the coefficient of generalizability in multi-facet decision studies', *Psychometrika*, 38(2): 173–81.

Wright, B.D. (1998) 'Estimating measures for extreme scores', *Rasch Measurement Transactions*, 12(2): 632–3.

Chapter 11

Multilevel modelling

Hans Luyten and Pam Sammons

University of Twente and University of Oxford (respectively)

Introduction

In this chapter we present a brief introduction to the theory behind multilevel modelling. We illustrate the main points in our discussion with examples from our own and other research experience. These include examples of multilevel models with random slopes, growth curve models, multivariate models and cross-classified models. We do, however, limit our discussion to multilevel analysis with continuously distributed outcome variables. Readers interested in multilevel analysis with discrete (dichotomous and ordinal) rather than continuous outcome variables are referred to more extensive and advanced publications on multilevel analysis (Bryk and Raudenbush 1992; Goldstein 1995; Hox 2002; Snijders and Bosker 1999). Moreover, some effectiveness studies have made use of this type of multilevel model, so such further reading might be of particular use to readers of this volume (Kyriakides *et al.* 2009; Pustjens *et al.* 2004)

Hierarchically structured data sets

Research in the field of educational effectiveness often involves the analysis of data sets that are hierarchically structured. In these cases, two or more levels can be distinguished, with the units at the lower levels nested within the higher level units. The most well-known example of this is a data set of students nested within classrooms within schools. The hierarchical structure may be extended even further, for example, if one takes into account the nesting of schools within geographical units (such as local communities, regions or nations).

It is not necessarily the individual level that constitutes the lowest level in the hierarchy. In many applications of multilevel analysis, multiple measurements per individual on the outcome variable(s) represent the lowest level. These may be repeated observations over time on the same variable (so can be used in longitudinal analyses, see Chapter 5), but they may also relate to scores on different measures (for example, reading and mathematics scores) for the same individual. In these cases, individuals represent the second level units, which may in turn be nested within higher level units. If the observations per individual relate to the same variable but are measured at different points in time, multilevel analysis can be employed to model individual growth patterns. The main advantage of multilevel analysis for this purpose is its flexibility and capability to deal with unbalanced data. Multilevel software does not require the same number of measurements for each individual and can easily handle data with incomplete records on the outcome measures. Nor does it require that all individuals are measured at the same points in time. In addition to the analysis of longitudinal data, the multilevel approach may also be useful for analysis of data with two or more distinct outcome measures per individual. This approach is usually referred to as multivariate multilevel modelling. It is less frequently applied as it is more complicated than conducting separate analyses for each outcome variable. Only with respect to specific research questions does the multivariate approach yield a clear advantage over separate analyses per dependent variable. For more details see the relevant following section on multivariate multilevel models.

Multilevel analysis is highly useful when the analysis relates to data that derive from multistage sampling. From a data collection perspective, it is often convenient to make use of the fact that individuals are clustered within higher level units. A two-stage sampling design with schools as the 'primary sampling units' in particular may be quite efficient. This means that in the first stage, a random sample of schools is drawn and in the second stage, a sample of students within the schools may then be selected, but more frequently a sample of intact grades or classes. In other cases of multistage sampling, geographic units (for example, regions or municipalities) may be the primary sampling units. Application of such multistage sampling methods has its consequences for computing appropriate confidence intervals and performing statistical significance tests. The basic formulas for computing the standard errors used for statistical inference that are discussed in most statistical textbooks assume that the data were obtained through a simple random sampling procedure. In practice, multistage sampling is applied much more frequently, especially in educational studies.

If a researcher ignores the fact that the data analysed were collected through multistage sample, she or he is bound to overestimate the statistical significance of the findings. In this case the interdependence of observations within primary sampling units (such as students within schools) is not taken into account. A simple random sampling design implies that the selection of one unit does not affect the chance of another unit to be selected, and this clearly does not apply for multistage sampling. Selection of certain primary sampling units (for example, schools) increases the chance of being selected for the lower level units (for example, students) nested within these primary units.

The most widely used statistical software programs by educational effectiveness researchers (SPSS, SAS, Stata) provide the possibility to obtain appropriately estimated standard errors by taking into account the sampling scheme. One might argue that these facilities solve the problems presented by multistage sampling. However, multilevel analysis is based on the notion that hierarchical structures in a data set present an interesting phenomenon that deserves special attention in itself. The various levels present distinct sources of variation. In educational research, the contributions of these levels (such as school, classroom and student) to the variance in the outcome measures are of particular interest. The percentage of variance in student achievement situated at the school level is usually referred to as the 'school effect'. Multilevel analysis often starts with a so-called 'zero model', which includes no explanatory variables and only involves a partitioning of the variance in the outcome measure into two or more components (for example, the student and the school level). For students nested within schools, this model merely conveys that an individual score can be considered to be the sum of the average score and the school and student specific deviations. This is expressed formally in the equation below:

$$Y_{ij} = \beta_{00} + u_{0j} + r_{ij}, \tag{1}$$

where:

Y_{ij} = score on the outcome measure for student i in school j

β_{00} = average score across schools and students ('Grand Mean')

u_{0j} = deviation from Grand Mean for school j

r_{ij} = deviation from school average for student i in school j.

The variances of the school-specific and student-specific deviations (u_{0j} and r_{ij}) are of particular interest. Let us denote the variance of u_{0j} as τ^2_{00} and the variance of r_{ij} as σ^2. In EER a question of special interest often relates to the percentage of school-level variance. This may also be expressed in terms of an intraclass correlation coefficient (ICC or ρ), which is defined as follows:

$$\rho = \frac{\tau^2_{00}}{(\tau^2_{00} + \sigma^2)}. \tag{2}$$

The variances computed for each level through the fitting of a zero model may also provide a basis for estimating the percentage of variance explained per level. In subsequent stages of the analysis, explanatory variables are added to the model and by comparing the variances per level of these models to the variance components in the zero model one can assess the variance explained for each separate level. The next equation presents an example of a multilevel model that includes an explanatory variable:

$$Y_{ij} = \beta_{00} + \beta_{10}X_{ij} + u_{0j} + r_{ij}. \tag{3}$$

The model described through equation (3) includes just one explanatory variable (X), which is measured at the student level. This is revealed by the double subscripts (i for students and j for schools). Scores on a school level variable would be denoted by only a single subscript. In practice the analysis usually involves more complex models with multiple variables measured at both levels. Equation (3) is highly similar to a regression equation and one may conceive of multilevel analysis as an extension of regression analysis. The Grand Mean (β_{00}) is analogous to the intercept in ordinary least squares (OLS) regression. It denotes the expected score on the dependent variable (Y) if the scores on the independent variables are equal to zero. In order to facilitate the interpretation of the intercept, the independent variables may be centred on the mean score. Thus, the intercept expresses the expected score on the dependent variable for individuals with an average score on all explanatory variables. In most cases a zero score on the independent variable(s) may represent a non-existing or highly exceptional situation, as most explanatory variables (for example, pre-test score or parents' education) do not take negative values.

The main extra feature of multilevel analysis in comparison to the most commonly used OLS regression is the identification of distinct levels of variance. It should be noted that lower level variables may explain variance at higher levels, but not the other way around. Student background characteristics may account for variation between schools with regard to student achievement, but school characteristics can only account for variation between schools. Sometimes one may even be confronted with the paradoxical finding that adding new explanatory variables to the model leads to *more* variance at the higher level(s). This would seem to indicate a *negative* percentage of variance explained. An example would be that including student achievement at school entry in the model produces an increase in the estimated school-level variance. This would imply that, if students of similar entry levels are considered, the differences between schools are larger than they appear without taking student background into account. This could be the case if the variation between schools with regard to the progress of the students is larger than it is for the post-test scores. Note that such negative percentages of explained variance only relate to higher level units and that the *total* amount of variance explained is never negative.

The way multilevel analysis deals with the various sources of variance (such as the school level) can be considered equivalent to controlling for the membership of a higher level unit (that is, being a student at a particular school). In ordinary regression analysis this might be dealt with through the introduction of numerous dummy variables into the statistical model, each of which denotes membership of a particular school. Dealing with the school level in this way would be rather inefficient, as in most cases the number of schools would be a few dozens at least. For the interpretation of the estimated effects it is important to realize that in multilevel analysis these estimates relate to effects when controlling for membership of higher level units. As a result, the effects of explanatory variables in multilevel analysis may deviate from outcomes obtained through a more straightforward analysis. On the next pages we will present an example of the gender effect on mathematics achievement for Dutch 15-year-olds in multilevel analysis that clearly deviates from a straightforward comparison of mean scores for male and female students. In this case, multilevel analysis shows a substantial male advantage, whereas the straightforward comparison only shows a minor and statistically insignificant difference between boys and girls. The distribution of male and female students across schools turns out to be an important factor. The multilevel results point to a male advantage *within* schools. Which outcome should be considered most relevant mainly depends on the specific research questions that the analysis is supposed to answer.

Another important feature of multilevel analysis is the possibility of modelling random slopes in addition to random intercepts. In the models described so far the intercept (Grand Mean) is allowed to vary randomly across higher level units, which allows for the estimation of variance components. In the case of random slopes, the effect of an explanatory variable is decomposed into a fixed effect and a random effect as well. The fixed effect denotes the average effect, whereas the random effect indicates to what extent the effect varies between higher level units. A relevant topic in educational research might be how much the effects of student background characteristics vary between schools. Random effects models are also highly appropriate when growth curves are the main focus of analysis (see Chapter 12). In these cases the lowest level relates to repeated measurements, which are typically modelled as a function of time. Usually the growth patterns will vary across individuals and possibly also across higher level units. The basic random effects model is presented in the equation below:

$$\Upsilon_{ij} = \beta_{00} + \beta_{10}X_{ij} + u_{0j} + u_{1j}X_{ij} + r_i. \tag{4}$$

In equation (4) the coefficient β_{10} represents the average effect of the explanatory variable (X) across higher level units. The new addition to the model in comparison to equation (3) is presented by u_{1j}, which expresses that the effect of X varies across higher level units. If the model relates to students nested within schools, u_{1j} denotes the school specific deviation of the effect. In the case of a random slopes model the higher level units can be characterized not only by the unit specific deviations of the intercept but also by deviations from the average effect of the explanatory variable. The variance of the latter deviation (u_{1j}) can be denoted as τ^2_{11}. One should also take into account that u_{0j} and u_{1j} may covary to some extent. This covariance can be denoted as τ_{01}. A positive covariance implies that positive deviations from β_{00} tend to coincide with positive deviations from β_{10} and negative deviations with negative ones. If we are dealing with students and schools, such a positive covariance indicates that the effect of the explanatory variable is particularly strong in schools with a high score on the outcome variable. For the sake of interpretation it may be helpful to express the covariances as correlations. For more details we refer to the section on random slopes models.

With regard to interpretation it should also be emphasized that in random slopes models the estimated variances and covariances relate to those cases with a zero score on the explanatory variables. Centring the independent variables on the mean score is therefore often very helpful. Most importantly, the zero scores on the explanatory variables should have a well-interpretable meaning (it is to be preferred that they relate to a relevant reference situation). In growth models, it may be suitable that the zero score corresponds to the first (or last) measurement.

Multilevel analysis was initially developed to deal with data sets that are structured in a way that is perfectly hierarchical. This means that membership of a certain unit determines membership of a corresponding higher level unit. For example, if a student belongs to a certain class this also implies that he attends a certain school. This is the essence of lower level units being nested within higher level units. In some situations, however, the nesting is not perfectly hierarchical. If one wants to include the nesting of schools within geographical units (such as neighbourhoods) in the analysis, it should be taken into account that some schools attract students from various neighbourhoods, while at the same time students from the same neighbourhood may attend different schools. In those cases the nesting of schools within geographical units is not perfectly hierarchical. Multilevel analysis can deal with such cross-classifications, although the models are technically and computationally more demanding than perfectly hierarchical models. Analysis that involves cross-classified multilevel models therefore requires powerful statistical software (for example, MLwiN).

In the next sections we provide real-life examples of the types of multilevel analysis described above. We start with an analysis that relates to gender effects on mathematics achievement. This example illustrates that the effects of explanatory variables estimated in multilevel analysis express their effects when controlling for membership of higher level units. The second example involves a random slopes model and the third relates to an analysis of individual growth curves. In this (third) case the repeated measurements present the lowest level and the individuals are higher level units. The same applies to the next (fourth) example, which presents a multivariate multilevel model. In this case the lowest level relates to distinct outcome measures (language and mathematics) per individual. The fifth example illustrates that the multivariate multilevel model is also highly useful for conducting meta-analysis. Our final examples relate to cross-classified multilevel models.

Example 1: gender effects on mathematics

In this section we illustrate that multilevel analysis may produce estimated effects that differ substantially from an analysis that does not take the hierarchical structure of the data set into account. The analyses focus on the effect of gender on mathematics scores for 15-year-olds in the Netherlands. The data derive from the PISA 2003 survey. PISA, which started in 2000, is a three-yearly international comparative study into student performance on reading, mathematics and science (OECD 2004). The Dutch data set contains 3,992 students in 154 schools. The results of a multilevel analysis with gender as the explanatory variable and the score on the mathematics test as the dependent variable are reported in Table 11.1. The computations were conducted with the SPSS software. Gender is by definition a dichotomous variable. In the analyses presented, female students get a zero score on the gender variable and the score for males is 1. Therefore, the intercept denotes the average mathematics score for girls, while the effect of gender reflects the male (dis)advantage.

A remarkable result is the relatively high amount of variance at the school level. This even exceeds the student-level variable. Expressed as an intraclass correlation coefficient, this yields a value equal to 0.64, which is much higher than what is usually found in EER. Table 11.1 further shows that multilevel analysis produces a highly significant male advantage of more than 15 points. When the data are analysed with OLS regression analysis, as reported in Table 11.2, the gender effect is less than five points and by no means statistically significant, if the standard errors are computed taking the sample design into account. The regression coefficient is exactly equal to the difference in achievement scores between male and female students and the regression intercept equals the mean score for girls. In this case, regression analysis and multilevel analysis yield clearly different results. This means that although the overall difference between boys and girls with regard to mathematics achievement is very small, *within schools* girls are outperformed by their male counterparts to a considerable extent. Some more specific knowledge with regard to the Dutch system of secondary education is required to explain these somewhat surprising and confusing findings.

Table 11.1 Gender effect on mathematics in multilevel analysis

Fixed effects	Effect	Standard error	Significance
Intercept	531.49	6.21	0.000
Male advantage	15.28	1.86	0.000
Random effects			
School-level variance	5,674.54	664.01	0.000
Student-level variance	3,166.01	72.34	0.000

Table 11.2 Gender effect on mathematics in OLS regression analysis

	Effect	Standard error	Significance
Model 1:			
Gender effect only			
Intercept	540.11	6.29	0.000
Male advantage	4.79	3.93	0.225
Model 2:			
Gender and school type			
Intercept	482.20	4.93	0.000
Male advantage	14.59	2.51	0.000
Senior secondary and pre-university track	129.65	5.53	0.000

After primary education (at the age of twelve) Dutch students are selected for various tracks on the basis of their (presumed) academic aptitudes. Most secondary schools provide several tracks, but usually not the entire range. Important is the distinction between schools providing the most advanced tracks, namely senior secondary and pre-university education vs. schools providing pre-vocational tracks. It is also important to note that boys are overrepresented in the less advanced, pre-vocational tracks, where they make up 55 per cent of the student population, whereas girls make up 55 per cent of the population in the more advanced tracks. The bottom part of Table 11.2 shows the outcomes of a regression analysis that takes into account whether a student is in one of the advanced tracks. The outcomes show that the difference in achievement between these two groups of students is enormous (nearly 130 points). It is also important to note that including this variable in the regression model produces a gender effect that is similar to the effect obtained with multilevel analysis.

The present example illustrates that regression analysis and multilevel analysis may produce clearly different outcomes. In this case it is caused by the unequal gender distribution across pre-vocational and more advanced schools. However, in other instances it will not always be possible to identify the underlying causes. In such cases multilevel analysis can provide highly valuable findings, because it takes into account that the nesting of lower level units within higher level units may produce distinct sources of variation in the outcome variables. However, it is also important to interpret multilevel findings correctly. In the present example it would be a mistake to interpret the gender effect estimated with multilevel analysis straightforwardly as an indication of the difference in mathematics achievement between Dutch male and female students. The multilevel findings relate to the gender differences within schools.

Example 2: random slopes; test scores and secondary school recommendations

This example illustrates how a random slopes model can be applied to assess whether the effect of a student-level variable varies across schools. For the analyses we make use of the Dutch PRIMA data that were collected in the second half of the school year 2002–03. The findings reported in this section relate to students in the final grade of Dutch primary education. In the next section, which focuses on growth curve analysis, we report findings from analyses on longitudinal PRIMA data. The data derive from a sample of 7,887 Dutch students in the final grade of 354 primary schools.

As mentioned in the previous section, students in Dutch secondary education are assigned to distinct tracks. At the end of primary school each student gets a recommendation for a specific subsequent track from his/her primary school. This recommendation is the outcome variable of the analysis in the present example. This variable can take on 15 different values. There are eight different tracks and often a student gets the recommendation that either of two adjacent tracks may be suitable, which produces seven additional categories. Pre-university education is the most advanced track, and this is recommended to the students who are believed to be the most talented ones. The second most advanced track is senior secondary education, followed by four pre-vocational tracks. Two more tracks are specifically designed for students with serious learning problems and those that need individual support.

The main research question is to what extent the recommendations are determined by student performance and to what extent home background plays a role. Through the fitting of a random slopes model the analysis shows to what extent the effect of student performance varies across schools. An additional research question relates to the effect of schools using a specific test for their recommendation. Most schools (83 per cent) base their recommendation in part on the scores of a widely used standardized test (the CITO test). The analysis addresses the extent to which the level of the recommendation is more positive when schools do not use the CITO test and to what extent not using the CITO test interacts with the effect of student performance on the recommendation. One might conjecture that the effect of student performance on the recommendation is less strong in the absence of the CITO test. Furthermore, it is conceivable that use of the CITO test accounts to some extent for a variation in the effect of student performance.

Student performance is measured by a test that correlates strongly ($r = 0.87$) with the CITO test. It relates to skills and knowledge in both reading and mathematics. The scores on this variable are transformed into z-sores, so that their mean equals zero and the standard deviation is equal to one. Home background is assessed by means of four categories that relate primarily to the highest level of education attained by either parent. The category that involves the lowest level (lower vocational education or less) is split into two categories on the basis of the parents' country of birth. Students with parents born in either Turkey or Morocco make up a special category. Most other students with poorly educated parents are Dutch. The largest category contains the students with parents of whom no one has attained a higher level than upper secondary education. The highest category relates to students of whom at least one parent has successfully finished tertiary education. The frequency distribution of the home background characteristics is presented in Table 11.3.

Table 11.3 Frequency distribution of home background (parents' education and origin)

	(%)
Lower vocational education or less; parents born in Turkey or Morocco	6.0
Lower vocational education or less; others	23.4
Upper secondary education (reference group)	44.3
Tertiary education	26.3

For the analysis, three dichotomous home background variables ('dummy variables') were created. These variables can take on either the value one or zero. If a student belongs to a particular category, the student gets a score equal to one on the dummy variable that indicates the category. All other students get a zero score. For example, the students with at least one parent having attained a tertiary education level get a score equal to one on the tertiary education dummy, whereas all others get a zero score on this dummy variable. There is no dummy variable for the upper secondary education category. The students in this category are identified by the fact that they get a zero score on all three home background dummy variables. This category serves as the reference group. The intercept in the multilevel model expresses the score for this category of students (if their scores on the other variables equal zero as well). The advantage of using dummy variables is that the analysis specifically reveals the differences among the categories. This is especially appropriate for discrete non-dichotomous variables.

Whether a school makes use of the CITO test for their recommendations is also indicated by means of a dummy variable. Schools that do not make use of this test (17 per cent) get a score equal to one and the others get a zero score. To assess whether the effect of student performance is weaker in schools that do not use the CITO test, an interaction term was created of student performance with the dummy variable that indicates use of the CITO test. This is, in fact, the multiplication of both variables. Schools that do not use the test get a zero score on the interaction term.

In order to answer the research questions two multilevel analyses were conducted. In the first analysis, use of the CITO and its interaction with student performance are not yet included as explanatory variables. Thus, one can observe to what extent including these terms affects the variance across schools of the student performance effect. The results of the analyses are reported in Tables 11.4a and 11.4b.

We can conclude from the tables that nearly all the effects included in the models are statistically significant. The only exception is the effect of the parents' educational level for Turkish and Moroccan students. The effects of the other two background dummy variables show significant effects. This means that students with similar performance levels but different home backgrounds still get different recommendations. The intercept in Table 11.4a indicates that students with an average performance level and parents with an educational level no higher than upper secondary (the reference group) get a recommendation of 10.74 on average. This is slightly below the highest pre-vocational track. A student with poorly educated parents, but an average performance level, gets a recommendation 0.61 lower, which corresponds to a recommendation between the highest and the second highest pre-vocational level. If the student's parents are highly educated, however, the student would get a recommendation 0.31 higher. The difference between students with poorly and highly educated parents is 0.92 on a scale that ranges from 1 to 15. This difference applies to students with similar performance levels. It should also be noted that the effect of

Table 11.4a Predictors of school recommendations – first model

Fixed effect	Effect	Std error	Significance
Intercept	10.74	0.05	0.000
Student performance	2.86	0.04	0.000
Low education parents; Turkish/Moroccan	−0.01	0.12	0.912
Low education parents; others	−0.62	0.06	0.000
High education parents	0.31	0.06	0.000
Random effects			
School-level variance	0.56	0.06	0.000
Variance of student performance effect	0.32	0.04	0.000
Correlation student performance/school intercept	−0.41	0.08	0.000
Student-level variance	3.79	0.06	0.000

Table 11.4b Predictors of school recommendations – second model

Fixed effect	Effect	Std error	Significance
Intercept	10.66	0.06	0.000
Student performance	2.90	0.04	0.000
Low education parents; Turkish/Moroccan	0.01	0.12	0.907
Low education parents; others	−0.61	0.06	0.000
High education parents	0.31	0.06	0.000
CITO test not used	0.43	0.12	0.001
Interaction student performance/CITO test not used	−0.22	0.11	0.041
Random effects			
School-level variance	0.53	0.06	0.000
Variance of student performance effect	0.31	0.04	0.000
Correlation student performance/school intercept	−0.39	0.08	0.000
Student-level variance	3.79	0.08	0.000

performance largely outweighs the effects of home background. If we compare the recommendation for students that score one standard deviation above and below average, we get a difference equal to 5.72 (2×2.86), which is more than six times as large as the difference between students from advantaged and disadvantaged backgrounds. In a standard normal distribution 16 per cent of the cases have a score less than one standard deviation below the mean. The same goes for the opposite tail of the distribution.

The random effects in Table 11.4a show that the intercept variance at the school level (0.56) is much smaller than the variance at the student level (3.79). This indicates that the variance in recommendations between schools is much smaller than the variance between students within schools. The intraclass coefficient (ρ) equals 0.13. Table 11.4a also show a significant variance of the effect of student performance across schools. The negative correlation (−0.41) expresses that in schools with relatively high recommendations, the effect of performance on the recommendation is relatively low (and vice versa). In order to enhance the interpretation of the performance effect variance (0.32) it is advisable to express it as a standard deviation. This yields 0.57 as a result ($\sqrt{0.32}$ = 0.57). This indicates that in schools where the size of the effect is one standard deviation below average, the effect of student performance on the recommendation equals 2.11 (2.86 − 0.57 = 2.29). In schools where the effect is one standard deviation above average the effect is 3.61 (2.86 + 0.57 = 3.43).

Table 11.4b shows the effects related to the use of the CITO test. The main effect (0.43) indicates that schools not using this test tend to give slightly higher recommendations when taking into account the effects of student performance and home background. The interaction effect shows that the effect of student performance is also slightly smaller in schools that do not use the CITO test. The effect is 2.90 in schools that use this test and 2.78 (2.90 − 0.22 = 2.78) in schools that do not use the test. This interaction effect accounts for just a rather limited portion of the variance in the effect of student performance across schools. The variance of this effect equals 0.32 in model 4a, and including the effects of CITO use reduces this to 0.31. The impact of including the interaction term on the correlation of the performance effect with the intercept is also very limited, as it decreases from −0.41 to −0.39. Although use of the CITO test can account for some part of the variation in the effect of student performance, its impact turns out to be quite limited.

Example 3: growth curve analysis

Multilevel analysis is also highly useful when it comes to analysing data that relate to individual growth. In this application of the technique, repeated measurements per individual constitute the lowest level. The present example involves a three-level structure. Schools represent the highest level units. Students nested within schools represent an intermediate level and at the lowest level we find repeated language scores measured over a range of six years. One important advantage of using multilevel analysis is that it can easily handle incomplete records with regard to the outcome measures (again, compare to Chapter 12).

For the analyses we make use of the Dutch PRIMA data that were collected in February of the years 1995, 1997, 1999 and 2001. Starting with the school year 1994–95, every two years data have been collected at a few hundred primary schools in the Netherlands. Since 2007 this has changed to a three-year cycle. Each year data on student achievement were collected in grades 2, 4, 6 and 8. In the Netherlands, kindergarten and primary education are integrated into a single structure that comprises eight grades. Children enter into the first grade at the age of four. Most of the students in grade 2 are six years old at the time of testing. Our analyses relate exclusively to students in schools that participated in all four waves of data collection from 1995 until 2001.

The design of the PRIMA cohorts allows for the analysis of individual student growth trajectories. Grade 2 students in 1995 will reappear as fourth graders in 1997, as sixth graders in 1999 and as eighth graders in 2001. However, each year a substantial number of schools end their participation in PRIMA, and these are then substituted by new ones. The representative samples comprise approximately 400 schools each year, but only 149 schools participated each and every year from 1995 through 2001. More detailed analyses of schools leaving and entering the PRIMA cohorts show no signs of systematic dropout (Roeleveld and Van der Veen 2007).

The analyses focus on the growth trajectories for language skills of 5,150 students. To be included in the analyses a valid score on at least one point of measurement was required. Only 41 per cent of all 5,150 students that were included in the analyses took part in the data collection at all four points in time. The general language skills of the students present the dependent variable in this study. The language tests taken in each grade have been equated according to IRT (see Chapters 8 and 9) so that student scores in different grades can be related to a common scale. This allows for the estimation of individual growth trajectories. Table 11.5 presents descriptive statistics for the assessed language skills at the four points in time.

Three levels are specified in our multilevel model (school, student and measurement occasion). Time is the only explanatory variable in the analyses presented here. Thus, it is estimated how much progress students make per year. As the growth in language skills may follow a curvilinear pattern, a quadratic effect of time is estimated in addition to the linear effect. The effect of time is allowed to vary both at the school and student level, as it seems likely that growth trajectories vary both between schools and individuals. Time is coded in such a way that its effects as estimated in the analyses express the progress made per year. Language scores measured in grade 2 are denoted by a zero score on the time variable. The scores from grade 4, which are measured two years later, are denoted by a score of 2 and the scores in grade 6 and 8 are denoted by scores of 4 and 6 respectively. The MLwiN software was used to conduct the analyses reported.

The findings are summarized in Table 11.6. The fixed effects reflect the average growth pattern across all schools and students, whereas the random effects denote the variation across schools and students. The fixed intercept (Grand

Table 11.5 Descriptive statistics for language skills

	Mean	Std. deviation	Number
Measurements in 1995 (grade 2)	969.98	34.59	3,565
Measurements in 1997 (grade 4)	1,040.70	36.18	3,425
Measurements in 1999 (grade 6)	1,080.75	34.84	3,224
Measurements in 2001 (grade 8)	1,118.52	34.60	3,188

Mean) provides an estimate of the average score in grade 2 (that is, when the value of the time variable equals zero). The analyses further yield significant linear and quadratic effects of time. The positive sign of the linear term and the negative quadratic effect suggest a pattern of declining growth, which is in line with the figures presented in Table 11.5.

The random effects are particularly interesting as they reveal to what extent the growth patterns differ across schools and students. The variances of the time effects indicate how growth in language skills differs between schools and students. The correlations indicate to what extent a high starting level coincides with the rate of improvement. The school- and student-level intercept variances indicate to what extent the starting level of the language scores varies between and within schools. The variance at the lowest level denotes the remaining variation. The school- and student-level variances indicate considerable difference in language scores both between and within schools at the first measurement. The school-level variance (170.119) corresponds with a standard deviation equal to 13.04. The student-level variance corresponds with a standard deviation equal to 20.90. With regard to the schools this implies a range of over 26 points (twice the standard deviation) for the middle 68 per cent in grade 2. On either

Table 11.6 Growth in language skills over time

	Effect	Standard error	Significance
FIXED EFFECTS			
Intercept (Grand Mean)	969.730	1.218	0.000
Time – linear effect	36.749	0.761	0.000
Time – quadratic effect	−2.121	0.114	0.000
RANDOM EFFECTS			
School-level variances			
Intercept	170.119	25.342	0.000
Time – linear effect	63.250	9.865	0.000
Time – quadratic effect	1.376	0.222	0.000
School-level correlations			
Intercept – Time linear	−0.34		0.003
Intercept – Time quadratic	0.25		0.029
Time linear – Time quadratic	−0.98		0.000
Student-level variances			
Intercept	436.665	23.074	0.000
Time – linear effect	4.607	1.229	0.000
Student-level correlation			
Intercept – Time linear	−0.04		0.686
Measurement-level variance			
Intercept	596.272	11.367	0.000

tail of the distribution, 16 per cent of the cases lie outside the range of one standard deviation from the mean. For students within schools the range is close to 42 points. These are substantial gaps, as students gain about 71 points in the first two years after the first measurement (see Table 11.5).

The analyses show significant variance at both the student and school level of the linear time effect. The quadratic effect turns out to vary only at the school level. Fitting a model with random quadratic effects of time at the student level yields a zero estimate. These results are not reported in the table. The random effects at the school level point to a remarkable pattern. The negative covariance between the intercept and the linear time effect indicates that linear growth is less strong in schools with a relatively high starting level. The correlation coefficient (r) between the linear effect and the intercept equals –0.34. The quadratic effect is positively correlated with the intercept ($r = 0.25$), which suggests less decline in growth for schools with a high starting level. The findings also reveal an almost perfectly negative correlation ($r = -0.98$) between the linear and quadratic effects of time. This implies that if linear growth is strongly positive, the quadratic effect is strongly negative (that is, strong linear growth also implies a strong decline in growth in the higher grades and vice versa). This remarkable finding has previously been reported for partly the same cohort of students by Guldemond and Bosker (2005).

The variance in growth at the student level is rather modest in comparison to the school level (4.607 vs. 63.250). The correlation between the linear time effect and the intercept at this level is very small (–0.04) and statistically insignificant. The moderate variance implies that within schools, students progress at a fairly similar pace. The negligible correlation between the intercept and time effect at the student level indicates that the limited variation in learning gain within schools is largely unrelated to the students' starting levels.

Example 4: multivariate multilevel models

Multivariate multilevel regression models have been described by Goldstein (1995, 2003). They are multilevel regression models that contain more than one response variable. Hox (2002) suggests they are comparable to classical MANOVA, where there are several outcome measures.

This present example also involves a further analysis of the Dutch PRIMA data. In this case we are dealing with two distinct outcome measures per individual (language and mathematics achievement). The data were collected in 2001 and relate to 3,232 students in 149 schools. Similar to the repeated measurement models, the scores per student constitute the lowest level. Often researchers will choose to conduct separate analyses for each dependent variable, but for a number of reasons, a joint analysis may be advisable (Snijders and Bosker 1999: 201):

- Multivariate multilevel analysis yields estimates of the correlations between the outcome measures. The findings indicate to what extent the correlation is situated at the individual level or at a higher level.

- Only by means of multivariate multilevel analysis is it possible to test whether the effect of an explanatory variable differs from one dependent variable to the next.
- Testing the joint effect of an independent variable on a number of outcome measures requires a multivariate analysis.
- If the dependent variables are strongly correlated and at the same time the data on the outcome measures are incomplete for a large number of cases, the tests of the effects for the explanatory variables are more powerful.

The example presented in this section focuses on the first two reasons listed above. The analyses relate to how far the school- and student-level variances are different for language and mathematics and to what extent the effects of home background differ for both outcome variables. Home background was operationalized by means of the same dummy variables that were used for the analyses of the school recommendations (see the section on random slopes models). The test scores were transformed into z-scores, so that the mean and standard deviation for both variables are identical. The data were analysed using the MLwiN software. The next section then presents an example of the multivariate multilevel model for meta-analysis. In these cases, the third and fourth reasons listed above apply as well.

The first stage in the analyses entails the fitting of a multivariate zero model. The results are reported in Table 11.7a. Besides a partitioning of the variances into a student- and a school-level component, the analyses produce the correlation between both outcome variables for each level separately. The analyses also involve the estimation of an intercept for language and mathematics. Neither of the intercepts differ significantly from zero, which is hardly surprising given the transformation into z-scores. The partitioning of the variances into a student

Table 11.7a Language and mathematics – zero model

	Effect	Standard error	Significance
FIXED EFFECTS			
Intercept, language	−0.027	0.033	0.409
Intercept, mathematics	−0.040	0.037	0.275
RANDOM EFFECTS			
School-level variance, language	0.108	0.018	0.000
School-level variance, mathematics	0.138	0.022	0.000
School-level correlation, language/ mathematics	0.532		0.000
Student-level variance, language	0.894	0.023	0.000
Student-level variance, mathematics	0.876	0.023	0.000
Student-level correlation, language/ mathematics	0.534		0.000

and a school component yields a slightly larger amount of school-level variance for mathematics than for language (0.138 vs. 108). At the student level it is the other way around (0.894 vs. 0.876). This implies that the intraclass coefficient (ρ) for language equals 0.11, while for mathematics $\rho = 0.14$. The correlation between language and mathematics is virtually the same at the school and student level ($r = 0.53$).

An important feature of multivariate multilevel modelling is that it provides an opportunity (by means of χ^2-tests) to assess whether the fixed and random effects differ significantly between the outcome measures. The results of these tests are displayed in Table 11.8. For the zero model none of the differences between language and mathematics (with regard to the intercept and the variances) are statistically significant.

In the second stage, the home background dummy variables are included in the model. The outcomes of this analysis are presented in Table 11.7b. The analyses show virtually identical effects on language and mathematics for students with parents whose educational level is high and for students with parents whose educational level is low, unless one of the parents was born in Turkey or Morocco. In that case the effect is much stronger for language than it is for mathematics (−0.839 vs. −0.335). The intercept, which denotes the average achievement level of the students in the reference group (namely students with parents whose educational level is medium), is higher for language than it is for mathematics (0.034 vs. 0.092). For language the difference between the Turkish and Moroccan students with poorly educated parents and the reference group is particularly large. The difference between the reference group and the other groups is highly similar for both outcome measures. The findings reported in Table 11.7b indicate that nearly all effects in the model that include the home background dichotomies as explanatory variables are statistically significant. The only exception is the intercept for mathematics. This means that with regard to mathematics, the average score for the students in the reference group does not deviate significantly from zero, which is the mean score. For language, the average of the reference group is significantly larger than zero. This is probably due to the particularly large language disadvantage for the Turkish and Moroccan students. The correlations at the school and student level in model 1 differ only slightly from the correlations in the zero model.

Three out of the four variance components in model 1 show no more than modest decreases in comparison to the zero model. The main exception is the school-level variance for language achievement, which has decreased by 64 per cent (from 0.108 to 0.039). This means that controlling for home background accounts for nearly two thirds of the school-level variance in language scores. This is largely due to the strong concentration of Turkish and Moroccan students in a limited number of urban schools. The decrease for the other three variance components amounts to a modest 7 per cent in each case.

Table 11.8 reports to what extent the differences between language and mathematics are statistically significant for the effects presented in Table 11.7b.

Table 11.7b Language and mathematics – model I (home background characteristics)

	Effect	Standard error	Significance
FIXED EFFECTS			
Intercept, language	0.092	0.032	0.004
Intercept, mathematics	0.034	0.042	0.419
Low-education parents; Turkish/ Moroccan – lang.	−0.839	0.072	0.000
Low-education parents; Turkish/ Moroccan – math.	−0.335	0.077	0.000
Low-education parents; others – language	−0.380	0.040	0.000
Low-education parents; others – mathematics	−0.383	0.042	0.000
High-education parents – language	0.359	0.044	0.000
High-education parents – mathematics	0.360	0.046	0.000
RANDOM EFFECTS			
School-level variance, language	0.039	0.009	0.000
School-level variance, mathematics	0.128	0.021	0.000
School-level correlation, language/mathematics	0.538		0.001
Student-level variance, language	0.829	0.021	0.000
Student-level variance, mathematics	0.815	0.022	0.000
Student-level correlation, language/mathematics	0.501		0.000

Table 11.8 Difference of effects for language and mathematics

	Model 0		Model I	
	Diff.	Sign.	Diff.	Sign.
FIXED EFFECTS				
Intercept	0.013	0.710	0.059	0.128
Low-education parents; Turkish/Moroccan	—	—	0.504	0.000
Low-education parents; others	—	—	0.003	0.982
High-education parents	—	—	0.001	0.999
RANDOM EFFECTS				
School-level variance	0.030	0.227	0.089	0.000
Student-level variance	0.017	0.531	0.014	0.868

With regard to the fixed effects, the only significant difference relates to the effect for the Turkish and Moroccan students. Their disadvantage is much larger for language than it is for mathematics. In fact, with regard to mathematics their disadvantage hardly differs from the disadvantage for the other students with poorly educated parents (−0.335 for the Turkish and Moroccan students; −0.383 for the others). With regard to the random effects, we can conclude that the school-level variance for language is significantly smaller than it is for mathematics, whereas this is not the case for the student level. This results from the fact that home background accounts for a large part of the school-level variance.

Example 5: multivariate multilevel meta-analysis

Chapter 13 of this volume focuses in detail on the topic of meta-analysis and its potential value in EER. It also provides an example of a multilevel meta-analysis used to test the dynamic model. Here we provide a further example of a multivariate multilevel meta-analysis used to test the impact of specific educational interventions. The study of self-concept research in school settings using a multivariate multilevel model meta-analysis by O'Mara *et al.* (2005) provides an example of new developments in multivariate multilevel models. The use of multilevel approaches that incorporate random error variance is desirable because participants can be seen to be clustered (nested) within the different studies included in a meta-analysis (for further discussion see Hox and De Leeuw 2003). Multivariate analyses allow the researcher to incorporate a range of different outcomes of interest. O'Mara *et al.* (2005) argue that an advantage of such a multilevel multivariate approach is that it also addresses the issue of independence that has affected traditional meta-analysis approaches and provides better estimates of the effect sizes of interventions and their statistical significance.

Meta-analysis uses statistical results from a range of studies that address a similar research question and often seeks to establish an average effect size and estimate of the statistical significance of a relationship. In EER this might be the effects attributable to a particular approach to teaching or of a school reform programme. However, one might also be interested in the variation in effect sizes across studies of interest, as in a random effects analysis that seeks to distinguish variance that is the result of sampling variance and that is attributable to real differences between studies. It is, thus, explicitly acknowledged that study outcomes may be heterogeneous. Thus, meta-analysis can be viewed as a special case of multilevel analysis. In meta-analysis there is typically limited access to original data – usually results are published in the form of selected statistics, such as effect sizes, means, standard deviations or correlation coefficients. O'Mara *et al.* (2005) argue that the advantage of a multilevel approach to meta-analysis is its flexibility to include a range of potential explanatory variables and multiple outcomes. They illustrate this ability by using data on various interventions intended to enhance self-concept. They also point to the importance of recognizing the existence of different domains of self-concept, including academic and behavioural (Marsh 1993; Marsh and Craven 1997).

O'Mara *et al.* (2005) note that there is evidence of a reciprocal relation between self-concept and skill building, such that direct self-concept interventions can enhance both students' self-concept and related performance outcomes. They cite the reciprocal relationship between academic attainment and academic self-concept, and findings that prior levels of academic self-concept lead to higher levels of later academic achievement, beyond what can be explained by prior levels of academic achievement. The advantages of using multilevel modelling include that:

> ... improved modelling of the nesting of levels within studies increases the accuracy of the estimation of standard errors on parameter estimates and the assessment of the significance of explanatory variables.
>
> (O'Mara *et al.* 2005: 5)

The meta-analysis of O'Mara *et al.* (2005) included studies published in English, involving children and adolescents with a mean age of 18 or younger, and including a control group drawn from the same population as the intervention group with a global- or domain-specific measure of self-concept. The following hierarchical model was used for comparison with a traditional fixed effects analysis as shown in equation (5):

$$d_{ijk} = \beta_{000} + \beta_1 W_{1j} + \beta_2 W_{2j} + \ldots + \beta_s W_{sj} + v_{0k} + u_{0jk} + e_{ijk}, \tag{5}$$

where d_{ijk} is the mean effect size, $\beta_0 \ldots \beta_s$ are the regression coefficients, $W_{1j} \ldots W_{sj}$ are the study characteristics (predictor or moderator variables), v_{0k} is the systematic variability in study k not captured by the s predictors, u_{0jk} is the systematic variability in intervention j not captured by the s predictors, and e_{ijk} is the sampling error for study k (Bryk and Raudenbush 1992). The intercept (β_{000}) is the estimated effect size for a study with zero values for all moderator variables. The remaining regression weights ($\beta_0 \ldots \beta_s$) indicate the amount of expected variation in the effect size for a one-unit change on each variable.

The findings revealed that self-concept was enhanced through various intervention treatments. Interestingly, the estimated mean effect size of 0.31 identified in the fixed-effects model increased to 0.47 in the multilevel analysis. Significant heterogeneity was also found in the effect sizes between different studies and a number of predictor variables were tested that improved the model fit. The results confirm that the fixed-effects model was less accurate in identifying statistically significant relationships, and the findings from the multilevel models supported the construct validity approach. In summary, O'Mara *et al.* conclude that:

> ... multilevel modelling has proven to be a useful new direction for meta-analysis. It affords greater confidence in the accuracy of the results than a traditional fixed effects model, and also allows the results to be generalised to the greater population of studies.
>
> (2005: 10)

Example 6: cross-classified models

The development of multilevel modelling techniques and appropriate statistical programs has been crucial to the development and expansion of EER over the last two decades. Having introduced the underlying basic principles of multilevel design and demonstrated their value in EER for the study of the size of institutional effects on student outcomes at different levels (for example, school board or neighbourhood, school, department and classroom/teacher level), including elaborations such as multilevel growth curve models, this section focuses on two further approaches that enable researchers to address more complex questions about institutional effects that reflect the realities of students' educational experiences. These are cross-classified multilevel models and multivariate multilevel models.

The principles underlying cross-classified models and their analysis have been described by Goldstein (1995, 2003) and Rasbash and Goldstein (1994) and a useful guide to their application is given by Hox (2002). Such an approach allows the researcher to study two sources of higher level influence simultaneously. In EER this is of particular interest because students may be clustered in (that is, be members of) different institutions or other higher level units at the same time point or at different time points. As has been noted elsewhere in this chapter, multilevel problems must be explained with the aid of theories that recognize the existence of multilevel structures. If it is hypothesized that there are effects of social context on individuals (in EER, effects on students are of particular interest), 'these effects must be mediated by intervening processes that depend on characteristics of the social context' (Hox 2002: 7). Creemers and Kyriakides (2008) have elaborated a dynamic model that seeks to advance such theoretical understanding building on the earlier comprehensive model developed by Creemers (Sammons 2009). Nonetheless, as yet EER theories have paid little attention to the notion of multiple institutional influences operating simultaneously, rather than merely sequentially.

For example, a student may live in one neighbourhood and attend one school at the same time for a period of years. Both are forms of clustering that are of interest to those studying the sources of variation in individual students' educational outcomes over time. We can hypothesize (as social geographers do) that the neighbourhood a student lives in may shape students' outcomes, perhaps through peer influences or other opportunities that vary on a spatial scale. In addition, the school a student attends is also likely to have an influence on their outcomes as evidenced by multilevel studies discussed earlier in this chapter. Although there may be a strong relationship between the neighbourhood and school attended, in most systems young people in some neighbourhoods will attend a range of schools, while in any one school students may come from homes in a number of different neighbourhoods. This is especially likely to occur in education systems that encourage choice and diversity of provision or that involve selection of some kind.

Similarly, over the course of their education, students typically attend more than one school at different times (most commonly there is a transition according to phases of education with a primary/elementary school followed by a secondary/high school, though in some systems a middle school may be attended after primary and before a move to secondary school). In addition, some students move schools within phase for various reasons such as a parent's house/ employment change or family break-up leading to relocation. We cannot assume, therefore, that only one institution (school) influences students' outcomes. Each institution previously attended as well as the current school is likely to help shape a student's subsequent outcomes. It is of substantive interest to explore the relative importance of primary and secondary-school effects on students' longer term educational outcomes – for example, whether primary-school effects 'last' (the question of continuity in effects). This is because we want to know whether the primary school attended still shapes students' progress trajectories while they are at secondary school, over and above their impact on students' attainment levels when they transfer to secondary school. We may miss-specify any secondary school models if we ignore such possible continuing effects in the longer term. In addition, the outcomes of mobile students (those who change schools once or more during a particular phase of education) similarly may be affected by the various schools they have attended as well as by having moved school.

In the scenarios described above there is a need for a modelling approach that can take into account these different group memberships simultaneously and identify their separate effects on student outcomes. Cross-classified multilevel models enable the different group memberships (sources of clustering) to be specified at higher levels. Without cross-classified models it was implicitly assumed that the impact of primary schools operated only while students attended the primary school and influenced the final level of attainment (or other outcomes) a student achieved at the end of primary school. In studies of secondary-school effects it was assumed that good control for students' prior attainment at entry to secondary school was sufficient to allow the identification of secondary-school effects on later outcomes, such as examination results without further consideration of primary school influences. Similarly, prior to the development of cross-classified models, EER studies generally excluded mobile pupils from analyses of school effects, or otherwise the effects of mobility were modelled only in the fixed effects part of a traditional two-level model (in terms of the number of months or terms a student had attended their current institution, or the number of previous schools attended). While this enabled identification of overall mobility effects on individual students to be explored, it ignored any possible effects of the previous institution (school) because these were not estimated as they were not specified in the random parameter matrix.

Hox (2002) notes that cross-classification can occur at any level in a hierarchical data set. The examples noted above concern cross-classification at a higher level (typically level two), but cross-classification can also occur at lower levels, such as the student. Hox (2002) illustrates this point with an example of students in a computer class where there are several parallel classes taught by different teachers. As a result, at the student level, students obtain grades for several different exercises given by several different teachers, because the exercises are graded by all available teachers. Here therefore, students are nested within classes, with a cross-classification of teachers (graders) and exercises nested within classes. Since there are likely to be differences between classes and students, in this example the cross-classification of exercises and teachers would be defined at the lowest level, nested within pupils, nested within classes.

An early example of a cross-classified multilevel study in the EER field is provided by Goldstein and Sammons (1997) who sought to address the question of the continuity of school effects measured at different stages of a student's school career. They conducted a re-analysis of an existing data set (Mortimore *et al.* 1988) to examine possible long-term effects of previous institutional membership (for example, primary school attended) on students' later attainment at secondary school. The analysis built on earlier published research by Sammons *et al.* (1995) that had attempted to address the issue of continuity in primary-school effects using traditional multilevel approaches. This earlier study was limited in that it did not consider the full cross-classification of individual students in terms of their secondary by primary school attendance. Goldstein and Sammons (1997) re-analysed the data set to provide a more detailed investigation of the question of continuity of school effects, by simultaneously estimating the joint contributions of primary and secondary schools using the newly (at that time) developed MLwiN program extension to enable cross-classifications to be studied.

Sammons *et al.* (1995) had presented data on the secondary school examination attainment (GCSE results) for students at age 16 who had originally been included in a classic early EER study conducted in the 1980s in 50 inner-London primary schools called the Junior School Project (JSP; Mortimore *et al.* 1988). These students had been followed-up in secondary education to the end of compulsory schooling at age 16. Two types of two-level analysis had been carried out, one with students classified by their secondary school and one with students classified by their junior (primary) school. They included in these models two measures of student prior-attainment at age 11 as baselines in their analyses of secondary-school effects – the London Reading Test (LRT) score and a verbal reasoning (VR) band (as well as other student level one predictors for each student, including free school meals, social class and ethnic group as covariates) – to evaluate student progress and estimate the size of the school effect. The level two variance for primary and that for secondary schools was found to be approximately the same in both analyses. They thus modelled junior and secondary-school effects separately, but what they could not do using standard two-level models was examine their influence simultaneously. Sammons *et al.* (1995) concluded that there was evidence that the primary school attended still affected students' later attainment at age 16, because they found significant level two variance in the junior school analysis even after controlling for student attainment at the end of primary school (age 11). However, they could not distinguish the separate contributions of primary and secondary schools in accounting for the variance in students' examination outcomes at age 16.

Goldstein and Sammons (1997) later extended the original analysis by Sammons *et al.* (1995) to illustrate the application of newly developed cross-classified approaches, although they omitted some of the student-level explanatory variables in the original study for simplicity and due to sample size, given the greater complexity of the models. They extended the multilevel models by including both the primary school and secondary school, identified in the same analysis as two random cross-classified factors. The basic model is shown in equation below (6):

$$y_{ij1j2} = \Sigma_k \beta_k x_{kij} + u_{j1} + u_{j2} + e_{ij} \tag{6}$$

$$var(u_{j1}) = \sigma^2_{u1}, var(u_{j2}) = \sigma^2_{u2}, var(e_{ij}) = \sigma^2_{e}.$$

Thus the outcome variable (GCSE total examination score at age 16, y) is modelled as a function with an overall intercept, together with residual error terms for both junior and secondary schools and an individual residual error term for students (e). The subscript 1 in the equations for u refers to junior (primary) and subscript 2 refers to secondary schools. The sample size in the analysis was only 758 students with 48 junior and 116 secondary schools, so the authors noted that results where there is a lack of statistical significance or lack of variation should be treated carefully, because the number of students in the individual secondary schools was typically very small in this sample.

To specify a cross-classified bivariate model, level one was used to define the bivariate structure, that is with up to two units (the GCSE or LRT response) within each level two unit (student) within a cross-classification of junior by secondary schools. The junior-school classification was specified at level three, and the secondary-school classification at level four, where every secondary school was assigned a dummy variable whose coefficient is random (with a single variance term) at level four, and these variances were constrained to be equal. Because the response was bivariate at levels two and three, the variances of GCSE and LRT and their covariance were parameters to be estimated.

To simplify the analysis and make it more manageable Goldstein and Sammons (1997) reported that all cells of the cross-classification with only one student were omitted. In total this omitted 31 secondary schools, 1 junior school and 146 students from the data set. Analyses were conducted for both the full and reduced data sets, using the purely hierarchical models and revealing no substantial differences in the results. Table 11.9 (reproduced from Goldstein and Sammons) gives results for fitting this model with different fixed coefficients and assumptions about the level one variance. It can be seen that the between-junior variance is always larger than that between secondary schools. As further explanatory variables are incorporated that measure achievement at the end of junior schooling, so relatively more of the junior-school variance in GCSE attainment at age 16 is explained, as might be expected.

In model C the size of the variances attributable to primary (junior) and secondary schools are compared. Analyses A and B (model A is a better-specified model) of Table 11.9 present a measure of the 'value added' by secondary schools

Table 11.9 Variance components cross-classified model for GCSE exam score as response analyses/models

	A	B	C
Fixed			
Intercept	0.51	0.50	0.25
Males	−0.21 (0.06)	−0.19 (0.06)	−0.34 (0.07)
Free school meal	−0.22 (0.06)	−0.23 (0.06)	−0.37 (0.08)
VR2 band	−0.39 (0.08)	−0.38 (0.08)	
VR3 band	−0.71 (0.13)	−0.71 (0.13)	
LRT score	0.31 (0.04)	0.32 (0.04)	
Random			
Level 2:			
(Junior) σ^2_{u1}	0.025 (0.013)	0.036 (0.017)	0.054 (0.024)
(Secondary) σ^2_{u2}	0.016 (0.014)	0.014 (0.014)	0.019 (0.02)
Level 1:			
σ^2_{e0}	0.50 (0.06)	0.554 (0.06)	0.74 (0.05)
σ_{e01}	0.092 (0.03)	0.064 (0.03)	0.10 (0.05)
σ_{e02}	0.093 (0.018)		
σ^2_{e2}	0.033 (0.022)		
−2Log likelihood	1,848.8	1,884.1	2,130.3

Note: The exam score and LRT score have been transformed empirically to have $N(0, 1)$ distributions. FSM is a binary (yes, no) variable. At level 2 the subscript 1 refers to junior and 2 to secondary school. At level 1 the subscript 0 refers to the intercept, 1 to males and 2 to LRT.

Source: after Goldstein and Sammons 1997

after adjusting for student intake performance *and* the effect of the junior school attended, which is not captured by the LRT and VR band variables that measure attainment at the end of primary school/beginning of secondary school. Nonetheless, although analysis A or B provides the better estimates of secondary-school effects than analysis C, the junior and secondary variances cannot be compared directly, because end-of-junior attainments have been fitted.

Another more recent and far more complex example of the use of cross-classified models is provided by Leckie (2009). This sought to examine the complexity of school and neighbourhood effects and study the impact of student mobility, as well using data from the national pupil database in England. Multiple membership models allow for pupil mobility, and Leckie (2009) builds on the work of Goldstein *et al.* (2007) to present a more detailed study of pupil mobility between schools and between neighbourhoods to allow the relative importance of secondary schools, neighbourhoods and primary schools to be investigated on both achievement and progress using a very large data set. Leckie (2009) argues that

> Until recently, research into pupil mobility has been held back by both a lack of data on pupil movements and also by the absence of appropriate

multilevel methodology. However, the recently established national pupil database in England and the development of cross-classified and multiple-membership multilevel models now make it possible to analyse a wide range of complex non-hierarchical data structures in models of educational achievement (Fielding and Goldstein, 2006; Rasbash and Browne, 2001).

(Leckie 2009: 4)

Leckie (2009) illustrates how the actual contribution of secondary schools to the variance in outcomes for a given student varies as a function of the number of schools that the student attends and the time they spend in each school. He argues that models that ignore the multiple membership structure lead to biased estimates of school effects and that the bias increases with the degree of student mobility. Leckie (2009) based his analysis on data for over 4,200 students in 264 secondary schools living in 3,175 neighbourhoods and had previously attended 3,107 primary schools. As students can move between both schools and between neighbourhoods, the models examined multiple membership structures. In all, 8 per cent changed schools, but a much higher proportion moved home (27 per cent) and neighbourhood (23 per cent). Leckie (2009) reports a succession of models of increasing complexity and shows how taking account of complex non-hierarchical structures in the data set affect the estimates of both school and neighbourhood effects. It is shown that neighbourhoods and schools attended in previous phases of education help to explain variation in students' test scores and their progress. In addition, the results show how student mobility between schools and between neighbourhoods also affects outcomes. After taking into account the impact of mobility, primary schools and secondary schools are shown to have similar size effects on student progress.

Conclusions and future directions

Methodological debates were particularly evident in the early development of the EER field as Sammons and Luyten (2009) discuss. Early seminal SER studies such as *Fifteen thousand hours* (Rutter *et al.* 1979) were criticized on a number of important features of the methodology, and this stimulated significant advances in subsequent SER designs. Most notably, the development of hierarchical regression approaches using multilevel modelling that recognized the important implications of clustering in educational data sets and the need for longitudinal samples with individual student-level data to compare school performance were led by authors such as Goldstein (1995) and Bryk and Raudenbush (1992).The advent of accessible software packages such as HLM and MLWin encouraged improvements in the size, scale and statistical approaches used in SER during the late 1980s and 1990s. Those who wish to learn more on the statistical under-pinnings and more advanced applications are encouraged to consult Goldstein (2003), Hox (2002) or Snijders and Bosker (1999). Multilevel modelling is a powerful tool that has particular advantages for the study of institutional effects using longitudinal data sets with measures at a variety of levels, due to the ability to take account of the role of clustering in educational data and identify variance at different levels in hierarchical structures. This provides more efficient and accurate estimates of the effects of predictor variables and their associated standard errors. It also allows the estimation of overall size of effects at higher levels (for example, school or classroom/teacher) in terms of the proportion of unexplained variance attributable to each level using the intra-class correlations. Good control for student's prior attainment and background characteristics remains essential for value-added analyses of such effects, however, because poorly specified models may lead to overestimates of institutional effects through failure to control sufficiently for pre-existing student intake differences. In addition, multilevel models allow for estimation of the effects of individual schools (and/or teachers if appropriate data are collected) with their associated confidence intervals (CIs). This can be helpful to distinguish more or less effective institutions and those that are typical in their effectiveness in promoting student academic progress or other outcomes for further case study (see also Chapter 7). In addition, the way models can explore random effects (providing evidence of internal variations in effectiveness, often termed differential effects) has been illustrated. This is important because it recognizes the complexity in defining educational effectiveness if some schools or teachers are more effective in promoting better outcomes for some student groups or in promoting only some outcomes. Multilevel models allow researchers to address questions of stability (over time), consistency (across different outcomes) and differential effectiveness (for specific student groups).

In this chapter we have discussed several applications of multilevel modelling in an educational context. The first example illustrated that multilevel analysis may produce outcomes that differ substantially from an analysis that does not take into account the nesting of lower level units within higher level units. The second example showed how random effects models may be used to estimate variations in the effect of a student-level variable across schools. The next example illustrated the usefulness of the multilevel approach for modelling individual growth and the fourth example showed the merit of multivariate models, which may be appropriate for analysing data with multiple outcome measures per student. The fifth example illustrated how the multivariate model can also be used for meta-analysis. The final example illustrated that the approach can also be applied when the nesting of lower level units within higher level units is not strictly hierarchical, using cross-classified models.

The wider availability of large scale longitudinal sets has facilitated the use of increasingly sophisticated multilevel models in EER in a number of countries in recent years. The results of such research point to complexity in the study of institutional and also neighbourhood effects on students outcomes. The further advances in such statistical modelling applications allow EER to address a wider range of questions about the role of educational and other influences (for example, personal characteristics, family and home, or neighbourhood factors) in shaping students' educational trajectories at different ages and across different phases of education. Further, these models reveal the way that educational influences may compound or help ameliorate existing inequalities in educational achievement that are linked with socio-economic disadvantage.

Elsewhere, in a special issue of the *School Effectiveness and School Improvement Journal*, we have discussed a number of recent methodological developments in EER approaches to studying the size of school effects that utilize multilevel analyses but adopt some innovative new approaches in terms of design and application (Sammons and Luyten 2009). Despite the important contribution of multilevel value-added studies of the variation in educational effectiveness over the last 20 years, there is growing recognition of the need to advance further the methodology of the study of school effects and to investigate the absolute as well as the relative effects of schools and schooling. The articles making up the special issue were drawn together to provide examples of recent innovative studies based on a number of alternative research methods to assess the effectiveness of education in terms of a range of outcomes and in different contexts.

Three different approaches were illustrated in discussing the recent development of the field in this special issue: regression-discontinuity, growth-curve analysis and seasonality of learning. We have discussed growth-curve modelling in this chapter already because this approach is becoming more widely applied and represents a further refinement of more traditional multilevel analysis by modelling student growth across more than two time points. A brief summary of the other two approaches is described below.

Regression-discontinuity is based on a comparison of students' outcomes in adjacent grades. This approach capitalizes on the fact that date of birth is the primary criterion for assignment to grades in most countries. The difference in achievement between students from adjacent grades minus the effect of age is therefore assumed to be a valid measure of the overall effect of extra time in schooling. This implies that the effect of education is equal to zero if the difference in achievement can be accounted for solely by the effect of students' ages in the statistical model. An important practical advantage of the approach is that it does not require longitudinal data (a major inhibitor of SER in many countries). Although longitudinal student-level data are indispensible for some specific research questions (for example, on the reciprocal relation between attitudes and achievement, or mapping changes in students' progress or growth trajectories), they also require more time and resources to collect. Kyriakides and Luyten (2009) and Luyten *et al.* (2009) provide illustrations of the application of regression-discontinuity to the study of the absolute effects of time in school. Their results point to the potential value of the regression-discontinuity approach in allowing analyses of the absolute effects of schooling with a meaningful zero level, as well as estimates of variation between individual schools (relative school effects) in the grade effect in the same analysis.

Seasonality-of-learning research can be seen as a special case of growth-curve analysis and examples are provided by Verachtert *et al.* (2009) and von Hippel (2009). In these studies, learning rates during the school year and the summer vacation are compared. The basic assumption is that during the school year learning gains are affected both by in- and out-of-school influences, whereas during the summer vacation it is assumed that only out-of-school factors operate. The effect of schooling is assumed to be zero if the rate of learning during the school year does not exceed the rate of learning during the summer vacation. In addition, if there is no school-level variance in summer learning but significant school variance in school-year learning this provides further evidence of school effects. While providing possibly more precise estimates of the size of school effects and illustrating the way summer learning rates may differ for students from different groups (for example, advantaged/disadvantaged), a potential disadvantage is the need for additional points of assessment at the start and end of the school year to allow vactation learning (or fall back) to be examined.

This chapter showed that multilevel models provide a powerful tool for the detailed investigation of variation in students' educational outcomes and the way various sources of influence help to shape students' learning and developmental outcomes over time. However, as with all research, the potential of such models also rests on the collection of appropriate data, careful measurement of relevant concepts and guidance from theoretical models as discussed in the first part of this volume.

References

Bryk, A.S. and Raudenbush, S.W. (1992) *Hierarchical linear models: Applications and data analysis methods*, Newbury Park: SAGE Publications.

Creemers, B.P.M. and Kyriakides, L. (2008) *The dynamics of educational effectiveness: A contribution to policy, practice and theory in contemporary schools*, London/New York: Routledge.

Fielding, A. and Goldstein, H. (2006) 'Cross-classified and multiple membership structures in multilevel models: An introduction and review', research report No. 791 for DfES: London.

Goldstein, H. (1995) *Multilevel statistical models*, 2nd edn, London: Edward Arnold.

Goldstein, H. (2003) *Multilevel statistical models*, 3rd edn, London: Edward Arnold.

Goldstein, H. and Sammons, P. (1997) 'The influence of secondary and junior schools on sixteen year examination performance: A cross-classified multilevel analysis', *School Effectiveness and School Improvement*, 8(2): 19–230.

Goldstein, H., Burgess, S. and McConnell, B. (2007) 'Modelling the effect of pupil mobility on school differences in educational achievement', *Journal of the Royal Statistical Society*, 170: 941–94.

Guldemond, H. and Bosker, R.J. (2005) *Ontwikkelingen in de groei van achterstanden? Op zoek naar de rol van de school (Developments in the growth of disadvantages? In search of the school role)*, Groningen, The Netherlands: GION.

Hox, J.J. (2002) *Multilevel analysis: Techniques and applications*, Mahwah, NJ: Lawrence Erlbaum Associates.

Hox, J.J. and De Leeuw, E.D. (2003) 'Multilevel models for meta-analysis', in S.P. Reise and N. Duan (eds) *Multilevel modelling: Methodological advances, issues, and applications*, Mahwah, NJ: Lawrence Erlbaum Associates.

Kyriakides, L., Antoniou, P. and Maltezou, E. (2009) 'Investigating the short- and long-term effects of secondary schools upon academic success and development', paper presented at the AERA conference, San Diego, CA, April 2009.

Kyriakides, L. and Luyten, H. (2009) 'The contribution of schooling to the cognitive development of secondary education students in Cyprus: An application of regression discontinuity with multiple cut-off points', *School Effectiveness and School Improvement*, 20(2): 167–86.

Leckie, G. (2009) 'The complexity of school and neighbourhood effects and movements of pupils on school differences in models of educational achievement', *Journal of the Royal Statistical Society*, Part 3, 172: 537–54.

Luyten, H., Tymms, P. and Jones, P. (2009) 'Assessing school effects without controlling for prior achievement', *School Effectiveness and School Improvement*, 20(2): 145–66.

Marsh, H.W. (1993) 'Relations between global and specific domains of self: The importance of individual importance, certainty, and ideals', *Journal of Personality and Social Psychology*, 65: 975–92.

Marsh, H.W. and Craven, R. (1997) 'Academic self-concept: Beyond the dustbowl', in G. Phye (ed.) *Handbook of classroom assessment: Learning, achievement and adjustment*, Orlando, FL: Academic Press.

Mortimore, P., Sammons, P., Stoll, L., Lewis, D. and Ecob, R. (1988) *School matters: The junior years*, Somerset: Open Books.

OECD (2004) *Learning for tomorrow's world, first results from PISA 2003*, Paris: OECD.

O'Mara, A.J., Marsh, H.W. and Craven, R.G. 'Self-concept intervention research in school settings: A multivariate, multilevel model meta-analysis', paper presented at the AARE Conference, University of Western Sydney, Parramatta, Australia, December 2005.

Pustjens, N., Van de Gaer, E., Van Damme, J. and Onghena, P. (2004) 'Effect of secondary schools on academic choices and on success in higher education', *School Effectiveness and School Improvement*, 15: 281–311.

Rasbash, J. and Browne, W. (2001) 'Modelling non-hierarchical structures', in A.H. Leyland and H. Goldstein (eds) *Multilevel modelling of health statistics*, Chichester: Wiley.

Rasbash, J. and Goldstein, H. (1994) 'Efficient analysis of mixed hierarchical and cross-classified random structures using a multilevel model', *Journal of Educational and Behavioural Statistics*, 19(4): 337–50.

Roeleveld, J. and Van der Veen, I. (2007) 'Kleuterbouwverlenging in Nederland: omvang, kenmerken en effecten (Scope, characteristics and effects of kindergarten retention policy in the Netherlands)', *Pedagogische Studiën (Dutch Educational Research Journal)*, 84(6): 448–62.

Rutter, M., Maughan, B., Mortimore, P., Ouston, J. and Smith, A. (1979) *Fifteen thousand hours: Secondary schools and their effects on children*, Cambridge, MA: Harvard University Press.

Sammons, P. (2009) 'The dynamics of educational effectiveness: A contribution to policy, practice and theory in contemporary schools', *School Effectiveness and School Improvement*, 20(1): 123–9.

Sammons, P. and Luyten, H. (2009) 'Editorial for special issue on school effects and schooling effects', *School Effectiveness and School Improvement*, 20(2): 133–43.

Sammons, P., Nuttall, D., Cuttance, P. and Thomas, S. (1995) 'Continuity of school effects: A longitudinal analysis of primary and secondary school effects on GCSE performance', *School Effectiveness and School Improvement*, 6(4): 285–307.

Snijders, T.A.B. and Bosker, R.J. (1999) *Multilevel analysis: An introduction to basic and advanced multilevel modelling,* London: SAGE Publications.

Verachtert, P., Van Damme, J., Onghena, P. and Ghesquiere, P. (2009) 'A seasonal perspective on school effectiveness: Evidence from a Flemish longitudinal study in kindergarten and first grade', *School Effectiveness and School Improvement,* 20(2): 215–34.

Von Hippel, P. (2009) 'Achievement, learning and seasonal impact as measures of school effectiveness: It's better to be valid than reliable', *School Effectiveness and School Improvement,* 20(2): 187–214.

Chapter 12

Structural Equation Modelling techniques

George A. Marcoulides and Leonidas Kyriakides

University of California, Riverside and University of Cyprus
(respectively)

Introduction

Structural Equation Modelling (SEM) currently enjoys widespread popularity in the behavioural, educational, medical and social sciences. Contributions to the literature in terms of books, book chapters and journal articles applying SEM or developing new SEM methodology are appearing at an incredible rate. There is even a scholarly journal devoted exclusively to SEM, entitled *Structural Equation Modeling: A Multidisciplinary Journal*. According to one review of the literature, SEM is the fastest growing and dominant multivariate statistical technique of the past two decades (Hershberger 2003). A major reason for this popularity is that SEM permits researchers to study complex multivariate relationships among observed and latent variables whereby both direct and indirect effects can be evaluated. Another reason for this popularity is the availability of specialized SEM programs. For example, programs such as Amos (Arbuckle 2006), EQS (Bentler 2004), LISREL (Jöreskog and Sörbom 1996), Mplus (Muthén and Muthén 2006), Mx (Neale *et al.* 1999), SAS PROC CALIS (SAS Institute 1989), SEPATH (Steiger 1995) and RAMONA (Browne and Mels 1990) are all broadly available for the analyses of various models.

In this chapter, we provide an overview of SEM and elaborate on some conceptual and methodological details related to analysing school effectiveness research data via this modelling approach. The term SEM is used throughout the chapter as a generic notion to refer to various types of possible models (for example, CFA; structural regression; path analysis; models for time-dependent data; recursive and non-recursive models for cross-sectional, longitudinal and multilevel data; covariance structure analysis; and latent class or mixture analysis). For obvious space limitations, we selectively introduce just a few of the more commonly encountered and recently popularized models. The various models are illustrated throughout the chapter using the Mplus (Version 5; Muthén and Muthén 2006) software program (although other programs such as Amos, EQS, LISREL, Mx and SAS PROC CALIS can also be readily used to complete some of the analyses). A frequent assumption made when using the SEM methodology illustrated in this chapter is that the relationships among observed and/or latent variables are linear (although modelling nonlinear relationships is also becoming increasingly popular; for details see Schumacker and Marcoulides 1998).

The chapter is organized in several sections as follows. In the first section, we provide an overview of the general process for defining a structural equation model and introduce some of the basic mathematical details associated with two commonly analysed models. In the second section we discuss model identification issues. In the next section we elaborate on model estimation issues. This is followed by a section on model assessment and evaluation of fit. Subsequently, the notion of model modification is introduced, along with a discussion regarding the potential ramifications for undergoing such strategies. In the next section, we provide an illustration of a data analysis that involved both a CFA model and a structural regression model. We finally expand the discussion to new modelling techniques. Throughout the chapter we use a notational system and equations generally considered to be consistent with the so-called Jöreskog-Keesling-Wiley framework (Jöreskog and Sörbom 1984), although this choice is to some extent arbitrary as specialized variants of the equations (for example, the Bentler-Weeks model; Bentler and Weeks 1980) can produce the same results.

The definition of a structural equation model

The definition of a structural equation model begins with a simple statement of the verbal theory that posits the hypothesized relationships among a set of studied variables (Marcoulides 1989). In its broadest sense, a structural equation model represents a translation of a series of hypothesized cause–effect relationships between variables into a composite hypothesis concerning patterns of statistical dependencies (Shipley 2000). The relationships are thereby described by parameters that specify the magnitude of the effect (regardless of whether the effect is direct or indirect) that independent variables have on dependent variables (both of which can be either observed or latent). Hypothesized relationships are translated into mathematical models and a researcher can use SEM to test a wide variety of proposed models. A structural equation model is typically represented by a path diagram, which is essentially a mathematical representation of the proposed theoretical model in graphical form. Figure 12.1 presents some of the most commonly used graphical notations to represent a structural equation model.

Once a theory has been proposed, it can be tested against empirical data. The process of proposing and testing a theoretical model is commonly referred to as the confirmatory aspect of SEM. Although in principle researchers should fully specify and deductively hypothesize a model prior to data collection and testing, in practice this often may not be possible, either because a theory is poorly formulated or because it is altogether nonexistent. Consequently, another aspect of SEM is the exploratory mode, in which theory development can occur. The theory development mode often involves repeated analyses on the same data in order to explore potential relationships among either observed or latent

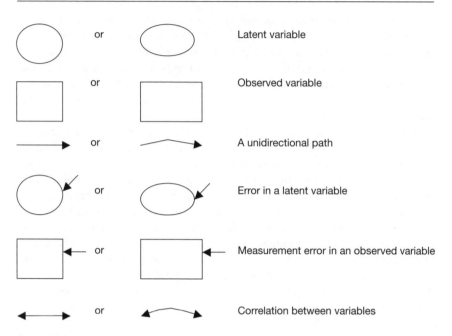

Figure 12.1 Commonly used symbols to represent SEM models in path diagrams

variables of interest (see Model modification section below). We emphasize that results obtained from such exploratory actions may be unique to the particular data set, and that capitalization on chance can occur during such analyses. For this reason, any models that result from exploratory searches must be cross-validated before real validity can be claimed from such findings.

A related utilization of SEM is with regards to *construct validation*. In these applications, researchers are mainly interested in evaluating the extent to which particular instruments actually measure one or more latent variables they are supposed to assess. This type of SEM use is most frequently employed when studying the psychometric properties of a given measurement device. Latent variables are hypothetically existing or theoretical variables (constructs) that cannot be directly observed. Although latent variables play a central role in many substantive areas, they often lack an explicit or precise way with which to measure their existence. For example, in the educational effectiveness arena, researchers study the constructs of organizational climate and culture and their potential impact on student achievement outcomes (Heck and Marcoulides 1996; Marcoulides and Heck 1993). Because organizational climate and culture cannot be explicitly measured, manifestations of the constructs are instead observed by measuring specific features of the behaviour of studied subjects in a particular environment and/or situation. Measurement of behaviour is usually carried out using appropriate devices and instrumentation. For example, devices such as a scale, self-reports, inventories or questionnaires are often used to measure the observable aspect of such latent variables. The measure or score obtained from the device would then be specified as an indicator of the latent variable or construct. Researchers often use a number of indicators or observed variables to examine a latent variable. It is generally recommended that multiple indicators for each studied latent variable be utilized so that a more psychometrically sound picture is obtained.

Figure 12.2 presents a CFA model, which is the simplest structural equation model that involves latent variables. A CFA model is most commonly used for assessing the extent to which particular indicators actually measure one or more latent variables that they are supposed to assess. The model in Figure 12.2 represents assumed relationships among two latent variables (achievement and motivation) and their indicators. The observed variables represent six scores that were obtained from a sample of elementary school students. The variables are denoted by the labels x_1 through x_6. The correlated latent variables achievement and motivation are denoted ξ_1 and ξ_2 (a lower-case Greek letter xi). Each latent variable is reflectively measured by three indicators, with each path in Figure 12.2 symbolizing the loading of the observed variable on its applicable latent variable. There is also a residual (error) term attached to each indicator, which

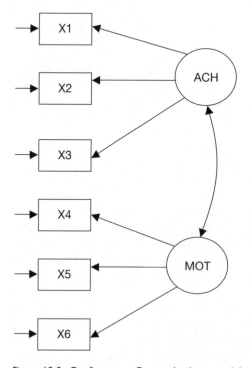

Figure 12.2 Confirmatory Factor Analysis model with two latent variables

ACH = Achievement   MOT = Motivation

is denoted by a δ (a lower-case Greek letter delta) and followed by the index of the variable to which it is attached. Each residual represents the amount of variation in the indicator that is due to measurement error or remains unexplained by variation in the corresponding latent variable that the indicator loads on.

The CFA model is mathematically defined as:

$$x = \Lambda_x\xi + \delta, \tag{1}$$

where Λ_x is a matrix of factor loadings, ξ represents factors with a covariance or correlation matrix Φ, and δ represents residuals with a covariance matrix Θ.

Based upon equation (1), the proposed model can also be written down as 'model definition' equations. These equations are for each observed variable in terms of how it is explained in the model and can either be written separately (one equation per variable) or in matrix form as:

$$
\begin{aligned}
x_1 &= \lambda_{11}\xi_1 + \delta_1 \\
x_2 &= \lambda_{21}\xi_1 + \delta_2 \\
x_3 &= \lambda_{31}\xi_1 + \delta_3 \\
x_4 &= \lambda_{42}\xi_2 + \delta_4 \\
x_5 &= \lambda_{52}\xi_2 + \delta_5 \\
x_6 &= \lambda_{62}\xi_2 + \delta_6
\end{aligned}
\tag{2}
$$

or

$$
\begin{bmatrix} x_1 \\ x_2 \\ x_3 \\ x_4 \\ x_5 \\ x_6 \end{bmatrix}
=
\begin{bmatrix} \lambda_{11} & 0 \\ \lambda_{21} & 0 \\ \lambda_{31} & 0 \\ 0 & \lambda_{42} \\ 0 & \lambda_{52} \\ 0 & \lambda_{62} \end{bmatrix}
\begin{bmatrix} \xi_1 \\ \xi_2 \end{bmatrix}
+
\begin{bmatrix} \delta_1 \\ \delta_2 \\ \delta_3 \\ \delta_4 \\ \delta_5 \\ \delta_6 \end{bmatrix}
\tag{3}
$$

where λ_{11} to λ_{62} denote the factor loadings in the matrix Λ_x. The covariance (or correlation) structure of the observed variables implied by the model can also be shown to be as follows:

$$\Sigma(\theta) = (\Lambda_x\xi + \delta)(\Lambda_x\xi + \delta)' = \Lambda_x\Phi\Lambda_x' + \Theta, \tag{4}$$

where $\Sigma(\theta)$ corresponds to the model-based covariance matrix, Λ_x is as displayed above,

$$
\Phi = \begin{bmatrix} 1 & \phi_{12} \\ \phi_{21} & 1 \end{bmatrix}
$$

represents the covariance or correlation among the latent variables, and

$$\Theta = \begin{bmatrix} \theta_{\delta 11} & 0 & 0 & 0 & 0 & 0 \\ 0 & \theta_{\delta 22} & 0 & 0 & 0 & 0 \\ 0 & 0 & \theta_{\delta 33} & 0 & 0 & 0 \\ 0 & 0 & 0 & \theta_{\delta 44} & 0 & 0 \\ 0 & 0 & 0 & 0 & \theta_{\delta 55} & 0 \\ 0 & 0 & 0 & 0 & 0 & \theta_{\delta 66} \end{bmatrix}$$

refers to the covariance or correlation matrix of residuals (and since in this model the residuals are unrelated, it is a diagonal matrix). The coefficients or parameters to be estimated from the collected data are considered to be *free*, whereas those set to some selected value (for example, in the case of some of the elements of the Λ_x matrix, they are set to zero because they do not measure a particular latent variable) are considered to be *fixed* (we note that such coefficients can also be considered *constrained* if they are set to one or more other parameters). Another example of fixed coefficients would include the setting of the variances of the two considered latent variables (ξ_1 and ξ_2) to a value of 1. This is done in order to establish a metric for the latent variables. Since latent variables cannot be directly measured, it is difficult to work numerically with them without first assigning them some scale of measurement. A common approach is to standardize these variances to a value of 1.

Figure 12.3 presents an example of a so-called structural regression model of variables assumed to influence school outcome variables. Structural regression models closely resemble CFA models except that, rather than the latent variables only being interrelated, they also postulate specific explanatory relationships among the latent variables. Structural regression models are frequently used to test or disconfirm theories about explanatory relationships among various latent variables under investigation, and for this reason are regularly just generically referred to as structural equation models. We refrain from using this taxonomy and prefer the term structural regression models, to differentiate them from other types of models such as latent change models, multilevel models, and so on, that may also involve explanatory relationships among various latent variables.

Another useful distinction with regards to the latent variables involved in structural regression models is the differentiation between dependent and independent variables. In graphical terms, dependent variables (whether latent or whether observed) are those that receive at least one path (one-way arrow) from another variable in the model. In mathematical terms this implies that when a model with dependent variables is represented in a set of model definition equations, each dependent variable appears in the left-hand side of at least one equation. Independent variables (whether latent or observed) are those from which a path or paths originate. In mathematical terms, no independent variable will appear in the left-hand side of an equation, in that system of model definition

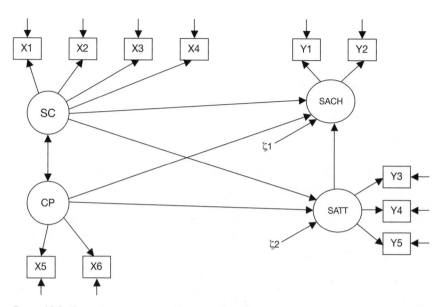

Figure 12.3 Example structural regression model

SC = School climate as perceived by each student
CP = Classroom processes as perceived by each student
SACH = Student achievement
SATT = Student attitudes

equations. Independent variables can of course be correlated among each another. In addition, a dependent variable may even act as an independent variable with respect to another variable, but this does not change its dependent-variable status. As long as there is at least one path ending at the latent variable, it is a dependent variable no matter how many other variables in the model are explained by it. We also note that the terms exogenous and endogenous variables are also frequently used to describe independent and dependent variables. The terms exogenous and endogenous are derived from the Greek words *exo* and *endos*, for being correspondingly of external or internal origin to the system of variables under consideration.

As mentioned above, a structural regression model can contain elements of a CFA model, and for this reason it is usually divided into two parts, the measurement and the structural part. The measurement part of the model is the section that involves the CFA (the model that explains how the indicators and latent variables are tied together). The structural part of the model details the explanatory relationships among the latent variables. Similar to the CFA model described in equation (1), the measurement part of a structural regression model is mathematically defined by two specific measurement equations, one for the x indicators associated with the exogenous latent variables (ξ) and one for the y indicators of the endogenous latent variables (η):

$$x = \Lambda_x \xi + \delta$$
$$y = \Lambda_y \eta + \varepsilon,$$
(5)

where Λ_x and Λ_y are matrices of factor loadings, and δ and ε are residuals with respective covariance matrices Θ_δ and Θ_ε.

The structural part of the model detailing the explanatory relationships among the latent variables is written as:

$$\eta = \beta\eta + \Gamma\xi + \zeta,$$
(6)

where B contains the regression coefficients among the η endogenous latent variables, Γ represents the matrix of regression coefficients for the prediction of the η endogenous latent variables by the ξ exogenous variables, and ζ represents residual errors in the prediction of the η variables with a covariance matrix Ψ. In matrix notation, the structural part of the model depicted in Figure 12.3 would be represented as:

$$\begin{bmatrix} \eta \\ \eta \end{bmatrix} = \begin{bmatrix} 0 & \beta12 \\ 0 & 0 \end{bmatrix} \begin{bmatrix} \eta1 \\ \eta2 \end{bmatrix} + \begin{bmatrix} \gamma11 & \gamma12 \\ \gamma21 & \gamma22 \end{bmatrix} \begin{bmatrix} \xi_1 \\ \xi_2 \end{bmatrix} + \begin{bmatrix} \varsigma1 \\ \varsigma2 \end{bmatrix}.$$
(7)

Model identification

Once the definition of a model is completed, the next consideration is the identification of the model. The definition of a model corresponds to a mathematical specification of the model-based covariance matrix $\Sigma(\theta)$ that will be tested against the covariance matrix Σ obtained from the empirical data (also sometimes referred to as the observed covariance matrix). The amount of unique information in the observed covariance matrix is what will determine whether a proposed model is identified. We note that this verification procedure must be performed before any model can be appropriately tested. The amount of unique or non-duplicated information in the observed covariance matrix is determined as $p(p + 1)/2$, where p is the number of observed variables in the model (since the covariance matrix is symmetric this amount includes only the diagonal elements and those elements either above or below the main diagonal). For example, in the above-mentioned CFA model with six indicators, this value would be equal to 21.

The amount of unique information in the observed covariance matrix must then be examined with regards to three different levels of identification for a model. The most problematic is that of an 'under-identified model', which occurs when the number of parameters in the model to be estimated are greater that the amount of unique information available in the observed covariance matrix. The parameters in such a model cannot be uniquely estimated from the observed covariance matrix. A 'just-identified model' (also sometimes referred to as a 'saturated model') is a model that utilizes all of the uniquely estimable parameters. Because there is no way that one can test or disconfirm the model, such a model will always result in a perfect fit to the observed data. As it turns out, the most desirable level of identification is the 'over-identified model'. This type of model occurs when the amount of information available in the observed covariance matrix is greater that the number of parameters to be estimated in the model. This ensures that there is more than one way to estimate the specified parameters in the model. The difference between the number of nonredundant elements of the observed covariance matrix and the number of parameters to be estimated in a model is known as the degrees of freedom (df) of the model. For example, in the CFA model presented in Figure 12.2 the degrees of freedom would be equal to 8 (that is, the 21 nonredundant elements in the observed covariance matrix minus the 13 parameters to be estimated in the model).

The topic of model identification in SEM is an extremely complicated issue and requires several procedures to verify the status of a proposed model (for further discussion, see Marcoulides and Hershberger 1997; Raykov and Marcoulides 2006, 2008). One of the most frequently used identification rules is the so-called t-rule. The t-rule, which is only a necessary condition for identification, simply requires that the number of degrees of freedom with regards to a proposed model be nonnegative. We emphasize, however, that the condition of positive degrees of freedom is only a necessary but not a sufficient condition for model identification. As it turns out, there can be situations when the degrees of freedom for a proposed model are positive and yet some of its parameters are unidentified. Consequently, just passing the t-rule does not guarantee identification. Others rules that examine identification include the order condition (also just a necessary condition) and the rank condition (which is both a necessary and sufficient condition – for further details on identification issues, see Hayashi and Marcoulides 2006). Model identification is in general a very complex issue that requires careful consideration and handling.

Model estimation

It was noted above that the definition of a model corresponds to a mathematical specification of the model-based covariance matrix $\Sigma(\theta)$ that is going to be tested against the observed covariance matrix Σ obtained from the data. However, the model-implied covariance matrix must first be computed from optimal estimates of the parameters. To simplify the discussion of model estimation, consider again the path diagram in Figure 12.2 and equation 4 in the previous section. This proposed model has specific implications for the variances and covariances of the involved observed and latent variables. As it turns out, these implications can be worked out using the relations listed below (for complete details see Raykov and Marcoulides 2006).

Let us denote the variance of a variable under consideration by using the notation 'Var' and covariance between two variables by the notation 'Cov'. For any one variable x, the first relation is:

Relation 1: $\text{Cov}(x, x) = \text{Var}(x)$,

and states that the covariance of a variable with itself is that variable's variance.

The second relation considers the covariance of two linear combinations of variables. Suppose that x, y, z and u are four variables (for example, those denoting the scores for each indicator in Figure 12.2) and that a, b, c and d are four constants. Then the following relation holds:

Relation 2: $\text{Cov}(ax + by, cz + du) = ac\,\text{Cov}(x, z) + ad\,\text{Cov}(x, u) + bc\,\text{Cov}(y, z) + bd\,\text{Cov}(y, u)$.

Based on relations 1 and 2, one obtains the next relation:

Relation 3: $\text{Var}(ax + by) = \text{Cov}(ax + by, ax + by)$
$= a^2\,\text{Cov}(x, x) + b^2\,\text{Cov}(y, y) + ab\,\text{Cov}(x, y) + ab\,\text{Cov}(x, y)$,

or simply

$$\text{Var}(ax + by) = a^2\,\text{Var}(x) + b^2\,\text{Var}(y) + 2ab\,\text{Cov}(x, y).$$

In the case that the variables x and y are uncorrelated (that is, $\text{Cov}(x, y) = 0$), then $\text{Var}(ax + by) = a^2\,\text{Var}(x) + b^2\,\text{Var}(y)$.

Now let us consider the model presented in Figure 12.2 using the above relations. For example, with regards to the first two variables x_1 and x_2 that load on the same latent variable ξ_1 this leads to the following:

$$\begin{aligned}
\text{Cov}(x_1, x_2) &= \text{Cov}(\lambda_1\xi_1 + \delta_1, \lambda_2\xi_1 + \delta_2) \\
&= \lambda_1\lambda_2\,\text{Cov}(\xi_1, \xi_1) + \lambda_1\,\text{Cov}(\xi_1, \delta_2) + \lambda_2\,\text{Cov}(\delta_1, \xi_1) \\
&\quad + \text{Cov}(\delta_1, \delta_2) \\
&= \lambda_1\lambda_2\,\text{Cov}(\xi_1, \xi_1) \\
&= \lambda_1\lambda_2\,\text{Var}(\xi_1) \\
&= \lambda_1\lambda_2.
\end{aligned}$$

The above result is based upon the fact that (a) the covariance of the residuals δ_1 and δ_2, and the covariance of each of them with the factor ξ_1, are equal to 0 and (b) the variance of ξ_1 was set to be equal to 1.

The covariance between the observed variables x_1 and x_4 could also similarly be determined as follows:

$$\begin{aligned}
\text{Cov}(x_1, x_4) &= \text{Cov}(\lambda_1\xi_1 + \delta_1, \lambda_4\xi_2 + \delta_4) \\
&= \lambda_1\lambda_4\,\text{Cov}(\xi_1, \xi_2) + \lambda_1\,\text{Cov}(\xi_1, \delta_4) + \lambda_4\,\text{Cov}(\delta_1, \xi_2) + \\
&\quad \text{Cov}(\delta_1, \delta_4) \\
&= \lambda_1\lambda_4\Phi_{21},
\end{aligned}$$

where ϕ_{21} denotes the covariance between the two latent variables.

If this process were continued for every combination of observed variables in a given model, one would then actually obtain every element of the model-implied matrix $\Sigma(\theta)$. For the entire model displayed in Figure 12.2, the following reproduced symmetric covariance matrix $\Sigma(\theta)$ is obtained:

$$\Sigma(\theta) = \begin{array}{llllll} \lambda_1^2 + \theta_1 & & & & & \\ \lambda_1\lambda_2 & \lambda_2^2 + \theta_2 & & & & \\ \lambda_1\lambda_3 & \lambda_2\lambda_3 & \lambda_3^2 + \theta_3 & & & \\ \lambda_1\lambda_4\phi_{21} & \lambda_2\lambda_4\phi_{21} & \lambda_3\lambda_4\phi_{21} & \lambda_4^2 + \theta_4 & & \\ \lambda_1\lambda_5\phi_{21} & \lambda_2\lambda_5\phi_{21} & \lambda_3\lambda_5\phi_{21} & \lambda_4\lambda_5 & \lambda_5^2 + \theta_5 & \\ \lambda_1\lambda_6\phi_{21} & \lambda_2\lambda_6\phi_{21} & \lambda_3\lambda_6\phi_2 & \lambda_4\lambda_6 & \lambda_5\lambda_6 & \lambda_6^2 + \theta_6. \end{array}$$

Thus, the matrix $\Sigma(\theta)$ represents the relationships among the variables determined according to a proposed model. As will be detailed in the next section, if the model is correct, then the estimates obtained from the model-implied matrix $\Sigma(\theta)$ will be close to those contained in the observed sample covariance matrix. Fortunately, researchers do not really have to worry about all these computations, as every SEM program available has built into its memory the exact way in which these functions of model parameters in $\Sigma(\theta)$ can be obtained. In fact, this occurs quite automatically once a researcher has communicated to the program the model with its parameters to be estimated.

Model assessment and evaluation of fit

The evaluation of model fit utilizes both the model-implied covariance matrix computed from the optimal estimates of the parameters considered and the observed covariance matrix. Evaluation of model fit is then just a function of determining how close the two matrices are. If the difference between these matrices is small, then one can conclude that the proposed model represents the observed data reasonably well. If the difference is large, then the model is not consistent with the observed data. There are at least two reasons for these inconsistencies: (a) the proposed model may be deficient, in the sense that it is not capable of emulating well enough the observed matrix of variable interrelationships even with most favourable parameter values, or (b) the data may not be good (that is, are deficient in some way, maybe by not validly/reliably measuring the aspects of the studied phenomenon that are reflected in the model). There are two types of tests that can be used to evaluate the fit of a model, exact fit tests and approximate fit tests. The exact fit tests answer the question dichotomously with a simple yes or no, while the approximate fit tests determine the degree of the closeness between the observed and model-implied matrices. Approximate fit tests have also been classified into a variety of different categories (for example, absolute, incremental and residual based). Due to space limitations, we do not give detailed description of each of these categories, and suggest that interested readers refer to a number of other available resources on the topic (Bollen 1989; Marcoulides and Hersberger 1997; Raykov and Marcoulides 2006).

One way to conceptualize model fit is akin to a distance measure between matrices. If the compared values were just a single number, then a simple subtraction of the two could suffice to evaluate the distance between them. However, this cannot be done directly with the two matrices Σ and $\Sigma(\theta)$. As it turns out, there are some meaningful ways with which to evaluate the distance between two matrices, with the resulting distance measure still ending up being a single number. For example, one straightforward way to obtain a single number involves taking the sum of the squares of the differences between the corresponding elements of the two matrices. Other more complicated ways involve the multiplication of these squares with some appropriately chosen weights and then taking their sum. In either case, the single number obtained represents a generalized measure of the distance between two matrices considered. The bigger the number, the more different the matrices, and the smaller the number, the more similar they are. Because (in SEM) this number results from the comparison of the elements of observed and model-implied covariance matrices, the generalized distance is a function of the model parameters as well as the elements of the observed variances and covariances. It is customary to refer to the relationship between the matrix distance, the model parameters and observed covariance matrix as a 'fit function'. Since the fit function is the distance between two matrices, it is always positive or zero (if the matrices considered are identical).

Before the particular measures for evaluating model fit are discussed in detail, a word of caution is warranted. Even if all possible model fit indices point to an acceptable model, one can never claim to have found the true model that has generated the analysed data (excluding of course the cases were data were specifically simulated according to a preset known model). SEM approaches are mostly concerned with supporting a deductively proposed model that does not contradict the data. That is to say, in SEM one is typically interested in retaining the proposed model whose validity is the essence of the null hypothesis. In statistical terms, this implies that one is interested in not rejecting the null hypothesis. In general terms, this follows along with Karl Popper's ideological process of 'falsification', the logical consequence of which is that no theory can ever be proved true from data, it can only be corroborated.

It turns out that depending on how the matrix distance is defined, several fit functions result. There are four main estimation methods and types of fit functions in SEM that are typically considered: (a) unweighted least squares (ULS), (b) maximum likelihood (ML), (c) generalized least squares (GLS), and (d) asymptotically distribution free (also called weighted least squares – WLS). In recent decades, research has shown that the ML method can also be employed with minor deviations from normality (Bollen 1989; Jöreskog and Sörbom

1993), especially when one is primarily interested in parameter estimates. With more serious deviations from normality and with fairly large sample sizes, the WLS method can be used.

One of the most widely used statistics for assessing the fit of a model is the χ^2 (chi-squared) goodness-of-fit statistics. This statistic is an assessment of the magnitude of the difference between the observed covariance matrix and the model-implied matrix. The probability level that is associated with this statistic indicates whether the difference is significant. When a significant value is found, the difference is due to sampling error or variation. We note that in SEM, researchers are generally interested in non-significant χ^2 values. Such non-significant values indicate that there are no differences between the observed and model-implied covariance matrices, which suggest a good fit of the model to the data. It should be emphasized that the χ^2 is well known to be sensitive to sample size issues and has a tendency to reject proposed models that are even only marginally inconsistent with the data. Thus, it is suggested that researchers examine a number of alternative fit criteria in order to assess the fit of a proposed model (Hu and Bentler 1999).

Other fit criteria include the comparative fit index (CFI), Akaike's information criterion (AIC), and the root mean square error of approximation (RMSEA) along with its associated confidence intervals. It is generally recognized that to support model fit a consensus among the following is needed: a CFI value above 0.90; an AIC value closer to the value of the index for the saturated model rather than the independence model; an RMSEA value below 0.05 and the left endpoint of its 90 per cent confidence interval is markedly smaller than 0.05 (with this interval not excessively wide). Detailed discussions of additional fit indices and criteria for model evaluation can be found for example in Bollen (1989), Byrne (1998), Hu and Bentler (1999), Marcoulides and Hershberger (1997), and Raykov and Marcoulides (2006, 2008).

Because many of these indices are mainly concerned with evaluating the fit of the entire model, one should also consider how well various parts of the model fit. It is quite possible that the model as a whole fits the data well, but individual sections do not fit so well. In the event that a proposed model does not fit the data well, such information is also useful in determining which parts of the model may be contributing to the misfit. One of the most common ways to determine the fit of specific sections of a proposed model is to examine the residual matrix (Bollen 1989). The residual matrix results from the difference between the observed covariance matrix and the model-implied matrix. A positive residual value of an element in this difference matrix would suggest that the model under predicts a particular covariance, whereas a negative value suggests that the model over predicts. Although these residuals elements are informative, some researchers (Joreskog and Sorbom 1996) believe that examining the residual correlation matrix or the normalized residuals matrix should be preferred because they convey a better sense of the fit of a specific part of a model.

Model modification

The general approach in SEM is that the details of a proposed theoretical model be specified before it is tested on data. Some theories, however, are often poorly developed and other may require changes or adjustments. In addition, fitting a model can be difficult, particularly when the number of variables is large. For example, a model with 25 variables has 325 variances and covariances that must be correctly modelled. One can envision that many models may not be perfect and might need some modification in order to better fit the data. There are three types of situations that can be considered with regards to model fitting and testing. The first situation is the so-called strictly confirmative approach in which the initial proposed model is tested against data and is either accepted or rejected. The second situation is one in which a researcher considers competing or alternative models. All proposed models are assessed and the best is selected based upon which model more appropriately fits the observed data. The third situation is the so-called model-generating approach in which a researcher repeatedly modifies an initially proposed model until some level of fit is obtained. We believe that the decision with regards to which approach to follow should be based on the initial theory. A researcher who is firmly rooted in his or her theory will elect a different approach than one who is quite tentative about the various relationships being modelled. We note that once a researcher re-specifies an initially proposed model after it has been ascertained to not fit the data, the modelling approach is no longer confirmatory. Indeed, the modelling approach has now entered an exploratory mode in which revisions or modifications to the model occur that will most significantly improve model fit. Such modifications can entail either adding and/or removing parameters in the model. The process of exploration is commonly referred to as a specification search (Marcoulides and Drezner 2001).

Most SEM programs come equipped with various test statistics to assist in conducting a specification search. Two of the most popular test statistics are the Lagrange multiplier test (more commonly referred to as a modification index – MI), and the t-ratio (Joreskog and Sorbom 1996). The MI is basically used to examine the parameters that have been fixed to zero in the model (that is, they have not been included in the originally proposed model) and determines whether or not the parameters should be added to the model (that is, should be freely estimated). The MI simply indicates the amount the χ^2 goodness-of-fit index would change (decrease) if a specific parameter were included in the model. We note that the MI is also available as a multivariate test in which more than one parameter in the model can be considered simultaneously. t-ratios can be used to assess the significance of individual parameters in the model, whereby values less than 2 are considered to be non-significant (that is, with $p > 0.05$). In all likelihood, parameters that are found to be non-significant may be removed from the model without causing model fit to deteriorate.

Recent research has provided some search procedures (for example, using genetic algorithms, ant colony optimization and Tabu search) that can automate the process of conducting a specification search (Marcoulides *et al.* 1998; Marcoulides and Drezner 2001). Nevertheless, it is important to note that results obtained from any specification search may be unique to the particular data set, and that capitalization on chance can occur during the search (MacCallum 1986). Even if adding a specific parameter leads to model improvement, it should be theoretically meaningful. Similarly, even if parameter does not appear to be important (based, for example, on its *t*-ratio), it should not be removed from the model if it is considered theoretically and logically important. Consequently, it is imperative that any model that results from a specification search should be cross-validated before the validity of its findings can be claimed.

Some example Mplus analyses

The first and most critical step in conducting a structural equation model analysis is communicating the model to the particular program being used. Mplus has ten main commands that can be used to fit a wide variety of models. The main commands also include a number of additional options, subcommands and keywords (for complete details, see Muthén and Muthén 2006). For example, the command file displayed in Appendix A can be used to fit the CFA model in Figure 12.2.

The command file begins with a title. We note that each command line ends with a semicolon, except the title line. The DATA command indicates the name and directory location of the file containing the observed covariance matrix. The subcommand TYPE indicates that it is a covariance matrix and NOBS provides the sample size. The VARIABLE command is for naming the variables. The MODEL command states each latent variable in the model with its corresponding indicators. In order to override some default options imposed in Mplus and obtain estimates of factor correlations and fix their variances to 1 (as opposed to the default, which fixes at 1 the loading of the first listed indicator for each latent variable), the subcommand F1-F2@ 1 is added. In addition, we add an *1 after each first listed indicator, which essentially frees all factor loading for each latent variable and simply provides a start value for initial estimation. Finally, the OUTPUT command requests the printing of modification indices, which might be useful to examine if the fit of the proposed model turns out not to be satisfactory.

The file produces the selectively presented output provided in Table 12.1. It is evident that all the fit criteria presented in Table 12.1 suggest that the model is a good fit to the data. The chi-squared is non-significant, the CFI is above 0.90, the RMSEA index is below 0.05 and the left end-point of its 90 per cent confidence interval includes 0. Given the good model fit, one can then proceed to examine the individual parameter estimates provided next in Table 12.1. Each parameter estimate is provided (first column) along with the standard error (second column), and their corresponding statistical significance using *t*-values (which are evaluated using ±1.96 for a significance level of $\alpha = 0.05$). It is evident

Table 12.1 Selective output from Mplus analysis of example CFA model

TESTS OF MODEL FIT

Chi-Square Test of Model Fit

Value	9.240
Degrees of Freedom	8
P-Value	0.2055

CFI/TLI

CFI	0.991
TLI	0.990

Information Criteria

Number of Free Parameters	8
Akaike (AIC)	2998.381
Bayesian (BIC)	3079.398
Sample-Size Adjusted BIC	3012.778

RMSEA (Root Mean Square Error Of Approximation)

Estimate	0.033	
90 Percent C.I.	0.000	0.058
Probability RMSEA <= .05	0.859	

MODEL RESULTS

		Estimates	S.E.	Est./S.E.
ACHI	BY			
X1		0.990	0.060	16.500
X2		0.962	0.063	14.630
X3		0.985	0.063	15.732
MOT	BY			
X4		0.980	0.050	19.600
X5		0.925	0.060	15.466
X6		0.987	0.066	15.015
ACHI	WITH			
MOT		44.557	6.633	6.717

that each indicator is a good measure of the considered latent variables of achievement and motivation.

The model examined above can also be modified to consider the case in which the factor loadings on either (or both) of the latent variables are equal. In the psychometric literature, such a model is referred to as a model with tau-equivalent measures. A tau-equivalent indicator model suggests the indicators are assessing the construct in the same units of measurement. To test this model, an equality of loadings constraint can be introduced into the model. For example, to test this for the achievement indicators in Figure 12.2, the statement, 'F1 BY X*1 X2 X3 (1)' can be added to the input statement in Appendix A. Running such a model in Mplus would provide a new set of fit criteria, which can then be examined by evaluating the chi-squared value against the previously obtained value without the constraints. In this case, the result of introducing the restriction in the original model results in a chi-squared value of 11.28 with df = 10, which compared to the original value of 9.24 with df = 8 provides a difference of 2.04 for df = 2, and is non-significant (that is, the critical value of the chi-squared with 2 degrees of freedom is 5.99 at the 0.05 significance level). Thus, we conclude that the imposed achievement factor loading identity is plausible, and hence that the achievement measures are tau-equivalent.

The model presented in Figure 12.3 represents a simple structural regression model in which school outcomes are predicted. The two latent variables of 'school climate' and 'classroom processes' (both as perceived by each student) are used as predictors of the latent variables of 'student attitudes' and 'student achievement'. The main difference in this file (relative to the Mplus command file for the CFA model examined previously) is that now explanatory predictions between latent variables are declared using the keyword 'ON' – see the command file provided in Appendix B.

Using the command file provided in Appendix B produces the output presented in Table 12.2. All of the fit criteria obtained indicate that the proposed model is a plausible means of data description and explanation. Given the good model fit one can then examine in greater detail the obtained individual parameter estimates. For example, it is quite clear that both school climate and classroom processes appear to be good predictors of student achievement and student attitudes. Beyond this, it would appear that the student attitude latent variable also functions as a good predictor of student achievement.

Statistical tests dealing with hypotheses about potential group differences are also quite common in SEM and are referred to as tests of model invariance (Heck and Marcoulides 1989; Marcoulides and Heck 1993). The terms 'interaction modelling' or 'multi-sampling' are also sometimes used to refer to such comparisons with regards to similarities of proposed models across different samples or subgroups of samples (Schumacker and Marcoulides 1998). Suppose for example that data have been obtained from G groups and that we are interested in studying the CFA model defined in equation (4) across these groups. From equation (4), it follows that the implied covariance matrix in each considered group is

$$\Sigma(\theta_g) = \Lambda_g \Phi_g \Lambda_g' + \Theta_g. \tag{8}$$

In general terms, evaluating this model across multiple samples consists of the following steps. The analysis first begins by fitting a model to the data for each sample considered separately, with none of the parameters constrained to be equal across groups. This unconstrained model serves as the baseline model. Subsequently, in a stepwise fashion, more stringent constraints are placed on the model by specifying the parameters of interest to be constrained across groups. The model is then examined using a chi-squared (χ^2) difference test between the less restrictive and more restrictive model to determine whether

Table 12.2 Selective output from Mplus analysis of example structural regression model

TESTS OF MODEL FIT

Chi-Square Test of Model Fit
Value	32.889
Degrees of Freedom	36
P-Value	0.4062

CFI/TLI
CFI	0.994
TLI	0.992

Information Criteria
Number of Free Parameters	36
Akaike (AIC)	22998.381
Bayesian (BIC)	23079.398
Sample-Size Adjusted BIC	23012.778

RMSEA (Root Mean Square Error Of Approximation)
Estimate	0.033	
90 Percent C.I.	0.000	0.058
Probability RMSEA <= .05	0.859	

MODEL RESULTS

		Estimates	S.E.	Est./S.E.
SC	BY			
X1		1.000	0.000	0.000
X2		0.926	0.063	14.630
X3		0.985	0.063	15.732
X4		0.977	0.063	15.507
CP	BY			
X5		1.000	0.000	0.000
X6		0.987	0.066	15.015
SACH	BY			
Y1		1.000	0.000	0.000
Y2		0.972	0.044	22.090
SATT	BY			
Y1		1.000	0.000	0.000
Y2		0.962	0.053	18.150
Y3		0.985	0.053	18.584
SC	WITH			
CP		44.557	6.633	6.717
SACH	ON			
SC		0.992	0.146	6.776
CP		0.674	0.180	3.747
SATT		0.758	0.100	7.617
SATT	ON			
SC		0.980	0.080	12.030
CP		0.96	0.020	43.400

the model and the individual parameter estimates (for example, factor loadings, factor inter-correlations, error variance, structural relations) are invariant across the samples. A significant difference in χ^2 represents a deterioration of the model and the null hypothesis that the parameters are equal is rejected. A non-significant χ^2 difference is consistent with model invariance; that is, the parameters examined are equal across groups.

More advanced SEM models

A latent change model

A CFA model can also be used to model change over time. Such a CFA model entails having the latent variables interpreted as chronometric variables representing individual differences over time. Traditionally two different codings of time can be used, the so-called level and shape (LS) model and the intercept and slope (IS) model. The LS model was first described by McArdle (1988) and is considered to have a number of advantages over the IS model (Raykov and Marcoulides 2006). In particular, because the IS model assumes that the change trajectory being studied occurs in a specific fashion (that is, is linear, quadratic, cubic, and so on), the actual process may be quite difficult to model precisely utilizing any specific trajectory shape. For this reason, the less restrictive (in terms of the change trajectory) LS model is preferable because it would be expected to fit the data better.

As an example of a longitudinal study, assume that a series of seven repeated ordered waves of measurements on a measure of student achievement is represented as Υ_{it} (where the index i corresponds to each observed individual in the study and t corresponds to each obtained measurement). The following equation can be used to describe these repeated measurements:

$$\Upsilon_{it} = \alpha_{yi} + \beta_{yi}\lambda_t + \varepsilon_{it}, \tag{9}$$

where α_{yi} is the initial measurement obtained at time 1, β_{yi} is the shape of the change trajectory, λ_t corresponds to the measured time points, and ε_{it} to the model residual for each individual. Because α_{yi} and β_{yi} are random variables, they must be represented by a group of mean values for the intercept ($\mu_{\alpha y}$) and slope ($\mu_{\beta y}$), plus the component of individual intercept variation ($\zeta_{\alpha yi}$) and slope variation ($\zeta_{\beta yi}$). In equation form these would be:

$$\alpha_{yi} = \mu_{\alpha y} + \zeta_{\alpha yi} \text{ and } \beta_{yi} = \mu_{\beta y} + \zeta_{\beta yi}. \tag{10}$$

Alternatively, in general matrix form the model defined by the above equations would be expressed as below, which is essentially similar to equation (5):

$$y = \Lambda_y \eta + \varepsilon \tag{11}$$

or simply as

$$
\begin{bmatrix} y_{i1} \\ y_{i2} \\ y_{i3} \\ y_{i4} \\ y_{i5} \\ y_{i6} \\ y_{i7} \end{bmatrix} = \begin{bmatrix} \lambda_{11} & \lambda_{12} \\ \lambda_{21} & \lambda_{22} \\ \lambda_{31} & \lambda_{32} \\ \lambda_{41} & \lambda_{42} \\ \lambda_{51} & \lambda_{52} \\ \lambda_{61} & \lambda_{62} \\ \lambda_{71} & \lambda_{72} \end{bmatrix} \begin{bmatrix} \alpha_1 \\ \beta_2 \end{bmatrix} + \begin{bmatrix} \varepsilon_1 \\ \varepsilon_2 \\ \varepsilon_3 \\ \varepsilon_4 \\ \varepsilon_5 \\ \varepsilon_6 \\ \varepsilon_7 \end{bmatrix} . \tag{12}
$$

As indicated previously, a number of different approaches to the coding of time (that is, the Λ matrix) can be utilized to examine this model. Using the LS approach, the loadings on the first factor (called the 'level factor') are also set to a value of 1, but the component of time is coded by fixing the loadings on the second factor (called the 'shape factor') as follows (where * corresponds to a freely estimated loading):

$$
\Lambda = \begin{bmatrix} 1 & 0 \\ 1 & * \\ 1 & * \\ 1 & * \\ 1 & * \\ 1 & * \\ 1 & 1 \end{bmatrix} .
$$

By fixing the loading of the first and last assessment occasion on the second factor to a value of 0 and 1, respectively, one ensures that this factor is interpreted as a change factor (regardless of the shape of the encountered trajectory, be it linear, quadratic, cubic, and so on). Freeing the loadings of the remaining time periods on the same factor captures the change that occurs between the first and each of these later measurement occasions. In other words, specifying the change trajectory in this manner ensures that the freed loadings reflect the cumulative proportion of total change between two time points relative to the total change occurring from the first to the last time point, and the correlation between the level and shape factors reflects their degree of overlap. Thus, this particular manner of specifying the level and shape factors tends to focus on the change over the length of the longitudinal process measured.

As an example analysis, consider the longitudinal model depicted in Figure 12.4. The data are from a study of 130 individuals that participated in the Fullerton Longitudinal Study. To evaluate model fit, the overall χ^2 goodness-of-fit test, the CFI and the RMSEA (along with its associated confidence intervals) are once again used. The proposed LS model using equation (6) provided the

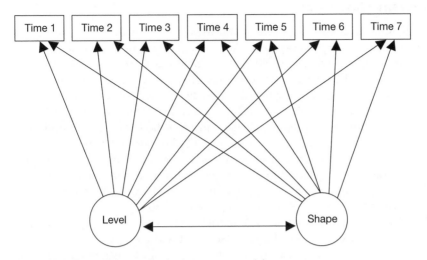

Figure 12.4 Example longitudinal achievement model

following fit criteria: $\chi^2 = 6.55$, $p = 0.45$; CFI = 0.99; and RMSEA = 0.02 (0.0; 0.06). An examination of the fit criteria based upon the previously outlined guidelines indicates that the proposed longitudinal model fit the data well. The Mplus modelling statements for examining the proposed model in Figure 12.4 are provided in Appendix C (where 'I' denotes level and 'S' denotes shape).

Based upon the good model-to-data fit results, we can then readily proceed to interpret the parameters to address the substantive focus of the study with respect to the change trajectories. First, we observed that the mean value of the shape factor is negative and significantly different from zero ($\mu_{\beta y} = -22.71$, t-value $= -8.63$, $p < 0.05$), indicating that there is a steady decline in scores over time from the initial measured mean value on the level factor ($\mu_{\alpha y} = 89.00$, t-value $= 61.00$, $p < 0.05$). Indeed, looking specifically at the estimated coefficients of the shape factor loadings of 0, 0.22, 0.47, 0.66, 0.70, 0.81, 1 that were obtained, it is evident that there is a decline in the achievement scores over time. The decline of the motivation scores is approximately 20 per cent each year for the first three measured time periods and appears to start levelling off at the remaining time periods. The specific average decline at any time point can be easily calculated. For example, the specific decline in achievement at time 2 is computed by taking the value of the shape factor loading (0.22) at that age and multiplying it by the mean value of the shape factor (−22.71) to produce −4.996. This value is then added to the mean value of the level factor (89.00) to provide the average achievement at this time period of 84.004. We also note that significant variance exists in both the level ($s^2 = 159.16$, t-value $= 5.308$, $p < 0.05$) and the shape factors ($s^2 = 505.67$, t-value $= 5.257$, $p < 0.05$), reflecting variability in the average initial and change scores of individuals over time.

A latent class model

Latent Class Analysis also operates much as a CFA model (in a conceptual manner similar to Exploratory Factor Analysis and cluster analysis). When running CFA models, it is often assumed that the observed scores obtained from the considered variables correspond to the distributional characteristics of a single sample or that group membership can be readily defined based on an observable variable (for example, male and female, or experimental and control groups). In some cases, however, group membership may not be known beforehand or is not observable. In such cases, the groups can be considered latent – sometimes also called mixtures. As an example of a Latent Class Analysis, consider the data distribution for a single continuous observed variable X with a mean value μ. Now consider the case in which the data consist of two different groups or classes of individuals but that the group membership is not directly observed. The observed data distribution of X actually corresponds to the mixture of the data distributions of the two latent classes $c = 1$ and $c = 2$, each with different means (μ_1 and μ_2). In other words, the two separate distributions are not observed but only their mixture is observed. In such a case, a Latent Class Analysis can be used to determine the presence and nature of the mixture and its associated parameter estimates. The basic assumption of such a latent class model is that the population from which the sample was taken consists of k latent classes of unknown size (postulated to be mutually exclusive and collectively exhaustive). For example, a proposed CFA model for $k = 1, \ldots, K$ latent classes can be specified similarly to equation (4) as follows:

$$\Sigma(\underline{\theta}) = \Lambda_k \Phi_k \Lambda_k' + \Theta_k. \tag{13}$$

Consider the CFA model examined previously with the six observed variables and two latent variables measuring achievement and motivation. To evaluate model fit in a Latent Class Analysis another index, called the Bayesian Information Criterion (BIC) index (Schwartz 1978), is generally used because it provides an ideal way to examine the relative fit of any proposed latent class model against the model for just one class (that is, the case for which the considered sample is homogeneous with respect to the model considered). The BIC values for the various alternative or competing models are compared and the model with the smaller value is considered the preferred model. Although some researchers also suggest the use of the likelihood ratio goodness-of-fit test to evaluate model fit, recent research has suggested that such an approach only works well in cases where there are not large numbers of sparse cells (Nylund *et al.* 2007).

The following illustrative results would be obtained when fitting the proposed CFA model to data using Mplus (Muthén and Muthén 2006). Model fit criteria based on the BIC values are examined for one-, two-, three- and four-class models and indicate that fitting a three-class model consistently results in the best BIC fit values. The proposed three-class measurement model fit criterion is BIC = 3,343.885, compared to model fit criteria of BIC = 3,368.539, BIC = 3,361.895

Table 12.3 Average posterior probabilities from the three-class model

Class	1	2	3
1	0.955	0.000	0.045
2	0.048	0.952	0.000
3	0.030	0.000	0.970

and BIC = 3,392.692 for the one-, two- and four-class models, respectively. Additional information obtained would include the information provided in Table 12.3, which provides evidence with regards to the quality of the classification, using average posterior probabilities for the three-class model considered. The fit of the model to the data suggests that three latent classes seem to classify individuals very nicely (in terms of percentage accuracy) into exclusive categories optimally based on the CFA model proposed. If desired, membership in these latent classes can be further investigated according to various individual characteristics such as gender or ethnicity. In addition, various other types of mixture models can be considered, such as latent growth mixture models, multilevel growth mixture models, latent transition analysis models, Markov chain models and latent variable hybrid models.

Concluding comments: application of SEM to EER

In this chapter, the background and some examples of basic SEM models were presented. These models are essential for running effectiveness studies, especially since they are able to test the construct validity of instruments used to measure effectiveness factors operating at different levels. More specifically, Example 1 refers to the use of a CFA model with two latent variables that are expected to be related to each other. In various effectiveness studies such models are used to generate latent variables, which are then treated as predictors of student achievement. For example, a CFA model can be used in a study testing the extent to which the five dimensions included in the dynamic model (Creemers and Kyriakides 2008) can help us measure a school-level factor such as school policy on partnership or teacher collaboration. Data emerging from a questionnaire administered to teachers can be analysed by using a CFA model in order to find out whether a first-order five-factor model fits the data. This model can also be compared with a more parsimonious model (for example, a single first-order factor model) in order to test the proposed measurement framework. Similarly, the regression model presented in the second example can be found useful by researchers who are searching for relations between factors operating at the same level (see also Chapter 10). Furthermore, researchers within the field of EER who undertake longitudinal studies can make use of more advanced SEM models such as the latent change/growth model, and the advantages of longitudinal studies and the importance of using latent change models are also discussed in Chapter 5. Finally, this chapter focused on single-level SEM models, but based on the same assumptions, a number of researchers have developed methods to apply SEM on multilevel data (Goldstein and McDonald 1988; Muthén 1989; Muthén and Satorra 1989). Hox (2002) gives an overview of the different approaches to multilevel SEM. The basic idea for this technique is the decomposition of the individual scores in an individual component (the deviation of the individual score from the group's mean score) and a group component (the disaggregated group mean score) (Heck 2001). This decomposition is used to calculate two independent covariance matrices: a between- and a within-matrix. To test a multilevel SEM model, both matrices are used. Different authors describe this technique more extensively (Heck 2001; Heck and Thomas 2000; Hox 2002; Muthén 1994; Stapleton 2006). Multilevel SEM models can especially help EER to develop and test its theoretical models further since the current EER theoretical models refer both to direct and indirect effects of school-level factors on student learning outcomes. Some studies employing this technique have been undertaken (de Maeyer *et al.* 2007; Palardy 2008) and their results are promising for the further theoretical development of EER.

References

Arbuckle, J.L. (2006) *Amos 7.0 user's guide*, Chicago: SPSS.

Bentler, P.M. (2004) *EQS 6.1 structural equations program manual*, Encino, CA: Multivariate Software.

Bentler, P.M. and Weeks, D.G. (1980) 'Linear structural equations with latent variables', *Psychometrika*, 45(3): 289–308.

Bollen, K.A. (1989) *Structural equations with latent variables*, New York: Wiley.

Browne, M.W. and Mels, M.G. (1990) *RAMONA user's guide*, Columbus: Department of Psychology, Ohio State University.

Byrne, B. (1998) *Structural Equation Modeling with LISREL, PRELIS, and SIMPLIS: Basic concepts, applications and programming*, Mahwah, NJ: Lawrence Erlbaum.

Creemers, B.P.M. and Kyriakides, L. (2008) *The dynamics of educational effectiveness: A contribution to policy, practice and theory in contemporary schools*, London: Routledge.

De Maeyer, S., Rymenans, R., Van Petegem, P., van den Bergh, H. and Rijlaarsdam, G. (2007) 'Educational leadership and pupil achievement: The choice of a valid conceptual model to test effects in school effectiveness research', *School Effectiveness and School Improvement*, 18(2): 125–45.

Goldstein, H. and McDonald, R. (1988) 'A general model for the analysis of multilevel data', *Psychometrika*, 53: 455–67.

Hayashi, K. and Marcoulides, G.A. (2006) 'Examining identification issues in factor analysis', *Structural Equation Modeling*, 13(4): 631–45.

Heck, R.A. and Marcoulides, G.A. (1989) 'Examining the generalizability of administrative personnel allocation decisions', *The Urban Review*, 21(1): 51–62.

Heck, R.A. and Marcoulides, G.A. (1996) 'School culture and performance: Testing the invariance of an organizational model', *School Effectiveness and School Improvement*, 7(1): 76–106.

Heck, R.H. (2001) 'Multilevel modelling with SEM', in G.A. Marcoulides and R.E. Schumacker (eds) *New developments and techniques in structural equation modeling* 89–127, Mahwah, NJ/London: Lawrence Erlbaum Associates Publishers.

Heck, R.H. and Thomas, S.L. (2000) *An introduction to multilevel modeling techniques,* Mahwah, NJ: Lawrence Erlbaum Associates.

Hershberger, L.S. (2003) 'The growth of Structural Equation Modeling: 1994–2001', *Structural Equation Modeling,* 10(1): 35–46.

Hox, J. (2002) *Multilevel analysis. Techniques and applications,* Mahwah, NJ/London: Lawrence Earlbaum Associates Publishers.

Hu, L.T. and Bentler, P.M. (1999) 'Cutoff criteria for fit indices in covariance structure analysis. Conventional criteria versus new alternatives', *Structural Equation Modeling,* 6: 1–55.

Jöreskog, K. and Sörbom, D. (1984) *LISREL VI: Analysis of linear structural relationships by maximum likelihood, instrumental variables, and least squares methods,* 3rd edn, Mooresville, IN: Scientific Software.

Jöreskog, K. and Sörbom, D. (1993) *LISREL 8: Structural equation modeling with the SIMPLIS command language,* Hillsdale, NJ: Lawrence Erlbaum Associates.

Joreskog, K. and Sorbom, D. (1996) *LISREL 8: User's reference guide,* Lincolnwood, IL: SSI.

MacCallum, R. (1986) 'Specification searches in covariance structure modeling', *Psychological Bulletin,* 100: 107–20.

Marcoulides, G.A. (1989) 'The application of Generalizability Theory to observational studies', *Quality & Quantity,* 23(2): 115–27.

Marcoulides, G. and Drezner, Z. (2001) 'Specification searches in structural equation modeling with a genetic algorithm. New developments and techniques in structural equation modeling', in G.A. Marcoulides and R.E. Schumacker (eds) *New developments and techniques in structural equation modeling,* Mahwah, NJ: Lawrence Erlbaum Associates Publishers, pp. 247–68.

Marcoulides, G.A., Drezner, Z. and Schumacker, R.E. (1998) 'Model specification searches in Structural Equation Modeling using Tabu search', *Structural Equation Modeling,* 5(4): 365–76.

Marcoulides, G.A. and Heck, R. (1993) 'Organizational culture and performance: Proposing and testing a model', *Organization Science,* 4(2): 209–25.

Marcoulides, G.A. and Hershberger, S.L. (1997) *Multivariate statistical methods: A first course,* Mahwah, NJ: Lawrence Erlbaum Associates.

McArdle, J.J. (1988) 'Dynamic but structural equation modeling of repeated measures data', in J.R. Nesselroade and R.B. Cattell (eds) *Handbook of multivariate experimental psychology,* 2nd edn, New York, NY: Plenum, pp. 561–614.

Muthén, B. (1989) 'Latent variable modeling in heterogeneous populations', *Psychometrika,* 54: 557–85.

Muthén, B. (1994) 'Multilevel covariance structure analysis', *Sociological Methods & Research,* 22: 376–98.

Muthén, L.K. and Muthén, B.O. (2006) *Mplus user's guide,* 4th edn, Los Angeles, CA: Muthén & Muthén.

Muthén, B.O. and Satorra, A. (1989) 'Multilevel aspects of varying parameters in structural models', in R.D. Bock (ed.) *Multilevel analysis of educational data,* San Diego, CA: Academic Press.

Neale, M.C., Boker, S.M., Xie, G. and Maes, H.H. (1999) *Mx: Statistical modelling*, 4th edn, Richmond, VA: Virginia Commonwealth University, Department of Psychiatry.

Nylund, K.L., Asparouhov, T. and Muthén, B.O. (2007) 'Deciding on the number of classes in mixture modelling: A Monte Carlo simulation', *Structural Equation Modeling*, 14(4): 535–69.

Palardy, G. (2008) 'Differential school effects among low, middle, and high social class composition schools: A multiple group, multilevel latent growth curve analysis', *School Effectiveness and School Improvement*, 19(1): 21–49.

Raykov, T. and Marcoulides, G.A. (2006) *A first course in structural equation modeling*, 2nd edn, Mahwah, NJ: Lawrence Erlbaum Associates.

Raykov, T. and Marcoulides, G.A. (2008) *An introduction to applied multivariate analysis*. Routledge: New York.

SAS Institute (1989) *SAS PROC CALIS user's guide*, Cary, NC: SAS Institute.

Schumacker, R.E. and Marcoulides, G.A. (1998). *Interaction and nonlinear effects in Structural Equation Modelling*. Mahwah, NJ: Lawrence Erlbaum.

Schwarz, G. (1978) 'Estimating the dimension of a model', *Ann. Statist.*, 6: 461–4.

Shipley, B. (2000) *Cause and correlations in biology: A user's guide to path analysis, structural equation and causal inferences*, Cambridge: Cambridge University Press.

Stapleton, L.M. (2006) 'Using multilevel structural equation modeling techniques with complex sample data', in G.R. Hancock and R.O. Mueller (eds) *Structural equation modeling: A second course* 345–84, Greenwich, CT: Information Age Publishing.

Steiger, J. (1995) 'SEPATH structural equation modelling', *Statistica*, 3: 3,539–689.

Chapter 13

Meta-analyses of effectiveness studies

Leonidas Kyriakides and Bert P.M. Creemers
University of Cyprus and University of Groningen (respectively)

The foundation of science is the accumulation of knowledge from the results of many studies. There are two steps to the accumulation of knowledge: (a) the analysis of results across relevant studies to establish the 'facts' – that is, the extent of consistency in results and the strength of evidence – and (b) the formation of theories to organize the consistent findings into a coherent and useful form to enhance understanding. Meta-analysis is concerned with the first step – that is, with the resolution of the basic 'facts' from a set of studies that all bear on the same relationship of interest. Meta-analysis is rapidly increasing in importance in the behavioural and social sciences because it offers a way to make sense of findings from a range of different studies conducted in different contexts. The increasing importance of meta-analysis is discussed in the first part of this chapter and special emphasis is given to using meta-analyses for testing the validity of theoretical models in EER. The second and third parts of this chapter are concerned with some practical suggestions on how to conduct a meta-analysis. Specifically, several different methods that can be used in order to select and classify studies are outlined in the second part of the chapter, whereas the use of multilevel modelling techniques to conduct meta-analyses in the field of effectiveness is discussed in the third part. The use of multilevel modelling techniques to conduct a meta-analysis is described in more detail by referring both to the principles underlying the use of this approach as well as to practical decisions that have to be taken in order to apply this approach. In the fourth part of this chapter, an example of a meta-analysis conducted in order to test the validity of the dynamic model of EER is given. The fact that this meta-analysis was guided by a specific theoretical framework enables us to see how researchers can deal with one of the main issues concerning coding the studies, taken into account for a meta-analysis, and at the same time contribute to the development of the theoretical framework of EER. For further discussion and another example, see Chapter 11 on multilevel modelling.

The importance of using meta-analyses

The goal in any science is the production of cumulative knowledge. Ultimately, this means the development and testing of theories that explain the phenomena that are the focus of the scientific area in question. One example is theories that identify the school factors associated with student achievement. Unless we can precisely calibrate relationships among variables (for example, leadership style or school climate and student achievement), we do not have the raw materials out of which to construct theories. There is nothing consistent for a theory to explain. For example, if the relationship between instructional leadership and student achievement varies capriciously across different studies from a strong positive to a strong negative correlation and everything between, we cannot begin to construct a theory of how leadership might affect achievement. This implies that there is a need for researchers in any field to conduct reviews of research and in particular meta-analyses (which are a more rigorous means of review) to examine and integrate the findings across studies and reveal the simpler patterns of relationships that underlie research literatures, thus providing a more robust basis for theory development. Moreover, meta-analysis can correct for the distorting effects of sampling error, measurement error and other artefacts that can produce the illusion of conflicting findings and obscure 'real' underlying patterns (Hunter and Schmidt 2004) by means of the calculation of average effect sizes for relationships.

It is important to note here that an *effect size* is a measure of the strength of the relationship between two variables in a *statistical population*, or a sample-based estimate of that quantity. Sample-based effect sizes are distinguished from test statistics used in hypothesis testing, in that they estimate the strength of an apparent relationship, rather than assigning a significance level reflecting whether the relationship could be due to chance. In scientific experiments and observational studies, it is often useful to know not only whether a relationship is statistically significant, but also the *size* of the observed relationship. In practical situations, effect sizes are helpful for making decisions, since a highly significant relationship may be uninteresting if its effect size is very small. For this reason, measures of effect size not only play an important role in statistical power analyses but also in meta-analyses that summarize findings from a specific area of research. More specifically, the effect size is a standardized measure of the effect of one variable on a dependent variable. For example, one can search for the effect of one intervention (treatment) on student outcomes. In this example, the effect size represents the change (measured in standard deviations) in an average student's outcome that can be expected if that student is given the treatment. Because effect sizes are standardized, they can be compared across studies. It is finally important to note that 'Cohen's d' is an effect size used to indicate the standardized difference between two means and is used, for example, to accompany t-test and ANOVA results. Cohen's d is widely used in meta-analysis and is defined as the difference between two means divided by a pooled standard deviation for the data. The pooled standard deviation is defined as follows:

$$s = \sqrt{\frac{(n_1 - 1)s_1^2 + (n_2 - 1)s_2^2}{n_1 + n_2}},$$

with S_k as the standard deviation for group k, for $k = 1, 2$.

Before meta-analysis, the usual way in which scientists made sense of research literature was by use of the narrative subjective review of literature. In many research literatures, there were not only conflicting findings but also large numbers of studies. This combination made the standard narrative subjective review a nearly impossible task. The answer, as developed in many narrative reviews, was what came to be called the 'myth of the perfect study'. Reviewers convinced themselves that most of the available studies were methodologically deficient and should not be considered in the review. These judgements of methodological deficiency were often based on idiosyncratic ideas. For example, textbook authors would often pick out what they considered to be the two or three 'best' studies and then base textbook conclusions on just those studies, discarding the vast bulk of the information in the literature.

In this context, the myth of the perfect study emerged. However, in reality, there are no perfect studies. All studies are conducted in a specific context (in both place and in time) and contain measurement errors in all measures used. Independent of measurement error, no measure in a study will have perfect construct validity (Cronbach 1990). Furthermore, there are typically other artefacts that can also distort study findings. Even if a hypothetical study suffered from none of these distortions, it would still contain sampling error, for example. Therefore, it can be claimed that no single study (or even a small number of studies) can provide an optimal basis for scientific conclusions about cumulative knowledge.

However, this does not mean that since there is no perfect study that all studies should be included in a meta-analysis. Only those studies that meet some basic quality criteria, such as the provision of information regarding the validity of the study, should be taken into account for a meta-analysis. Nevertheless, we do not support the idea that only studies using specific approaches, such as true experimental approaches, should be selected or given more emphasis than survey studies, as proposed by those who advocate the best-evidence approach (Slavin 1986, 1987; Chapter 6 in this volume), since reliance on 'perfect studies' does not provide a solution to researchers when they are confronted with the problem of conflicting research findings. On the contrary, characteristics of the studies used to conduct the meta-analysis (for example, research design employed, country-context, statistical techniques employed) can be taken into account, and researchers may try to find out the extent to which these characteristics can predict variation in observed effect sizes. The use of multilevel modelling techniques to provide answers to this question is recommended by this chapter. A brief description of this technique is also provided below.

The impact of meta-analysis on accumulation of knowledge

Looking at the history of the use of meta-analysis in the social sciences, one could observe that starting in the late 1970s, new methods of combining findings across studies on the same subject were developed. These methods were referred to collectively as meta-analysis, a term coined by Glass (1976). Applications of meta-analysis to accumulated research literatures (Schmidt and Hunter 1977) showed that research findings were not nearly as conflicting as had been previously thought (Cronbach 1975; Meehl 1978) and that useful and sound general conclusions could in fact be drawn from the systematic study of bodies of existing research. In fact, meta-analysis has even produced evidence that the cumulative weight of research findings in the behavioural sciences is typically as great as that in the physical sciences (Hedges 1987). The major lesson drawn during the last two decades from the attempts of researchers to conduct meta-analysis in different subject areas of social sciences is that many discoveries and advances in cumulative knowledge are being made not by those who do primary research studies but by those who use meta-analysis to discover the latent meaning of existing research literatures (Hunter and Schmidt 2004). It was also found that the meta-analytic process of cleaning up and making sense of research literatures not only reveals cumulative knowledge but also provides clearer directions about the remaining research needs, and so guides future research.

Reasons for conducting meta-analyses

Usually meta-analyses are conducted for two main reasons. First, researchers are interested in finding out at what certain stage is the cumulative knowledge in a field, and the main aim is to provide an insight into the state of the art that can be used by both researchers and practitioners. Second, researchers may also be interested in using the findings of a meta-analysis as an argument or starting point for building a theory or for designing further studies.

In the case of EER, a large number of reviews were conducted in the 1990s, but most of them did not follow the quantitative approach to estimate the average effect sizes of school factors on student achievement. As mentioned above, their main purpose was to provide the research community and policymakers with an indication of the state of the art of the field (Creemers and Reezigt 1996; Levine and Lezotte 1990; Sammons et al. 1995; Teddlie and Reynolds 2000). On the other hand, Scheerens and Bosker (1997) conducted for the first time a quantitative synthesis of effectiveness studies in order to determine the estimated effect size of variables mentioned in the school effectiveness literature on student outcomes. By applying this approach to the field of EER, a significant contribution to the knowledge base was made. Following this meta-analysis, a number of quantitative syntheses of studies were conducted that focused on either the impact of specific factors or on a group of factors operating at either the teacher or the school level (Creemers and Kyriakides 2008; Scheerens et al. 2005; Seidel and Shavelson 2007). Interest in policy and practice has driven the inclusion of specific educational factors such as leadership (Robinson et al. 2008; Witziers et al. 2003), parental involvement (Fan and Chen 2001; Jeynes 2007; Senechal and Young 2008), homework (Cooper et al. 2006) and class size (Goldstein *et al.* 2000) in a number of meta-analyses. However, these meta-analyses were not conclusive but resulted in diverse answers with respect to the impact of the factor under study on student outcome measures. For example, three meta-analyses revealed that leadership has only a very weak direct impact on student outcomes (Creemers and Kyriakides 2008; Scheerens *et al.* 2005; Witziers *et al.* 2003), whereas another recent meta-analysis claimed to find a very strong impact (Robinson *et al.* 2008). One of the reasons behind these discrepancies may be the use of different classification schemes and, especially, the fact that the last study lacks a clear theoretical framework for classifying variables included in the studies involved in the meta-analysis. Another possible reason concerns differences in the methods used to analyse the data that emerged from the studies that were included, especially since multilevel modelling techniques were used in all three earlier studies, where no support for the impact of leadership has been provided. By contrast, in the more recent meta-analysis study, not enough information was given about the processes that were used to estimate effect sizes. In this context, the next two parts of this chapter are concerned with the process of selecting studies and coding variables involved and with the methods that can be used to estimate effect sizes.

Conducting a meta-analysis: collecting and coding studies

Because of the expansion in interest in conducting meta-analyses over the last fifteen years, no single book can cover all aspects of meta-analysis. Therefore, this section does not cover all issues associated with the processes of locating, selecting, evaluating and coding studies (for further details on these aspects see Hall and Rosenthal 1995; Schmidt and Hunter 1998; Stock 1994). The material in this section is selective rather than comprehensive.

Selection of studies

Cooper (1998) illustrates how to conduct a thorough literature search, including through the use of conference papers, personal journals, libraries, electronic journals, research report reference lists, research bibliographies and reference databases (for example, using ERIC, ERA, PsycInfo, Social Science Citation Index). The limitations of computer-based literature searches are also acknowledged, and methods for assessing the adequacy and the completeness of a literature search have also been developed (Reed and Baxter 1994; Rosenthal 1994; Rothstein 2003). However, a main issue that has to be considered in the process of selecting studies refers to how one can deal with studies that have methodological weaknesses. Many reviewers wish to eliminate from their analyses studies that they perceive as having methodological inadequacies (Slavin 1986). However, this may not be as desirable as it might seem. The assertion of 'methodological inadequacy' always depends on theoretical assumptions about what might be methodologically 'appropriate' in a study. One could claim that these assumptions may not be well founded themselves, and it should at least be acknowledged that these assumptions are rarely tested in their own right. Those who 'believe' these methodological assumptions usually feel no need to test them. It should also be acknowledged that no research study can be tested against all possible counter-hypotheses, and this means that no study can be without any 'methodological inadequacy'.

However, methodological inadequacies do not always cause biased findings, and prior to the analysis of the full set of studies on the topic, it is difficult to identify when methodological inadequacies have caused biased findings and when they have not. Some reviewers are inclined to use the simple strategy of eliminating all studies believed to have methodological inadequacies. However, because most studies have some weaknesses, their reviews refer to inferences drawn from a very small number of studies deemed to be methodologically robust. In this chapter, it is argued that the hypothesis of methodological inadequacy should be tested in two ways. First, one should determine if the variation across all studies can be accounted for by sampling error and other artefacts, such as differences in reliability. If the variation is due to these artefacts, one could argue that there is no variance due to method-ological inadequacy. Second, if there is substantial variation across studies, then theoretically plausible moderator variables should be identified. If these moderator variables do not explain the variance in the reported effect sizes, then method-ological inadequacies may be present. If this is the case, the researchers should rate the internal and external validity of each study or code the characteristics of the studies that might produce inadequacy and identify the extent to which these characteristics of the studies included in the meta-analysis explain variation in the reported effect sizes.

Cooper (1998: 81–4) pointed out another reason for not excluding studies considered as methodologically weak. To make such decisions, evaluators must judge and rate each study on methodological quality. However, Cooper claimed that research on inter-rater agreement for judgements of research quality revealed that the average correlation coefficient between experienced evaluators is not higher than 0.50. This finding reveals that there is a substantial amount of subjectivity in assessments of methodological quality.

Obviously, the question of methodological weaknesses addressed above should be separated from the question of relevant and irrelevant studies. Relevant studies are those that search for the existence of a relationship between variables that are the focus of the meta-analysis. For example, if one is interested in the impact of teacher behaviour in the classroom upon student achievement, studies that report relationships between teacher behaviour in the classroom and parents' views about the effectiveness of teachers should be excluded because they are not looking at the impact of teacher behaviour in the classroom on student learning outcomes. Obviously, if enough such studies are encountered, researchers may also consider the possibility of conducting a separate meta-analysis that will be concerned with the impact of teacher behaviour in the classroom upon the perceived effectiveness of teachers by parents. Measures of different constructs of the dependent variable that is the focus of our meta-analysis should not be combined in the same meta-analysis, but if the researchers like to draw attention to the use of different constructs then different meta-analyses for each construct should be conducted and their results could be compared.

In general, meta-analyses that do not mix different independent variables are also likely to be more informative. However, the issue raised here has no simple answer. More specifically, one should bear in mind that measures that assess different constructs from the same perspective (for example, using frameworks arising from the trait theory to measure leadership style) may also assess the same construct from the perspective of another theory (for example, using frameworks arising from the situational theory to measure leadership). Furthermore, the second theory may represent an advantage in understanding the functioning of the independent variable. In this context, we draw attention to the results of the example meta-analysis given below, which uses different dependent variables by looking at studies that investigate the impact of school factors on different outcomes of schooling such as cognitive, psychomotor and affective disorders. This example did not reveal substantial variations in the impact of most factors upon student achievement when different outcomes were taken into account (Kyriakides et al. 2008). Therefore, the question of how varied the independent and dependent variable measures that are included in a meta-analysis should be is more complex than it appears at first glance. The answer depends on the specific hypotheses, theories and aims of the researcher(s) who conduct the meta-analysis. Glass et al. (1981) argued that there is nothing wrong with mixing apples and oranges, if the focus of the research interest is fruit. However, they also go beyond even the theory-based rationale supported here in arguing that it may be appropriate to include in the same meta-analysis independent and dependent variables that appear to be different constructs. Specifically, it is argued that such broad meta-analysis might be useful in summarizing the literature in broad strokes. However, here we argue, at least initially, meta-analyses in a given area within EER should be focused enough to correspond to the major constructs recognized by the researchers in this area. Then, as focused meta-analyses help us develop our understanding, we can move to conduct meta-analyses that may have a broader scope, especially if that is shown to be theoretically appropriate.

Coding studies

The process of coding data from primary studies is usually complex, tedious and time-consuming. It is, however, one of the most critical components of meta-analysis and it is essential that it be done appropriately and accurately. Stock (1994) and Orwin (1994) provided detailed discussions of the many considerations, decisions and subtasks that can be involved in coding information from each empirical study. First, the complexity of the coding needed depends on the hypotheses and purposes underlying the meta-analysis. For example, if the studies included in a meta-analysis differ on many dimensions and the meta-analysis focuses on several different relationships, the coding task will be quite complex. Similarly, the coding task will be complex if there is reason to believe that many particular study characteristics may affect its results. On the other hand, coding can be relatively easy in research literature where studies are quite similar in terms of the methods adopted, their population(s) and the constructs used to measure independent and dependent variables. In such a case, relatively few study characteristics may need to be coded, greatly reducing the scope of the coding task. This distinction bears on the issue of coder agreement. In this latter example, there is some evidence supporting the conclusion that inter-coder agreement and inter-coder reliability can be extremely high (Whetzel and McDaniel 1988). Moreover there is also some evidence supporting the view that even in more complex coding tasks (such as in our first example), the coder agreement and reliability have still commonly been quite good (Cooper 1998). Nevertheless, these arguements refer to the coding of more objective-specific aspects of studies rather than on judgments of the overall methodological quality of studies included in a meta-analysis. Finally, it is important to note that although readers can have access to different code schemes that have been used for conducting different types of meta-analyses (Hunter and Schmidt 2004), there is no illustrative coding scheme that can be taken as a perfect example, especially since each coding scheme should be tailored to the purposes of each specific meta-analysis.

Methods of meta-analysis: the use of multilevel modelling techniques

Although different methods are often used to conduct a quantitative synthesis of studies, the use of multilevel modelling techniques is recommended in this book especially since it can help explain variation in the reported effect sizes of different factors. By identifying sources that explain variation in the reported effect sizes of an effectiveness factor (moderators), the extent to which this factor can be considered generic is identified. For example, if variation in the reported effect sizes of a factor cannot be explained by the fact that the studies that are included in a meta-analysis were conducted in different countries, we could argue that this factor is more generic and its impact on student achievement can be viewed as independent of the country context. As a consequence, one could also claim that the results are likely to be relevant for countries that are not represented in the original studies. On the other hand, we could identify factors that have differential effects. For example, if variation in the reported effect sizes of a factor can be explained by the age group of students involved in the original studies, the factor is treated as more differential, meaning that it is seen as more important for specific age groups of students or phases of education. This approach is also in line with the multilevel structure of the theoretical models used to describe educational effectiveness (Creemers 1994; Scheerens 1992; Stringfield and Slavin

1992) and is thereby familiar to researchers within EER, and it can also give more efficient estimates of overall effect sizes and their standard errors.

Therefore, the approach described below is based on the assumption that it is important to identify the impact that the characteristics of each study may have on effect sizes. By providing answers to these research questions, we get a clear insight into the potential impact of independent variables upon the dependent variable of interest – for example, the extent to which the impact of specific teacher effectiveness factors depends on the criteria used for measuring effectiveness. If specific characteristics of the studies (such as the country where the study was conducted, the age group of students involved or the type of school) explain variation in the reported effect sizes, the theories might further be developed by acknowledging the impact of contextual factors.

The multilevel model can be applied to analyse the observed effects from studies and the sources of variance among the findings that emerge from different studies investigating the effect of a specific factor on a dependent variable such as student achievement (Raudenbush and Bryk 1985). Specifically, studies that are found to investigate the effect of a factor on student achievement can be considered to be a sample from the population of studies investigating the relationship between this factor and student achievement (where schools are nested within each study). Each study can then be viewed as an independent replication. This concept could be used, but it does not solve the problem of multiple results from one study, such as when effects are reported for more than one outcome of schooling (for example, mathematics and language achievement or mathematics and development of positive attitudes towards the school) while using the same sample of schools and students. To deal with this problem, the two-level model for meta-analysis can be expanded to a three-level model. As a consequence, the highest level of the studies is then referred to as the 'across-replication' level, and the multiple results within a study as the 'within-replication' level. The main advantage of this statistical meta-analysis is that the information from each study is weighted by the reliability of the information, in this case the sample size. Moreover, the multilevel model helps us identify factors that predict variation in observed effect sizes of each of the main school-level factors on student achievement that emerge from this synthesis of school effectiveness studies. Therefore, differences in reported effect sizes are modelled as a function of study characteristics, such as differences in the type of outcomes used to measure student achievement, the level of education over which the study was conducted, and the nature of the study. Some further information about the statistical modelling technique is given below.

It is first important to indicate that the multilevel model for the meta-analysis (Raudenbush and Bryk 1985; Raudenbush 1994), starting with the 'within-replications' model, is given by the following equation:

$$d_{rs} = \delta_{rs} + e_{rs}.$$

The above equation implies that the effect size d in replication r in study s (d_{rs}) is an estimate of the population parameter (δ_{rs}) and the associated sampling error (e_{rs}). The sampling error is attributed to the fact that in each replication, only a sample of schools is studied. As far as the between-replications model is concerned, the following equation is used:

$$\delta_{rs} = \delta_{s} + u_{rs}.$$

In the above model, it is acknowledged that the true replication effect size is a function of the effect size in study s and sampling error u_{rs}. Finally, the between-studies model is formulated as follows:

$$\delta_{s} = \delta_{0} + v_{s}.$$

The above formula basically implies that the true unknown effect size as estimated in study s (δ_{s}) is a function of the effect size across studies (δ_{0}) with random sampling error v_{s}, which is attributed to the fact that the studies are sampled from a population of studies.

To assess the effects of particular study characteristics, we extend the between-replication model to one that takes into account the effect of explanatory variables that refer to the special characteristics of each study. Since the explanatory variables are likely to be grouping variables, they can be entered into the model as dummies, with one of the groups as baseline. For example, within EER it is possible to classify studies into groups according to the phase of education (for example, pre-primary, primary, secondary) in which each of them took place. In such a case, we extend the between-replication model into the model shown below, where the level of education is taken into account:

$$\delta_{rs} = \delta_{0} + \gamma_{1} \text{ pre-primary}_{rs} + \gamma_{2} \text{ secondary}_{rs} + v_{s},$$

where for

pre-primary 0 = primary and 1 = pre-primary

secondary 0 = primary and 1 = secondary.

Where the researcher is looking for the impact of other study characteristics (for example, the country where the study was conducted or the design of the original studies) other relevant dummy variables can be added to the above equation. Finally, we stress the importance of conducting the multilevel meta-analyses twice. In the first case, all the original studies are included, whereas in the second case, the so-called 'sensitivity analysis', the outliers are removed from the samples to check the robustness of the findings.

Conducting meta-analysis to test and develop theories on educational effectiveness

In this chapter, it is argued that meta-analyses can also be conducted to test theories on educational effectiveness. By following this approach, the theoretical framework that is tested can be used to generate the structure upon which the selection of studies and the classification of the factors/variables used within each study are based. A meta-analysis using this approach is presented below. It is shown that this approach helps researchers not only to integrate the findings across studies but also to test the validity of a theory in a systematic way. Thus, such meta-analyses are very likely to contribute significantly in providing robust answers to policymakers and to establishing a better basis for theory development in the area of educational effectiveness. Moreover, this type of meta-analysis may reveal which aspects of a theory that is tested have not yet been addressed in primary studies and can therefore identify the need for future research on particular topics. In this context, the methods and the main results of a meta-analysis that uses the dynamic model as a theoretical framework are presented below. Implications for further research on developing and expanding the model are identified.

A quantitative synthesis of studies searching for school factors: testing the validity of the dynamic model at the school level

The meta-analysis reported here used the dynamic model of educational effectiveness (Creemers and Kyriakides 2008) as a framework in order to organize and structure the list of factors reported in the studies included in the review. The dynamic model was developed in order to establish strong links between EER and improvement of practice and refers to specific factors, which are presented below. The review used a quantitative approach to synthesize the findings of multinational research studies conducted during the last 20 years in order to estimate the effect size of various school effectiveness factors on student achievement. The focus is on the substantive findings that emerged from the meta-analysis, specifically, the extent to which the findings of the review justify the importance of the school factors included in the dynamic model. In this way, the meta-analysis reported here not only provides answers about the importance of isolated factors, but also attempts to contribute to the establishment of the theoretical model by generating evidence supporting some factors of the model and pointing out possible weaknesses. It also attempts to identify the factors (or moderators) that account for the variation between studies in reported effect sizes. This is due to the fact that the effect sizes of studies involved in a meta-analysis are very likely to vary due to differences in procedures, instrumentation, study contexts and treatments. Identifying the impact that these factors have on effect sizes gives a clearer insight into the potential impact of school factors because it helps to clarify the conditions under which each of them is able to influence effectiveness. For this reason, the extent to which the impact of the various factors depends on the criteria used for measuring effectiveness is identified. Thus, this analysis can reveal school factors that may be termed generic and/or others that have differential effects.

School factors in the dynamic model

The dynamic model accounts for the fact that effectiveness studies conducted in several countries have indicated that influences on student achievement are multilevel (Teddlie and Reynolds 2000). As a result, the dynamic model refers to factors operating at the four levels shown in Figure 13.1. The teaching and learning situation and the roles of the two main actors (that is, teacher and student) are analysed. Above these two levels, the dynamic model also refers to school- and context-level factors. It is expected that school-level factors influence the teaching-learning situation through the development and evaluation of school policies on teaching and on creating a learning environment. The context level refers to the influence of the educational system at large, especially through development and evaluation of the educational policy at the regional and/or national level. The model also accounts for the teaching and learning situation being influenced by the wider educational context in which students, teachers and schools are expected to operate. Factors such as the values of the society in terms of learning and the importance attached to education may play an important role both in shaping teacher and student expectations as well as in the development of perceptions of various stakeholders about what constitutes effective teaching practice.

Since this meta-analysis is concerned with school-level factors, a description of the dynamic model at the school level is provided below. Figure 13.1 reveals that the definition of the school level is based on the assumption that school factors are expected to influence classroom-level factors, especially teaching practices. Therefore, the dynamic model refers to factors at the school level that are related to the key concepts of quantity of teaching, quality of teaching and provision of learning opportunities, which are the same factors used to define the classroom-level factors (Creemers and Kyriakides 2006). Specifically, the dynamic model emphasizes two main aspects of school policy that are hypothesized to affect learning at both the teacher and student level: (a) school policy for teaching and (b) school policy for creating a learning environment. These factors do not imply that each school should simply develop formal documents to articulate and install its policy; instead, the factors concerned with the school policy mainly refer to actions taken by the school to help teachers and other stakeholders have a clear understanding of what is expected from them. Support offered to teachers and other stakeholders to implement the school policy is also an aspect of these two factors.

Based on the assumption that the search for improvement underpins and defines the essence of a successful organization in the modern world (Kyriakides

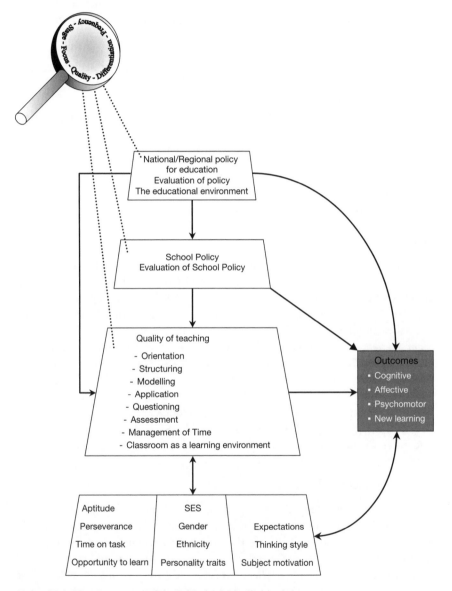

Figure 13.1 The dynamic model of educational effectiveness

and Campbell 2004), we examine the processes and the activities that take place in the school to improve teaching practice and the learning environment. It is for this reason, that the processes used to evaluate school policy for teaching and the learning environment are also investigated. The following four factors at the school level are included in the model:

- School policy for teaching and actions taken for improving teaching practice.
- Policy for creating a school learning environment and actions taken for improving the school learning environment.
- Evaluation of school policy for teaching and of actions taken to improve teaching.
- Evaluation of the school learning environment.

Methods used in the meta-analysis testing the dynamic model

Selection of studies

The following databases were examined to identify school effectiveness studies: Educational Resources Information Centre (ERIC), Social Sciences Citation Index, Educational Administration Abstracts, SCOPUS, Pro Quest 5000 and PsycArticles. We also paged through volumes of educational peer-reviewed journals with interest in EER, such as the journals: *School Effectiveness and School Improvement, British Educational Research Journal, Oxford Review of Education* and *Learning Environment Research*. Finally, relevant reviews of school effectiveness studies (Creemers and Reezigt 1996; Fan and Chen 2001; Fraser *et al.* 1987; Hallinger and Heck 1998; Levine and Lezotte 1990; Sammons *et al.* 1995; Scheerens and Bosker 1997) and handbooks focused on effectiveness (Teddlie and Reynolds 2000; Townsend *et al.* 1999) were also examined for references to empirical studies.

Criteria for including studies

The next step consisted of selecting studies from those collected in the first stage. The following three criteria for including studies were used. First, we only selected studies conducted during the last 20 years that had been purposely designed to investigate the effect of school factors on student outcomes. Second, these studies had to include explicit and valid measures of student achievement in relation to cognitive, affective or even to psychomotor outcomes of schooling. Third, studies that used more global criteria for academic outcomes, such as drop-out rates, grade retention and enrolment in top universities, were also selected. Finally, the meta-analysis reported here focused on studies investigating the *direct effects* of school effectiveness factors on student achievement.

Analysis of data

The multilevel model was applied to analyse the observed effects of each study and the sources of variation among the findings that emerged from different studies investigating the effect of the same school-level factor on student achievement (Raudenbush and Bryk 1985). Specifically, the procedure presented earlier was followed and the effects of the study characteristics were examined.

Main findings

Table 13.1 provides information about the characteristics of studies investigating the relation of different school effectiveness factors to student achievement. In order to demonstrate the empirical support given to the factors of the dynamic model and the possible importance of factors yet to be included, school factors were classified into those included in the dynamic model and those not included. The average effect size of each factor is also provided. The values of the average effect sizes of the school effectiveness factors support the argument that effective schools should develop a policy on teaching as well as a policy on establishing a learning environment. The six factors that belong to these two overarching school-level factors of the dynamic model were found to have an effect larger than 0.15. On the other hand, not enough data are available to support the importance of investigating the evaluation mechanisms that the schools develop to examine their own policies on these matters. The lack of studies investigating the evaluation mechanisms of schools and the resulting improvement decisions may be attributable to the fact that only 8 out of 67 studies are longitudinal studies that took place for more than two school years.

The last part of Table 13.1 refers to the average effect size of factors not included in the dynamic model. We can see that a relatively high percentage of studies (42.0 per cent) measured the relationship between leadership and student achievement. However, the average effect size of this factor is very small. This implies that leadership has a very weak direct effect on student achievement. Moreover, the figures in this part of the table do not reveal support from this meta-analysis for including any other school factor in the dynamic model.

The next step in the meta-analysis was to use the multilevel approach to estimate the mean effect sizes of the following five factors: (a) policy on school teaching, (b) partnership policy (that is, the relations of school with community, parents and advisors), (c) collaboration and interaction between teachers, (d) leadership, and (e) school climate and culture. The multilevel analysis allows us to estimate the mean effect size of the first three factors of the dynamic model as well as the effect size of the two factors not included in the dynamic model that received significant attention in educational research (that is, leadership and school climate and culture). In this way, we might then be able to justify our decision to include the first three factors in the model and exclude the other two. This approach also allowed us to examine whether the observed effect sizes vary across and within studies. Table 13.2 shows the results of analyses that

Table 13.1 Characteristics of studies investigating the effect of school-level factors on student achievement and types of effects identified

School-level factors	Average effect	Number of studies*	Outcomes**			Studies per sector			
			Cogni-tive	Affec-tive	Psycho-logical	Primary	Secondary	Both	Other
FACTORS INCLUDED IN THE DYNAMIC MODEL									
1) Policy on teaching									
A) Quantity of teaching	0.16	18	14	6	2	9	6	2	1
B) Opportunity to learn	0.15	13	11	3	2	7	4	1	1
C) Quality of teaching	0.17	26	22	4	1	13	7	5	1
C.1) Student assessment	0.18	12	10	4	0	8	3	1	0
2) Evaluation of policy on teaching	0.13	6	8	1	0	4	1	1	0
3) Policy on the school learning environment									
A) Collaboration	0.16	31	27	5	1	11	14	6	0
B) Partnership policy	0.17	21	14	9	0	8	10	3	0
4) Evaluation of policy on the school learning environment	—	0	0	0	0	0	0	0	0
FACTORS NOT INCLUDED IN THE DYNAMIC MODEL									
1) Leadership	0.07	29	22	10	0	16	8	4	1
2) School climate	0.12	24	22	5	0	9	8	6	1
3) Autonomy	0.06	3	3	0	0	1	1	1	0
4) Teacher empowerment	0.17	2	2	0	0	0	2	0	0
5) Resources and working conditions (for example, salary)	0.14	13	10	3	1	7	4	1	1
6) Admission policy, selection tracking	0.18	5	4	1	0	0	4	1	0
7) Staff experience (teachers and headteachers)	0.08	4	4	0	0	1	0	3	0
8) Job satisfaction	0.09	3	3	0	0	1	1	0	1

*Some studies reported more than one observed effect.

**Some studies search for effects on more than one type of schooling outcome.

Table 13.2 Predicting difference in effect sizes of each of the five school factors

Predictors	Policy on teaching Estimate (p value)	Policy on SLE: Partnership policy Estimate (p value)	Policy on SLE: Collaboration between teachers Estimate (p value)	Leadership Estimate (p value)	School climate and school culture Estimate (p value)
Intercept	0.18 (0.001)	0.17 (0.001)	0.16 (0.001)	0.07 (0.001)	0.12 (0.001)
Language	−0.02 (0.778)	−0.02 (0.710)	0.01 (0.834)	−0.01 (0.812)	−0.02 (0.792)
Drop out	0.01 (0.482)	0.02 (0.549)	0.01 (0.793)	0.00 (0.962)	0.02 (0.781)
Non-cognitive	−0.05 (0.005)*	−0.06 (0.041)*	0.00 (0.951)	0.04 (0.082)	−0.02 (0.542)
Secondary	−0.03 (0.117)	−0.04 (0.058)	0.01 (0.741)	−0.05 (0.038)*	0.03 (0.41)
The Netherlands	−0.04 (0.141)	0.01 (0.812)	0.03 (0.179)	−0.03 (0.042)*	−0.07 (029)*
United Kingdom	0.02 (0.791)	0.00 (0.955)	0.01 (0.817)	0.01 (0.816)	0.00 (0.971)
Asian countries	0.02 (0.548)	0.05 (0.041)*	0.04 (0.042)*	0.04 (0.102)	0.03 (0.041)*
All other countries	0.02 (0.729)	0.01 (0.805)	N.A.	0.04 (0.115)	0.00 (0.958)
Longitudinal	0.02 (0.005)*	0.00 (0.901)	0.01 (0.829)	0.02 (0.812)	0.01 (0.712)
Experimental	N.A.	0.03 (0.011)*	0.00 (0.919)	N.A.	N.A.
Outlier	N.A.	0.01 (0.887)	N.A.	−0.03 (0.048)*	0.04 (0.050)*
Uni-level vs. multilevel	−0.06 (0.103)	0.02 (0.656)	0.01 (0.804)	0.01 (0.789)	0.02 (0.612)

N.A.: It was not possible to test the effect of this explanatory variable since almost all the studies that assessed the impact of this factor belong to only one of the two groups that are compared.

*A statistically significant effect at level 0.05 was identified.

attempted to predict differences between effect sizes with such study character-istics as criteria of measuring effectiveness (that is, the use of different outcomes of schooling for measuring effectiveness), sector of education, country, study design employed, and the use of multilevel rather than uni-level statistical techniques.

The following observations arise from Table 13.2. First, the results show that moderators only had infrequent significant relationships with effect size. Moreover, no moderator was found to have a significant relationship with the effect size of all five factors. This provides support for viewing the school factors as more generic in nature. In regard to the effect of the two factors not included in the dynamic model, this table also reveals that their effect sizes are very small and also suggests that in some countries they do not even exist. For example, in the Netherlands, the effect size of leadership is nearly zero and the effect size of school climate is very small (that is, smaller than 0.06). It is also important to note that the sensitivity study revealed that the effect of leadership is greatly reduced when outliers are removed from the sample. Although this implies that there is still a positive and statistically significant relationship between leadership and student outcomes, the indicator loses much of its relevance. On the other hand, the sensitivity study suggested that the factors from the dynamic model do remain relevant even when outliers are removed.

Implications for the contribution of meta-analysis to EER

Methodological implications for conducting meta-analyses can be drawn from the example presented above. However, it is also important to note that meta-analyses are usually conducted for two main reasons. First, researchers are interested in appraising the cumulative existing knowledge in a field, and the main aim is therefore to give specific answers about the effect of certain factors or of specific interventions on some other variables. In this way, both policymakers and practitioners can make use of the results. For example, a meta-analysis that is concerned with the impact of different forms of homework on student achievement can help stakeholders to develop policies at the national or local level in order to improve teaching practice. Second, researchers may also be interested to use the findings to build a new theory or for designing future studies. However, the approach used in the multilevel meta-analysis reported here was relatively new. For the purposes of this meta-analysis, we used a theoretical framework based on the dynamic model to guide the structure and classification of factors and to interpret the findings. Based on the results, evidence supporting the validity of this framework was generated and suggestions for the further development of the model emerged. It can, therefore, be claimed that using this approach to conduct meta-analyses helped us not only to integrate the findings across studies, but also to systematically test the validity of a theory and thereby better contribute to theory development in the area of educational effectiveness.

The theoretical framework used for this meta-analysis also refers to relatively new factors and for the first time introduces a multidimensional approach to measuring the functioning of school factors. Due to the fact that a theoretical model is expected to introduce new ways of understanding educational effectiveness, some limitations of using meta-analysis to test a theoretical model may emerge. For example, the meta-analysis reported here could not test the validity of the two school-level factors concerned with the school evaluation mechanisms since relevant studies were not identified. However, this meta-analysis points to the importance of examining the effects of school evaluation mechanisms in a more systematic way rather than by looking at student results alone. The two relatively new school-level factors included in the dynamic model (and the operational definition attached to them) may have significant implications for the design of future effectiveness studies. Specifically, the fact that the dynamic model emphasizes actions taken to evaluate and change school policy seems to imply that longitudinal studies should be conducted to measure the impact of these factors on the effectiveness status of schools rather than investigating the relation between the existing practice and student achievement. Thus, this chapter not only drew attention to the use of meta-analysis for the synthesis of research, but also for the development of theoretical frameworks of EER. Implications for designing better studies that are able to describe the complex nature of effectiveness can also be drawn.

References

Cooper, H. (1998) *Synthesizing research: A guide for literature reviews*, Thousand Oaks, CA: Sage.

Cooper, H., Robinson, J.C. and Patall, E.A. (2006) 'Does homework improve academic achievement? A synthesis of research, 1987–2003', *Review of Educational Research*, 76(1): 1–62.

Creemers, B.P.M. (1994) *The effective classroom*, London: Cassell.

Creemers, B.P.M. and Kyriakides, L. (2006) 'A critical analysis of the current approaches to modelling educational effectiveness: The importance of establishing a dynamic model', *School Effectiveness and School Improvement*, 17(3): 347–66.

Creemers, B.P.M. and Kyriakides, L. (2008) *The dynamics of educational effectiveness: A contribution to policy, practice and theory in contemporary schools*, London: Routledge.

Creemers, B.P.M. and Reezigt, G.J. (1996) 'School level conditions affecting the effectiveness of instruction', *School Effectiveness and School Improvement*, 7(3): 197–228.

Cronbach, L.J. (1975) 'Beyond the two disciplines of scientific psychology revisited', *American Psychologist*, 30: 116–27.

Cronbach, L.J. (1990) *Essentials of Psychological Testing*, 3rd edn, New York: Harper & Row.

Fan, X.T. and Chen, M. (2001) 'Parental involvement and students' academic achievement: A meta-analysis', *Educational Psychology Review*, 13(1): 1–22.

Fraser, B.J., Walberg, H.J., Welch, W.W. and Hattie, J.A. (1987) 'Syntheses of educational productivity research', *International Journal of Educational Research*, 11: 145–252.

Glass, G.V. (1976) 'Secondary and meta-analysis of research', *Educational Researcher*, 11: 3–8.

Glass, G.V., McGraw, B. and Smith, M.L. (1981) *Meta-analysis in social research*, Beverly Hills, CA: Sage.

Goldstein, H., Yang, M., Omar, R., Turner, R. and Thompson, S. (2000) 'Meta-analysis using multilevel models with an application to the study of class size effects', *Journal of the Royal Statistical Society Series C – Applied Statistics*, 49: 399–412.

Hall, J.A. and Rosenthal, R. (1995) 'Interpreting and evaluating meta-analysis', *Evaluation and the Health Professions*, 18: 393–407.

Hallinger, P. and Heck, H.R. (1998) 'Exploring the principal's contribution to school effectiveness: 1980–1995', *School Effectiveness and School Improvement*, 9(2): 157–91.

Hedges, L.V. (1987) 'How hard is hard science, how soft is soft science: The empirical cumulativeness of research', *American Psychologist*, 42: 443–55.

Hunter, J.E. and Schmidt, F.L. (2004) *Methods of meta-analysis: Correcting error and bias in research findings*, 2nd edn, Thousand Oaks, CA: Sage.

Jeynes, W.H. (2007) 'The relationship between parental involvement and urban secondary school student academic achievement – A meta-analysis', *Urban Education*, 42(1): 82–110.

Kyriakides, L. and Campbell, R.J. (2004) 'School self-evaluation and school improvement: A critique of values and procedures', *Studies in Educational Evaluation*, 30(1): 23–36.

Kyriakides, L., Creemers, B.P.M. and Charalambous, A. (2008) 'Effective schools in facing and preventing bullying', paper presented at the EARLI SIG 18 Conference, Frankfurt Main, Germany.

Levine, D.U. and Lezotte, L.W. (1990) *Unusually effective schools: A review and analysis of research and practice*, Madison, WI: National Centre for Effective Schools Research and Development.

Meehl, P.E. (1978) 'Theoretical risks and tabular asterisks: Sir Karl, Sir Ronald and the slow progress of soft psychology', *Journal of Applied Psychology*, 46: 806–34.

Orwin, R.G. (1994) 'Evaluating coding decisions', in H. Cooper and L.V. Hedges (eds) *Handbook of research synthesis*, New York: Russell Sage, pp. 139–62.

Raudenbush, S.W. (1994) 'Random effects models', in H. Cooper and L.V. Hedges (eds), *The handbook of research synthesis*, New York: Russell Sage, pp. 301–23.

Raudenbush, S.W. and Bryk, A.S. (1985) 'Empirical Bayes meta-analysis', *Journal of Educational Statistics*, 10: 75–98.

Reed, J.G. and Baxter, P.M. (1994) 'Using reference database', in H. Cooper and L.V. Hedges (eds) *The handbook of research synthesis*, New York: Russell Sage, pp. 57–70.

Robinson, V.M.J., Lloyd, C.A. and Rowe, K.J. (2008) 'The impact of leadership on student outcomes: An analysis of the differential effects of leadership types', *Educational Administration Quarterly*, 44(5): 635–74.

Rosenthal, R. (1994) 'Parametric measures of effect size', in H. Cooper and L.V. Hedges (eds) *The handbook of research synthesis*, New York: Russell Sage, pp. 231–45.

Rothstein, H.R. (2003) 'Progress is our most important product: Contributions of validity generalization and meta-analysis to the development and communications of knowledge in I/O psychology', in K.R. Murphy (ed.) *Validity generalization: A critical review*, Mahwah, NJ: Lawrence Erlbaum, pp. 115–54.

Sammons, P., Hillman, J. and Mortimore, P. (1995) *Key characteristics of effective schools: A review of school effectiveness research*, London: Office for Standards in Education and Institute of Education.

Scheerens, J. (1992) *Effective schooling: Research, theory and practice*, London: Cassell.

Scheerens, J. and Bosker, R.J. (1997) *The foundations of educational effectiveness,* Oxford: Pergamon.

Scheerens, J., Seidel, T., Witziers, B., Hendriks, M. and Doornekamp, G. (2005) *Positioning and validating the supervision framework,* University of Twente: Department of Educational Organisation and Management.

Schmidt, F.L. and Hunter, J.E. (1977) 'Development of a general solution to the problem of validity generalization', *Journal of Applied Psychology,* 62: 529–40.

Schmidt, F.L. and Hunter, J.E. (1998) 'The validity and utility of selection methods in personnel psychology: Practical and theoretical implications of 85 years of research findings', *Psychological Bulletin,* 124: 262–74.

Seidel, T. and Shavelson, R.J. (2007) 'Teaching effectiveness research in the past decade: The role of theory and research design in disentangling meta-analysis results', *Review of Educational Research,* 77(4): 454–99.

Senechal, M. and Young, L. (2008) 'The effect of family literacy interventions on children's acquisition of reading from kindergarten to grade 3: A meta analytic review', *Review of Educational Research,* 78(4): 880–907.

Slavin, R.E. (1986) 'Best-evidence synthesis: An alternative to meta-analytic and traditional reviews', *Educational Researcher,* 15(9): 5–11.

Slavin, R.E. (1987) 'Ability grouping and student achievement in elementary schools: A best-evidence synthesis', *Review of Educational Research,* 57: 293–326.

Stock, W.A. (1994) 'Systematic coding for research synthesis', in H. Cooper and L.V. Hedges (eds) *The handbook of research synthesis,* New York: Russell Sage, pp. 125–38.

Stringfield, S.C. and Slavin, R.E. (1992) 'A hierarchical longitudinal model for elementary school effects', in B.P.M. Creemers and G.J. Reezigt (eds) *Evaluation of educational effectiveness,* Groningen: ICO, pp. 35–69.

Teddlie, C. and Reynolds, D. (2000) *The international handbook of school effectiveness research,* London: Falmer Press.

Townsend, T., Clarke, P. and Ainscow, M. (eds) (1999) *Third millennium schools. A world of difference in school effectiveness and school improvement,* Lisse: Swets & Zeitlinger.

Whetzel, D.L. and McDaniel, M.A. (1988) 'Reliability of validity generalization data bases', *Psychological Reports,* 63: 131–34.

Witziers, B., Bosker, J.R. and Kruger, L.M. (2003) 'Educational leadership and student achievement: The elusive search for an association', *Educational Administration Quarterly,* 39(3): 398–42.

Methodological advances and EER

Retrospect and prospect

Chapter 14

Conclusions for the development of EER

Introduction

In this book we have sought to provide an authoritative account of the history and the current state of the methodology of EER and the way it has been developed and applied in research and evaluation to study teacher and institutional effects. By doing so, we have attempted to promote the further development of theory and research in educational effectiveness, which, at least in part, depends on the further development of appropriate research methodology to study the multilevel and complex interlinked features of educational systems and institutions. At the same time, it has been shown that the knowledge base of EER and its attempt to establish theoretical models continue to offer several challenges to researchers in the design of methodologically appropriate studies, such as ways of analysing clustered and longitudinal data. Next to this more theoretical perspective of the book, we have discussed the appropriate use of more advanced and recently developed research techniques by educational effectiveness researchers. Our aim was to provide sufficient background for students and researchers to gain a better understanding of the main features of each method and to discuss examples of the use of each method in the context of EER. In this way, both students and researchers can be helped to refine their own research agendas and identify appropriate methods that can be used for the design of their studies and the analysis of their data.

Therefore, in the last part of this volume, we seek to link the themes of the first two parts of the book by relating the further development of theory and research in educational effectiveness (presented in Part A) to current trends and advances in the methodology of research in the social sciences, discussed in Part B. We also draw on (and link together) the main conclusions that emerged from the various chapters of the book to create a conceptual map for conducting methodologically appropriate effectiveness studies, which we believe will contribute to the future development of EER. Finally, a number of research topics are identified that are likely to prove fruitful avenues of enquiry for further advances in the EER knowledge base.

Main issues emerging from Part A and Part B

In the first part of the book, it was shown that EER has benefited greatly from the gradual evolution and application of more methodologically rigorous approaches in conducting effectiveness studies. For example, some of the studies conducted during the third and fourth phases of EER were only made possible due to further advances in research methodology, such as the use of advanced multilevel modelling and Structural Equation Modelling techniques. As a result we can identify *reciprocal improvements* in both the methodology of EER and in the establishment of the knowledge base of the field. Part of this ongoing process of gradual improvement has involved a movement away from raising largely descriptive questions concerned with the characteristics of effective and ineffective schools to searching for direct and indirect associative and causal relations between factors and learning outcomes. As a consequence of this shift in the research agenda of EER, the methodological issue of how to conceptualize and measure *causality* is becoming a critical one for the future development of the research methods used within EER. Moreover, a stronger emphasis on establishing *theories* to promote greater understanding of the processes of educational effectiveness has emerged. However, this again highlights the need for further development of the methodology of EER in order to test, further refine and expand these theoretical models. Furthermore, in the last chapter of Part A, it was argued that EER should ultimately attempt to influence policy and practice by establishing *theory-driven* and *evidence-based* approaches to school improvement. It was also argued that EER is likely to have a greater impact on policy and practice if theory-driven evaluation studies based on theoretical models of EER are conducted. A framework for conducting such studies was provided based on methodological advances that are also useful for conducting basic research on effectiveness. It is expected that the results of such evaluation studies will also contribute to the further theoretical development of the field.

In the second part of the book, the use of different types of research design was discussed. It was shown that different research methods can address specific research questions in a more or less appropriate way and that researchers need to consider the advantages and limitations of alternative methods when designing EER studies. Beyond the use of specific research designs (that is, longitudinal studies, experimental studies and mixed methods research) to collect original data, we argued for the importance of conducting quantitative syntheses of effectiveness studies in order to enhance and refine the existing evidence base and to test and further develop different theoretical models of EER. As a consequence, methodological issues that need to be considered in conducting meta-analyses were then discussed. The importance of conducting secondary analyses of data from major international comparative studies was then raised before it was argued that researchers within EER should make use of advanced measurement theories (such as Item Response Theory and Generalizability Theory) in order to investigate the construct validity of their measurement instruments and develop psychometrically appropriate scales to measure key constructs of interest. By making use of Generalizability Theory, D studies can also be conducted in order to help researchers take decisions on designing their studies. Finally, it was then argued that the complex nature of educational effectiveness and the need to elaborate on it by drawing on empirical data that can emerge from any kind of study (from basic research to evaluation), necessitates the use of advanced techniques in analysing data. A particular emphasis was given to the role of multilevel modelling and Structural Equation Modelling techniques. For the purposes of analysing longitudinal data, both of these approaches can prove useful, but a number of suggestions were made about how to identify the particular conditions that will help a researcher decide which of them is most appropriate in a given study (not that they are mutually exclusive).

In this section, we raise three issues that have emerged from analysing and comparing the arguments and conclusions drawn in each of the preceding chapters. First, although each chapter addressed a specific methodological topic, we can conclude that there are interrelationships among the different method-ological tools that can be used to promote the aims of EER. For example, in Chapter 5 (concerned with conducting longitudinal studies) the readers were shown how different advanced statistical techniques such as multilevel analysis and Structural Equation Modelling can be applied to analyse data collected across a series of time points – for example, following cohorts of students in a longitudinal study. It was also shown that in specific circumstances, one approach rather than the other can be a more appropriate choice. Similarly, in the chapter on meta-analysis, readers were shown how multilevel modelling can be adopted to enable conclusions to be drawn about the characteristics of the studies included in a meta-analysis that help to explain variations in the observed effect sizes identified for interventions of interest. These two examples illustrate some coherence and similarities in the issues raised across the various chapters of this book and how researchers within the EER tradition may benefit from knowledge about a broad spectrum of interrelated methodological tools.

Second, these earlier chapters can also be seen as complementary. It is clear that not all the contributors share the same views about the appropriateness of using different methodological tools within EER. For example, the importance of using experimental studies to demonstrate causal relations was stressed in Chapter 6, which saw them as a 'gold standard', whereas the reasons for using other approaches to demonstrate causality such as longitudinal studies and cross-sectional (large-scale) studies were discussed in Chapters 3 and 5. Readers can therefore evaluate the various arguments made in each chapter to reach conclusions about what may prove most fruitful for research designs in their own projects to assist them in building appropriate models and searching for cause-and-effect relations. Similarly, the chapters on IRT and on the use of Generalizability Theory presented different measurement theories that are based on different underlying assumptions. Again, we take an instrumental perspective and suggest that readers seek to identify which of the different theories of measurement can be used to help them test the validity of their instruments rather than advocating the use of a specific measurement theory. Similarly in Chapter 7, the use of mixed methods research was advocated as a way of enriching existing EER studies by illustrating ways that the combination of quantitative and qualitative approaches and the integration and synthesis of different sources of evidence can produce new and synergistic understandings. This implies that under specific circumstances, researchers may choose to integrate these two approaches rather than treating them as contradictory. Instead of giving emphasis to the different ontological, epistemological and methodological assumptions (Cohen *et al.* 2000; Robson 1993) upon which each is based and emphasizing incompatibility, the chapter promoted the idea that we can improve our understanding of the nature of educational effectiveness in different contexts by making use of both approaches in designing EER studies. However, researchers need to decide whether both approaches should be treated as equally important in addressing a particular type of research question or whether to make use of alternative approaches to address different questions. Much will depend on the research aims but a fully integrated mixed method design that involves ongoing dialogue between the two approaches at all stages of an enquiry was seen as more authentic and potentially more illuminating.

Third, a topic that was important across almost all chapters is the issue of statistical power (Cohen 1988). If researchers underestimate the importance of this issue, they may conduct a study that is not powerful enough to identify potential associative and causal relations and, thereby, will be unable to draw any implications from their findings for the further testing and refinement of the drawn upon theoretical framework of EER. Usually, statistical power is seen as a particularly important issue in conducting experimental studies (see Chapters 3 and 6). However, in this volume, we also tried to make explicit that the issue of power is important in designing any type of study and also in using advanced statistical techniques to analyse quantitative data. For example, statistical power is a crucial element in deciding on appropriate sample sizes where propensity score-matching techniques are used to analyse data to demonstrate possible cause-and-effect relations (see Chapter 3) and requires large initial samples. Without a sufficiently large sample at the start, a study may, for example, end up with two comparable groups of subjects (for example, students, teachers, schools) but the size of the final sample may be insufficient to demonstrate any statistically significant relations because a small sample size increases the possibility of a type II error. Similarly, statistical power is also an issue that has to be taken into account in designing studies that are expected to produce nested data analysed through multilevel modelling approaches (see also Cools *et al.* 2009). Here, it is typically recommended that at least 40 higher level units (for example, schools) be sampled in order to tap sufficient variance. In addition and depending on research purposes, sufficient numbers of lower level units (for example, classes and students) are also required to produce robust estimates, confidence limits and to enable examination of interaction effects across levels. In the next section, the main issues for designing a rigorous effectiveness study that have emerged from the first two parts of the book are taken into account in establishing a guide or road map for researchers aiming to contribute to the future theoretical and methodological development of the EER field.

Guidelines for conducting a rigorous effectiveness study

Based on issues raised in Part A with respect to the theoretical development of EER, in this section we classify the research topics that need further investigation into three major areas, and under each, specific research topics that need to be addressed are mentioned. In this section, we also refer to the sequence of decisions that have to be taken in planning a competent effectiveness study. These decisions address the six steps that researchers have to follow in designing and implementing a study and reporting its results. Methodological approaches that can be used to provide answers to each type of research question are also here identified. In this way, a road map for conducting more rigorously planned effectiveness studies is provided. In the next section we then move a step forward by suggesting a future research agenda for the field by indicating the research topics that we believe need more attention at this stage of the development of EER.

In the first chapter of this book, it was made explicit that the main research question underlying most educational effectiveness studies is to identify factors at different levels (for example, school, class/teacher) that are associated directly or indirectly with students' learning outcomes and to seek to explain (through reference to theory) why these factors influence students' learning outcomes. This implies that EER attempts to establish and test theories that explain why and how some schools and teachers are more effective than others in promoting better outcomes for their students. Thus, the first area of investigation for EER is concerned with the development and validation of the theoretical framework of educational effectiveness. This framework aims to explain how, why and under what conditions specific factors operating at different levels of the educational system have an impact on student learning outcomes. By doing so, researchers attempt to establish and validate a knowledge base that can be used for improving educational practice and that is of relevance to both policymakers and practitioners.

The relevance of the knowledge base generated by researchers for use by policymakers and practitioners suggests that beyond modelling effective practices, a second area of investigation that needs to be examined is the use of this knowledge base for improvement purposes. The importance of this second area of investigation reflects the fact that the ultimate aim of EER is to improve practice, and it is argued that improvement is most likely to be achieved by helping schools and teachers to make use of the research-generated knowledge base of EER in order to develop their improvement strategies and actions (Mortimore 1998; Sammons 1999). In this chapter, we move a step forward and suggest that the research agenda of EER should be expanded by not only attempting to develop a valid theoretical framework, but also by investigating under which conditions this framework can be used for improvement purposes.

Since EER is also expected to influence policy, the third area of investigation is concerned with the need to identify how the theoretical framework of EER can be used for designing evaluation mechanisms for measuring teacher and school effectiveness either for summative or for formative reasons. For example, studies attempting to generate evaluation criteria that emerged from various models of EER have already been conducted (Kyriakides *et al.* 2006) but further studies are needed to identify how policy conditions (and changes in these, such as specific education reforms) can influence the improvement of practice and student outcomes (Dobert and Sroka 2004; Sammons 2008). Through these kinds of studies, EER can identify better ways to promote the use of its knowledge base for developing reform policies to improve the quality of teaching and raise educational standards.

Figure 14.1 illustrates the six steps that we recommend researchers follow in designing, implementing and reporting the results of their studies. These six steps provide suggestions on how researchers can make use of advanced methodological techniques in taking decisions on how to conduct their studies.

The first step is concerned with the identification of the area of investigation to which the study belongs. A study could attempt to contribute to the modelling of educational effectiveness (first area of investigation) or to search for a use of the knowledge base of EER in order to improve either the practice (second area of investigation) and/or the design of evaluation reform policies (third area of investigation). Under each of these three areas, some specific research topics are mentioned that may help researchers develop their plans for future studies. Although the importance of investigating specific research topics associated with each of these three areas of investigation is discussed in the next section of this chapter, at this step researchers should not only identify their area of investigation but also clarify their own research questions. In order to identify important research questions, they should conduct a systematic review of the relevant literature, which will also give attention to methodologies used and the strengths/limitations of the designs and analyses of previous studies. In this way, important research question will be identified.

At the second step, researchers are expected to identify the most appropriate type of research that has to be used in order to provide answers to their research questions. Specifically, in this step the decision has to do with the extent to which an experimental, longitudinal, cross-sectional (large-scale) or mixed methods study should be conducted and whether the researcher will conduct a secondary analysis of existing data sets or collect new empirical data. Beyond conducting an original study, researchers could also consider the possibility of undertaking a quantitative synthesis of original studies (for example, meta-analysis). In Part B, the main advantages and disadvantages of using each type of study were presented. In addition, in Chapter 3 we discussed how each type of study can be used in order to demonstrate causal relations. We stress that

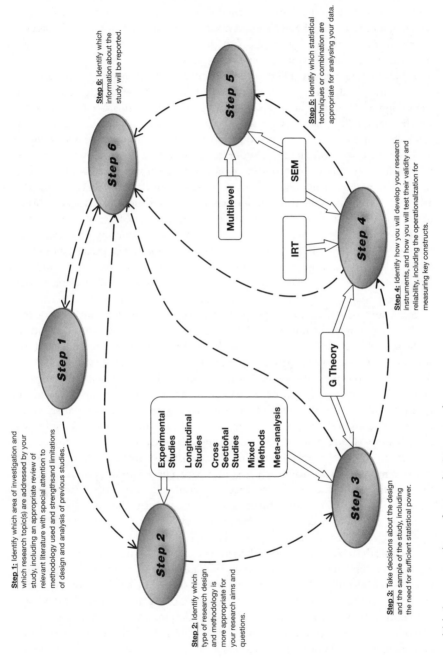

Figure 14.1 A conceptual map for conducting research

none of these types of studies can be considered unique in demonstrating cause-and-effect relations, but researchers should take into account the circumstances under which their studies can be carried out. In choosing the type of research we are going to undertake, we should not only take into account the theoretical development of the field in relation to the research questions raised but also practical considerations (for example, cost, time).

Beyond taking some general decisions about the type of study that could be used, at the third step researchers need to take more specific decisions about the design and the sample of their study. In respect to this need, the chapter on Generalizability Theory (Chapter 10) revealed how this measurement theory can help us take decisions on how to conduct an effectiveness study. For example, a D study can be conducted in order to identify how many observations are needed in order to generate reliable data about the teaching skills of a sample of teachers without spending too many resources on data collection. Similarly, a D study can help us identify the optimal number of observers that can be used to collect reliable data on the quality of teaching. A special type of decision that has to be taken in regards to this is concerned with the sampling procedure and the sample size. With regard to the sampling procedure, researchers should be aware of the nested character of data in educational effectiveness studies and the statements that they may like to make about the size of teacher, classroom, school and system effects. Moreover, studies making use of an experimental design need to make sure that random sampling takes place at the appropriate level of the study. For example, a study investigating the impact of interventions conducted at the school level needs to allocate *schools* randomly rather than teachers and/or students (the advantages of group randomization studies are discussed in Chapters 3 and 6). In the previous section of this chapter, the importance of statistical power was again raised, and decisions about the size of the sample should be based on the results of simulation studies that search for the optimal size that can produce enough statistical power in relation to the parameter of interests in each study (Cools *et al.* 2009). For example, a study investigating differential teacher effectiveness in relation to the characteristics of students should attempt to select more students from each class in order to have enough power to search for random slope(s) at the lowest level. By contrast, more classes/schools are needed in studies where the estimation of the intercept is the main focus of the research, such as studies attempting to classify teachers/schools in different groups by taking into account their effectiveness status.

The fourth step is concerned with identifying key constructs that an EER study needs to address, the development of research instruments and the testing of their validity and reliability. At this step, researchers should make clear how the main constructs of their study relate to existing EER models and theories. In this way, the contribution of the study to the theory development of the field will be identified. Further, researchers should also make use of measurement theories described in Part B in order to develop new instruments and/or find out whether available instruments can produce valid and reliable data in different educational contexts. Unless the construct validity of a study's instruments is demonstrated, no claim about the effect of any constructs can be made. Therefore, this is an important step since it provides data to help researchers clarify the structure of the constructs that are used to describe different types of variables. For example, a study searching for the impact of teacher perceptions towards teaching upon student outcomes should not only develop instruments to measure perceptions but also use appropriate techniques to clarify the various latent variables that are used to measure the perceptions. In this respect, researchers can consider the possibility of using either Item Response Theory or Confirmatory Factor Analyses within SEM to investigate the factor structure of their research instrument and clarify the meaning of their explanatory variables. Advantages and limitations of each approach are discussed in Chapters 8, 9 and 12, and researchers should consider them in choosing their own approach. Moreover, in almost all effectiveness studies it is likely that student learning outcomes may need to be measured. Therefore, researchers should make use of different measurement theories in order to produce psychometrically appropriate scales and use a pre- and post-test design over two or more time points to measure change and identify the progress that each student makes. In particular, special attention should be given to establishing appropriate scales of learning outcomes in longitudinal studies. In this case, test-equating approaches can also be used to help researchers develop instruments that can be administered to different age groups of students, which, though not identical, can nonetheless produce comparable scores. Although both Classical Test Theory and IRT produce different test-equating approaches, the advantages of using IRT for this purpose are clearly pointed out in Chapter 9.

At the fifth step, researchers are expected to make use of appropriate advanced techniques, such as SEM and/or multilevel modelling, to analyse their quantitative data (in mixed methods designs there are additional considerations as discussed in Chapter 7). Obviously, decisions taken at the earlier steps are likely to affect decisions on using a specific approach to analyse the data. For example, in cases where data from a longitudinal study design will be collected, researchers could consider the possibility of using either SEM techniques to estimate a growth model or a multilevel regression analysis model treating measurement occasion (time) as the first level. These two techniques have their unique advantages. As shown in Chapter 5, with multilevel regression models you can have, in principle, as many levels as your nested data imply (that is, student, teacher, school, district, and so on). Moreover, you can also take into account that students can move from one group to another group (for example, from one classroom to another or from one school or neighbourhood to another) and develop a cross-classified model. On the other hand, the SEM technique allows researchers to treat variables as having a double role, and this makes it possible to set up and test chains of variables that may influence each other both directly and indirectly (thus testing hypotheses of mediation). Obviously such SEM models must be specified by taking into account either an underlying theory supporting the existence of such relations or results of previous original studies and/or meta-analyses. This comparison shows that decisions taken at step 1 dealing with the research questions and the theoretical framework underlying an effectiveness study play an important role not only in choosing to conduct a specific type of study (that is, in the above example a longitudinal study) and the design of a study (steps 3 and 4) but also in choosing the appropriate method of analysing the resultant data (step 5).

At the final step, researchers should make decisions on how to report their results and on how to design further studies that can test the generalizability of their findings and/or raise further questions. Reporting is not always treated seriously, but it is stressed here that it is an important step in the research process especially since it provides future readers with the necessary information to evaluate the strength of the knowledge claims that are made and take further steps either by: conducting a new investigation such as a replication study; using it for conducting a meta-analysis; building on its findings to define new research questions; or for taking decisions on how to build a reform policy or an improvement strategy. For this reason, in this chapter we discuss in more detail the issue of reporting and provide some guidelines for reporting original studies and meta-analyses.

The issue that has to be considered here is the identification of the information that it is necessary to report. From the view point of research, information on the *effect size* of each factor that is examined should be clearly reported since a study that does not provide enough information cannot be used for conducting a meta-analysis. In particular, within Chapter 13 the importance of conducting meta-analyses within EER was stressed. However, researchers conducting meta-analyses usually find some relevant original studies that do not report enough information about the effect size of each factor involved in the study, and as a consequence, these studies cannot be included in their meta-analyses. Moreover, in Chapter 13 it was demonstrated that a meta-analysis can also be used in attempting to identify whether specific characteristics of the original studies explain variation in the reported effect sizes. This implies that researchers should provide enough information about the *type of their study* and about the *processes used to collect data*. For example, claiming that an experimental study was conducted is not enough unless the process of formulating the different experimental groups and the treatments offered to them is reported as well. In this way, readers can see whether an experimental or a quasi-experimental study was conducted and can also evaluate the internal and external validity of the reported findings. Information that should also be reported is concerned with the *process used to demonstrate the validity and reliability of the data*. In Chapter 13, it was stressed that one of the major criteria for selecting studies to include in a quantitative synthesis has to do with the information provided about the validity of the instruments used to collect data. This implies that the step concerned with the reporting of studies is related to all the other steps presented in Figure 14.1, since information should be reported about the type of study that was carried out, the processes used to collect data, the processes used to investigate the validity of the data and the effect sizes that emerged from using different techniques to analyse the data.

With respect to reporting the actual findings of a study, we emphasize the importance of reporting information concerned with the processes used to analyse data by using advanced statistical techniques such as SEM and multilevel modelling. For example, in the chapter on SEM (Chapter 12), we stressed the importance of reporting relevant covariance matrices used to develop and test a model, and the importance of reporting different fit indices. In the case of multilevel modelling, Dedrick *et al.* (2009) conducted a review about the quality of the reporting of studies using this technique and a set of guidelines on their reporting was advocated. Specifically, it was argued that researchers should state explicitly whether centring was used, whether and how the distributional assumptions were tested and whether the data were complete. Obviously, it is also important to provide either standard errors or confidence intervals for the parameter estimates that emerged from the multilevel analysis. In this way, the effect sizes of the factors included in the study will be estimated and the quality of the analysis carried out can be evaluated.

By providing such information, the quality and the relevance of a study can be evaluated and other researchers can incorporate the study in subsequent meta-analyses. In addition, they can also use it for conducting a replication study or treating it as a starting point for further research. In regard to the importance of conducting replication studies in EER, very few direct replication studies have been conducted despite the development of a validated knowledge base (that is, the first area of investigation mentioned above), depending on replication studies that can test the generalizability of the reported findings. As far as the use of an original study as a starting point for designing further studies is concerned, we advocate the need for gradually building a research programme by taking into account the results of earlier studies. In this way, a strong contribution to the development of a theoretical framework of EER can emerge. For example, a study investigating the impact of specific factors on student achievement by drawing data from a specific phase of education (for example, primary education) and focusing on a specific type of learning outcome (for example, mathematics) could be seen as the starting point to search for the existence of generic factors that can explain variation in achievement in different types of outcomes (for example, affective as well as cognitive) and for different groups of students (for example, secondary students; see also Kyriakides and Creemers 2009a). By reporting original studies in a way that has implications for conducting further studies, readers are better placed to identify any limitations in the original studies and so be stimulated to search for ways to design subsequent studies that address these limitations.

So far the discussion of reporting has been concerned with original studies and their use for conducting other empirical studies and/or meta-analyses. However, the issue of reporting is also very important in presenting the results of a meta-analysis (see Chapter 13), and we have emphasized the need to use specific criteria to select the original studies. These criteria have to be reported in order to provide the reader with enough information about the quality of the meta-analysis. Unless the reader is aware of the reasons why specific studies were excluded, doubts about the generalizability of a meta-analysis may emerge. For example, the review of the quality of the reporting of the results of studies using multilevel modelling mentioned above did not include any study reported in the *School Effectiveness and School Improvement* journal, but no reason for this was given. Due to this omission, Dedrick *et al.* (2009) did not cover many important EER studies that have used multilevel modelling and provide good examples of informative reporting of results. This seems to reflect a lack awareness of the important contribution of European researchers (and other researchers in non-American contexts) and of the widespread use of multilevel modelling in EER in particular (Sammons 2009). Second, the process used to analyse effect sizes reported in different studies has to be explicitly reported. In Chapter 13, we suggested the use of multilevel modelling to conduct a meta-analysis. Irrespective of whether multilevel modelling is applied, researchers need to provide information about each technique used to conduct their meta-analysis, especially where a meta-analysis is set up to search for the impact of more than one factor upon student achievement. In such a case, researchers should not only report the technique(s) used to analyse their data, but also the studies included in each type of analysis. Some meta-analyses in the area of EER are not reported as following the above guidelines, and it is thereby difficult for the research community to evaluate their conclusions. For example, a meta-analysis of 27 studies carried out by Robinson *et al.* (2008) does not refer to the criteria used to select 27 out of more than 100 school effectiveness studies identified by other meta-analyses looking at the effect of the same school factors (Scheerens *et al.* 2005; Kyriakides *et al.* in press). Moreover, it is not clear what kind of analysis was carried out and whether the nested character of data was taken into account. Furthermore, it is not reported which studies were used to estimate the average effect size of each factor. Therefore, it is difficult to interpret the results of this meta-analysis, especially since two other similarly recent meta-analyses (Scheerens *et al.* 2005; Kyriakides *et al.* in press) found much smaller effects of the school factors concerned with leadership on achievement that were the subject of the Robinson *et al.* (2008) meta-analysis, and these alternative meta-analyses reported their results by following the guidelines mentioned here.

In this section, we have referred to decisions that have to be taken about the reporting of results and have formulated some guidelines with respect to reporting results of original studies and meta-analyses. Following these guidelines should enhance the research community's ability to evaluate the quality of any reported study. It is therefore suggested that primary researchers should take these guidelines into account and thoroughly describe their methods and results, especially since more complex types of research and advanced statistical techniques are increasingly used in EER. Moreover, these guidelines could be taken into account by manuscript reviewers and journal editors in order to promote the quality of the scientific papers and allow readers to evaluate the quality of reported studies. Finally, those academics teaching research methodology courses and courses on conducting evaluations should include discussion of best practice in research reporting in their courses and especially those dealing with the use of advanced statistical techniques such as SEM and multilevel modelling.

From the viewpoint of policymakers and practitioners, it is also important that the results of a study are reported by following the above guidelines. Providing information about the methods used to conduct a study can help policymakers to evaluate the quality of the study (which might not be their prime interest) and to see the relevance of the study for the specific decisions that they have to take in order to develop and implement an improvement strategy. Moreover, reporting the effect sizes of different factors on specific learning outcomes may help them select the improvement strategies most likely to achieve the educational goals they want to promote. This is due to the fact that their decisions may be based partly on comparing the efficiency and costs of different strategies, and in order to draw such a decision, they will find it helpful to compare the reported effect sizes in different studies.

Future directions for the development of educational effectiveness: suggestions for a research agenda

This book illustrates that educational effectiveness remains a dynamic field of enquiry and, if no longer in its adolescence, one that is still certainly in an early stage of maturity. EER remains an exciting area with many possibilities to influence not only policy and practice but also the development of advanced methodological approaches with which to study education. There are numerous opportunities to consolidate, refine and extend the existing knowledge base of school and teacher effectiveness and, in particular, to develop its methodology further. Moreover, the need for better links with (and contributions to) thoughtful school improvement and evaluation studies remains urgent. In this chapter, we have distinguished three areas of investigation that need further development, but we acknowledge that some studies or research programmes may address research questions that are concerned with more than one area (see Figure 14.1). Below, we refer to the importance of investigating ongoing research topics associated with each of these three areas of investigation and which are also related to the current methodological developments in social science.

First, topics related to the development and testing of theoretical models need to be taken into account. Specifically, beyond searching for the impact of factors operating at different levels (such as measures of the quality of teaching and various school organizational variables) it is important to elaborate their ways of functioning and develop validated constructs. For example, Creemers and Kyriakides (2008) developed a framework to measure the functioning of factors in relation to five dimensions: frequency, focus, stage, quality and differentiation. Although some studies testing the validity of this measurement framework have been conducted (Kyriakides and Creemers 2008a), further studies are needed to develop this framework or to produce alternative approaches in conceptualizing teacher and school factors rather than treating frequency as the only measurement dimension of effectiveness.

Second, another topic that has to be considered is the nature of the impact that each factor may have on student outcomes. In this respect, one could search for direct and/or indirect effects of factors on student achievement or other outcomes and/or for the existence of generic and/or differential factors. Some studies have already made use of the advanced statistical techniques such as SEM and multilevel modelling to search for direct and/or indirect effects of school factors (De Maeyer *et al.* 2007; Creemers and Kyriakides forthcoming, 2010) but further studies are needed, especially since strong indirect effects were rarely found, whereas theoretical models argue that school factors are expected to have mainly indirect rather than direct effects (Creemers and Kyriakides 2008; Scheerens 1992; Stringfield and Slavin 1992). A similar problem seems to have emerged in studies testing the validity of models promoting differential teacher and school effectiveness (Campbell *et al.* 2004), which revealed that contrary to expectations, factors had mainly generic effects for different groups of students (Kyriakides 2007; Muijs *et al.* 2005). With respect to this topic, researchers could search for the impact of contextual variations influencing effectiveness at school, regional and national levels through conducting comparative international research studies. Such studies may not only provide support to the generalizability of theoretical models but may also reveal that some factors have differential effects (Reynolds 2006; Teddlie *et al.* 2006).

A third research topic that needs to be addressed is whether there are factors that have situational effects, leading them to be more important in particular contexts. One study has demonstrated that school policy for teaching and actions taken to improve teaching have stronger effects in schools with poor teaching practice at the classroom level (Creemers and Kyriakides 2009). However, further studies are needed to test the generalizability of these findings and identify other school and/or system factors that may also have situational effects.

Fourth, a research topic that is very closely related to current methodological advances is the identification of nonlinear relations between specific factors and learning outcomes. Although some argue that the difficulties in demonstrating the impact of some factors on student achievement is due to possible nonlinear relations (see for example the arguments about the impact of teacher subject knowledge supported by Darling-Hammond 2000), as far as we are aware, there are no studies demonstrating such relations. Identifying significant nonlinear effects might not only reveal the need to use better methods to analyse our data but also to design more appropriate types of studies, such as longitudinal studies that last for longer time periods.

A fifth topic that needs further attention is the concept of the grouping of factors, such that factors operating at the same level may be related to each other. This concept was initially introduced by the educational productivity model of Walberg (1984) and developed further in the third phase of EER (Creemers 1994; Scheerens 1992; Stringfield and Slavin 1992). However, only recently a study has shown that the grouping of teacher factors can be related to student outcomes (Kyriakides *et al.* 2009). This study made use of IRT to develop stages of teaching skills, and then the relations of these stages to outcomes was demonstrated by using multilevel modelling. Further studies making use of advanced methodological techniques are yet needed to see whether groupings of school factors can also be established and whether such groupings of factors may be useful for developing strategies to improve practice.

Sixth, in respect to modelling effectiveness, we can see that there is almost no empirical study treating equity as a dimension for measuring effectiveness. Given that existing evidence suggests that school effects vary most for disadvantaged groups (Scheerens and Bosker 1997), it is argued here that further studies are needed to establish whether particular approaches to teaching and methods of organization promote better outcomes for disadvantaged students. For example, a review by Van der Werf (2006) argued that direct instruction is more beneficial than constructivist approaches to teaching low SES children and younger and lower attaining groups. In this respect, issues of differential effectiveness and stability and consistency of effects also require further investigation. Student and family background factors that predict educational outcomes and the size of the equity gap in achievement remain foci of continued interest – particularly how they may interact with school and classroom processes (Sammons *et al.* 2008). By searching for schools that manage not only to promote educational achievement for their students (quality) but also to reduce the initial gaps (equity), EER can provide better responses to those criticizing schooling as not able to reduce inequality in education (Sammons 2007; 2010).

Seventh, researchers need to identify the long-term effects of teachers and schools in terms of both quality and equity. Research concerned with the long-term effect of schools is of great importance not only for establishing the theoretical framework of EER but also for political and accountability reasons. If a teacher turns a student off mathematics for life then this would be a disastrous consequence and probably more important than any other short-term achievement loss. On the other hand, if a teacher is able to motivate a student to be interested in science and this leads to a long-term career, then that is of far greater importance than a few gains in points on science, as research on the short-term effect of schools has demonstrated. However, relationships may well also be reciprocal. If poor teaching leads to low attainment in some subjects, students are likely to struggle, lose academic self-concept and are then more likely to drop subjects they find difficult. The experience of poor teaching in successive school years is particularly disadvantageous and may compound existing disadvantages. By contrast, attending a more effective school for several years has measurable benefits (Goldstein and Sammons 1997). Through long-term benefits, schools may play an important public role in helping children overcome the cognitive, social and emotional deficits that frequently accompany growing up in economically deprived homes (Spielhagen 2006). However, in order to measure the long-term effect of teachers and schools, high quality longitudinal data with appropriate controls are needed, and the use of advanced multilevel modelling approaches should be considered (Kyriakides and Creemers 2008b) in order to generate valid estimates of long-term teacher and school effects.

Moving to the second area of investigation, we can identify four research topics that can help us understand the conditions and the means by which schools can make use of the theoretical framework of EER to improve their effectiveness status. The first topic that has to be addressed is concerned with the impact that changes in the functioning of teacher/school/system effectiveness factors may have for the improvement (or decline) of teacher/school/system effectiveness. This topic also draws attention to the importance of looking at changes in the effectiveness status of schools. Rather than treating the achievement of a single group of students as the dependent variable (thus implying stability in school effectiveness) studies attempting to explain changes in the effectiveness status of schools will reveal that the main aim of effectiveness studies should be a better understanding of the *change* of the effectiveness status of schools. By collecting data in more than two periods from the same schools and if possible following them during a long period, EER should produce a better picture of the complex process of institutional change and of the associative and causal factors that predict improvement or decline. Moreover, mixed research methods can be employed for studying schools where dramatic changes in their effectiveness status are observed, and this is likely to be important in increasing our understanding of the processes of change.

The second topic is focused on the development of intervention programmes that are based on a theory-driven and evidence-based approach – although the impact of these interventions on student learning outcomes must also be measured. For example, experimental studies can be conducted in order to identify the extent to which the use of a theoretical framework may help us to design an effective intervention strategy to improve either teacher or school effectiveness. Such studies may also help us to identify under which conditions such an approach is more effective rather than approaches promoting the improvement of practices based on action research (for example, by encouraging teachers and schools to develop their own actions without considering the existing knowledge base of the EER field).

Third, one of the most difficult topics that needs to be considered concerns the obstacles that schools face in introducing an improvement strategy. In this respect, mixed method research might be employed to find out how teachers and schools could move from being resistant to change to becoming committed to school improvement strategies. Such studies may help us expand the theoretical framework of educational effectiveness by helping us identify variables that are associated with the effective implementation of an improvement strategy, especially in a context of difficult circumstances where performance is very low and resistance to change is very high. Purely quantitative studies testing the validity of this framework will also be needed since they allow the possibility of developing more generic models for understanding the process of change and implementing it effectively.

Fourth, a topic that looks at the other end of the continuum is concerned with the efforts that the most effective schools take in order to remain effective. Currently, there are almost no studies looking at the improvement strategies that effective schools take in order to remain effective. However, a study following 50 schools for a period of five years has shown that schools that were more effective had to act to improve the functioning of school factors in order to remain among the *most* effective, otherwise they dropped to a typical level (Kyriakides and Creemers 2009b). Moreover, a mixed method study by Day *et al.* (2009) investigated schools that remained academically effective over at least three years and pointed to the importance of adopting a range of strategies to improve. Further studies testing these findings are needed in order to help us better understand the dynamic nature of educational effectiveness and in supporting actions that should be taken to enable schools to remain effective.

The third proposed area of investigation is concerned with the use of EER for establishing evaluation mechanisms and designing theory-driven evaluation studies. The importance of conducting theory-driven evaluation studies was discussed in Chapter 4, however, it is also argued here that the research community should have a greater impact on the design of evaluation policies by using the knowledge base of EER and its methodological advances to build teacher and school evaluation mechanisms. Different mechanisms and evaluation processes should be designed in order to achieve the formative purpose of evaluation which aims to contribute to the improvement of teaching quality and the functioning of schools. For accountability reasons, other evaluation mechanisms and evaluation processes should also be considered. For example, in cases where multiple sources of data are used to collect data for summative evaluation, researchers should make use of different measurement theories to find out whether a unidimensional psychometrically appropriate scale can be developed in order to allow comparisons among schools and/or teachers. This is a topic that reveals that the methodological and conceptual advances within EER should be seen as related to each other in order to generate valid suggestions for the development of reform policies in evaluation. Finally, researchers can investigate the extent to which EER can be used to inform and evaluate the impact of school improvement initiatives and educational policy reforms to enhance our understanding of the processes of educational and institutional change.

Based on the description of the research topics associated with each area of investigation and by taking into account the theoretical and methodological developments of EER presented in this book, we argue that the field is mature enough not only to develop its theoretical models further (first area of investigation) but also to undertake studies addressing topics associated with the second area of investigation. In Chapter 4, the importance of using an evidence-based and theory-driven approach to school improvement was stressed. It is argued here that we need various projects investigating under which conditions schools can make use of the knowledge base of EER in order to improve their effectiveness. In this respect, experimental and longitudinal studies have to be designed, and the impact of this type of approach to school improvement has to be compared with other approaches currently used within the field of school improvement. With regard to the third area of investigation, it is acknowledged that there are some difficulties for those engaged in EER in affecting the development of educational policy. This is due to the political dimension of evaluation, implying that reforms in evaluation policy are unlikely to be based on only research-validated knowledge since any reform is very likely to cause changes in the power relations within any educational system (Kyriakides and Demetriou 2007; Hoyle and Skrla 1999). Nonetheless, there have been some examples of teacher and school effectiveness studies influencing education reforms in England (Sammons 2008) particularly in approaches to the improvement of poorly performing schools and literacy and numeracy teaching. This remains an area for further study.

The description of different research topics that are situated within the three research areas concerned with the conceptual development and the knowledge base of educational effectiveness reveals that there is also a need to develop further our methodological approaches and techniques. In this book, it has been shown that advancements in the methodology of research have helped us to study the processes of effectiveness and raise more complex research questions about the nature of the impact that effectiveness factors can have on student achievement. We believe that future research can make use of such EER approaches and instruments and develop them further by using more complicated techniques to study different educational effects. For example, the effect of schooling can be examined by using both the regression discontinuity approach and cross-sectional data. Further, both direct and indirect effects of school factors can be investigated by using multilevel SEM approaches. Another topic that needs to be considered is the use of a broader range of student outcomes covering new educational goals that can be achieved by making use of measurement theories such as Generalizability Theory and IRT to develop psychometrically appropriate instruments and relevant measurement scales.

Finally, further advances in research designs and methodology are underway within the social sciences and will help us within EER to develop and test theories of educational effectiveness and educational change, which will contribute to the improvement of policy and practice at both the school and the system level. We hope that this book has increased awareness of the focus of EER, has increased understanding of the growing suite of methodological approaches that are available and has highlighted key issues that require consideration in designing EER studies. We have sought to stress the importance of theory-driven research designs, the use of appropriate techniques, and we have suggested a range of topics for further study in this important and growing field.

References

Campbell, R.J., Kyriakides, L., Muijs, R.D. and Robinson, W. (2004) *Assessing teacher effectiveness: A differentiated model*, London: RoutledgeFalmer.

Cohen, D., Manion, L. and Morrison, K. (2000) *Research methods in education*, 5th edn, London: RoutledgeFalmer.

Cohen, J. (1988) *Statistical power analysis of the behavioural sciences*, 2nd edn, New York: Academic Press.

Cools, W., de Fraine., B., Van den Noortgate, W. and Onghena, P. (2009) 'Multilevel design efficiency in educational effectiveness research', *School Effectiveness and School Improvement*, 20(3): 357–73.

Creemers, B.P.M. (1994) *The effective classroom*, London: Cassell.

Creemers, B.P.M. and Kyriakides, L. (2008) *The dynamics of educational effectiveness: A contribution to policy, practice and theory in contemporary schools*, London: Routledge.

Creemers, B.P.M. and Kyriakides, L. (2009) 'Situational effects of the school factors included in the dynamic model of educational effectiveness', *South African Journal of Education*, 29(3): 293–315.

Creemers, B.P.M and Kyriakides, L. (forthcoming, 2010) 'School factors explaining achievement on cognitive and affective outcomes: Establishing a dynamic model of educational effectiveness', *Scandinavian Journal of Educational Research*, 54(2).

Darling-Hammond, L. (2000) 'Teacher quality and student achievement: A review of state policy evidence', *Education Policy Analysis Archives*, 8(1). Online. Available at: http://epaa.asu.edu/epaa/v8n1/ [accessed 17 January 2010].

Day, C., Sammons, P., Hopkins, D., Harris, A., Leithwood, K., Gu, Q., Brown, E., Ahtaridou, E. and Kington, A. (2009) 'The impact of school leadership on pupil outcomes', *DCSF Research Report – RR108*, London: Department for Children, Schools and Families.

De Maeyer, S., Rymenans, R., Van Petegem, P., van den Bergh, H. and Rijlaarsdam, G. (2007) 'Educational leadership and pupil achievement: The choice of a valid conceptual model to test effects in school effectiveness research', *School Effectiveness and School Improvement*, 18(2): 125–45.

Dedrick, R.F., Ferron, J.M., Hess, M.R., Hogarty, K.Y., Kromrey, J.D., Lang, T.R., Niles, J.D. and Lee, S.R. (2009) 'Multilevel modeling: A review of methodological issues and applications', *Review of Educational Research*, 79(1): 69–102.

Dobert, H. and Sroka, W. (2004) *Features of successful school systems, a comparison of schooling in six countries*, Munster: Waxmann.

Goldstein, H. and Sammons, P. (1997) 'The influence of secondary and junior schools on sixteen year examination performance: A cross-classified multilevel analysis', *School Effectiveness and School Improvement*, 8(2): 219–30.

Hoyle, R.J. and Skrla, L. (1999) 'The politics of superintendent evaluation', *Journal of Personnel Evaluation in Education*, 13(4): 405–19.

Kyriakides, L. (2007) 'Generic and differentiated models of educational effectiveness: Implications for the improvement of educational practice', in T. Townsend (ed.) *International handbook of school effectiveness and improvement*, Dordrecht, The Netherlands: Springer, pp. 41–56.

Kyriakides, L. and Creemers, B.P.M. (2008a) 'Using a multidimensional approach to measure the impact of classroom level factors upon student achievement: A study testing the validity of the dynamic model', *School Effectiveness and School Improvement*, 19(2): 183–205.

Kyriakides, L. and Creemers, B.P.M. (2008b) 'A longitudinal study on the stability over time of school and teacher effects on student learning outcomes', *Oxford Review of Education*, 34(5): 521–45.

Kyriakides, L. and Creemers, B.P.M. (2009a) 'The effects of teacher factors on different outcomes: Two studies testing the validity of the dynamic model', *Effective Education*, 1: 61–86.

Kyriakides, L. and Creemers, B.P.M. (2009b) 'Explaining stability and changes in schools: A follow-up study testing the validity of the dynamic model', paper presented at the EARLI conference. Amsterdam.

Kyriakides, L., Creemers, B.P.M. and Antoniou, P. (2009) 'Teacher behaviour and student outcomes: Suggestions for research on teacher training and professional development', *Teaching and Teacher Education*, 25(1): 12–23.

Kyriakides, L., Creemers, B.P.M., Antoniou, P. and Demetriou, D. (in press) 'A synthesis of studies searching for school factors: Implications for theory and research', *British Educational Research Journal*.

Kyriakides, L. and Demetriou, D. (2007) 'Introducing a teacher evaluation system based on teacher effectiveness research: An investigation of stakeholders' perceptions', *Journal of Personnel Evaluation in Education*, 20(1): 43–64.

Kyriakides, L., Demetriou, D. and Charalambous, C. (2006) 'Generating criteria for evaluating teachers through teacher effectiveness research', *Educational Research*, 48(1): 1–20.

Mortimore, P. (1998) *The road to improvement: Reflections on school improvement*, Lisse, The Netherlands: Swets & Zeitlinger.

Muijs, D., Campbell, R.J., Kyriakides, L. and Robinson, W. (2005) 'Making the case for differentiated teacher effectiveness: An overview of research in four key areas', *School Effectiveness and School Improvement*, 16(1): 51–70.

Reynolds, D. (2006) 'World class schools: Some methodological and substantive findings and implications of the International School Effectiveness Research Project (ISERP)', *Educational Research and Evaluation*, 12(6): 535–60.

Robinson, V.M.J., Lloyd, C.A. and Rowe, K.J. (2008) 'The impact of leadership on student outcomes: An analysis of the differential effects of leadership types', *Educational Administration Quarterly*, 44(5): 635–74.

Robson, C. (1993) *Real world research*, Oxford: Blackwell.

Sammons, P. (1999) *School effectiveness: Coming of age in the twenty-first century*, Lisse, The Netherlands: Swets & Zeitlinger.

Sammons, P. (2007) 'School effectiveness and equity: Making connections, a review of school effectiveness and improvement research and its implications for practitioners and policy makers', report commissioned by CfBT, London. Available online at: www.cfbt.com/evidenceforeducation/Default.aspx?page=372.

Sammons, P. (2008) 'Zero tolerance of failure and new labour approaches to school improvement in England', *Oxford Review of Education*, 34(6): 651–64.

Sammons, P. (2009) 'Current achievements and future directions for school effectiveness research'. Keynote paper presented at the Educational Effectiveness SIG D Session EARLI conference, Amsterdam, August 28, 2009, submitted to *School Effectiveness and School Improvement*.

Sammons, P. (forthcoming, 2010) 'Equity and educational effectiveness', in *International Encyclopedia of Education*, Oxford: Elsevier.

Sammons, P., Anders, Y., Sylva, K., Melhuish, E., Siraj-Blatchford, I., Taggart, B. and Barreau, S. (2008). 'Children's cognitive attainment and progress in English primary schools during Key Stage 2: Investigating the potential continuing influences of pre-school education', *Zeitschrift für Erziehungswissenschaften*, 10. Jahrg. special issue (Sonderheft) November, 179–98.

Scheerens, J. (1992) *Effective schooling: Research, theory and practice*, London: Cassell.

Scheerens, J. and Bosker, R.J. (1997) *The foundations of educational effectiveness*, Oxford: Pergamon.

Scheerens, J., Seidel, T., Witziers, B., Hendriks, M. and Doornekamp, G. (2005) *Positioning and validating the supervision framework*, University of Twente: Department of Educational Organisation and Management.

Spielhagen, R.F. (2006) 'Closing the achievement gap in math: The long-term effects of eighth-grade algebra, *Journal of Advanced Academics*, 18(1): 34–59.

Stringfield, S.C. and Slavin, R.E. (1992) 'A hierarchical longitudinal model for elementary school effects', in B.P.M. Creemers and G.J. Reezigt (eds), *Evaluation of educational effectiveness*, Groningen: ICO, pp. 35–69.

Teddlie, C., Creemers, B.P.M., Kyriakides, L., Muijs, D. and Fen, Y. (2006) 'The International System for Teacher Observation and Feedback: Evolution of an international study of teacher effectiveness constructs', *Educational Research and Evaluation*, 12(6): 561–82.

Van der Werf, M. (2006) 'General and differential effects of constructivist teaching', lecture presented at ICSEI 2006 conference, Fort Lauderdale, FL, USA.

Walberg, H.J. (1984) 'Improving the productivity of America's schools', *Educational Leadership*, 41(8): 19–27.

Appendices to Chapter 10

Appendix A

Sample **GENOVA** programs

Program with raw data input

```
 1  GSTUDY          P X I DESIGN – RANDOM MODEL
 2  OPTIONS         RECORDS 2
 3  EFFECT          *P        5        0
                    +I        5        0
 4  FORMAT          (5f2.0)
 5  PROCESS
 .  data set placed here
20  COMMENT         D STUDY CONTROL CARDS
21  COMMENT         FIRST D STUDY
22  DSTUDY          #1  – PI DESIGN   I RANDOM
23  DEFFECT         $  P
24  DEFFECT         I  1  5  10  20
26  DCUT
27  ENDSTUDY
28  FINISH
```

Program with mean squares as input

```
 1  GMEANSQUARES    PI DESIGN
 2  MEANSQUARE      P        9.48      20
 3  MEANSQUARE      I        6.34       5
 4  MEANSQUARE      PI       0.84
 5  ENDMEAN
20  COMMENT             D STUDY CONTROL CARDS
 .  same as above D studies
28  FINISH
```

Program with variance components as input

```
 1  GCOMPONENTS       PI DESIGN
 2  VCOMPONENT        P          1.73      30
 3  VCOMPONENT        I          0.27      5
 4  VCOMPONENT        PI         0.84
 5  ENDCOMP
20  COMMENT           D STUDY CONTROL CARDS
 .  same as above D studies
28  FINISH
```

Appendix B

SAS PROC VARCOMP setup program for estimating variance components in two-facet study

```
DATA EXAMPLE;
INPUT PERSON RATER SUBJECT SCORE;
PROC ANOVA;
CLASS PERSON RATER SUBJECT;
MODEL SCORE = PERSON|RATER|SUBJECT;
PROC VARCOMP METHOD = REML;
CLASS RATER OCCASION PERSON;
MODEL RATING = RATER|OCCASION|PERSON;
```

Appendix C

Example LISREL program code to examine two-facet model

```
LISREL CODE TO ESTIMATE THE G-COEFFICIENT IN A TWO-FACET
CROSSED DESIGN
DA NI = 8 NO = 50 ! (SEE MARCOULIDES, 1996, P. 295)
CM
10
3 10
3 3 10
3 3 3 10
3 2 2 2 10
2 3 2 2 3 10
2 2 3 2 3 3 10
2 2 2 3 3 3 3 10
```

MO NY = 8 NE = 16 BE = FU,FI PS = DI,FR TE = ZE
LA
R1O1 R2O1 R3O1 R4O1 R1O2 R2O2 R3O2 R4O2
LE
Y1 Y2 Y3 Y4 Y5 Y6 Y7 Y8 PERSONS RATER1 RATER2 RATER3 C
RATER4 OCCASN1 OCCASN2 Y
FI PS(16) ! NO RESIDUAL ATTACHED TO DUMMY VARIABLE FOR
SCALE SCORE Y
EQ PS(1)-PS(8)
VA 1 LY 1 1 LY 2 2 LY 3 3 LY 4 4 LY 5 5 LY 6 6 LY 7 7 LY 8 8
VA 1 BE 1 9 BE 2 9 BE 3 9 BE 4 9 BE 5 9 BE 6 9 BE 7 9 BE 8 9
VA 1 BE 16 1 BE 16 2 BE 16 3 BE 16 4 BE 16 5 BE 16 6 BE 16 7 BE 16 8
VA 1 BE 1 10 BE 2 10 BE 3 10 BE 4 10 BE 5 11 BE 6 11 BE 7 11 BE 8 11
VA 1 BE 1 12 BE 2 13 BE 3 14 BE 4 15 BE 5 12 BE 6 13 BE 7 14 BE 8
OU ALL! CORRELATION BETWEEN (TRUE SCALE SCORE, SCALE
SCORE) PROVIDE IN OUTPUT

Appendices to Chapter 12

Appendix A

Example CFA model Mplus input statements

TITLE: CFA MODEL OF ACHIEVEMENT AND MOTIVATION
DATA: FILE = DATA.COV;
                 TYPE = COVARIANCE;
                 NOBS = 250;
VARIABLE: NAMES = X1 X2 X3 X4 X5 X6;
MODEL: ACH BY X1*1 X2 X3;
                 MOT BY X4*1 X5 X6;
                 F1-F2@1;
OUTPUT: MODINDICES;

Appendix B

Example structural regression model Mplus input statements

TITLE: STRUCTURAL REGRESSION MODEL
DATA: FILE = DATA.COV;
                 TYPE = COVARIANCE;
                 NOBSERVATIONS = 300;
VARIABLE: NAMES ARE X1 X2 X3 X4 X6 X8 X7 Y1 Y2 Y3 Y4 Y5;
MODEL: SC BY X1 X2 X3 X4;
                 CP BY X5 X6;
                 SACH BY Y1 Y2;
                 SATT BY Y3 Y4 Y5;
                 SACH ON SC CP SATT;
                 SATT ON SC CP;
OUTPUT: MODINDICES;

Appendix C

Level and shape model Mplus input statements

TITLE: LEVEL AND SHAPE MODEL
DATA: FILE = DATA;
            TYPE = MEANS COVARIANCE;
            NOBSERVATIONS = 130;
VARIABLE: NAMES ARE Y1 Y2 Y3 Y4 Y5 Y6 Y7;
ANALYSIS: TYPE = MEANSTRUCTURE;
MODEL: I S|Y1@0 Y2 Y3 Y4 Y5 Y6 Y7@1;
OUTPUT: RESIDUAL;

Index

absolute error variance 224, 225, 228–9
achievement *see* student achievement
across-/between-/within-replication
 models 311–12
active teaching model 10
affective outcomes 30
age/achievement study 81–2, 85, 87
aggregation 89, 90
Akaike's information criterion (AIC) 289
alternative treatment comparison 109,
 110
anchor test designs 184–5
Andersen, Erling 174–7
ANOVA (analysis of variance) designs
 222–4, 227–9
approximate/exact fit tests 287–8
aptitude variables 43
attrition 50–2, 82–3
autoregressive models 95–7

background *see* home background effects
balanced incomplete block (BIB) designs
 186
Bayesian estimation 196–7
Bayesian Information Criterion (BIC)
 index 298–9
behaviour problems study 94
bivariate/univariate measures 95–6, 230
block-interlaced anchoring designs
 184–5
Bock, R. Darrell 171–4
Bosker, Roel 26, 306
Bub, Kristen 94

Campbell, Donald 125
Campbell, Jim 25–6
category response functions: GRM 177–8;
 NRM 171–4; PCM 174–7

causality (cause–effect relations) 8, 19,
 37–40, 54–5, 329; and cross-sectional
 studies 41–7; and experimental studies
 47–52; and longitudinal studies 41,
 79–80; and meta-analysis 52–3; and
 outlier studies 40–1; role of theory
 53–4
causality, reversed *see* selection bias
'cause', defining the term 37–8
CFA *see* Confirmatory Factor Analysis
CFI *see* comparative fit index (CFI)
change scores 81–2, 91–2
changes, effectiveness status 342
chi-squared tests 199–205; goodness-of-
 fit 289, 291–5, 296
CITO test 186, 254–7
Classical Test Theory 32, 153, 164, 225,
 233; compared with Generalizability
 Theory 219–22
class size, and 'selection bias' 44
cluster analysis 30
clustering 7, 91, 266–7
CML estimation 193–6
coding data, meta-analysis 309–10
coefficients: free/fixed/constrained 282;
 generalizability 224–7, 231; reliability
 220–2
cognitive outcomes, schooling 30
Cohen's d 304
coin-tossing example 197–8
Coleman, James 4–5
collapsing categories, PCM/GRM
 176–7
comparative fit index (CFI) 289, 291–2,
 294, 296–7
compensatory models 180
compensatory programmes, failure of 5
compensatory resource allocation 90